British Columbia
1847-1871

0   50   100   150
SCALE IN MILES

D1554572

Peace River

Parsnip River

RT ST. JAMES

ako R

FORT
GEORGE

Fraser River

BARKERVILLE

QUESNEL

ALEXANDRIA

YELLOWF
PASS

TETE JAUNE
CACHE

Quesnel Lake

Chilcotin R

SODA CREEK

WILLIAMS
LAKE

North Thompson River

Columbia River

BIG
BEND

LAC
LA HACHE

Fraser River

SEYMOUR
CITY

Death
Rapids

Shuswap
Lake

CLINTON

Bridge R

CACHE CREEK

SAVONA'S FERRY

Thompson R

LILLOOET

KAMLOOPS

SPENCES
BRIDGE

Nicola
Lake

Okanagan
Lake

Kootenay
Lake

Wild
Horse Cr

PEMBERTON

LYTTON

BOSTON
BAR

Harrison
Lake

YALE

PRINCETON

Smilkameen River

KEREMEOS

NEW
WESTMINSTER

HOPE

ROCK
CREEK

FORT
SHEPHERD

Kootenay River

HBA

FORT
LANGLEY

OSOYOOS

FORT
COLVILE

VICTORIA

Vancouver, B.C
May 1978.

British Columbia

CHRONICLE

1847-1871

SIR JAMES DOUGLAS

British Columbia

CHRONICLE

1847-1871

GOLD & COLONISTS

G. P. V. Akrigg and Helen B. Akrigg

DISCOVERY PRESS

1977

ISBN 0-919624-03-0

Published by
DISCOVERY PRESS
P.O. Box 46295
Vancouver, British Columbia v6R 4G6

Canadian Cataloguing in Publication Data

Akrigg, G. P. V., 1913-
    British Columbia chronicle, 1847-1871

    Companion volume to the authors' British
Columbia chronicle, 1778-1846.
    Bibliography: pp. xxii + 439.
    Includes index.
    ISBN 0-919624-03-0

    1. British Columbia — History — To 1871.*
I. Akrigg, Helen B., 1921-   II. Title.
FC3822.A39   971.1'02   C77-002090-9
F1088.A57

By G. P. V. Akrigg
Jacobean Pageant or The Court of King James I
Shakespeare and the Earl of Southampton
HARVARD UNIVERSITY PRESS & HAMISH HAMILTON LTD.

By G. P. V. Akrigg & Helen B. Akrigg
1001 British Columbia Place Names
British Columbia Chronicle, 1778-1846: Adventurers by Sea and Land
DISCOVERY PRESS

Designed and printed in Canada by
MORRISS PRINTING COMPANY LTD.
Victoria, British Columbia

TO THE MEMORY OF

Sir James Douglas

GOVERNOR
OF THE CROWN COLONIES OF

Vancouver's Island

&

British Columbia

WHO BY HIS COURAGE, INDUSTRY AND
UNDERSTANDING, PRESERVED THESE
TERRITORIES FOR BRITAIN

Contents

Prologue   1

1847   Paul Kane paints at Fort Victoria — Quest for an all-   4
British brigade route — John Tod saves Fort Kamloops
from Nicola's war party — Bishop Demers.

1848   Fort Yale — Nightmare journey of a brigade using the   12
Anderson River route — Henry Peers discovers the Co-
quihalla-Tulameen route — Fort Hope — H.M.S. *Constance* at Esquimalt.

1849   Vancouver Island granted to the Hudson's Bay Company   19
— The Company attempts to colonize it — Captain
Grant, the first settler — Scottish coal miners at Fort
Rupert — An Anglican clergyman "full of frills" — Bri-
gade route problem solved.

1850   Richard Blanshard, first royal governor of Vancouver   28
Island — The immigrant ship *Norman Morison* — Dr. J.
S. Helmcken — Trouble at Fort Rupert — Douglas' In-
dian treaties — Measles decimate the Indians.

1851   High jinks at Bachelors' Hall — Captain Cooper, entre-   38
preneur — The immigrant ship *Tory* — Captain Lang-
ford and his pretty daughters — Governor Blanshard
resigns and Douglas takes over — Gold in the Queen
Charlottes.

1852   The Nanaimo coalfields — American goldseekers in the   48
Queen Charlottes are frustrated by the HBC — H.M.S.
Thetis visits the "gold diggings establishment" — Haidas
capture the *Susan Sturges* — Dr. Helmcken's wedding.

1853   Expedition against the Cowichans and the Nanaimos —   55
Douglas' tax on grog shops — The Hon. C. W. Wentworth Fitzwilliam at Fort Victoria — The Fort Simpson
bootlegger — Northern cruises by H.M.S. *Virago* — Festivities at Beacon Hill — Vancouver Island's first settler
takes his final departure — A bad regime in New Caledonia.

1854   A "drouthy" New Year's Day at Fort Victoria — Death   71
by drowning for a demagogue — Douglas plans to take
the Alaskan Panhandle from Russia — The *Princess
Royal's* miners at Nanaimo.

1855   Douglas orders a census — Adam Horne comes upon an   80
Indian massacre — And finds a way across Vancouver
Island — The strange death of Paul Fraser.

1856   An expedition against the Cowichans — The first legisla-   88
tive assembly meets at Victoria — Gold is found on
Thompson River.

1857   Amateur theatricals — Goldseekers from the United   95
States — Douglas extends his governorship to the British
mainland — Captains Prevost and Richards — The San
Juan Islands, British or American?

1858   British Columbia's wonderful year — Negroes seek free-   104
dom on Vancouver Island — Americans hunt for gold on
the bars of the Fraser River — Royal Engineers — British
Boundary Commission and the Sumas mosquitoes —
Harrison-Lillooet Trail — Steamboats on the Fraser —
Reinhart's Okanagan journey — "The Fraser Canyon
War" — Royal Navy strengthens the Governor's hand —
Mr. Nugent, "Special Agent of the United States" — A
new crown colony — Sir Edward Bulwer Lytton, its
foster father — Inauguration of British Columbia.

1859   "Ned McGowan's War" — Colonel Moody ends the   145
trouble — Founding of Queenborough *alias* New West-

minster — Methodist missionaries from Canada — Early
newspapers — Amor De Cosmos — Northern Indians
descend on Victoria — Wealth of the Fraser gold bars —
Similkameen and Rock Creek — Explorations of William Downie — Judge Begbie on circuit — Lieut. Mayne
and Chief Lolo — "The Pig War" — General Harney
frustrated.

1860   The first Anglican Bishop of British Columbia — Un-   184
usual election tactics in Victoria — Indians evicted from
Alberni sawmill site — Gold discovered in Cariboo — A
boy's adventure on the Hope-Similkameen trail —
"The Rock Creek War" — Governor Douglas' tour — A
changing population — Achievements of the Royal Engineers — Gunboats *Forward* and *Grappler* permanently
stationed at Esquimalt — A pioneer geologist — Indian
troubles at Victoria — "Captain John" slain in Victoria
jail.

1861   More gold finds in Cariboo — Fantastic wealth — Cari-   211
boo Wagon Road is begun — Bella Coola and Bute Inlet
routes — Judge Begbie's "Bowie Knife Address" — Hazards of steamboat travel on the Fraser — Indian troubles
— "Battle of Cape Mudge" — The Victoria Rifle Volunteers — Indian policemen — Death of Lieut. Robson —
An embezzling Colonial Treasurer — Douglas plans to
invade the United States.

1862   British Columbia's severe winter — The Cariboo Gold   232
Rush — The "Overlanders" — Billy Barker strikes it rich
— Wealth and destitution in the goldfields — James
Thomson's letters home — Road-building — Cariboo
camels — The Bentinck Arm Company and the Bute
Inlet Company — Smallpox — Stikine a "humbug" —
Esquimalt becomes a fortified naval base — The bride-
ship *Tynemouth* — The Bank of British Columbia —
Begbie vs. Robson — The three greenhorns pre-empt
"The Brickmakers' Claim" — William Duncan founds
Metlakatla.

1863   "Cariboo" Cameron brings out his dead wife — Her four   267
funerals — The Gold Escort — Stagecoaches and roadhouses — Viscount Milton and Dr. Cheadle come overland from Canada — Whites murdered on Saturna Island by Lamalchi Indians — Punitive expedition by the
Royal Navy — Governor Douglas learns of his retirement
—Receives knighthood—Prize essay embroglio—Royal
Engineers and their service in British Columbia.

1864   Sir James Douglas retires — Rivalry between Victoria   291
and New Westminster — Governor Kennedy acquires a
Government House — The convivial Governor Seymour
— The Chilcotin Uprising — Pursuit of Klatsassin —
Ahousats capture the *Kingfisher* — Indian submissiveness
and their addresses to Seymour and Kennedy — The
Wild Horse goldfield.

1865   The last of the "Golden Years" of the Cariboo — Cari-   316
boo Wagon Road completed — *Cariboo Sentinel* — The
tragic, ironic death of a son of Simon Fraser — Britain
fails to purchase the Alaska Panhandle — Admiral Denman favours disposing of British Columbia — Economic
depression in Victoria and New Westminster — End of
the Wild Horse Diggings — The Big Bend gold rush —
Moberly finds Eagle Pass — The Collins Overland Telegraph — Christmas Squaw Race at Takla Lake.

1866   End of the overland telegraph — Fenians threaten British   328
North America — S.S. *Marten*'s maiden voyage on Shuswap Lake — The Big Bend gold rush peters out —Economic crisis forces union of British Columbia and Vancouver Island — Murder on the Cariboo Road.

1867   Constitution of the enlarged colony of British Columbia   340
— New Westminster or Victoria for capital? — Found-
ing of the Dominion of Canada — The Americans buy
Alaska and eye British Columbia — Colonial Secretary
Birch, the Governor's "dry nurse" — "The Grouse Creek
War" — Continued depression — Last days of the Har-
rison-Lillooet route — "Gassy Jack" comes to Burrard
Inlet.

1868   New Westminster loses a battle and Victoria becomes   354
        the capital — Moves towards confederation with Canada
        — "The Victoria Memorial" — The Yale Convention —
        Anti-confederationist strength in Victoria — Death at the
        Mystic Spring — The Barkerville fire — Indian reserves
        reduced in size — Philip Hankin, the new Colonial Secre-
        tary.

1869   The wreck of the *John Bright* and the subsequent hang-   371
        ings at Hesquiat — Governor Seymour's northern cruise
        — He is killed by a bottle of brandy — The Granville
        Despatch — The Annexationist Petition — Renewed Fe-
        nian threats — Gold in the Omineca.

1870   The terms for confederation drafted — Trutch, Helm-   385
        cken and Carrall journey to Ottawa — Agreement on the
        terms of union — The Flying Squadron at Esquimalt
        — Governor Musgrave takes an American wife — The
        Nanaimo coal strike — An election to ratify the terms of
        confederation.

1871   Robert Dunsmuir discovers the Wellington coalfield —   396
        British Columbia and Canada ratify the Terms of Union
        — "The glorious Twentieth of July".

Epilogue   The Hon. H. L. Langevin arrives from Ottawa — His   403
        report on British Columbia — Some events of 1871-1878
        — David Sallosalton, the amazing Indian boy — "The
        Carnarvon Terms" — Loss of the *Pacific* — Lord Duffer-
        in's visit — Death of Douglas — March 1878: The cen-
        tennial of Captain Cook's landing at Nootka.

Bibliography   411

Index   421

List of Illustrations

1. Sir James Douglas. (Frontispiece).
   Provincial Archives of British Columbia.

FOLLOWING PAGE 58

2. A Babine Chief.
   Painting by Paul Kane, *Royal Ontario Museum, Toronto.*

3. Saw-se-a, A Cowichan Chief.
   Painting by Paul Kane, *Royal Ontario Museum, Toronto.*

4. Indian Family at House Entrance.
   Metropolitan Toronto Library Board.

5. Two Coastal Indians.
   Metropolitan Toronto Library Board.

6. Indian Chiefs at New Westminster. *PABC.*

7. Indians and Houses at Cape Caution. *PABC.*

8. Indian Grave near Chapman's Bar, Fraser Canyon.
   Public Archives of Canada.

9. Roman Catholic Priests Leading Indians in Prayer, Fraser Valley.
   PABC.

10. H.M.S. *Termagant* Aground in Active Pass. (H.M.S. *Alert*,
    centre; H.M.S. *Plumper*, right). *PABC.*

11. H.M.S. *Sutlej* Gun Deck. *PABC.*

12. H.M.S. *Virago* on Rocks.
    Mitchell Library, Sydney, Australia.

13. H.M.S. *Virago* Being Repaired, Fort Simpson.
    Mitchell Library, Sydney, Australia.

14. View of Victoria, July 1858. *PABC.*

15. H.M.S. *Plumper* Surveying in Johnstone Strait.
From *Illustrated London News*, 1 March 1862.

16. Captain and Mrs. G. H. Richards with Officers of H.M.S. *Plumper*. *PABC*.

17. British Boundary Commission Party at Colvile, W.T. *Royal Engineers Corps Library, Brompton Barracks, Chatham, England.*

18. British Boundary Commission — Observatory Tent. *Royal Engineers Corps Library, Brompton Barracks, Chatham, England.*

19. Governor Richard Blanshard. *PABC*.

20. Governor Sir James Douglas. *PABC*.

21. Members of the First House of Assembly, Vancouver Island, 1856. *PABC*.

FOLLOWING PAGE 186

22. Colonel Richard Clement Moody, R.E. *PABC*.

23. Chief Justice Sir Matthew Baillie Begbie. *PABC*.

24. The Rt. Rev. George Hills, Bishop of British Columbia. *PABC*.

25. Amor De Cosmos. *PABC*.

26. The Royal Engineers' Camp, Sapperton. *PABC*.

27. View of New Westminster in the 1860s. *New Westminster Public Library.*

28. Hyack Volunteer Fire Brigade, New Westminster. *New Westminster Public Library.*

29. Coal Workings and Bastion at Nanaimo. *Metropolitan Toronto Library Board.*

30. The Town of Hope. *Canadian Illustrated News*, 18 May 1872.

31. View of Yale. *Illustrated London News*, 12 May 1866.

FOLLOWING PAGE 194

32. A Way-side House — Arrival of Miners.
Milton and Cheadle, *North-West Passage by Land.*

33. A Way-side House at Midnight.
Milton and Cheadle, *North-West Passage by Land.*

34. Tenas Lake (Little Lillooet Lake) on the Harrison-Lillooet Route.
Metropolitan Toronto Library Board.

35. Lillooet. *Metropolitan Toronto Library Board.*

36. Miner's Cabin, Williams Creek, Cariboo. *PABC.*

37. Bill Phinney working at Old Caledonia Mine, Cariboo. *PABC.*

38. Rafting through the Grand Canyon of the Fraser. *PABC.*

39. Lord Milton and Dr. Cheadle with guides. *PABC.*

FOLLOWING PAGE 250

40. Barnard's Stage at Yale. *PABC.*

41. Alexandra Bridge, Fraser Canyon. *PABC.*

42. Seventeen Mile Bluff, Fraser Canyon. *PABC.*

43. Boothroyd's Hostelry, north of Boston Bar. *PABC.*

44. The Cariboo Road at Jackass Mountain. *PABC.*

45. View of Lytton. *PABC.*

46. Spence's Bridge, Thompson River. *PABC.*

47. Cariboo Road at the Great Bluff, Thompson River. *PABC.*

48. Approaching Cache Creek. *PABC.*

49. Clinton Hotel. *PABC.*

50. Soda Creek, showing Colonial Hotel and river steamer. *PABC.*

51. Quesnelmouth. *PABC.*

52. Barkerville, the main street, before the fire of 1868. *PABC.*

53. Barkerville, the Hotel de France. *PABC.*

FOLLOWING PAGE 298

54. Waddington's Road, at head of Bute Inlet. *PAC.*

55. Rifle pit dug by packers during Chilcotin Uprising. *PAC.*

56. John A. ("Cariboo") Cameron. *PABC.*

57. Mrs. John A. Cameron. *PABC.*

58. "Steve" Tingley. *PABC.*

59. A Chinese in British Columbia.
Metropolitan Toronto Library Board.

60. The original Parliament Buildings ("The Birdcages"),
Victoria. *PABC.*

61. Government Street, Victoria. *PABC.*

62. Victoria, view from Parliament Buildings towards James Bay
Bridge. *PABC.*

63. Sir Edward Bulwer Lytton. *PABC.*

64. Governor Frederick Seymour. *PABC.*

65. Governor Arthur Edward Kennedy. *PABC.*

66. Governor Anthony Musgrave. *PABC.*

FOLLOWING PAGE 306

67. Victoria Pioneer Rifle Corps ("The African Rifles"). *PABC.*

68. Queen Victoria's birthday, New Westminster [?]. *PAC.*

69. Government House, New Westminster. *PABC.*

70. Croquet party at Fairfield House, Victoria. *PABC.*

71. Indian bridge, Hagwilget, built with wire abandoned by Collins
Overland Telegraph. *PAC.*

72. A Vancouver Island passport.
Rare Book Department, McGill University Libraries.

73. H.M.S. *Sparrowhawk. PABC.*

74. Ships loading lumber at Moodyville, Burrard Inlet.
New Westminster Public Library.

Maps and Diagrams

Map of British Columbia   end papers

Early Trails in the Hope-Tulameen-Princeton Area 14

Queen Charlotte Islands 45

Victoria and Esquimalt, c. 1858 62

San Juan Boundary Dispute 100

Fraser River Gold Bars from Hope to Lytton c. 1858 110

Routes to Upper Fraser 1859 116

Royal Engineers' Plan for New Westminster 156

Cariboo 1865 192

Early Roads and Trails on Burrard Peninsula 262

Abbreviations

B.C.	British Columbia
BCHQ	*British Columbia Historical Quarterly*
CMS	Church Missionary Society (England)
HBC	Hudson's Bay Company
HBCA	Hudson's Bay Company Archives
H.M.S.	Her Majesty's Ship
NMM	National Maritime Museum (Greenwich, England)
PABC	Provincial Archives of British Columbia
PAC	Public Archives of Canada
PRO	Public Record Office (London, England)
R.E.	Royal Engineers
RGS	Royal Geographical Society
R.M.	Royal Marines
R.N.	Royal Navy
UBC	University of British Columbia
U.S.S.	United States Ship
V.I.	Vancouver Island

Acknowledgements

After the drudgery of often unrewarding research and the labour of polishing successive drafts of the resulting book, real pleasure comes when, preparing the statement of acknowledgements at the end of the venture, we realize how much friendliness, co-operation and generosity we have found in those who helped us along the way.

First, we would like to express our thanks to those libraries and archives which have made their resources available to us: the Public Archives of Canada, the Provincial Archives of British Columbia, the Archives of the Hudson's Bay Company (now in the keeping of the Provincial Archives of Manitoba), the Provincial Archives of Ontario, the Metropolitan Toronto Central Library, the Archives of the United Church of Canada (also in Toronto), the Rare Book Department of McGill University, the Special Collections division of the University of British Columbia Library, the Vancouver City Archives, the pictorial collections of the Royal Ontario Museum, and of the Vancouver and New Westminster Public Libraries. Proceeding beyond Canada, we must acknowledge our debts to the Bancroft Library of the University of California, Berkeley; to the Huntington Library, San Marino, California, and to the Library of the Oregon Historical Society, Portland. Looking beyond the seas, we recall with pleasure the time we spent in Britain working in the Public Record Office, the Scottish Record Office, the British Library, the Navy Library (formerly the Admiralty Library), the Office of the Hydrographer of the Navy, the National Maritime Museum, the Archives of the Church Missionary Society, and the libraries of the Royal Geographical Society and the University of Nottingham. Ranging even farther afield, we must record our hospitable reception both at the University of Otago in New Zealand, where unfortunately we found the papers of Sir James Hector almost entirely illegible, and at the Mitchell Library in Sydney, Australia, where we received permission to reproduce the pictures of H.M.S. *Virago* to be found in this book.

We are under special obligation to the University of Texas Press for permitting us to reprint from *The Golden Frontier: The Recollections of Herman Francis Reinhart*, Reinhart's account of the gold-hunters' expedition through the Okanagan in 1858, and to the McGill-Queen's University Press for similar permission to reprint lengthy excerpts from James Thomson's Cariboo letter of 1862 (originally printed in R. A. Preston, ed., *For Friends at Home* (Montreal: McGill-Queen's University Press, 1974), pp. 297-304.) To the University of British Columbia Press we are indebted for permission to use the transcripts of Dr. Helmcken's writings printed by our old friend Dr. Dorothy Blakey Smith in *The Reminiscences of Doctor John Sebastian Helmcken*.

We come finally to the invidious task of singling out for mention some of the scores of people who, in one way or another, have helped us with this book. We record our thanks to such persons as our Celista neighbours Mr. and Mrs. Alfred Gardner, who accompanied us on a field reconnaissance through the Chilcotin to the Pacific at Bella Coola. Thanks to their four-wheel-drive truck, our van was safely hauled out of an enormous frost-boil, turned to mud, near Anahim Lake. We are grateful to Mr. Gabriel Bayliff who on this same expedition led us to the site, on his ranch, of Fort Chilcotin. We are grateful too to our old Celista friends Mr. and Mrs. Ed Riley for taking us along a stretch of the Big Bend gold rush trail of the 1860s. Mr. Robert C. Harris, whose incredible energy has sent him on innumerable forays to find old trails, in intervals of accumulating a wealth of maps and other documentation, was most helpful in the preparation of the map showing the trails in the Hope-Tulameen-Princeton area. We owe much also to his comments after reading over drafts of our passages relating to the Fraser Canyon trails. Shirlee Anne Smith of the Hudson's Bay Company Archives checked our references to their manuscripts cited in this book. Mrs. Anne Yandle and Miss Frances Woodward of the University of British Columbia Library's Special Collections, and Miss Maureen Wilson of its Map Division, gave us every assistance. Others whom we must mention include Rear-Admiral P. W. Brock, R.N., (retd.), Lieutenant-Commander A. C. F. David, R.N., Mr. R. W. Sandilands of the federal hydrographic office in Victoria, Colonel G. S. Andrews, former Surveyor-General of British Columbia, Professor A. L. Farley, Miss E. M. I. Cayley, Mr. A. M. Channer, and Dr. J. Roberts.

One final and perhaps slightly unusual acknowledgement must be made to the men and women of the Morriss Printing Company of Victoria, the creators of this book as an artifact. It was a happy day indeed when, eight years ago, we took our first book over to Victoria. Here we dealt initially with Charlie Morriss, founder of the firm, relaxed, canny, humorous, a man who loves fine books and good printing. Later, as Charlie spent more of his time in retirement at his beautiful estate at Sooke, we found just as good a friend and helpful an adviser in his son Dick, who was taking over. Nor is our debt limited to the principals. The whole atmosphere of the plant is one of friendliness and of respect for each other's craftsmanship. We would like to thank not only Bev Leech, who designed this book; Ron Smith ("Smitty"), who was in charge of its production; and Frank Frawley, who was responsible for the binding; but every other member of the company who worked on *British Columbia Chronicle*.

Celista, B.C.   G.P.V.A.

                                             H.B.A.

Prologue

In 1845 the threat of an impending Anglo-American war hung over the Pacific North-west. During twenty-seven years of intermittent negotiations, Britain and the United States had failed to agree upon a common boundary west of the Rocky Mountains. Deadlocked, they had settled for a vague interim co-occupation of all that vast territory which extended from the Russian border (now the British Columbia-Alaska boundary) and the then Mexican border (today's Oregon-California state line).

For most of these twenty-seven years the superior organization and discipline of the Hudson's Bay Company had enabled their officers largely to exclude American traders from the co-dominion, while a network of HBC trading posts, extending from the Arctic to southern Oregon, had maintained British *de facto* supremacy in the area.

In the early 1840s the situation changed drastically when thousands of American immigrants journeyed westward over the Oregon Trail. Now, when the officers of the Hudson's Bay Company crossed the lower Columbia from their principal base, Fort Vancouver, they could see the river's southern bank and the valley of the nearby Willamette being settled by ardently expansionist Americans. Many of these newcomers were convinced that an auspicious destiny had assigned to the United States everything between the North Pole and Panama. Few or none would concede anything to the British when the latter argued that both present possession and past history entitled Britain to the lands to the north of the Columbia River, and that the long overdue boundary should leave the 49th parallel of latitude close to today's Trail, and follow the Columbia in its south-westerly course to the Pacific. The least that the Americans would

settle for was the 49th parallel all the way to the sea. The more
militant, seeking all the land up to Russian America, shouted "Fifty-
four Forty or Fight".[1]

When, early in 1846, the belligerent Polk became President of the
United States, everybody knew that a showdown on the Oregon
boundary was imminent. The militia units formed among the
American settlers readied themselves to storm and burn the "forts"
of the Hudson's Bay Company, knowing them quite incapable of
withstanding anything more than Indian raids. The United States
Army was expected to bring troops up the River Platte, and then
send them overland to Walla Walla, which was seen as the gateway
for invasion. Nor were the British idle. Thinly disguised as tourists,
Lieut. Henry James Warre, A.D.C. to the Commander-in-Chief,
British North America, and Lieut. Mervin Vavasour of the Royal
Engineers, travelled overland to Fort Vancouver, made a careful
reconnaissance of the North-west, and sought to assure that the
British would have control of the mouth of the Columbia when war
came. Meanwhile the Royal Navy mustered a squadron in Esquimalt
harbour.

But the anticipated war was never fought. The British government, at the urging of Lord Aberdeen its pacifist Foreign Secretary,
backed down and, on 15 June 1846, the Treaty of Washington was
signed, conceding to the Americans the 49th parallel as their boundary all the way from the Rockies to the Pacific. True, the Americans
had to agree that after the boundary line reached the sea it would
dip southwards and pass through the Strait of Juan de Fuca, leaving
Vancouver Island entirely British. Fort Victoria, established at its
southern tip in 1843, would remain under the Union Jack, ready to
replace Fort Vancouver as the Hudson's Bay Company's principal
Pacific depot. This concession was a small one, however, compared
with Britain's surrender of the Puget Sound area and much of the
interior of today's State of Washington.

"The hand that signed the paper . . . halved a country." Purely
arbitrary, the line of demarcation set forth by the signatories of the
Treaty of Washington was an absurdity in a land where natural

---

[1] For a detailed appraisal of the British and American claims, see *British
Columbia Chronicle, 1778-1846* (Vancouver, 1975), pp. 395-401.

boundaries such as rivers and mountain ridges were to be found in all directions. Like a great mindless giant, with a compass in place of a brain, the Boundary strode blindly westward from the Rockies to the Pacific. It marched up unscalable mountain precipices and plunged into swampland and bog. Ruthlessly it severed little prairies and jewel-like lakes. The sparkling Kootenay River, turning south, crossed the Boundary's path and suddenly became American. Turning north, it became British again. Coming to Point Roberts, the Boundary amputated its southern tip and left it American, even though it lacked all land connection with the United States.

Years would pass, of course, before survey parties could fix the boundary, erecting cairns or planting iron pillars at intervals, and slashing a swath through the forest at major points. Ultimately some of the treaty maps which fixed the final line would be found to be erroneous. To this day the official boundary across Point Roberts runs about two hundred and fifty yards north of the true 49th parallel.[2]

In 1846 this error and its detection alike lay in the future. What was important this year was that Great Britain and the United States had at last agreed on where the yet unmarked boundary should run. South of "The Line" lay most of the old HBC District of Columbia, shortly to be known as the Territories of Oregon and Washington. To the north lay that remnant of Columbia which had been saved for the British Crown, along with the northern district known as New Caledonia, today comprising most of central and northern British Columbia. In twelve years' time the name of "British Columbia" would be given to this part of the continental mainland which remained in Queen Victoria's empire. Vancouver Island would be added to British Columbia later.

This present chronicle addresses itself to the fascinating task of recording British Columbia's history during the twenty-five years that elapsed between the boundary treaty of 1846 and the entry of the Crown Colony of British Columbia into the Dominion of Canada in 1871. Those twenty-five years are so crammed with incident, excitement, discovery, high hopes and abject disappointments, that surely their like can be found nowhere else in Canada's history.

[2] See Canada, National Topographic Map 92G/3a (Scale 1:25,000), 1973.

1847

Paul Kane paints at Fort Victoria — Quest for an all-British brigade route — John Tod saves Fort Kamloops from Nicola's war party — Bishop Demers.

Early on the afternoon of April 9th a white visitor landed at Fort Victoria, stepping out of the canoe in which six Indians had paddled him from Puget Sound. The newcomer was a tall man, almost a six-footer, dignified and deliberate in his bearing. His voice was "gentle, rather grunty". From his weathered, pock-marked face a bushy red beard extended to his chest. A visored cap rose above two rather widely spaced, steady, blue eyes, slightly weakened by snow blindness suffered in the Alps and the Rockies. With him he carried a letter which he would show to Roderick Finlayson, the officer in command of Fort Victoria:

> Fort Frances — Lac à la Pluie,
> 31 May 1846
>
> Gentlemen,
>
> I have the pleasure to introduce to you the bearer hereof Mr. P. Kane an Artist who has come to the country on a professional tour; and I have to request the favor of your showing that gentleman your kind attentions and the hospitalities of such of the Company's posts as he may visit; and you will be pleased to afford Mr. Kane passages from post to post in the Company's craft — free of charge.
>
> I am,
> Gentlemen,
> Your very obedt. servt.,
> G. SIMPSON
>
> The Gentlemen of the
> Hon. Hudsons Bay Co.'s Service
> Ruperts Land and Elsewhere.[1]

---

[1] J. Russell Harper, ed., *Paul Kane's Frontier* (Toronto, [1971]), p. 327. Those who are interested in examining Kane's work cannot do better than to look at the splendid reproductions in this book. Some of Kane's pictures are to be found in *B.C. Chronicle, 1778-1846* and others in the present volume.

Born in Ireland and educated in York (later to be named Toronto), Paul Kane had started his career as a largely self-trained artist, earning a living by painting furniture in Canada West. Advancing in skill, he had travelled down to the United States, painting portraits in Michigan and Alabama. In 1841, having painfully accumulated the necessary funds, he had sailed for Europe where he painted copies of masterpieces in the galleries of Rome, Florence and Venice. From Italy he had gone to England and there, in London, came under an influence more potent than that of any of the Renaissance masters, that of George Catlin, who was exhibiting his paintings of Indian life in the American West. Becoming friendly with Catlin, Kane discovered his mission in life. He would do for the Indians of British North America what Catlin had done for the Indians of the United States.

Once back in Canada, Kane was eager to head west into the Indian Country, where the tribes still lived their own wild free life, not yet half-metamorphosed into white men. A crucial meeting with Governor Simpson followed. It yielded not only that precious letter just quoted, but a commission for twelve oil paintings. Paul Kane was soon on his way. In November he crossed the Rockies by the Athabasca Pass. In January he arrived at Fort Vancouver and now he had reached his ultimate destination, Fort Victoria. The next two months saw Kane, at the height of his powers, sketching and painting not only at Fort Victoria but also on frequent brief excursions along the Strait of Juan de Fuca and up around Haro Strait. Fort Victoria itself offered him subjects aplenty, with Indians from many tribes constantly coming and going; not only the local tribes but also Cowichans and Nootkas, northern Kwakiutls, Tsimpseans and Haidas, and visitors from the American shore. Directly across the inlet from Fort Victoria was the Songhees settlement, home of five hundred warriors. One of the finest of Kane's paintings shows a war party returning there, the leaders standing up in the canoes and triumphantly brandishing the heads taken from their victims.

Kane wanted to paint portraits of notable and representative Indians. The Indians, however, regarded with superstitious dread the artist's power of creating "second selves". Generally he managed to get Indians to sit for him, but occasionally difficulties arose. Later, in his *Wanderings of An Artist*, Kane recalled one such occasion.

In one of my daily excursions, I was particularly struck by the ugliness of an Indian whom I met. Upon inquiry, I found he was Shawstun, the head chief of the Sinahōmās. He inquired very earnestly if my sketching him would not involve the risk of his dying; and after I had finished the sketch, and given him a piece of tobacco, he held it up for some moments, and said it was a small recompense for risking his life. He followed me afterwards for two or three days, begging of me to destroy the picture; and at last, to get rid of him, I made a rough copy of it, which I tore up in his presence, pretending that it was the original.[2]

At least one grisly experience befell Kane during his sojourn at Fort Victoria:

One morning while I was sketching, I saw upon the rocks the dead body of a young woman, thrown out to the vultures and crows, whom I had seen a few days previously walking about in perfect health. Mr. Finlayson, the gentleman in charge of Fort Victoria, accompanied me to the lodge she belonged to, where we found an Indian woman, her mistress, who made light of her death, and was doubtless the cause of it. She told us that a slave had no right to burial, and became perfectly furious when Mr. Finlayson told her that the slave was far better than herself. "I," she exclaimed, "the daughter of a chief, no better than a dead slave!" and bridling up with all the dignity she could assume, she stalked out, and next morning she had up her lodge and was gone. I was also told by an eye-witness, of a chief, who having erected a colossal idol of wood, sacrificed five slaves to it, barbarously murdering them at its base, and asking in a boasting manner who amongst them could afford to kill so many slaves.[3]

On June 10th Kane left for Fort Vancouver, where he prepared for his long journey back East with an HBC express party. Looking over his magnificent harvest of sketches and paintings, he was struck by a disturbing thought — so bizarre were some of the sights that he had portrayed, so remote were they from anything ever seen in Canada, that he might very well find himself accused of romantic exaggeration, if not groundless invention, when he came to exhibit

---

[2] Paul Kane, *Wanderings of an Artist among the Indians of North America from Canada to Vancouver's Island and Oregon through the Hudson's Bay Company's Territory and Back Again*, (London, 1859), p. 240.

[3] *Ibid.*, pp. 215-16.

these works back East. Addressing himself to Chief Factor Douglas, he obtained a certificate:

I have seen Mr. Kane's faithful and spirited sketches of Oregon Scenery, and have been perfectly delighted with these masterly delineations of places, rendered familiar by a residence of 20 years on the banks of the Columbia and N. West Coast.

The Indian Portraits and Costumes are perfect and it is impossible to give a better idea, than they Convey, of the dress and appearance of the Native inhabitants of this Country.

JAMES DOUGLAS
C. Factor, Hudsons Bay Co.

Fort Vancouver
30th June '47[4]

Armed with this, Paul Kane was ready to face any sceptics in Toronto.

*　　*　　*

Very much on Chief Factor Douglas' mind this summer was the problem of finding an all-British route for the HBC's famous fur brigades. Annually these brought out, for shipment to England, the year's harvest of furs from the Interior forts in New Caledonia and Columbia. Each year, on their return, they resupplied the Interior forts with trade goods. Until now the brigades had used a long-established route down the Okanagan valley, then along the lower Columbia to Fort Vancouver. Unfortunately it appeared all too likely that the Americans would bar this route. In 1846 A. C. Anderson had investigated the Lillooet-Harrison Lake-Fort Langley route linking the Interior to the Coast. Travelling "haphazard" he had also found another all-British route of sorts which crossed the Cascade Mountains east of the Coquihalla River. Anderson himself, however, was the first to admit that neither of these routes was really practicable for the brigades with their hundreds of heavily laden horses.

This year Anderson made his second attempt to find a usable British route over the Cascade Mountains. Setting out along a well-

---

[4] Harper, *op. cit.*, p. 328.

known HBC trail from Kamloops on May 19th with a party of five, Anderson the next day reached "Lac de Nicholas" (Nicola Lake) amid the tawny grass, yellow pines and bare rock of its surrounding hills. From here it was for the most part a fairly easy journey along the Nicola River to where it joins the Thompson, though Anderson found troublesome the volcanic rock, the cactus, and the rattlesnakes along the way. On May 22nd Anderson, at the site of the modern village of Spences Bridge, sent his horses back to Kamloops under the care of some Indians and started on foot along the difficult path which led downstream through the canyon of the Thompson River. Arriving at last where the clear waters of the Thompson mingled with the muddy waters of the Fraser, Anderson and his men found an Indian chief awaiting them. He was Pahallak, engaged by Chief Trader Yale at Fort Langley to serve as their guide southwards.

On May 24th Anderson and his men, led by Pahallak, toiled through a long hot day following an Indian trail southwards into the Fraser Canyon. When they halted that evening they had travelled about twenty-eight miles and were approaching midpoint in the canyon. Anderson already realized that this route would be quite impossible for the brigades:

... though I do not condemn these passages as *impassable* with horses, in the strict acceptation of that term, I decidedly think them quite impracticable for a loaded brigade, or loaded horses, however limited in number. . . . [5]

Resuming his journey a little before 3 a.m. on the morning of May 25th, Anderson pushed down the Fraser Canyon until he reached the mouth of Squa-zowm (now Anderson) River. Now he left the Fraser and followed an Indian horse trail, leading south-east, high above the deep canyon of the Anderson River. Thus he arrived at the confluence of Uztlius Creek and Anderson River. Here the Indian trail which he had so far followed turned eastwards up Uztlius Creek and, by way of Maka Creek and the Coldwater River, reached the Nicola River and the trail to Kamloops. (The HBC

---

[5] This account of Anderson's 1847 expedition is based upon his own report contained in his *History of the Northwest Coast*. The quoted passage will be found on p. 78a of the UBC transcript.

already knew that this Uztlius route was suitable for brigade travel.) Crossing Uztlius Creek and the nearby East Anderson River at their mouths, Anderson continued southward up the main Anderson River for a couple of miles. Then he ascended the saddle, or low point, of the high ridge on his right and, descending on the other side, rejoined the Fraser River, having by-passed the worst stretch of the Fraser Canyon. Anderson knew that any future brigade which came up the Coldwater-Uztlius trail and then followed his route up the Anderson River would have a very hard time getting over this final ridge, but he was satisfied that, once a suitable zig-zag trail had been built along its slopes, the crossing would be possible.

From the point where he had struck the Fraser at Kequeloose (a mile above the old Alexandra suspension bridge), Anderson followed the river south for about three miles, then crossed it near Spuzzum. Anderson thought that a brigade could ferry itself or swim across the river here. Resuming his journey, he worked his way downstream until at last he emerged from the Canyon at "The Foot of the Rapids", otherwise known as "The Falls of the Fraser" (the area around Lady Franklin Rock above Yale). It seemed to him that future brigades could traverse this stretch by boat and portage. From this point on, the Fraser was navigable and Anderson and his men, taking to canoes, swiftly travelled down to Fort Langley.

To Chief Trader Yale, Anderson reported that he had at last found a possible brigade route. He made no secret that some stretches of it would prove very rough going, but he was confident that, with necessary work done on the worst stretches, the route would be feasible. Chief Factor Douglas, learning of Anderson's discovery, came and took a look at the stretch from the proposed ferry point near Spuzzum to the Foot of the Rapids. Deciding against Anderson's recommended alternate use of boats and portages through the lower Fraser Canyon, Douglas ordered that a horse-trail be constructed as a thirteen-mile detour to the west of the river. Later this trail became known as the "Douglas Portage".

En route back to his post at Fort Alexandria, Anderson had an opportunity to stop over at Fort Kamloops and talk there with the veteran Chief Trader Tod. Perhaps Anderson now learned of a notable exploit of John Tod's, one which had happened apparently during this year of 1847.

A band of strange Indians, ones who had never traded there before, turned up at Fort Kamloops. Identifying themselves as long-time enemies of neighbouring Chief Nicholas (or Nicola) and his people, they camped very close to the fort for protection in case of an attack. Nicola, learning of the arrival of the newcomers, summoned his warriors and in a long and fiery oration aroused them to revenge the wrongs that these people had inflicted upon their ancestors. Hostilities of course required munitions so Nicola, carefully conceal-ing his motive and pretending an eagerness to hunt, sent his people to Fort Kamloops to trade their furs for guns and ammunition. No sooner had the transaction been completed than one of the visiting band came to Tod and told him that he was being deceived by Chief Nicola, who was getting the arms not for hunting but for war against themselves. When Indians belonging to Nicola's band came a second time for arms, Tod asked them to accept blankets, beads and suchlike goods, alleging that he must keep a stock of guns and gunpowder so that other tribes could get their proper share. Refusing to barter for anything but arms, Nicola's braves returned to their chief with their furs. Furious at finding Tod had turned suspicious and uncooperative, Nicola told his warriors that they would go to Kamloops, capture the fort, and help themselves to the muskets and gunpowder which Tod would not let them have.

Somehow word reached Fort Kamloops that Nicola and his war party were on their way. The Indian strangers hurriedly decamped. Tod's engagés (the Company's hired hands) panicked and fled also. Only one, a cook named Lefevre, remained; but Tod told him that he too must depart. Similarly Tod ordered his wife and children to a place of concealment well away from the fort. Then, alone, Tod awaited the coming of Nicola. In preparation for that event he rolled out a hundred pound keg of gunpowder, placed it by the fort gate, kicked in its ends, and took his position by it, flint and steel in hand. Seeing what Tod had in mind, a passing Indian raced to where Chief Nicola and his war party were approaching. Once the braves realized that Tod meant to blow up the fort, himself and them once they drew close, they flatly refused to go any farther. His plans frustrated, Nicola told one of his men to wash off his war paint, and sent him to the fort bearing a white flag. The crisis was over.[6]

* * *

Late this year, on the last day of November, Father Modeste Demers (who had been the first Catholic priest to visit New Caledonia) was consecrated Bishop of Vancouver Island, with responsibility also for the British territories on the mainland. The consecration of the new bishop was conducted in the little church at Oregon City which had to serve as a cathedral for Archbishop Blanchet. After receiving Blanchet's benediction, Bishop Demers headed not for Vancouver Island but for Quebec and Europe to raise funds for the new diocese and to recruit clergy to serve under him. The need was urgent. Up in New Caledonia, after Father Nobili's departure in 1846, Indian "pseudo-priests" or "prophets" had arisen. Chief among these was a Babine named Uzakle who, like the others, preached a strange doctrine compounded of Christian elements and native superstitions. His influence was tremendous throughout New Caledonia, partly because of his claims that he could see, floating above each of his hearers, a bodiless head suspended by wings. These winged heads knew the innermost thoughts of every man, and these same innermost thoughts were equally known to him, Uzakle. Years later, when Father Morice came into the country, he found that every living witness, white as well as Indian, agreed that the prophecies of Uzakle had invariably been fulfilled.[7]

---

[6] For Tod's own account of this adventure, an account which one rather suspects had been lovingly elaborated over the years, see his *History of New Caledonia & the Northwest Coast*, PAC, MG29, B35, Vol. 8:63-68 (Bancroft transcript). Oddly enough, an identical tale was told to Paul Kane of how Archibald McKinlay had used these same tactics to save Fort Walla Walla from attack. (*v.* Kane, *Wanderings of an Artist* (1859), p. 194.)

[7] A. G. Morice, *The History of the Northern Interior of British Columbia* (Toronto, 1904), pp. 234-36.

1848

*Fort Yale — Nightmare journey of a brigade using the
Anderson River route — Henry Peers discovers the Coqui-
halla-Tulameen route — Fort Hope — H.M.S.* Constance *at
Esquimalt.*

Although in 1846 and 1847 the Hudson's Bay Company had been
anxious to find a practicable all-British route for its brigades to
travel between the Interior and the Coast, the discovery of such a
route had been of no real urgency, though a British one was desirable
as a means of freeing the Company from the burdensome customs
duties which the Americans were forcing it to pay. The situation
changed with the outbreak of the Cayuse War in American territory
late in 1847, for that war effectively closed the old Columbia route
for the HBC. The 1848 brigade would have to use the very difficult
route which A. C. Anderson had discovered the previous year.
Accordingly, the spring of 1848 saw everything possible being done
to complete Douglas' horse-trail from The Foot of the Rapids to
Spuzzum, and to make other improvements on the route. At The
Foot of the Rapids a new establishment came into existence this
spring, chiefly as a way-station for the brigade and only incidentally
as a trading post for the Indians. It consisted of a single sturdy log
building, without any palisades, but it was given the fine-sounding
name of "Fort Yale", after the veteran HBC officer at Fort Langley,
James Murray Yale. Fort Yale, or Yale, would figure prominently in
British Columbia's history in the coming decades.

June saw the new route being travelled by the three brigades from
New Caledonia, Fort Kamloops and Fort Colvile, amalgamated
under the command of Chief Trader Donald Manson, the superintendent of New Caledonia. For their guide they had Anderson himself. Their journey turned out to be a nightmare, especially after they

had crossed from Anderson River to the Fraser and were labouring to get four hundred horses and their loads across the surging current of the great river. Somehow, at long last, the exhausted men and animals struggled down to Fort Yale. Here boats were waiting to carry them and their furs down to Fort Langley. A few weeks later they were back at Fort Yale ready to attempt the return journey. This time the going was, if anything, even worse. The hardy engagés, whose cheerfulness under the most arduous difficulties was proverbial, now approached the breaking-point. One of them, unable to endure any longer, committed suicide.

On August 24th, having reached Kamloops on his way home, Manson did not mince words when delivering his verdict on the new route:

We have now tested its advantages and disadvantages thoroughly, and I have no hesitation in declaring it utterly impracticable for a large brigade such as ours. The rugged, rocky, mountainous and thickly wooded country which lies between Fraser River and the plains, say a distance of about forty-three miles, and which the brigade took ten days to pass, seven of which the horses were without food, is, in my opinion, sufficient in itself to condemn this route.[1]

In a subsequent letter to Governor Simpson he reported that, although he had taken every possible precaution, he had lost 70 horses and 25 pieces of merchandise on the appalling journey.

Anderson, sending in his own report this August, agreed that another route must be found and urged:

... immediate measures for ascertaining the practicability of certain improvements and partial alterations in my route by the Similkameen of 1846, which have been suggested by Old Blackeye [an Indian] and others. . . .[2]

For the new quest he recommended one of the Company's clerks, Henry Newsham Peers. Peers was set to work immediately and this autumn was able to report that he had found a route which he deemed feasible. From the lower Fraser it led up the Coquihalla River, Peers Creek and over Manson Mountain. After paralleling

---

[1] Quoted by Morice, *History of Northern Interior of B.C.*, p. 254.
[2] *History of Northwest Coast*, p. 99.

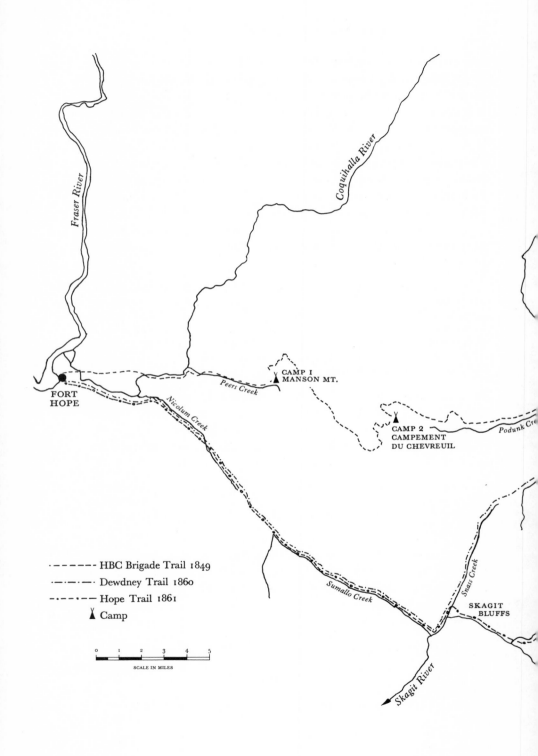

FORT
HOPE

Fraser River

Coquihalla River

Peers Creek

CAMP I
MANSON MT.

CAMP 2
CAMPEMENT
DU CHEVREUIL

Podunk Cr

Nicolum Creek

Sumallo Creek

Snass Creek

SKAGIT
BLUFFS

Skagit River

----- HBC Brigade Trail 1849
-·--·- Dewdney Trail 1860
-··--··- Hope Trail 1861
⛺ Camp

0   1   2   3   4   5
SCALE IN MILES

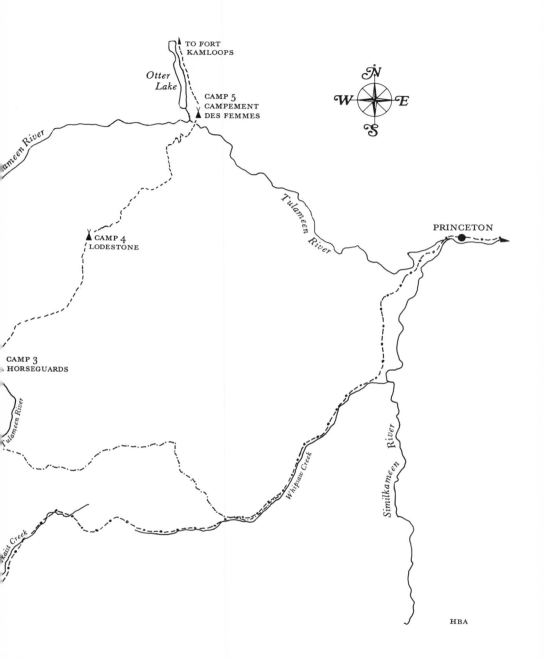

TO FORT
KAMLOOPS

*Otter
Lake*

CAMP 5
CAMPEMENT
DES FEMMES

Tulameen River

PRINCETON

Tulameen River

CAMP 4
LODESTONE

CAMP 3
HORSEGUARDS

Tulameen River

Whipsaw Creek

Similkameen River

Skaist Creek

HBA

Early Trails in the
Hope - Tulameen - Princeton Area

Sowaqua Creek for a time, the trail crossed it, went through a pass and down Podunk Creek. Here the trail utilized part of the Indian Blackeye's Trail which took it up over Lodestone Mountain and down to the Tulameen River near Otter Lake. Late this year, trusting that Peers' route would measure up to his expectations, the HBC built a new post at the junction of the Coquihalla and Fraser Rivers, where transshipment would be made next year between the brigade packtrain and the Fraser River boats. The new post was bravely given the name "Fort Hope."[3]

*   *   *

Despite the ending of the Oregon boundary dispute, Chief Factors Douglas and Ogden, who had the direction of the Hudson's Bay Company's Columbia Department, remained worried about the safety of Fort Victoria. They felt that, just as H.M.S. *Modeste* had long lain off Fort Vancouver on the Columbia affording it protection, so now a British warship should be stationed permanently at the Company's new headquarters at Fort Victoria. Douglas and Ogden did not get their wish but Rear-Admiral Phipps Hornby, Commander-in-Chief, Pacific, went some way to meet them this year when he sent H.M.S. *Constance* and H.M.S. *Pandora* on somewhat extended visits to Vancouver Island. First on the scene, late in July, was H.M.S. *Constance* (a frigate of 50 guns), Captain Courtenay. Anchoring in Esquimalt harbour (where Constance Cove preserves her memory), she made a valuable discovery, a fresh-water spring yielding five or six hundred tons of water in twenty-four hours. The find was the more important since the shortage of water in Victoria itself was already notorious.

This visit by H.M.S. *Constance* was almost certainly inspired by a warning that Samuel Cunard, the steamship magnate, had given the Admiralty in January. According to Cunard, unless action were quickly taken to protect the coal deposits on northern Vancouver Island, the Americans might very well take them over. In any event, the coal up-island seems to have been very much on Captain Cour-

---

[3] On this whole matter of the search for a new brigade route, see F. W. Howay, "The Raison d'Etre of Forts Yale and Hope", *Transactions of the Royal Society of Canada*, Sec. II, 1922, pp. 49-64.

tenay's mind. He instructed the HBC officers to erect a hut at Port McNeill as a token of occupancy, and to put up a notice there declaring that "the Lands adjacent together with the Coal and other Minerals were taken possession of for Her Majesty".[4] These instructions he ordered entered both into his own ship's log and into the journal of Fort Victoria. As for the coal which H.M.S. *Cormorant* had brought to Victoria from Port McNeill several years before, he took sixteen tons of it on board H.M.S. *Constance* for her own use, and had a log shed with a thatch roof built on shore for the storage of the remaining forty-one tons.

By and large, Captain Courtenay did not get on very well with the Hudson's Bay Company men whom he had come to support. True, he did land a force of 250 bluejackets and marines and march them, with rifles at the slope, past Fort Victoria's palisades — a useful demonstration that impressed the Indians. But he was impatient about the complaints the HBC men brought against the Americans and opined that " . . . having for years Lorded it over that Country — they cannot bring themselves to act in obedience to the Laws of the state as now established." Indeed, he felt that the HBC should forget about the rights guaranteed it under the Treaty of Washington and close down its establishments south of the new boundary.

Sensing Captain Courtenay's impatience and hostility, Roderick Finlayson and his assistants clammed up. In considerable dudgeon, the Captain reported to his Admiral:

I must remark that there appears to be the greatest reluctance or fear on the part of the Hudson's Bay Company's servants to afford information relating to their affairs or upon any subject connected with the North West Coast.[5]

To bring matters to a head, Captain Courtenay submitted a formal written questionnaire to Roderick Finlayson, who returned it with four of its questions pointedly unanswered. This document survives. The only information it yields of any interest is a table, tribe by tribe,

[4] National Maritime Museum (Greenwich, England), MS. PHI/3/5.

[5] *Loc. cit.*

which shows that Vancouver Island at this time had a native population totalling 11,463.[6]

With obvious relief Captain Courtenay sailed for San Francisco
where he found the entire American garrison had deserted in the
rush to the newly-discovered goldfields on the Sacramento River.
Behind him at Vancouver Island he left H.M. Survey Ship *Pandora*,
which for a short while was continuing the charting which she had
commenced in the Strait of Georgia two years earlier. The *Pandora*'s
men found a number of changes since their previous visit. A good,
substantial wooden bridge had been thrown across the narrows at
the upper end of Victoria harbour, and a road cut to Esquimalt,
where a sawmill was being erected at the upper end of the inlet.
Victoria was beginning to grow.

6 *Loc. cit.* The same table is printed in an article, almost certainly by Lieut.
Wood, commanding H.M.S. *Pandora*, in the *Nautical Magazine*, 18 (1849):
301.

1849

Vancouver Island granted to the Hudson's Bay Company — The Company attempts to colonize it — Captain Grant, the first settler — Scottish coal miners at Fort Rupert — An Anglican clergyman "full of frills" — Brigade route problem solved.

The Treaty of Washington had hardly been ratified and Vancouver Island in its entirety preserved for Britain when Earl Grey, Britain's Colonial Secretary, received a communication from Sir John Pelly, Governor of the HBC, informing him:

The Hudson's Bay Company having formed an establishment on the southern point of Vancouver's Island, which they are annually enlarging, are anxious to know whether they will be confirmed in the possession of such lands, as they may find it expedient to add to those which they already possess.[1]

Pelly took the opportunity to point out to the Colonial Secretary that his company already possessed a grant giving them, until 13 May 1859, the exclusive right to trade with the Indians west of the Rockies. Pelly's letter confronted the British government with an important question: just what should it do with that territory in the Pacific North-west to which, since 1846, it had enjoyed complete title? In the ensuing negotiations Earl Grey came out for an active policy of British immigration and colonization, and Governor Pelly expressed the HBC's hearty support for this policy as one which would help to secure the Company from further American aggression. Writing in October 1846, Pelly observed:

It would be a superfluous task to enter into a detail of the reasons which render the colonization of Vancouver's Island an object of great

[1] Pelly to Grey, 7 Sept. 1846. Great Britain, Parliament, House of Commons, Sessional Papers, 1847-48, No. 619, p. 3.

importance; I shall, at present, merely submit to Earl Grey's consideration whether that object, embracing as I trust it will, the conversion to
Christianity and civilization of the native population, might not be
most readily and effectually accomplished through the instrumentality
of the Hudson's Bay Company. . . . [2]

He subsequently suggested that, in return for the HBC undertaking
to promote colonization, Her Majesty should grant the Company, in
perpetuity, all her new domain west of the Rocky Mountains. Earl
Grey demurred — the Company was really asking for too much!
But Grey was ready to give the HBC title to Vancouver Island
provided the Company would colonize it. Further letters and meetings followed. And then the storm broke.

Word had got out that the government was intending to make a
gift of Vancouver Island to the Hudson's Bay Company and there
were plenty of people who thought that this was not at all a good
idea. Lord Lincoln (who as Duke of Newcastle would himself one
day be Colonial Secretary), and the Rt. Hon. W. E. Gladstone were
among those who asked questions and made speeches in Parliament
about Vancouver Island. Newspapers fulminated. The Manchester
Chamber of Commerce sent in a remonstrance. James Edward Fitzgerald, who wanted a joint stock company to take over the coal-fields
on Vancouver Island, and Charles Enderby, who wanted to base a
British whaling fleet there, joined in the debate. The objections to
the proposed grant were partly philosophical (that the great
monopolistic trading companies of the seventeenth and eighteenth
centuries were out of place in the brave new Victorian age of free
trade), and partly practical (that the HBC had shown precious little
aptitude for colonization in the past). Bowing before the storm, the
government released part of the Grey-Pelly correspondence and a
draft of the proposed grant.

Taken aback by the furor, the Hudson's Bay Company got a
rather superior hack, R. M. Martin, to rush into print a book entitled
The Hudson's Bay Territories and Vancouver's Island. Parts of the
Martin book were little more than an anthology of tributes to the
sagacity, even-handed justice, and Christian magnanimity of the
HBC. Section IV, entitled "Christian Conduct and Beneficent Policy

[2] Pelly to Hawes, 24 Oct. 1846. *Ibid.*, p. 5.

of the Hudson's Bay Company", prepared readers for the verdict reached in Martin's fifth and concluding section on "The Qualifications of the Hudson's Bay Company for the Colonization of Vancouver's Island". Fitzgerald retorted with his own book, *An Examination of the Charter and Proceedings of the Hudson's Bay Company with Reference to the Grant of Vancouver's Island*. The conclusions in that book were sufficiently foreshadowed by the Latin motto on its title page — *"Ubi solitudinem faciunt, pacem appellant"* ("Where they make a desert, they call it peace"). Unfortunately for Fitzgerald, his book did not appear until after January 13th, on which day Queen Victoria signed a grant making the Hudson's Bay Company "the true and absolute lords and Proprietors" of Vancouver Island, enjoying "all royalties of the Seas upon the Coasts within the limits aforesaid and all mines royal thereto belonging".[3]

Earl Grey believed in the Wakefield system of large-scale colonization administered on a corporate basis, a system which was to work well in New Zealand. Accordingly he remained firm in his opinion that, despite its faults, the Hudson's Bay Company was in the best position to get a British population established on Vancouver Island. However, to placate the opposition, he made certain changes in the charter as originally drafted. A new clause obligated the Company to sell land at a reasonable price to anybody wishing to settle on Vancouver Island. Moreover, while the HBC was allowed to retain 10% of all the money it obtained from the sale of lands, coal or other minerals, it was obligated to spend the remaining 90% on surveys, roads, bridges, churches, schools and other conveniences and amenities for the colonists. The final charter, like the original draft, provided for revocation of the grant of Vancouver Island if the HBC failed to establish there, within five years, a settlement of British colonists. In any event, the grant could be terminated in 1859, along with the Company's privilege of exclusive trade with the Indians west of the Rockies.

With this grant safely in its possession, the Hudson's Bay Company had to decide how it would set up its colonization scheme. One thing was clear to the Governor and Committee — they should recreate

[3] Provincial Archives of British Columbia (hereafter PABC), A/B/15/4.

on Vancouver Island the social structure of England, a stalwart squirarchy with the working class properly relegated to an inferior station. The HBC wanted British gentlemen of substantial means who would buy land, preferably in blocks of a hundred acres, at £1 per acre, and bring out one labourer for every twenty acres purchased. This scheme was doomed from the start. Why should anybody buy land, at a pound an acre (rocky outcrops, swamps and all) on Vancouver Island, when he could get a square mile free in the American territory, providing he homesteaded it for four years and filed the necessary legal forms?

Comedy was not lacking as the moguls of the great fur-trading company tried to function as land developers. Having set up their unrealistic scheme of land purchase which demanded that the money be paid in advance, the HBC advertised in the British papers. Alas, gentlemen of substance seemed to have little interest in travelling to a remote corner of North America to clear farms amid the dense forests. When prospective colonists called around at Hudson's Bay House on Fenchurch Street, they found to their surprise that there were neither surveys nor views for them to examine. They would have to travel half around the world, and then see what was available. (The HBC, incidentally, had decided that it was not going to allow any of these colonists to settle within the Fur Trade Reserve, twenty square miles, which contained the good land around Fort Victoria.) Under these circumstances, the Company's Governor and Committee should not have been surprised that colonists proved hard to come by.

Even before the grant of Vancouver Island was finally passed, however, the Hudson's Bay Company did have one colonist in sight. He was Captain Walter Colquhoun Grant, formerly of the 2nd Dragoons (Scots Greys) who, having lost his private means, had had to resign his commission and turn his thoughts to going out to the colonies. If ever there was a fine big braw Scotsman it was Captain Grant, twenty-six years old and six foot two inches high. He had a remarkably engaging personality, but precious little business sense. However his uncle, Sir Lewis Grant, was ready to put up money so that the captain could purchase two hundred acres on Vancouver

Island and buy passage for himself and the eight men who would work for him.

On 30 November 1848 the HBC's ship *Harpooner* sailed from Britain for Vancouver Island, carrying Captain Grant's eight men. In June 1849 it docked at Fort Victoria and here for two months they waited for their employer. Finally, on August 11th, the famous Captain Grant, British Columbia's first settler, stepped out of a canoe which had brought him to Fort Victoria from Nisqually on Puget Sound. Taking the Panama railway route so as to save himself the long voyage around Cape Horn, he had arrived in San Francisco flat broke. There the HBC agent had advanced him enough money to get to Fort Victoria. Fortunately Grant was not without the prospect of income in his new home since, before leaving England, he had been promised that once he arrived at Vancouver Island the HBC would pay him a retainer fee as a surveyor.

At Fort Victoria, after the first settler had had a couple of days' rest, James Douglas helped him to select his two hundred acres:

On the 14th [of August] . . . I started with Captain Grant, on an excursion along the coast, for the purpose of showing him the best points for settlement, and recommending him to the natives. He chose a place at Sy-yausung [Sooke] 25 miles distant from Fort Victoria, where he has the important advantage of a good Mill Stream, and a great abundance of fine timber. He is now busily employed putting up log houses for present use. . . . [4]

Captain Grant nostalgically named his homestead in the wilderness at Sooke "Mullachard", after his ancestral home in Strathspey, Scotland.

*   *   *

Samuel Cunard had been right the previous year in his tip to the Admiralty that Americans were taking an interest in Vancouver Island's coal. He was wrong, however, in thinking that they contemplated helping themselves to it. What had happened was that William Henry Aspinwall of New York, having secured a U.S. mail

---

[4] Hudson's Bay Company Archives (hereafter HBCA), A.11/72, quoted by Willard Ireland in his useful article "Captain Walter Colquhoun Grant", *British Columbia Historical Quarterly* (hereafter *BCHQ*) 17 (1953) :87-125.

contract between Panama and Oregon, had set up the Pacific Mail Steamship Company, and was considering using Vancouver Island coal for his steamers, instead of that transported by colliers from Wales. At the time of Cunard's overly suspicious message to the Admiralty, Aspinwall had, in fact, already begun negotiating with the Hudson's Bay Company for the purchase of its coal.[5]

The successful outcome of these negotiations resulted in the founding this spring of a new HBC post, Fort Rupert, on Beaver Harbour towards the north-eastern tip of Vancouver Island. Although Fort Rupert was intended primarily for the working of the adjacent coalfields, it also served as a fur-trading post.

The HBC did not feel that it could leave to untrained Indians the mining of the coal contracted for by the Pacific Mail Steamship Company. Accordingly seven Scottish coal-miners were enlisted in the Company's service and these, along with their "oversman", John Muir, came out from Britain this year in company with Captain Grant's men aboard the *Harpooner*. By September the Scots were installed in quarters which had been built for them at Fort Rupert.

*   *   *

Two other new arrivals of this year must not go unnoticed: the Rev. Robert John Staines, aged twenty-eight, and his wife Emma. Mr. Staines, B.A. (Cantab.), had shown himself a thoroughly competent schoolmaster in England before setting up his own school for English boys at Boulogne in France. According to his own declaration, he was competent to teach "Classics, Mathematics, and every branch of the usual routine of an English education". Of his wife he crisply noted:

Mrs. Staines is perfectly qualified to take every department in the usual course of a gentlewoman's education, including music and French, of both which she is *perfectly mistress*, and Italian and German sufficiently to read and translate.[6]

---

[5] On this arrangement with the Pacific Mail Steamship Company, see J. H. Kemble, "Coal from the Northwest Coast 1848-1850," *BCHQ* 2 (1938): 123-130. For an account of the discovery of this coal, see *British Columbia Chronicle, 1778-1846*, p. 288.

[6] See G. Hollis Slater, "Rev. Robert John Staines: Pioneer Priest, Pedagogue, and Political Agitator", *BCHQ* 14 (1950): 191.

The HBC obviously felt itself fortunate to obtain the services of so gifted a team to teach in the school which was to be opened at Fort Victoria, especially since Mr. Staines was ready to be ordained as a priest in the Church of England and serve also as the Company's chaplain. Staines having been duly ordained in Norwich Cathedral, he, his wife, a young nephew and two servants sailed for Vancouver Island aboard the HBC barque *Columbia*. On March 17th of this year the Staines party came ashore at Fort Victoria. Neither residence nor schoolhouse had yet been built for them, but work was hurriedly commenced on both these buildings. Meanwhile the Staines and their servants were put up at the fort.

Within the confines of the fort Roderick Finlayson had a good opportunity to become acquainted with the reverend gentleman. Later he recorded his impression of him, along with a pleasantly malicious little anecdote about what had happened during the *Columbia*'s stopover at Hawaii:

He [Staines] was a man full of frills, as we say, & liked displays, kept a servant &c. He called at the Sandwich Islands on the way out, sent a note to the King stating he wished to call on His Majesty. The King returned word he would be glad to see Mr. Staines on the next day. He dressed as a clergyman and dressed up his servant in livery, very showy of course. He had silver lace &c &c they went to call on "the King of the Cannibal of [*sic*] Islands"! The King came out to see his reverend visitor, rushed past him to shake hands with the servant in livery whom he took from the gorgeous dress, to be Mr. Staines. The latter was awfully disgusted, but matters were explained & everything passed off all right once more.[7]

Mr. Staines, in fact, was a snob and a prig. It was a little as if Jane Austen's Mr. Collins had arrived to take Fort Victoria in hand.

The reason why Staines had been despatched to Fort Victoria instead of Fort Vancouver was that this year the HBC, taking the action it had long contemplated, had transferred its Pacific headquarters to Fort Victoria from Fort Vancouver (increasingly untenable now it was in the United States). At the close of 1849 Chief

---

[7] Roderick Finlayson, *The History of Vancouver Island and the Northwest Coast*, Public Archives of Canada (hereafter PAC), MG29 B35 Vol. 6:47-48 (Bancroft transcript).

Factor Douglas, as part of that transfer, moved to Fort Victoria with his family and took over command there from Roderick Finlayson. Finlayson became the post's chief accountant, just as Douglas had for so many years been Dr. McLoughlin's chief accountant at Fort Vancouver.

The prosperity which might have come to Fort Victoria in consequence of its new importance did not occur. News had arrived of fantastic fortunes to be made in the California goldfields and nearly all of the HBC labourers had deserted and headed south, throwing into confusion both the Company's fur-trading and agricultural activities. Probably the flight southwards was precipitated by the arrival, early this year, of a party of California gold-miners (at first mistaken for pirates) who, desperate for supplies at reasonable prices, had come all the way thither and paid for their purchases with gold nuggets poured out of leather "pokes".

There were other arrivals by sea, for the Royal Navy continued to keep a protective eye on the infant colony. In May H.M.S. *Inconstant* (a frigate of 36 guns) anchored at Esquimalt. In a letter to Captain Shepherd, Douglas expressed his appreciation of the continued protection but noted that, whereas the HBC had hitherto had to be on constant guard against "the lawless American population in Oregon", the days of "anxiety and painful suspense"[8] had apparently passed now that a responsible American administration had been set up, headed by Governor Lane who had recently arrived from Washington, D.C.

*   *   *

This year, as for so many years in the past, the posts in the Interior baled their furs and started them on their journey to the Coast for shipment to Britain. Work had diligently proceeded on the Fort Hope-Tulameen trail laid out by Peers the previous year. Windfalls had been chopped away, gradients improved, the path cleared and broadened. All the same, not enough had been done for the route to be inaugurated and for a second year the brigade had to come out by the heart-breaking Anderson River-Spuzzum-Fort Yale route. On

[8] Douglas to Shepherd, 28 May 1849. National Maritime Museum, Greenwich, PHI/3/5.

their return journey, however, the brigade became a work force, finishing the essential work on the Fort Hope-Tulameen trail, and heading home over it. Their journey was not an easy one, but it was better than the one that had caused them such intolerable agony in 1848. At long last the HBC had a practicable all-British route for its annual brigades. Fort Hope's name had been justified.

*   *   *

This year a little pamphlet, *The Employment of the People and the Capital of Great Britain in her own Colonies* was published in London. Its contents were sensational, nothing less than a proposal to build across British North America an "Atlantic and Pacific Railway". The author was Major Robert Carmichael Smyth, who had just returned from the two colonies constituting Canada where he had been serving with the 93rd Highlanders. Smyth's booklet contained a map delineating the route for his proposed transcontinental railway. That route was in effect the one to be followed by the Canadian Pacific Railway thirty-five years later, when it linked the Province of British Columbia to the rest of the Dominion of Canada.[9]

---

[9] For early foreshadowings of the CPR, beginning with an editorial in a Toronto newspaper in 1834, see Pierre Berton, *The National Dream* (Toronto, 1970), pp. 11-15.

1850

Richard Blanshard, first royal governor of Vancouver Island — The immigrant ship Norman Morison *— Dr. J. S. Helmcken — Trouble at Fort Rupert — Douglas' Indian treaties — Measles decimate the Indians.*

This was not a happy year for Captain Walter Colquhoun Grant, British Columbia's first settler. Twenty-five miles out in the wilderness, at Sooke, he got some land cleared, planted it, kept a few cattle, and even built a small sawmill, but the enterprise faltered. Some of his men he had to discharge, and then the others deserted him. He earned a bit of money this summer surveying the Hudson's Bay Company's Fur Trade Reserve around Fort Victoria, but he never got the job completed. Chief Factor Douglas could not help noticing that the rudiments of surveying once taught to Grant at the Royal Military College, Sandhurst, really did not qualify him as a surveyor. In October Grant sailed on a visit to Hawaii.

When Vancouver Island became a Crown Colony with its settlement entrusted to the HBC, the British government, brushing aside an earlier decision in favour of Douglas, decided to appoint as the royal governor a man totally independent of the HBC who could report impartially to London. The Colonial Secretary and the Governor of the HBC agreed that the position should go to a young lawyer, an Oxford man, named Richard Blanshard. Blanshard was a man with a taste for travel (he had earlier visited Honduras and India), but he totally lacked experience as a colonial administrator. Grey, the Colonial Secretary, was not prepared to offer Blanshard any salary, but he informed him that the HBC would supply him with a house and give him a thousand acres of land. As for Blanshard, he obviously regarded his governorship as something of a sporting venture — if the new colony thrived there would, in time, be a civil list to provide him with a salary, and his thousand free acres might provide him with a future competence. Moreover, this initial appointment could lead to more rewarding ones, possibly the governorship of some really important place like Hong Kong or Jamaica, with an attendant knighthood.

On March 9th the paddlewheel sloop H.M.S. *Driver*, bringing the new governor from Panama, splashed into Fort Victoria's Inner Harbour, but not until March 11th did the new governor come ashore. The welcoming HBC men, standing in a foot of snow, greeted Blanshard to the accompaniment of a salute of seventeen guns from the little warship, which was answered by the guns of Fort Victoria. They found themselves shaking hands with a gentleman of agreeable manners and fairly tall stature, whose aquiline features were set off by a large military moustache. The *Driver*'s officers, those of the HBC, and the entire British population of Fort Victoria having assembled in the fort's mess-hall, His Excellency Governor Richard Blanshard read his commission. A British government had at last been formally established on the west coast of North America.

His Excellency soon found that his government was to be more nominal than real. The actual governing would be done by Chief Factor James Douglas who noted with some surprise, "Mr. Blanshard has neither Secretary nor Troops." He added, "I may say that his quiet gentlemanly manner is prepossessing."[1]

After the ceremony of his installation, Governor Blanshard, pulling on that long heavy pipe which was his invariable companion, took stock of his situation. It was a decidedly odd one — not only was he a governor without either a council or civil servants, he was also one without anywhere to live, construction having only just begun on his promised house. While this work proceeded, Blanshard remained aboard H.M.S. *Driver*. But at length she had to leave the coast, and then he moved into a room in the fort.

A minor crisis existed at Fort Victoria when Blanshard arrived. An immigrant ship was expected from England almost any day, and the fort lacked food for the newcomers. Fortunately an abundance of meat on the hoof was available at the HBC's Fort Nisqually farm

---

[1] Douglas to A. C. Anderson, 18 March 1850, quoted in Willard E. Ireland, "The Appointment of Governor Blanshard", *BCHQ* 8 (1944):224.

in Washington Territory, if only a ship could be found to fetch the animals hither. Complying with a request from Blanshard, Commander Johnson good-naturedly converted H.M.S. *Driver* into a cattle-boat. With the homeless governor still on board, the ship sailed into Puget Sound and returned with 86 cattle and 830 sheep.[2]

H.M.S. *Driver* got back to Victoria with the livestock just in time. Two days later, on March 24th, the expected immigrant ship put into Esquimalt harbour. She was the *Norman Morison*, the nearest thing to a *Mayflower* in British Columbia's history. Her arrival more than doubled the white population of Vancouver Island, for aboard her were more than eighty immigrants: mostly coal-miners and labourer-settlers under contract to the HBC, a few of them bringing wives. Their arrival had been delayed by calms in the Strait of Juan de Fuca, which had left the *Norman Morison*, her sails bereft of wind, drifting up and down the Strait with the tides and currents. This interval had given the newcomers ample leisure to inspect their new homeland:

> ... nothing but mountains on both sides wooded to the top — they appeared weird and gloomy.... Scarcely a foot of level land could anywhere be seen and we used to ask each other, "How can any of this be cultivated?" "Where is it possible to make any farms at all?"[3]

Among the newcomers was a brisk little medical man, Dr. John Sebastian Helmcken, London-trained but with a German background. He would become known to generations of Victoria children as "Dr. Heal-my-skin", would lead a very long life intertwined with British Columbia's history, and finally go to his rest in 1920. During the *Norman Morison*'s voyage, Dr. Helmcken had nursed twenty of her crew and passengers during a smallpox outbreak, losing only one of them. One other patient died of cancer. The latter was an elderly Highland schoolmaster whom the incredible Captain Grant had engaged to teach Gaelic on Vancouver Island.

Once ashore at Fort Victoria, Dr. Helmcken hastened to pay his respects to Governor Blanshard and to Chief Factor Douglas:

---

[2] NMM, PHI/3/5, Item 7.

[3] Dorothy Blakey Smith, ed., *The Reminiscences of Doctor John Sebastian Helmcken* (Vancouver, UBC Press, 1975), p. 79.

I saw Mr. Douglas — he did not impress me very favourably, being of very grave disposition with an air of dignity — cold and unimpassioned. A dark-complexioned man — with rather scanty hair, but not too scanty — muscular — broad-shouldered — with powerful legs a little bowed — common to strong men; in fact he was a splendid specimen of a man. His clothes were rather shabby and seedy looking. . . . [4]

As for Douglas' manner, Helmcken described it as "coldly affable".

If the young doctor was somewhat dashed by the distant manner of Douglas, he was cheered by the sight of one of his daughters:

. . . the room of Mr. Douglas, partly an office and partly domestic, stood open, and there I saw Cecilia his eldest daughter flitting about, active as a little squirrel, and one of the prettiest objects I had ever seen; rather short but with a very pretty graceful figure — of dark complexion and lovely black eyes — petite and nice. She assisted her father in clerical work, correspondence and so forth — in fact a private secretary. I was more or less captivated. Afterwards I heard her singing in the Church, and she had a beautiful voice tho uneducated. [5]

Not surprisingly, some little while later Miss Cecilia Douglas became Mrs. J. S. Helmcken.

While the young doctor was being captivated by Cecilia Douglas and being rather put off by her aloof papa, the *Norman Morison* was discharging her cargo. The latter included three puncheons of Scotch whiskey for Captain Grant, and possibly the cricket set which he later presented to the boys of Fort Victoria. Then she sailed to Fort Rupert and landed the remainder of her passengers, the little company of English miners who were to work there along with Muir and his Scots. These English coal-miners had hardly settled in before they contributed another "first" to British Columbia's history by going on strike. The spectacle of men actually refusing to do their work after they had accepted employment was a new experience for the HBC. [6] For a few days Captain McNeill, in command of the fort,

---

[4] *Ibid.*, p. 81.

[5] *Loc. cit.*

[6] A little later Chief Factor Douglas expressed his view of the Englishmen in his reply to a letter from Chief Trader Yale pleading for additional manpower for Fort Langley: *"I would have sent you some of my Englishmen, but they are such a troublesome, useless sett [sic], that I was certain you would prefer Indians to them. I have dispersed them amongst the ships, the coal mines, to*

kept the ringleaders shackled and imprisoned in one of its bastions but his action did not end the strike. The men became more militant. They swore that their contract was not being observed, that their food and quarters were not up to what the HBC had promised them in England, and that they would appeal to Governor Blanshard and have the law on McNeill for illegal imprisonment of their comrades.

The trouble came to fever-pitch with the arrival in Beaver Harbour of the barque *England*, which for days was anchored off the fort taking on coal. The strikers saw a wonderful opportunity to board her and head down to California where they could mine gold for themselves instead of coal for the HBC. Refused release from their contracts, they began to slip away from the fort. The *England*, it so happened, had on board four sailors who had deserted in Fort Victoria from the *Norman Morison*. Such was the situation when that most famous of early steamers, the Hudson's Bay Company's *Beaver*, came into the bay. Three of the deserters, panicking, decided that she had come to seize them. Taking their first opportunity, they slipped over the side of the *England* and sought a safe hiding-place ashore. Very soon rumours began to spread that, though one of the deserters had drowned during his flight, the other two had reached shore only to be murdered by the Indians. To learn what had really happened, Charles Beardmore, a Company officer at Fort Rupert, made contact with some Nahwitti Indians. The latter, while protesting that the murders had been committed by members of another tribe, told Beardmore where he would find the victims. Following their directions, he found beside a hollow tree the naked bodies of Charles and George Wishart with bullet holes through their hearts. Dragging their corpses into the open, Beardmore heaped brush over them and went to fetch the magistrate to conduct an inquest.

That magistrate was none other than young Dr. Helmcken, who after a month at Fort Victoria had been sent up to Fort Rupert to be the mine doctor. After word of the miners' strike had reached Fort Victoria, Governor Blanshard sent up a document appointing

---

Nisqually, the northwest coast, and have now only 11 remaining here. There is a perpetual growling about provisions, though they are better fed than ever they were in their own country." Douglas to Yale, 27 June 1850. HBCA B.113/c/1.

Helmcken a justice of the peace, and asked him to attend to the trouble. Dr. Helmcken had been totally unable to do so, since nobody would agree to be sworn in as a special constable to assist him. But now he had an inquest to conduct. Following Beardmore's directions, he headed towards Shushartie Bay. Many years later, in some fascinating recollections of his Fort Rupert days, Dr. Helmcken recalled that journey:

...I took a canoe, went to the island; found the bodies of the poor fellows as described; wrapped them in blankets, brought them to the fort, where they lay during the remainder of the day, being identified by some who had come out from England with them in the *Norman Morison*.
The following morning, July 16th, they were, with Christian rites, buried in the garden at the back of the fort; all the residents were sad and mournful.[7]

By now Dr. Helmcken felt that he had had enough of Fort Rupert. To Governor Blanshard he submitted his resignation as magistrate. To Chief Factor Douglas he wrote:

I cannot stop here; nothing but trouble day after day; not a moment's peace or quietness and now to add to our misfortunes, everyone is afraid of his life, and the fort, and not without reason, for certainly there is not a sufficient number to defend it against the large tribe of Indians here, who are becoming very saucy and the men are afraid of them. As far as I could, it has been my endeavor to check and remedy complaints; these have now grown beyond remedy and probably abandoning the fort shortly will be the cure. I was sent here on account of the miners. They have disappeared; so please allow me to do the same in the "Mary Dare".[8]

Later Dr. Helmcken would look back on this letter as one written by a panicky greenhorn, and realize that the 2500 Indians at Fort Rupert "in reality, were our best friends and wished to be on good terms with us." Still, at the time, he was a very badly shaken young physician.

At Fort Victoria there was a general realization that punitive action would have to be taken against the murderers, even if their

---

[7] Blakey Smith, *Helmcken Reminiscences*, p. 314.

[8] *Ibid.*, p. 316.

victims had been deserters from the HBC's service. Nothing could be done, however, until a warship showed up. In October H.M.S. *Daedalus*, 19 guns, having arrived, Governor Blanshard travelled upcoast on her to the village suspected of harbouring the murderers. There was a brisk exchange of riflefire, in which a British officer and several bluejackets were wounded. Then the natives fled inland, leaving their village and most of their possessions to be destroyed in the flames kindled by the avengers.

*   *   *

Chief Factor Douglas had much on his mind this year besides the troubles at Fort Rupert. The Americans, harrassing the HBC in the hope of coercing the Company into closing its posts south of the new international boundary, seized two of its ships, the *Cadboro* and the *Albion*, and some delicate negotiating was needed to obtain their release. Continual desertions by men heading for the California gold-fields left the Company almost entirely dependent upon Kanakas (Hawaiians) and Indians to keep its ships manned and its farms cultivated. Moreover, besides the continual problems caused by the labour shortage, Douglas was having to negotiate treaties with the Indians since London had decided that the colonists must be protected from any future disputes arising out of Indian land claims. The first of these treaties was signed in April. It read:

Know all men, We the Chiefs and People of the "Teechamitsa" Tribe who have signed our names and made our marks to this Deed on the Twenty ninth day of April, one thousand eight hundred and Fifty do consent to surrender entirely and for ever to James Douglas the Agent of the Hudsons Bay Company in Vancouvers Island that is to say, for the Governor Deputy Governor and Committee of the same the whole of the lands situate and lying between Esquimalt Harbour and Point Albert including the latter, on the straits of Juan de Fuca and extending backward from thence to the range of mountains on the Sanitch Arm about ten miles distant.

The Condition of, or understanding of this Sale, is this, that our Village Sites and Enclosed Fields are to be kept for our own use, for the use of our Children, and for those who may follow after us; and the land, shall be properly surveyed hereafter; it is understood however that the land itself, with these small exceptions becomes the Entire property of the White people for ever; it is also understood that we are at liberty to hunt over the unoccupied lands, and to carry on our fisheries as formerly.

We have received as payment Twenty seven pound Ten Shillings Sterling.

In token whereof we have signed our names and made our marks at Fort Victoria 29 April 1850.

		his mark	
1.	See-sachasis	X	
2.	Hay-hay kane	X	
3.	Pee shaymoot	X	
4.	Kalsaymit	X	
5.	Coochaps	X	Done in the presence of
6.	Thlamie	X	Joseph William McKay
7.	Chamutstin	X	(signed) RODERICK FINLAYSON[9]
8.	Tsatsulluc	X	
9.	Hoquymilt	X	
10.	Kamostitchel	X	
11.	Minayiltin	X	

Over the next four years Douglas negotiated thirteen other Indian treaties, the final one, on 23 December 1854, obtaining the "country [which] extends from Commercial Inlet twelve miles up Nanaimo River" in return for £350.[10]

The Nanaimo treaty was important because of the discovery of the Nanaimo coal-fields — a particularly fortunate discovery since there was a growing awareness of the inferior nature of the Fort Rupert coal. The latter, in fact, had proved so bad that this autumn the Pacific Mail Steamship Company stopped using it. The discovery of the Nanaimo coal-fields happened under circumstances curiously parallel to those which had revealed to the HBC the existence of coal at Fort Rupert.[11] In December 1849 one of the Company's

[9] Wilson Duff, "The Fort Victoria Treaties," *BC Studies* No. 3 (Fall 1969): 9-11.

[10] PABC, F/53/H86, "Return of Treaties made by Hudsons Bay Co with Indian Tribes shewing Lands conveyed and sums paid". In 1964 the Hon. Mr. Justice Norris found this treaty as binding as if it had been entered into by the Sovereign herself. The Supreme Court of Canada upheld this ruling.

[11] *British Columbia Chronicle, 1778-1846*, pp. 288-89.

officers was hurriedly summoned to the forge at Fort Victoria where he found an Indian who, pointing to some coal ready for the blacksmith's fire, had declared that there was plenty of that sort of stone where he came from. A reward was offered the Indian if he would bring some of this "stone that burns" to Fort Victoria, and finally in April of this year he arrived with a canoe loaded with coal. Little time was lost in making a reconnaissance of the area from which it came, that adjacent to what was then called "Winthuysen Inlet". In May the "Douglas Vein" was found, which yielded the first of the millions of tons of coal that would come from the Nanaimo-Wellington fields in the next century.

Nor was the Nanaimo coal the only discovery of this year, as British Columbia began gradually to reveal her wealth in minerals. On August 18th Governor Blanshard wrote to Earl Grey, "I have seen a very rich specimen of gold ore, said to have been brought by the Indians of Queen Charlotte's Island. . . . [12]

*   *   *

Other developments of this year must be mentioned. In September, Douglas wrote to London advising that the Company terminate its Fur Trade Reserve and allow settlers to buy the good land close to Fort Victoria. His recommendation was not made in any spirit of altruism but on the commonsense grounds that it would prove cheaper for the HBC to let settlers have this land than to provide protection for them in "distant and struggling settlements".

Wedding bells chimed in Fort Victoria this year for Dr. William Fraser Tolmie, the high-minded Scot who, back in 1834,[13] had agonized over his decision never to unite himself to an Indian woman in the most sacred of all human ties. His bride was Jane, one of the eight daughters of Chief Factor John Work and Susette, his half-Indian wife.

There was trouble at Fort Simpson this year, with the Haidas and

---

[12] Great Britain, Parliament, House of Commons, *Copies or Extracts of Correspondence relative to the Discovery of Gold at Queen Charlotte's Island*, London, 1853 (P.P. 788), p. 1, (hereafter referred to as "Correspondence re QCI Gold").

[13] *British Columbia Chronicle, 1778-1846*, p. 281.

the Tsimpseans pitted against each other in their final battle. Disease as well as war afflicted northern British Columbia, for a widespread epidemic of measles decimated the population. Among those who died was the dreaded Waccan, the enforcer used by the HBC in New Caledonia when it had serious trouble with the Indians.

This year may have seen the writing, allegedly by a visiting officer of the Royal Navy, of the earliest British Columbian verse to survive. In his old age Dr. Helmcken recalled a few of the stanzas, not because of their poetic distinction (for they have none), but because of the way they touched on the appalling remoteness of Fort Victoria with only one or two ships a year leaving for Britain:

> The groves of Blarney, that were so charming
>   By rason of their swateness, have had their day;
> For the Isle of Vancouver bates Blarney all over,
>   That iligant island beyond the grane sae.

> There's the Governor's mansion in a state of expansion
>   With three windows and a door, all in front;
> And Chief Trader Finlayson, seeking change for a shilling
>   And Port Admiral Nevins[14] in charge of a punt.

>   . . .   .

> Oh, the groves of Blarney, that were so charming
>   By rason of their swateness, have all lost their day;
> For the Isle of Vancouver bates Blarney all over:
>   Bedad, when you get there you can't get away![15]

[14] Nevin, who "liked whiskey too much," looked after the HBC's small boats and barges in Victoria harbour.

[15] *Daily Colonist*, 22 Dec. 1907, p. 56. (Several minor changes have been made in the interests of scansion and consistency.)

1851

High jinks at Bachelors' Hall — Captain Cooper, entrepreneur — The immigrant ship Tory *— Captain Langford and his pretty daughters — Governor Blanshard resigns and Douglas takes over — Gold in the Queen Charlottes.*

In February Captain Grant arrived home from his trip to Hawaii, bringing some broom seeds given him by the British consul there which he planted by his house at Sooke. From Sooke the broom spread all along the southern coast of Vancouver Island, and the masses of broom flowering each spring around Victoria remain as Captain Grant's sole but splendid monument. How much time Captain Grant now spent at Sooke is uncertain. Clearly he was a frequent visitor to Fort Victoria where he contributed notably to the high jinks in the Bachelors' Hall. On one occasion he had all the young clerks there bounding around like kangaroos, pretending to be coach horses drawing Queen Victoria through Windsor Park. The royal procession ended when some of the Rev. Mr. Staines' pupils, boarded at the fort, sent cold water cascading down through gaps in the floor of their dormitory above.

Poor Captain Grant, he needed his Scotch whiskey and the convivial life at Bachelors' Hall, for he was at the end of his means financially. But a solution occurred to him — gold was to be had for the finding down South. In July he set out for the goldfields, not of California but of the Klamath River in southern Oregon. Before departing he leased his farm at Sooke to Thomas Munro, formerly his servant.

On August 8th Grant wrote from Oregon City to an old family friend, Brodie of Brodie. His principal purpose was to ask if Brodie would use his influence with Lord Fife to get him a position "in the Austrian [Australian?] service." But in the course of this letter he had some interesting things to say about his experiences on Vancouver Island:

Until this year I was entirely alone as a settler, but within the last few months 3 old servants of the Hudson's Bay Coy. have taken claims of land, though none of them have as let either p[ai]d anything for the land or brought out men to cultivate it. The Hudson's Bay Coy. having claimed 40 Sqe. miles in the neighborhood of Victoria; although I had p[ai]d for my land in Eng[lan]d with the understanding that I was to have free choice on the island, I was obliged to go 25 miles off, where I have been living a totally solitary life ever since. I soon got tired of my own society & except when a stray ship came along the coast, never saw a creature save my own men and a few rascally Indians. I got quite weary of my existence, and if it had not been for the episode of a 2 months trip down to the Sandwich Islands last winter, I really believe I s[houl]d have committed Suicide, by hanging drowning or otherwise. I returned f[ro]m the Islands with fresh vigour, but soon got disgusted again, seeing that no other bona fide settlers were coming out to enliven my solitude, I therefore was glad enough to let my place, which I did on a lease of 5 years for £70 pr annum, I also let a flour & saw mill which I had built, for a similar sum & similar period. . . . I have had pretty hard work to keep afloat since coming out here, now selling a Spar, now a Potatoe etc. All my personal property had likewise to be made available, & guns, furniture, Books clothes etc successively found their way up the spout and were converted into dollars & cents. I have done better for the men I brought out with me than for [myself]. I employed them at high wages, and have now established them on plots of land of their own. . . . [1]

Just when British Columbia's first independent settler was leaving, its second was arriving. Captain James Cooper was a very different person from Captain Grant. For some years Cooper had commanded the HBC ship *Columbia* on voyages between Vancouver Island and England. He had sensed the potential wealth in the new country, and this year took up three hundred acres at Metchosin, part way between Fort Victoria and Sooke. As the superintendent of this property he installed a former Australian stockman, Thomas Blinkhorn. An ambitious, energetic man, Cooper had the previous year

---

[1] Letter of 8 Aug. 1857, pp. 12-14. Scottish Record Office, *Brodie of Brodie Papers*. We found this letter when working in Edinburgh in 1971. J. E. Hendrickson discovered it independently, and has published it complete in "Two Letters from Walter Colquhoun Grant", *BC Studies* 26 (Summer 1975) :9-14.

got British capitalists interested in putting up £10,000 for his Vancouver's Island Steam Sawing Mill and Agricultural Company.[2]
Cooper himself had a diversity of interests. He brought out to the
island with him, knocked down in sections, the *Alice*, an iron ship
intended for trading between Vancouver Island, California and
Hawaii. Seeking cargoes for his ship he even planned to export
barrels of cranberries from the Fraser Valley to San Francisco.[3]

Captain Cooper was only one of 120 passengers which the *Tory*
brought out from England this spring. In the autumn the *Norman
Morison* brought out about 35 more. But except for Cooper, none of
the new arrivals was an independent settler. The HBC, failing to
secure gentlemen of independent means who would create handsome estates, had decided to establish farms of its own and bring out
colonists who would be its own employees. There seemed to be no
other way of meeting the colonization requirement attached to the
charter granting it Vancouver Island.

One of the most important arrivals on the *Tory* was highly convivial Captain Edward E. Langford, formerly of the Black Watch,
the newly-appointed manager of one of these farms being set up by
the HBC's affiliate, the Puget's Sound Agricultural Company. When
Captain Langford came ashore, all eyes were fastened on his wife,
decked out in the latest London fashions, and on their five pretty
daughters. Although Mrs. Langford was shortly expecting another
child, the only accommodation the HBC had ready for her and her
family was a one-room log cabin. Fortunately Governor Blanshard
took pity on the family, and it was in the Governor's residence that
George Langford, probably the first child of entirely white descent
to be born in British Columbia, entered this world.[4] Subsequently the
Langfords were to dwell in a fine large house on Esquimalt Farm
(often called Colwood Farm), where the hospitable captain was
bailiff.

---

[2] For a statement submitted by this company in June 1850 to the British Board
of Trade, see Public Record Office, London (hereafter PRO) BT1/478/1952.

[3] In true monopolistic spirit the HBC, the only manufacturer of barrels, set
their price so high that Cooper could not afford to purchase them. The Company then took over his idea and itself initiated the California trade in
cranberries.

[4] Margaret A. Ormsby, *British Columbia: A History* (Toronto, 1958), p. 113.

Following the discovery of Captain Grant's inadequacies, the HBC had sought a thoroughly expert surveyor and had found him in Joseph Despard Pemberton, c.e. (1821-93). Pemberton, after extensive experience in railway construction, had served as Professor of Surveying, Civil Engineering and Mathematics at the Royal Agricultural College at Cirencester, Gloucestershire. Entering the HBC's employ, he arrived in Victoria this June. Almost immediately he made his own survey of the Fur Trade Reserve, one which would replace the botched work that Grant had attempted. Then, the Company having changed its policy and ended the Reserve, he laid out a plan for the "town of Victoria"[5] adjacent to the fort. Apart from occasional visits back to England, Pemberton would spend the rest of his life in British Columbia, and the Pembertons would find their place in the little colonial aristocracy of late nineteenth century Victoria.

*   *   *

The Royal Navy continued to play its role as guardian over the youthful colony. When Rear-Admiral Phipps Hornby handed over command in the Pacific to Rear-Admiral Fairfax Moresby, he informed him:

> ... I think it very desirable that one [warship] should be sent at least annually to Vancouvers Island to communicate and cooperate with H.E. the Governor (taking up an Anchorage at Esquimalt Harbour) and to afford protection to the Hudsons Bay Company.[6]

Hornby referred Moresby to Captain Wellesley of H.M.S. *Daedalus* for detailed information about the situation on Vancouver Island. When Admiral Moresby did so, he learned how the 1850 punitive expedition against the Nahwitti Indians had proved a semi-fiasco. Things should be attended to more effectively than that, decided the new Commander-in-Chief, Pacific. Accordingly this June he arrived at Esquimalt in person on his flagship H.M.S. *Portland*,

---

[5] Harriet S. Sampson, "My Father, Joseph Despard Pemberton: 1821-93", *BCHQ* 8 (1944):115. The west boundary of the town was the harbour, the east Government Street, the north Johnston Street and the south the fort itself. Outside these boundaries were cultivated fields.

[6] NMH, PHI/2/2 (Squadrons Letters).

accompanied by H.M.S. *Daphne*. Esquimalt so impressed Moresby that he wrote to the Admiralty urging that a royal reserve be placed upon the harbour and its shores since they were so admirably adapted for a future naval establishment.[7] Esquimalt would in time become a base first for the Royal Navy and then for the Royal Canadian Navy.

While the *Portland* swung at anchor at Esquimalt, the *Daphne* was sent north to attend to the unfinished business with the Indians. The Nahwittis were harried so effectively that at last they themselves executed the Wisharts' murderers and delivered their corpses to Fort Rupert.

When H.M.S. *Daphne* left Esquimalt for England on September 1st, she had on board Richard Blanshard, Esq., formerly Governor of Vancouver Island. Blanshard by now was a bitter and disillusioned man. Probably, in view of his poor health, he should never have accepted his governorship. The time he had spent earlier in the tropics had undermined his constitution, and he was afflicted with the *tic douloureux*, whose darting pains he treated with morphine. Not surprisingly he was generally depressingly pessimistic in outlook, even while maintaining the good manners of an English gentleman. But even a healthy optimist would have found Blanshard's assignment utterly impossible.

All through Blanshard's regime the real power had remained in the hands of Chief Factor Douglas. Even the treaties with the Indians had been made by Douglas. Totally unsalaried and limited to his own private means, Blanshard was compelled to buy all his necessities from the HBC store at Fort Victoria, where he was not given the discount enjoyed by all HBC employees. When the Governor asked Chief Factor Douglas for his promised thousand acres of land, he was coolly informed that the land, when granted, would not be his own personal property but would pass to future governors. Pressing the point, Blanshard demanded to know where the thousand acres might be, whereupon he was rewarded with a sardonic smile and a sweep of the arm towards the rocky slopes of Gonzales Hill.

---

[7] Letter of 3 July 1851, "Correspondence relating to the Establishment of a Naval Base at Esquimalt, 1851-57", *BCHQ* 6 (1942):280.

What had occurred, of course, was a personal falling out between the governor *de jure* and the governor *de facto*. Part of the trouble had arisen when Blanshard, a lawyer who had brought out his law books, instituted a court, presided over by himself. Douglas probably had no objections to Blanshard investigating the alleged theft of pigs which were the pride of the Rev. Mr. Staines, but he took a more serious view of matters when he found himself rebuked from the bench by Blanshard for having exceeded his powers. Eight months after his arrival, Blanshard did the only sensible thing and resigned. His resignation was promptly accepted and the Colonial Office sent out a commission appointing Chief Factor Douglas as his successor.

News of Douglas' appointment was not well received by that small group of colonists who were not in the service of the HBC. No longer would there be an independent authority from whom they could seek justice in dealing with the all-powerful Company. A few brave souls signed a petition:

To His Excellency Richard Blanshard Esq[ui]re Governor of Vancouver's Island:

May it please your Excellency we the Undersigned, inhabitants of Vancouver's Island, having learned with regret that your Excellency has resigned the Government of this Colony and understanding that the Government has been committed to a chief Factor of the Hudson's Bay Company cannot but express our unfeigned surprise at such an appointment.

The Hudson Bay Coy being as it is a great trading body must necessarily have interests clashing with those of independent Colonists. Most matters of a political nature will cause a contest between the Agents of the Company and the Colonists. Many matters of a judicial nature also will undoubtedly arise in which the Colonists and the Company or its Servants will be contending parties or the upper servants and the lower servants will be arrayed against each other. We beg to express in the most emphatical and plainest manner our assurances that impartial decisions cannot be expected from a Governor who is not only a member of the Company sharing its profits, his share of such profits rising and falling as they rise and fall but is also charged as their Chief Agent with the sole representation of their trading interests in this island and the adjacent coast.[8]

---

[8] James Cooper, "Maritime Matters on the Northwest Coast and Affairs of the Hudson Bay Company in Early Times", PAC MG29, B35, Vol. 4, p. 16 (Bancroft transcript).

Blanshard could do little to aid the petitioners, but that little he did. His commission authorized him to appoint a council to advise the governor in the exercise of his powers. So far, the population being so scanty, he had not appointed a council but, on August 27th, shortly before leaving Fort Victoria, in a last exercise of his gubernatorial power he appointed a Provisional Council of Vancouver Island. One member was Douglas (almost immediately to become Governor Douglas). A second member was John Tod who, having retired from the HBC service, had moved to Victoria from Kamloops. The third was Captain Cooper, one of the fifteen signers of the petition.

*   *   *

Following the discovery of gold in California in 1848, the HBC officers at Fort Simpson procured some gold dust and, showing it to the Indians, asked to be told if they ever found anything of the sort. Sure enough, in 1850 specimens of gold from the Queen Charlotte Islands began to show up at Fort Simpson, apparently including that large piece shown to Governor Blanshard at Victoria. One old Indian woman remembered having seen a large lump of the precious yellow metal years earlier. Setting out with her husband, she managed to find the place and the gold was still there. The upshot of her appearance at Fort Simpson with a 21-ounce specimen[9] was that Chief Factor Work in this May of 1851 headed by canoe to Englefield Bay. Here he did some test blasting and was sufficiently encouraged to return shortly with the HBC ship *Una*, Captain Mitchell. Although this second expedition failed to find gold, it met with Haidas who offered to barter some gold at exorbitant prices.

Undeterred, the *Una* returned in late October and this time her luck was in. At a place subsequently known as "Gold Harbour" or "Mitchell's Harbour", she discovered "a rich vein of gold, averaging 6½ inches in width, bedded in quartz rock, running 80 feet parallel with the coast."[10] For several days the HBC men conducted blasting,

---

[9] G. H. Inskip, "Remarks on Some Harbours of Queen Charlotte Islands, North-West Coast of America", *Nautical Magazine* 24 (1855):630.

[10] *Correspondence re QCI Gold*, p. 3.

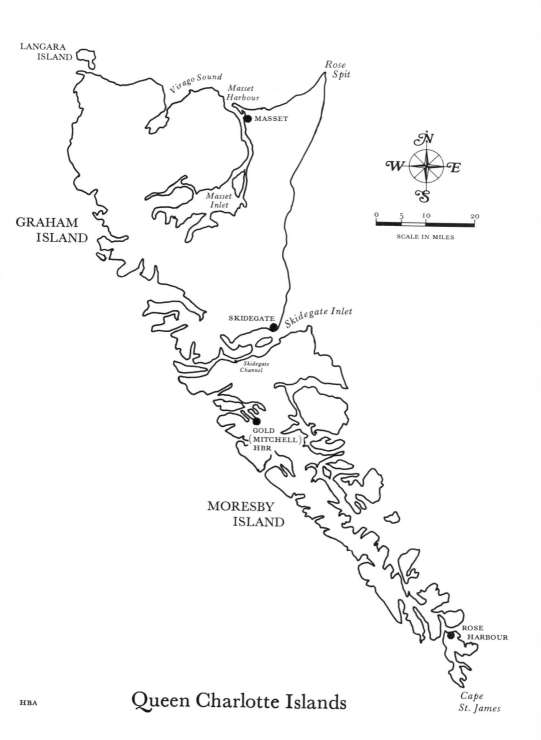

LANGARA
ISLAND

Virago Sound

*Masset
Harbour*

*Rose
Spit*

● MASSET

*Masset
Inlet*

GRAHAM
ISLAND

SKIDEGATE ● *Skidegate Inlet*

*Skidegate
Channel*

GOLD
(MITCHELL)
HBR

MORESBY
ISLAND

N
W ✦ E
S

0   5   10   20

SCALE IN MILES

ROSE
HARBOUR ●

HBA

Queen Charlotte Islands

*Cape
St. James*

and obtained specimens which yielded 25% pure gold. But there was trouble with the Haidas:

When they saw us blasting and turning out the gold in such large quantities, they became excited, and commenced depredations on us, stealing the tools, and taking, at least, one-half of the gold that was thrown out by a blast; they would be concealed until the report was heard, and then make a rush for the gold; a regular scramble between them and our men would take place; they would take our men by the legs, and hold them away from the gold: some blows were struck on those occasions; the Indians drew their knives on our men often.[11]

The *Una*'s men were not prepared to endure such hazards, and when they refused to go ashore any more the ship departed, only to be wrecked in a gale at Neah Bay. Another HBC gold-hunting party, headed by Pierre Legarre or Legace, failed to find treasure but made the incidental discovery that "Queen Charlotte's Island" was really two islands of approximately equal size.[12]

The news that gold had been found in the Queen Charlottes could hardly be confined to British territory. Late this autumn two American ships were off to the Queen Charlotte Islands with parties of prospectors. One, the *Exact*, achieved nothing beyond putting her name on the map at Exact Point. The other, the *Georgianna*, seeking shelter in Skidegate Inlet, was driven ashore when her cable parted. Those on board the *Georgianna* all managed to struggle ashore close to an Indian village whose occupants relieved them of their caps, their weapons, and much of their clothing. Strange scenes occurred as the Haidas looted the ship's cargo. Not knowing what flour was, they threw it away and confined their interest to the flour sacks; on the other hand, taking soap to be edible, they attempted to eat it. In December, four of the *Georgianna*'s men managed to reach Fort Simpson, where Captain McNeill gave them shelter. Meanwhile the authorities at Fort Steilacoom, Washington Territory, having learned of the *Georgianna*'s fate, chartered a rescue vessel on which they embarked an army lieutenant and a corporal's guard. When this ship, the *Demaris Cove*, arrived up north, the

---

[11] *Ibid.*, p. 4.

[12] Bessie D. Haynes, "Gold on Queen Charlotte's Island", *The Beaver*, Outfit 297 (Winter 1966):4.

Haidas released the rest of the *Georgianna*'s men in return for a ransom of five blankets for each.

*   *   *

Gradually the exploration of British Columbia was proceeding. In February this year Chief Factor Douglas asked Chief Trader Yale at Fort Langley to send a canoe party to investigate Indian statements concerning "an extensive plain lying between the North Branch of Fraser's River and Burrard Canal."[13] Yale was informed by Douglas that an Indian trail from Musqueam led into the area. One day, of course, this "extensive plain" would be the site of the city of Vancouver.

[13] HBCA, B.226/b/3.

1852

The Nanaimo coalfields — American goldseekers in the Queen Charlottes are frustrated by the HBC — H.M.S. Thetis visits the "gold digging establishment" — Haidas capture the Susan Sturges — Dr. Helmcken's wedding.

One day this year, when the rain was pouring down on Fort Victoria and the waves were running high in the Strait, an Indian canoe pulled into the safety of Cadboro Bay, a few miles from the fort. Out of the canoe stepped a white man who, stretching himself prostrate on the beach, kissed the ground. Rising, he went over to a driftwood log and knelt in prayer. The Most Reverend Modeste Demers, Bishop of Vancouver Island, had entered his diocese.

Although Fort Victoria now had the dignity of a royal governor and a Roman Catholic prelate, the colony was not progressing very rapidly. True, Pemberton having laid out a townsite, the HBC had ended its selfish and shortsighted policy of keeping independent colonists from settling near the fort, and had encouraged its own officers, active as well as retired, to buy land in the vicinity. Still there continued to be a sad lack of settlement. The HBC might send out scores of indentured labourers from England but, once these landed and found that the £17 per annum they had accepted before sailing was only one-quarter the wage that free labourers were earning,[1] they began to melt away, some of them hastening to American territory where they could do much better for themselves. Moreover, the little colony remained as isolated as ever. Most communication with the outside continued to be by the mail canoe, a huge one obtained from the northern Haidas which regularly carried mail and passengers between Fort Victoria and the head of Puget Sound.

[1] HBCA, B.226/b/7.

On the other hand, those who had hopes for the young colony were enormously cheered by the recent coal discovery made near Nanaimo River. In August Governor Douglas personally inspected the new coalfields. En route north by canoe, he was startled to find that the maps of Vancouver Island were so inexact that they showed islands such as Galiano and Valdes as part of Vancouver Island itself. When at length the coalfields were reached, he was delighted with what he saw:

One of those beds measured 57¾ inches in depth, of clean coal; and it was impossible to repress a feeling of exultation in beholding so huge a mass of mineral wealth, so singularly brought to light by the hand of nature, as if for the purpose of inviting human enterprise, at a time when coal is a great desideratum in the Pacific; and the discovery can hardly fail to be of signal advantage to the colony.[2]

Douglas knew whereof he spoke for now, the Fort Rupert coal having proved unsatisfactory, steamers were having to purchase imported Welsh coal at very high prices at San Francisco.

*   *   *

Despite the jubilation over the coal around Nanaimo, men's interest centered chiefly on the gold area at Mitchell Harbour up in the Queen Charlotte Islands. Early this year Governor Douglas received word that four American ships, with over five hundred goldseekers, were about to sail to the area. Seriously perturbed by this information, Douglas wrote to the Colonial Secretary in London:

These vessels are chartered by large bodies of American adventurers, who are proceeding thither for the purpose of digging gold; and if they succeed in that object, it is said to be their intention to colonise the island, and establish an independent government, until, by force or fraud, they become annexed to the United States.[3]

Douglas wanted help from the Royal Navy but, in the absence of a warship, all he could do was to despatch an HBC ship to Mitchell

---

[2] James Douglas, "Report of a Canoe Expedition along the East Coast of Vancouver Island", *Journal of the Royal Geographical Society* 24 (1854): 247.

[3] *Correspondence re QCI Gold*, p. 2.

Harbour as early as possible this year. Accordingly, having recruited men who, for a share in the gold, were willing to face hostile Indians, Douglas sent them north in the *Recovery*. Luck was with the HBC — the *Recovery* was the first ship of the season to enter Mitchell Harbour. Her men set to work with a will, blasting away at the *Una*'s vein of the previous year. Shortly she was joined by the American vessels *Susan Sturges, Tepic, Palerma* [*sic*], *Mexican, Eagle* and *Cecil*. With the one known vein being worked by men from the HBC ship, the Americans cast around, looking for other veins but finding none. American parties headed inland prospecting for gold but came back to report fruitless searches. Cutting their losses, the six American ships sailed away, some for California, others to look elsewhere along the coast of the Queen Charlotte Islands.

A week after the departure of the last of the disappointed Americans, H.M.S. *Thetis*, 38 guns, Captain Augustus L. Kuper, arrived in Mitchell Harbour. Alerted by the British consul in San Francisco that trouble might be expected in the Queen Charlottes, Rear-Admiral Moresby had lost no time in sending her north from the British base at Valparaiso. Finding only the HBC's operation proceeding routinely, with no interlopers to create problems, the *Thetis* made a survey of the adjacent waters, then headed for Esquimalt, calling briefly at Fort Rupert en route. In mid-August, when making a second visit to Mitchell Harbour, she found the "Gold digging Establishment broken up and the place deserted even by the Indians."[4] Without further ado, the *Thetis* sailed back to Esquimalt.

In September of this year a new Colonial Secretary, Sir John Pakington, sent Douglas a commission appointing him Lieutenant-Governor of the Queen Charlotte Islands. In an accompanying letter Pakington informed Douglas that, to insure that goldseekers recognized British sovereignty over the Queen Charlotte Islands, he was to require them to take out mining licences before going there. However, by the time Douglas received his commission, nobody was any longer interested in looking for gold in the Queen Charlottes. He never issued a single licence to any miner going there. However, the mining licence tactic remained in his memory, and it proved

---

[4] Royal Navy, Office of the Hydrographer of the Navy, Taunton, Somerset, *Master's Remark Book of H.M.S. Thetis, 1852*, p. 11.

extremely useful in asserting British control five or six years later when the Fraser River gold rush brought thousands of American prospectors north of the international boundary.[5]

We have mentioned the *Susan Sturges*, a little schooner of 150 tons, as one of the American vessels at Mitchell Harbour in the spring of this year. After returning to San Francisco her captain, in an ill-omened hour, decided to take her, with a crew of six, to the Queen Charlottes on a second voyage, partly bartering with the Indians and partly, no doubt, keeping a sharp lookout for gold. Calling at Langara Island, Captain Rooney asked for Chief Edensaw, with whom he had become acquainted on his previous voyage. Learning the chief was at Skidegate, Rooney took his schooner there, received on board the chief, his wife, child and two other Indians, then headed back to Edensaw's village on Langara Island. After rounding Rose Spit, at the extreme northeast of the Charlottes, the *Susan Sturges* met a Masset canoe returning from Fort Simpson. Edensaw engaged the newcomers in conversation. From this point on, we have two very different reports of what happened, the subsequent testimony of Captain Rooney and Edensaw, and the story told by the Masset Indians.

First for the Rooney-Edensaw version. According to this, the people in the canoe asked what trade goods the *Susan Sturges* carried, and what Captain Rooney sought in exchange. Chief Edensaw answered their questions. Then, continuing along the north coast of the Charlottes, the *Susan Sturges* had the bad luck on September 26th to become becalmed close to Masset Harbour. About twenty-five canoes had drawn up beside the little vessel and had begun to trade, when one of the Indians managed to climb over the ill-fitting boarding net which, as a standard precaution, encircled the boat. The next moment the *Susan Sturges* was aswarm with Indians. Muskets were leveled at Captain Rooney's breast and he was only saved by Edensaw's wife throwing herself between him and his would-be murderers. Edensaw, moving swiftly, got Rooney into a cabin and engaged in furious battle with one of the Massets while Rooney contrived to join four of his men in the aft cabin. Seeing that

[5] *Correspondence re QCI Gold*, pp. 12-13.

there was no hope of saving the boat from plunder, Edensaw then joined in the looting and in the process ingratiated himself with the Massets, hoping thereby to save the lives of Rooney and his crew. In this purpose he was successful and, though the *Susan Sturges* was set afire after being cleared of her cargo of blankets, calico and tobacco, Edensaw arranged for her seven men to be safely conveyed to Fort Simpson. Here Edensaw later restored to Rooney his chronometer and certain other objects, refusing all remuneration. The grateful Rooney then wrote a testimonial letter (still cherished by Edensaw's descendants) briefly setting forth what had happened, and certifying "he deserves well at the hands of every white man."[6]

So much for the Rooney-Edensaw version, which was later to be published by Rooney in a Boston magazine. This too was the story that Edensaw told in 1853 to the officers of H.M.S. *Virago* when the latter were investigating the whole affair. The impression the *Virago*'s officers had of Chief Edensaw is worth noting: " . . . he is decidedly the most advanced Indian to be met with on the coast: quick, cunning, ambitious, crafty, and, above all, anxious to obtain the good opinion of the white men."[7]

Now for the testimony of the Masset Indians. Some of them maintained that even while the *Susan Sturges* was en route from Skidegate a runner, following an overland trail, was on his way to tell the Massets that the boat, very weakly manned, was coming in their direction. The occupants of the canoe encountered off Rose Spit unanimously testified that what Edensaw had really told them (unknown to Rooney who could not understand their language) was that he, Edensaw, was only pretending to be a friend to the white men and was undecided as to whether or not he should try to seize their ship. One of the Masset chiefs, Scowell, said that it was he himself, on his own initiative, who got Rooney safely ashore and subsequently took him and his men to Fort Simpson. Such were the

---

[6] Kathleen E. Dalzell, *The Queen Charlotte Islands 1774-1966* (Terrace, B.C., 1968), pp. 61-62.

[7] "Account of the Plunder of the *Susan Sturges*", *Nautical Magazine* 23 (1854):210. Although unsigned, this account clearly comes from the pen of George H. Inskip, Master of the *Virago*, who published two other articles relating to the Queen Charlotte Islands in this same journal in March 1854 and December 1855.

two versions which would be put before the officers of H.M.S. *Virago* the following year when she arrived to investigate the attack on the *Susan Sturges*.

*   *   *

This year ended with wedding bells (or more exactly, the signal bell of Fort Victoria) ringing out in nuptial celebration. Young Dr. Helmcken, he who had pleaded so eloquently from Fort Rupert for a passage home to England, had changed his mind and fallen in love with Cecilia (petite, pretty and very musical), the eldest daughter of Governor Douglas. Many, many years later old Dr. Helmcken was to set down his recollections of his wedding on 27 December 1852. With gentlemanly reserve he wrote the account in the third person and never identified himself and his wife as the principals. To get the full point of that reminiscence, now to be quoted, one must remember that the rules of the Church of England then required that weddings be performed during the forenoon:

About Xmas 1852, a wedding in high life took place. The day before the time fixed it snowed and it snowed — lord, how it snowed! — so that a couple of feet of snow lay on the ground. The only thing approaching to a carriage was a two-wheeled light cart — the governor's carriage — useless, there not being any roads. The bridegroom goes to church. The bride and her maidens at home, waiting for the carriage. The cart was at the fort, had travelled a hundred yards the wheels no longer would turn and there was a dead stop. The charioteer, a lively, active, good natured French-Canadian gentleman, full of resource, got an idea. He sent to the store for a dry-goods box, cut off the top and one side, put a seat in and threw some scarlet cloth over all. Having hewn a couple of willows growing close at hand, of these he made shaft and runners all in one! The box arriving is fixed upon the willow runners, the horse harnessed, the sleigh hastens for the bride and maids.

The poor bridegroom is waiting impatiently in the mess-room church; the hour approaches twelve! His best man rushes into the mess-room, to put the clock hands back, when he suddenly discovers the chaplain's wife, dismayed he kicks out a dog, to disguise his intentions, and returns disappointed. The chaplain appears, and says, if the bride does not arrive before twelve; it only wants a quarter now, I will not be able to perform the ceremony to-day, it being illegal to do so. Here's a pretty kettle of fish; but just then the tinkle of sleigh bells are heard, and the bridesmaids and dry-goods box appear. The whole party hurry into the church, the ceremony is proceeding, the clock strikes twelve, just as the ring is put on the finger, etc.: the ceremony over, the bride and bridegroom leave the church to return to their parents' house for a good time, and then the guns roar from the bastions. The bell in the middle of the fort rings — the dogs howl thereunder — the men fire muskets — all hurrah. Grog is served out all round, there is feasting, revelling and jollity, and everybody heart and soul wishes the handsome, favorite, and favored couple very many happy new years.[8]

John and Cecilia Helmcken were to have only thirteen years together, before Mrs. Helmcken died, leaving seven young children. For the remaining fifty-five years of his life Dr. Helmcken remained a widower.

[8] Blakey Smith, *Helmcken Reminiscences*, pp. 296-97.

1853

Expedition against the Cowichans and the Nanaimos —
Douglas' tax on grog shops — The Hon. C. W. Wentworth
Fitzwilliam at Fort Victoria — The Fort Simpson bootlegger
— Northern cruises by H.M.S. Virago *— Festivities at Bea-*
con Hill — Vancouver Island's first settler takes his final
departure — A bad regime in New Caledonia.

New Year's Day saw H.M.S. *Thetis* anchored in Esquimalt harbour.
Her departure date was near, but she had still to perform a final
mission for Governor Douglas. On November 5th Peter Brown, a
Scottish shepherd employed by the HBC at its Saanich sheep station,
had been found murdered. The murderers had been identified as a
Cowichan brave and the son of a Nanaimo chief, both of whom had
fled to their tribal homes. Only a powerful force such as the *Thetis*
provided could make the Cowichans and Nanaimos surrender them.

The punitive expedition set forth from Fort Victoria on the
beautifully clear and frosty morning of January 5th. At the head was
the invaluable little *Beaver* carrying Governor Douglas, twenty
marines off the *Thetis*, and about ten of the Victoria Voltigeurs, the
tiny French-Canadian paramilitary constabulary that Governor
Blanshard had raised several years before. The *Beaver* had in tow a
second HBC vessel, the sailing ship *Recovery*, carrying four naval
officers and eighty bluejackets. Behind the *Recovery*, completing the
tow, were the launch, barge and pinnace of the *Thetis*, carrying
artillery.

The next afternoon this odd little armada, having travelled all of
two miles an hour, arrived at the mouth of the Cowichan River, and
the Cowichan Indians were summoned to a meeting the following
day. Many years later Lieut. John Moresby, R.N., now an admiral

enjoying retirement, set down his recollections of the happenings of January 7th:

Day broke wet and sullen, but in order to gain a choice of position we made an early start and landed our forces, anchoring our boats so that their guns dominated the situation. A small tent was pitched for the Governor, where were deposited presents for the tribe, besides his pistols and cutlass, the use of either to depend on circumstances. Then, guarded by the Canadians and Marines, he and Lieutenant Sansum advanced to the front and waited.

Soon rolling down the river came the melancholy boom of the war-drums, and far-off cries resolved themselves into war-songs, as a fleet of large canoes, lashed together in triplets, paddled furiously round a bend of the river and headed for our position at full speed. The strange and fascinating sight is present with me still. The whale-backed downs of Hampshire around me melt into air, and I see the snowy forests, the river, and over 200 tall warriors, their height exaggerated with head-plumes, faces terrifically painted with red ochre, decked with loin-ropes of shells which met their deer-skin leggings and clattered with every movement as they leaped from the canoes.

Instantly the Governor . . . lit the pipe of council and smoked, watching them indifferently, with Sansum and two aides-de-camp at his side.

The indifference covered some anxiety, for without an instant's hesitation a large body of braves rushed up the hill-side, taking higher ground and completely outflanking us, a knowledge of tactics rendered somewhat disquieting by the array of glittering eyes and gun-barrels covering us.[1]

Douglas now spoke briefly in Chinook, declaring that just as a white man must be punished if he killed an Indian, so an Indian must be punished if he killed a white. He concluded: "Give up the murderer, and let there be peace between the peoples, or I will burn your lodges and trample out your tribes!"[2] Two hours of impassioned oratory followed, but finally the Cowichans decided to surrender the murderer. Suddenly all the warriors sank to the ground, leaving standing only the wanted man and his old father. The two were immediately taken aboard the *Beaver*.

On January 9th the little flotilla was at anchor at Nanaimo. When the Nanaimos came down the river in their canoes, they had

---

[1] John Moresby, *Two Admirals* (London, 1909), pp. 129-30.

[2] *Ibid.*, p. 130.

white headplumes and wore no warpaint, thus indicating that they desired peace — but they did not have the murderer with them. The chiefs claimed that they had lost control of their young men, who had sworn not to give up the wanted man. Soon, however, the experienced half-breed trackers among the Victoria Voltigeurs were threading their way through the snowy forest following first the route of the young Nanaimo braves, and then the solitary trail of the murderer after he had split off from them. Working along the course of the Chase River, which now acquired its name, they caught up with the second murderer, finding him cowering under the roots of a fallen tree.

Once both the wanted men were prisoners aboard the *Beaver*, Governor Douglas held their trial. A verdict of guilty was brought in, and on January 17th a gallows was erected at Gallows Point on Protection Island and here the two Indians were hanged.

*   *   *

Back in Victoria, Governor Douglas turned his attention to another problem, the finances of the infant crown colony. Since nearly all the meagre funds from the sale of lands went into a trust fund in London for ultimate expediture on public works on Vancouver Island, Douglas himself was without any source of immediate income with which to finance his government. A plan to impose import duties was vetoed by London, which said that such duties could not be imposed until there was a local legislative assembly to approve such imposts. Another possible source of income suggested itself to Douglas — a heavy licensing fee to be paid by all those engaged in the liquor trade. Since the heavy drinking around Victoria was creating increasing problems, licensing would carry with it other benefits besides the supplying of funds. The difficulty lay in getting the consent of that Council which Douglas had inherited from Governor Blanshard. With two of its members, Chief Trader Roderick Finlayson (Douglas' replacement on the original council) and John Tod, the retired HBC officer, no trouble could be expected; but there would be a great deal of difficulty with the third member, Captain Cooper the "free settler", for Captain Cooper was himself engaged in the liquor traffic, as was his friend James Yates, a former HBC clerk who had set up in business on his own account.

To avoid Cooper's predictable opposition, Douglas resorted to a Machiavellian manoeuvre. On March 28th, aware that Cooper was off on a visit to his property at Metchosin, the Governor had his secretary deliver to Cooper's Victoria residence, late in the afternoon, written notice that a meeting of the Council was to be held at ten o'clock the next morning. Needless to say, given such short notice during his absence, Cooper was not present at that meeting and the liquor licensing measure was passed without difficulty.

When Cooper got back to Victoria on April 1st and learned what had happened, he was very angry indeed and shot off a letter of complaint to Douglas. The latter coolly replied that, since Metchosin was only eight miles from Victoria, he had every reason to think that Cooper could have attended if he had wanted to. Cooper retorted with a second letter in which he pointed out:

... in my judgment it is a great inaccuracy or at least much calculated to mislead to describe "Metchosin" as beng a distance of "eight miles". In a straight line across the water it may be only that distance: but your Excellency knows well that we are dependent on the canoes of the natives to perform this journey, and that even if the weather was always favourable (which it often is not) canoes are not to be had at *any time* and scarcely at 5. O.Clock P.M. By land the practicable journey is allowed to be fifteen miles at least and generally occupies about five hours in performing as is perfectly well known to those who have been accustomed to travel it. Besides in the *dark* the road is such that it is impossible to perform the journey with any degree of safety.[3]

No doubt Douglas smiled sardonically as he read what he had known so well when setting the time of the council meeting. Anyway, it was all water under the bridge now, and he had his liquor licensing revenue.

Cooper and his friends were not without their revenge. A wandering British aristocrat, the Hon. C. W. Wentworth Fitzwilliam, youngest son of Earl Fitzwilliam, was at this time a visitor in Victoria. Dissatisfied with his reception by Douglas, he had grown

---

[3] Text taken from the copy sent to the Duke of Newcastle by Earl Fitzwilliam, now in the Newcastle Papers on deposit at the University of Nottingham.

2. A Babine Chief

3. Saw-se-a, A Cowichan Chief

4. Indian Family at House Entrance

5. Two Coastal Indians

6. Indian Chiefs at New Westminster

Standing: Tak-o'task, Canoe Creek Chief; William, Williams Lake;

Seated: Nā-nāh, Dog Creek; Quil-quarlse, Alkali Lake; Se-as kut, Shuswap; Templ-khan, Babine Lake; Silkosalish, Lillooet; Kam-eo-saltze, Soda Creek; Sosastumpl, Bridge Creek.

7. Indians and Houses at Cape Caution

8. Indian Grave near Chapman's Bar, Fraser Canyon

9. Roman Catholic Priests Leading Indians in Prayer, Fraser Valley

10. H.M.S. *Termagant* Aground in Active Pass. (H.M.S. *Alert*, centre; H.M.S. *Plumper*, right)

11. H.M.S. *Sutlej* Gun Deck

12. H.M.S. *Virago* on Rocks

13. H.M.S. *Virago* Being Repaired, Fort Simpson

14. View of Victoria, July 1858

15. H.M.S. *Plumper* Surveying in Johnstone Strait

16. Captain and Mrs. G. H. Richards with Officers of H.M.S. *Plumper*
Sitting, left to right: Sub-Lieut. E. P. Bedwell, 2nd Lieut. R. C. Mayne,
Mrs. G. H. Richards, 1st Lieut. W. Moriarty.
Standing: Dr. Wood [?], Paymaster W. H. J. Brown, Capt. G. H. Richards,
Lieut. D. Pender.

17. British Boundary Commission Party, Colvile, W.T.
Left to right: muleteer, J. K. Lord, Dr. Bauerman.

18. British Boundary Commission — Observatory Tent
Captain Darrah and Assistant, Yahk River Observatory.

19. Governor Richard Blanshard   20. Governor Sir James Douglas

21. Members of the first House of Assembly, Vancouver Island, 1856
Back Row: J. W. McKay, J. D. Pemberton, J. Porter (clerk);
Front Row: T. Skinner, Dr. J. S. Helmcken, J. Yates.

sympathetic with the dissident group headed by Captain Cooper. Accordingly when he left Victoria he carried with him a statement of grievances against Douglas drawn up by Cooper (who did not fail to point out that under the HBC Vancouver Island had attained a white population of only 300 persons, whereas the American territory now had 30,000). Fitzwilliam was given a similar statement by Yates, together with a transcript of the correspondence between Cooper and Douglas concerning the council meeting of March 29th. Appended to the last was a note signed by the Rev. Mr. Staines, the HBC chaplain, testifying to the truthfulness of Cooper's allegations. These documents reached Earl Fitzwilliam in June, and were immediately forwarded by him to the Duke of Newcastle, the Colonial Secretary. They seem to have done Douglas no harm.

*   *   *

A liquor problem of a different kind developed at Fort Simpson on the northern coast. J. W. McKay, the officer in command there, was delighted this year to receive the services of an excellent cook, a Frenchman named Leon. His pleasure was short-lived, however, for a few months after the man arrived one of the Tsimpsean chiefs told McKay that he would have to send Leon away. Demanding why he should deprive himself of his excellent chef, McKay was told that Leon would prove the ruin of the Indians. Pressed for a more specific answer, the Indian at last confided that Leon had approached another chief with an interesting proposal: if the chief would hand over to Leon a large number of furs, and provide him with passage to Fort Victoria in a canoe, he would teach the chief how to make whiskey out of potatoes. Confronting his cook with the Indian's story, McKay had little difficulty in getting a confession from him, and in return agreed to keep him in his employ until he could transfer him to another post. The next morning, to his consternation, McKay found that Leon had fled. Since all the northern tribes raised abundant crops of potatoes, there would be really appalling consequences if Leon were left free to get rich by teaching them how to make alcohol out of their harvests. Learning that Leon was hiding at Bella Bella, McKay headed there with an armed party and announced a reward of $50 for anybody who would deliver the Frenchman to the

HBC officers at Fort Victoria. Four hours after McKay posted that reward, Leon, bound hand and foot, was lying at the bottom of a large Indian canoe en route to Victoria.[4]

*   *   *

As we have seen, the coal near Fort Rupert, after initial high expectations, had proved generally unsatisfactory. Accordingly mining was terminated there this year, though the fort continued to exist as a fur-trading post. The white miners who had been employed at Fort Rupert were taken south to Nanaimo to open up the superior coalfields there. The tall wooden bastion which to this day remains Nanaimo's most famous landmark was built this year to give protection to these miners. At the same time careful surveys were made of Nanaimo Harbour, initially by HBC men but then by H.M.S. *Virago*.

The *Virago*, a small paddlewheel sloop bearing only six guns, seems to have been a thoroughly happy ship despite her unattractive name. An agreeable account of her adventures in British Columbia waters this year is to be found in the diary kept by her rather timid surgeon, Henry Trevan. Almost as soon as the *Virago* entered Esquimalt harbour in mid-April, there was a visit paid by Governor Douglas, who left an invitation for Commander Prevost, Trevan, and a third officer to dine with him. Unfortunately, en route to the Governor's dinner, the three naval gentlemen got lost for a while in the forest while trying to follow the Esquimalt-Victoria trail. There was much laughter about this misadventure, and Douglas made a point of giving them Hall, the Fort Constable, as their guide back to their ship that night. Unfortunately, the night turned so black and rainy that even Hall got lost on the return journey and they blundered around in the forest until they ended up in a ditch by Macaulay's farm.

After this ill-omened start, things went well. The officers enjoyed deer-shooting parties, visits to Governor Douglas' dairy, and calls at the hospitable home of the Langfords and their pretty daughters.

[4] J. W. McKay, *Recollections of a Chief Trader in the Hudson's Bay Company*, PAC, MG29, B35, Vol. 7, pp. 13-14 (Bancroft transcript).

Captain and Mrs. Langford, along with Miss Mary, enjoyed a cruise aboard H.M.S. *Virago* to Bellingham Bay.

The ship then set about her serious business, first to Nanaimo to coal, then to Fort Rupert where Trevan vaccinated the children of Mr. Blenkinsop, the Cornishman in command of the fort. The crew, negotiating with the Indians here, "bartered for a Fine Old Eagle. God knows what they are going to do with it. They gave two fish-hooks and ten pearl buttons for it."[5] Complete with its new mascot the ship sailed up to the Queen Charlotte Islands and entered Skidegate Inlet. Here Commander Prevost met a local chief, Captain Bear Skin, and enlisted his son, Mr. Bear Skin, as an interpreter. Continuing to Fort Simpson, Prevost engaged Chief Edensaw to pilot H.M.S. *Virago* around the north end of the Queen Charlotte Islands. Obviously Edensaw was viewed with some distrust because of what had happened when he was aboard the *Susan Sturges* in 1852, for Trevan notes in his diary:

Possibly he anticipated getting us on shore and making a wreck of the Virago on his own shores where at first he was very anxious to pilot us. On drawing near the Land, We told him to be careful where he took the ship that we drew 16 feet of water and if the ship grounded or struck a rock we would hang him immediately to the yard arm. Shewed him the Rope he was to be hung with. At first he thought it was a joke. . . . [6]

Convinced that his life hung on his skill as a pilot, Edensaw safely brought the ship to Mitchell Harbour, where he was released from his duties. The gold excitement had long since ended and the *Virago* found not a single ship anchored where the goldseekers had congregated in 1851.

From here the *Virago* made a clear run back to Esquimalt. Shore leave was granted the ship's company, which found "some Strong Yankee Stuff which made them very tipsy. They were continually fighting, terrifying the Indians and keeping Hudson's Bay Company People in constant alarm." A number of the sailors became so

---

[5] *The Diary of Henry Trevan, R.N., Surgeon H.M.S. "Virago"*, PAC, MG24, F40, p. 291.

[6] Trevan, *Diary*, p. 300.

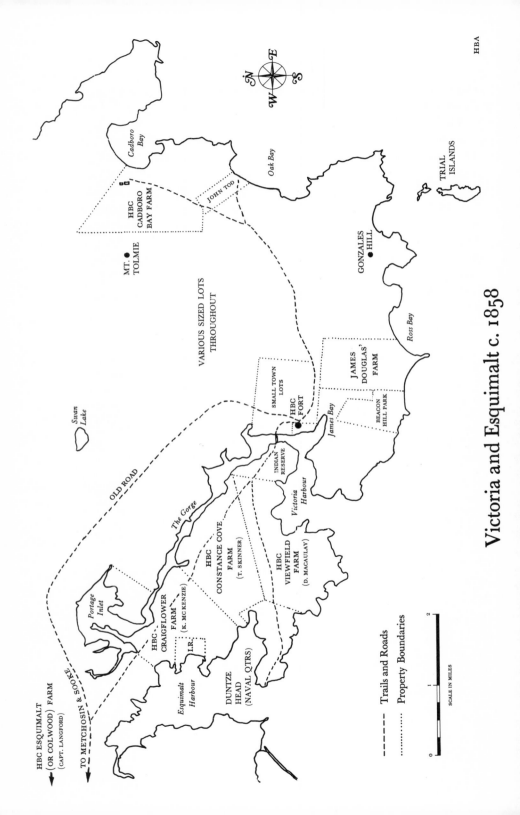

Victoria and Esquimalt c. 1858

HBA

Trails and Roads

·········· Property Boundaries

SCALE IN MILES

0   1   2

TRIAL ISLANDS

Oak Bay

Cadboro Bay

HBC CADBORO BAY FARM

JOHN TOD

MT. TOLMIE

GONZALES HILL

Ross Bay

VARIOUS SIZED LOTS THROUGHOUT

Swan Lake

SMALL TOWN LOTS

HBC FORT

JAMES DOUGLAS' FARM

BEACON HILL PARK

James Bay

OLD ROAD

The Gorge

INDIAN RESERVE

Victoria Harbour

HBC CONSTANCE COVE FARM (T. SKINNER)

HBC VIEWFIELD FARM (D. MACAULAY)

Portage Inlet

HBC CRAIGFLOWER FARM (K. MC KENZIE)

I.R.

Esquimalt Harbour

DUNTZE HEAD (NAVAL QTRS)

HBC ESQUIMALT (OR COLWOOD) FARM (CAPT. LANGFORD)

TO METCHOSIN & SOOKE

befuddled that they lost their way back to their ship and wandered around in the forest all night until Indians found them and led them to the Victoria-Esquimalt trail.

June 1st was a festive day for Fort Victoria, with Governor Douglas providing a magnificent picnic at Beacon Hill to celebrate his son's second birthday. The Royal Navy officers, the Hudson's Bay Company officers, the local populace and hundreds of Indians turned out for the occasion. After a copious lunch there was horse-racing. Then old John Tod got out his fiddle and "the most respectable of the party" danced a quadrille on the green. Meanwhile, in another part of the grounds, "the Scotch Piper in full costume was playing the Pipes to a Party of Scotch Mechanics & Labourers who are in the Company's Service. The latter were kicking away at Scotch Reels with great energy."[7] A couple of prizefight rings were set up where the opponents smashed at each other "most desperately."

Towards sunset the Douglas family, the naval officers and "the most respectable part of the Residents" withdrew to Government House for tea followed by quadrilles, polkas and waltzes — and the homely music of the fiddle and the bagpipes gave way to the more cultured tones of the pianoforte. The party broke up about eleven o'clock. The *Virago*'s officers had a hard time getting home, partly because the bagpiper, who was very drunk, kept falling down. Mr. Hassan, a Turkish naval officer attached to the British service, solicitously carried the pipes so that they would come to no harm. Hassan panicked when he thought he saw a grizzly bear in the woods, but this proved to be only Farmer Macaulay's white bull. Finally the little party straggled back to their ship about two o'clock in the morning.

Possibly H.M.S. *Virago* would now have terminated her visit to Vancouver Island, but Governor Douglas belatedly received instructions from London to launch an investigation into the Haidas' attack on the *Susan Sturges* the previous year. To conduct this inquiry the *Virago* had to make a second visit to the Queen Charlotte Islands. This time the ship was not so successful in navigating the treacherous British Columbia coast and ended up at Fort Simpson

---

[7] Trevan, *Diary*, p. 308.

so damaged, through striking Virago Rock in Cowichan Gap[8] (now Porlier Pass), that Commander Prevost had no choice but to head to Fort Simpson, have the ship lightened of everything that could be taken off her, get her beached at high tide, and set the carpenters repairing her keel during low water, work which would require almost three weeks' labour. About fifteen hundred Indians milled around the helpless warship, most of them filled with larcenous thoughts. As a safety measure, the grounded *Virago* was surrounded by a rope cordon beyond which natives were forbidden to pass. As an additional precaution, the ship's cannons had been put on rafts anchored three-quarters of a mile from the ship. Even so, an armed sentry was required to keep the Indians from cutting the rafts' cables and making off with Her Majesty's cannons. Despite these and other precautions, there were losses. Twenty-eight cannon shot which had been put in Fort Simpson for safe custody disappeared, and much negotiating was needed to get most of them back from the Indians.

While the *Virago* was being repaired, her crew had an opportunity to witness an Indian potlatch. This provided Surgeon Trevan with material for one of the most colourful parts of his diary:

Monday [July] 4th

There was a Great Indian Feast today when The Chief who glories in the name of Sweet William became higher in the estimation of his people by his acts of generosity. The principal thing given was large quantities of rancid grease. In the distribution there were from time to time broils and contentions because some had more than others. Blankets were torn up and distributed in strips in fact all the wealth he has been saving for several years was distributed today. . . . The Dance took place after the gifts had been distributed. . . . A Tribe from Skitigate Queen Charlotte's Island were invited to this feast and in the midst of the dance one of the Indian Ladies fainted under the pretence that she could not bear to see the Skitigate men dancing at Fort Simpson as it brought to her recollection the circumstance of the Skitigate men taking some of her relations and making slaves of them when she was a little girl. This was a signal for the Lady's party to pounce on one of the

---

[8] Royal Navy, Hydrographic Office, Taunton, Somerset, *Master's Remark Book of H.M.S. Virago, 1853,* no pagination. A detailed account of the damage to the *Virago* and the repairs made at Fort Simpson will be found in the manuscript *Private Remark Book* (now in private possession) of her master, George H. Inskip, pp. 15-21.

Skitigate men and take him prisoner. In the course of five minutes the different parties were armed with their muskets to the number of seven or eight hundred in array of each other. The Balls were whistling about but no person shot. The Skitigate man was kept a prisoner being the weaker party.[9]

Four days after these stirring happenings the *Virago*, repaired and once more seaworthy, was refloated and started taking on her cannons and supplies. A few days were spent in "wooding", laying in the stock of cordwood which would be needed to fire her boilers. On the evening of July 11th, this work being pretty much completed, the *Virago* treated the Indians to a display of her gunnery. For a target, the principal chief of the Tsimpseans provided a canoe in which the effigy of a man had been placed. Alas for H.M.S. *Virago*! When she opened fire the results were decidedly anticlimactic. First the warship fired one of her 32-pounders, loaded with cannister shot, at a range of some four hundred yards and missed the canoe entirely. Then the cannon was loaded with a round shot, and missed entirely for the second time. The 32-pounder tried again with a round shot, only to have it fall short, though on the ricochet it did manage to hole the canoe. Another 32-pounder was brought into action and in its turn missed the canoe. Finally a charge of grape shot managed to knock down the dummy and put a number of holes in the canoe. For a grand finale, the *Virago* fired two shells from a 68-pounder, only to have both of them fail to explode. When the display ended, with the 68-pounder managing to get off a round shot successfully, the Indians were unkind enough to say that the shooting had not been anything like as impressive as they had expected.[10] Certainly if the exhibition had been intended to overawe them with the might of a British warship, it had failed signally. The Tsimpseans had witnessed one of the Royal Navy's worse displays of inept gunnery.

On July 14th H.M.S. *Virago* steamed into Masset Harbour, piloted by Chief Edensaw. Two Indians who were believed to be ringleaders in the attack on the *Susan Sturges* were arrested but both, after they had been brought out to the ship, escaped by leaping overboard and swimming for the shore. One, as he went over the

[9] Trevan, *Diary*, pp. 326-27.

[10] Inskip, *Private Remark Book*, pp. 22-23.

side, left a sentry still hanging on to his blanket. The chiefs of the Masset Indians refusing thereafter to come on board the warship, Commander Prevost and Dr. Kennedy of the HBC (who was Douglas' personal representative) went ashore and parleyed with the Indians. Their investigation into the capture of the *Susan Sturges* found the Massets accusing Chief Edensaw of being the prime instigator, and Edensaw indignantly repudiating the charge. No clear proof could be found either way, but G. H. Inskip, one of the *Virago's* officers, showed a certain John Bull commonsense when he later bluntly summed things up:

They tried to implicate Edensaw; it was known that he saved the captain's life, but they held the stolen goods. They brought us the empty money chests, and gave up two boats, which were of no use to them.[11]

After this somewhat unsatisfactory winding up of the investigation, H.M.S. *Virago* sailed out from Masset Harbour, curtly firing a single cannon in response to an ironic farewell salute from the Masset Indians.

Travelling along the north shore of the Queen Charlottes, the *Virago's* men saw a bear, some four hundred yards away on the beach, turn and stare at their ship. For their entertainment, one of the gunners fired a 24-pound howitzer loaded with grape shot at bruin. Apparently the *Virago's* gunnery had not improved since the debacle at Fort Simpson, for the bear escaped this singularly unsporting attempt on his life by the Royal Navy, and gave his name to Bruin Bay, west of Virago Sound.[12] At the southern end of the Queen Charlottes, the *Virago* paused to complete a survey begun earlier of Houston Stewart Channel. While the ship's gig and cutter were off examining the entrance into Rose Harbour, they encountered canoes full of Indians who beckoned to them to come ashore. Aware of the bad reputation of the Haidas, the two little British boats turned and made the best speed they could with sail and oar, whereupon the Indians opened fire, the musket balls falling in the retreating gig and

[11] "Remarks on Some Harbours of Queen Charlotte Islands", *Nautical Magazine* 24 (1855):627.

[12] Letter of 3 June 1905 from Capt. G. H. Inskip to Capt. John H. Walbran. Canadian Permanent Committee on Geographical Names, Topon. file 0023.

cutter. Gladly they rejoined the *Virago* and said their last farewell to the Queen Charlotte Islands.

July 22nd saw the *Virago* again at Fort Rupert, where Henry Trevan blithely noted in his diary, "We were to have married Mr. Moffett one of the Company's officers to Miss Lucy McNeil at this place, but the Gentleman's heart failed him and the wedding was scuppered."[13] A couple of days later the *Virago* was at Nanaimo where she received word that a consort, H.M.S. *Trincomalee*, was impatiently awaiting her arrival at Esquimalt.

One ghastly experience marked the *Virago*'s final visit to Nanaimo. As evening was descending, a small northern canoe pulled up on a little island close to the warship. At four o'clock in the morning musket fire was heard: twenty-seven Nanaimo Indians had attacked the eight men and one woman in the northern party, hoping to rob them of the earnings that they were taking home from Victoria. Aware that they had no chance against such odds, the surviving northerners paddled desperately to the side of the *Virago*. Looking down into the canoe, the *Virago*'s crew saw an appalling sight — three men apparently already dead, blood everywhere, and shattered bones mixed with human brains. After the *Virago* had taken on board the injured Indians and hauled up their canoe, she took them back to Victoria to await a safer journey home in company with a larger band of their fellow Tsimpeans.

On August 10th H.M.S. *Virago* sailed for San Francisco, after having towed H.M.S. *Trincomalee* out of the Strait of Juan de Fuca where the latter hoisted sail in the open Pacific on a cruise to Sitka before returning to Esquimalt.

*   *   *

Surgeon Henry Trevan of the *Virago* was not the only diarist plying a pen this year. He had a counterpart in the person of young Martha Cheney, a niece of Thomas Blinkhorn, the manager of Captain Cooper's Metchosin farm. Martha seems to have been a lively girl who thoroughly enjoyed life. The earliest portion of her diary has been lost, and what survives is contained in a scribbler now in the

---

[13] Trevan, *Diary*, p. 337. Hamilton Moffat regained his courage and finally married Lucy McNeill in Victoria on 15 March 1856.

Provincial Archives of British Columbia. Martha's journal, erratic in capitalization and innocent of punctuation, often with very scrappy entries and gaps here and there, is hardly a model of its kind. It does however give an occasional insight into pioneer life at Victoria, with Martha scrawling down her record of experiences, ranging from Indian scares to dancing until 4 a.m. at a ball on board H.M.S. *Trincomalee*.

The earliest surviving entry in Martha's diary, that for 16 September 1853, notes that around ten o'clock in the evening, just when everybody was going to bed, four gentlemen including Captain Grant and Captain Cooper arrived and had to be put up overnight.[14] Captain Grant was, of course, that first independent settler on Vancouver Island, of whom we have made no mention since, more or less bankrupt, he headed down to the Oregon goldfields. That venture had yielded him no wealth and he had ended up in San Francisco, completely destitute. Here he gamely turned to humble manual labour to keep alive. With his strong Highlander frame, he was well fitted for work on the San Francisco docks. Still there is something piquant about a former captain of the Scots Greys toiling among the American stevedores. At length, having put by a little money, he managed to get a passage back to Vancouver Island, arriving just about the time of this first mention of him in Martha Cheney's diary. Vancouver Island's first settler no longer had any hopes for his Sooke establishment. His one concern was to sell it for the best price that he could get, and head home to Britain. A purchaser was found in John Muir, who with his family had immigrated a few years before to mine coal for the HBC at Fort Rupert. Muir in October agreed to pay $4000 for the Sooke property and Captain Grant took his final departure around mid-November of this year.

A few words may be said about the subsequent career of the gallant and irrepressible captain. He got back to Britain just as the Crimean War broke out, offered his services, and became Lieut.-Colonel of the Cavalry of the Turkish Contingent. In 1857 and again in 1859 he read papers on Vancouver Island to the Royal Geographical Society, of which he was elected a Fellow. The Indian

14 "The Diary of Martha Cheney Ella, 1853-1856", *BCHQ* 13 (1949):101.

Mutiny saw Grant serving in India, where he was present at the siege of Lucknow. He died in Saugor, Central India, in August 1861.

*   *   *

Several other events of this year must not go unchronicled. One was the arrival in Victoria this June of the fine new screw steamer *Otter*, acquired by the HBC to take over part of the work of the aging *Beaver*. Another was the appointment of a judge to preside over the newly-created Supreme Court of Civil Justice. The three or four local magistrates had proved too involved in local factionalism to be the sole source of justice, so the only solution was to find an impartial newcomer and make him a superior judge. For the new position Governor Douglas chose his own brother-in-law, David Cameron, who had recently arrived in the colony. Cameron lacked legal training — but so did everybody else on Vancouver Island — and the Colonial Office ratified his appointment. Douglas' choice brought angry charges of a "Family Compact" from the anti-Douglas faction headed by Cooper, Yates and Staines. But in fact Cameron proved a good judge, handing out an even-handed justice based on common sense rather than the quiddities of the lawyers, until his retirement as Chief Justice of Vancouver Island in 1865.

*   *   *

We have made little mention of events in New Caledonia during these years, chiefly because the fur trade there followed a tedious routine, varied only occasionally by a murder, a drowning, or a desertion. Since 1844 New Caledonia had been under the superintendency of Donald Manson. Normally that position carried with it the rank of Chief Factor, but Manson was denied that promotion year after year. The reason was that, although Manson successfully got out the furs and so was not replaced, he had a thoroughly bad reputation as a crude bully. Any HBC officer had to be ready to look after himself in a rough world, but Manson seemed to find a positive pleasure in threats and beatings, and encouraged his subordinates to imitate his own brutality. By and large the HBC had a very good record indeed in its administration of the vast savage areas over which it held sway, but Manson's regime in New Caledonia is a blot on that record. Governor Simpson contemptuously applied to Manson's methods the old English phrase of "club law". On June 18th of this year he wrote angrily to Manson from Norway House:

There is at present here a retired winterer from your district, one Francois Lacourse, who states that he was very severely beaten by Mr. Ogden [a son of the famous Peter Skene Ogden], who knocked him down, kicked him, and injured him so seriously that the man has since then been subject to epileptic fits. He states that on another occasion you aimed a blow at him with an axe. . . .

These are *ex parte* statements of Lacourse and they may be in part false; but taken in connection with other cases of late years, they afford ample evidence of the existence of a system of 'club law' which must not be allowed to prevail.[15]

Unfortunately Manson continued his brutal system, and Simpson never allowed him his Chief Factorship.

[15] Morice, *History of Northern Interior of B.C.*, p. 277.

1854

A "drouthy" New Year's Day at Fort Victoria — Death by drowning for a demagogue — Douglas plans to take the Alaskan Panhandle from Russia — the Princess Royal's *miners at Nanaimo.*

For an account of New Year's Day, 1854, at Fort Victoria, we may turn to the diary of a certain Robert Melrose. This bears the lugubrious heading:

ROYAL EMIGRANT'S ALMANACK

concerning

FIVE YEARS SERVITUDE

under the

HUDSON'S BAY COMPANY

on

VANCOUVER'S ISLAND

Melrose's entry for January 1st is notable for its brevity: "Drouthy New Year." Fortunately he explains in a footnote why this New Year's was a thirsty one:

New Year's Day, a day above all days, for rioting in drunkenness, then what are we to expect of this young, but desperate Colony of ours; where dissipation is carried on to such extremities my readers will be expecting to find nothing in my Almanack, from Christmas, till past the New Year, but such a one drunk, and another drunk, and so on; how different is the scene, then what must I attribute the cause of all this, too, must I prescribe it to the good morals of the people; no! no! my friends, no such thing could be expected here; the grog-shops were drained of every sort of liquor, not a drop to be got for either love or money, had it been otherwise the case, there is no saying whither my small Almanack would have contained them or not; it would almost take a line of packet ships, running regular between here, and San

Francisco to supply this Island with grog, so great a thirst prevails amongst its inhabitants.[1]

In fact, a fair amount of Melrose's diary consists of entries such as "James Downie ½ Drunk", "W. Veitch ¾ D. Enoch Morris ¾ D. J. Wilson ½ D. Fresh beef served out. John Russel ¾ D. Peter Bartleman ¾ D." Melrose has the honesty to admit upon occasion "The Author ¾ D."

*   *   *

March saw tragedy strike the small community. For several years we have had little occasion to mention the Rev. Robert J. Staines, who had arrived with his wife in 1849 to serve as chaplain and schoolmaster. Things had not gone badly for Staines at first. He had conscientiously attended to his ecclesiastical duties in Victoria, even though annoyed by Douglas' delay in getting a proper church built for him. He had found time to conduct services at Fort Langley and at several settlements in the United States. His little school had prospered. But unfortunately Staines allowed himself to become embroiled ever more deeply in the petty politics of Fort Victoria. Perhaps his involvement was inevitable. Dr. Helmcken later described him as "an excitable politician and a very dissatisfied man".[2] Captain James Cooper, even though one of Staines' allies, conceded "he would have made a very good parish lawyer instead of a parish priest".[3] Staines' first indiscretion was adding his signature to the petition taken by Blanshard to England, in which various free settlers protested against Douglas' appointment as Governor. In 1852 there was trouble over an anonymous letter, sent to the Colonial Office, accusing Douglas of oppression in his administration of affairs. Declared Douglas:

There is no doubt of Mr. Staines being the author of the letter in question the style and spirit of the production as well as common report mark it as one of his effusions.

He entertains a most unaccountable and unreasonable dislike to the Company, and has done so ever since his arrival in this country; and he

---

[1] "The Diary of Robert Melrose, Part II, 1853-54", *BCHQ* 7 (1943):199.

[2] Blakey Smith, *Helmcken Reminiscences*, p. 144.

[3] James Cooper, *Memoirs*, p. 5.

moreover endeavours to fill the minds of every stranger who arrives here, with the rancorous feelings of his own breast.[4]

Staines, in short, was deep in a parson vs. squire row, one of the kind so common in rural England but hardly to be expected in a tiny wilderness outpost.

While the battle raged, with Staines in concert with the malcontents who frequented Yates' grog shop getting up a new petition against Governor Douglas, the reverend gentleman's school began to falter. This was a serious matter since a good part of Staines' income depended upon the fees which HBC officers stationed at other posts paid him to board and educate their children. Early this year most of the parents of Staines' Victoria students sent Douglas a petition complaining of Staines' derelictions of duty both as a parson and as a teacher. At the beginning of February, Chief Factors Douglas and John Work (in their capacity as the Board of Management of the HBC's Western Department) sent Staines a letter brusquely informing him that his services as a schoolmaster were being dispensed with, and that his salary of £340 would end on June 1st.

Staines' apparent negligence in conducting his school may have been due to his deep involvement in such political activities as preparing a protest against Douglas' recent appointment of his brother-in-law, David Cameron, as judge of the newly-created Supreme Court of Civil Justice. Under the leadership of Cooper and Staines, seventy-one colonists signed a petition to the Queen calling for an investigation of this appointment. In an evil hour, Staines offered to carry this petition to England and money was raised to pay his expenses.

Staines had always had a streak of procrastination (laziness some people called it) and this made him miss the ship on which he had booked his passage to San Francisco on the first lap of the homeward journey. Instead, he had to board at Sooke a lumber barque, the *Duchess of San Lorenzo*. She ran into heavy weather and foundered off Cape Flattery where her hulk, dismasted and filled with water, was found wallowing in the water on March 19th by the barque *George Emery*. A sole survivor clinging to some rigging was taken

4 Slater, "Rev. R. J. Staines", *BCHQ* 14:208.

aboard the *George Emery* where he died, but not before telling how Staines, after cutting his way out of his cabin, had survived until a day or two previously.

Almost a year later Mrs. Staines and the children left for England, having been granted a free passage home by the HBC. Thus the Staines family departed from the scene, leaving however one good story behind concerning the days when the Rev. Mr. Staines and his lady had played a leading role in Victoria society. Mrs. Staines was very fond of inviting friends to salad dinners, with guests often staying for the night rather than risking the unlit and muddy roads of the village that was growing around the fort. Upon one such occasion there was much stirring during the night, with one guest after another heading down the corridor, candle in hand. So frequently indeed were lights seen within the house that the fort watchman knocked to ask if there was anything amiss. In the morning Mrs. Staines, investigating the disturbances during the night, asked old Mrs. Blinkhorn, who helped as a servant, where she had got the salad oil. "Out of the old salad oil bottle," staunchly replied Mrs. Blinkhorn. "Oh!" cried Mrs. Staines, "I forgot to tell you I had a fresh bottle, and had filled the one you used with castor oil — it is a mercy we were not all killed!"[5]

*   *   *

Governor Douglas had other worries this spring besides the Staines petition. As usual the northern tribes, Tongass Indians from Alaska, Tsimpseans and others, had made their annual journey down to Fort Victoria, threatening the peace and security of the little settlement. This year there was a special complication. An American at Nisqually had murdered "in a cowardly manner" a Tongass chief. His friends immediately returned to Victoria, mustered their numerous tribesmen and declared their intention to enter Puget Sound in quest of revenge. By sheer force of personality and his status with the Indians, Douglas managed to head off this invasion which could have embroiled the United States and Britain in hostilities. Frustrated, the Tongass Indians turned some of their wrath upon the HBC.

[5] Blakey Smith, *Helmcken Reminiscences*, p. 145.

Late in May, Thomas Grenham arrived posthaste at Fort Victoria with word that about two hundred northern Indians had attacked the HBC farm at Cadboro Bay. Douglas and five other men galloped off to the scene of the action. They found Mr. Baillie, the manager of the farm, badly beaten about the head and robbed of his gun, but the Indians had all moved off the scene. Every able-bodied man in Victoria was promptly put under arms until the next day when, with great relief, the embattled whites saw the northerners heading back up coast. On their way home the latter skirmished with the Cowichans with some loss of life on either side.[6]

*   *   *

This year brought a war infinitely greater in scale than any Indian hostilities, for the Crimean War broke out with Britain, France and Turkey taking up arms against Russia. To Fort Victoria came orders for Douglas to provide sanctuary for any French ships which might be in danger of capture by Russian warships. Unfortunately Fort Victoria, with its wooden palisades and a few ancient cannon useful only for overawing the Indians, was in no shape to protect French shipping from Russian pursuers, much less to withstand any Russian attack. Accordingly, on May 16th, Douglas wrote to the Colonial Office asking for 400 muskets and 100 "minie" rifles, along with full accoutrements, uniforms and military boots for 500 men whom he proposed to raise locally. He also asked for a twelve months' supply of victuals for the force, four light cannon mounted on field carriages, and a few heavy guns to defend the entrance to Victoria harbour. Finally, he requested that a detachment of the Pacific Fleet be stationed at Esquimalt. His letter was received very coldly and he was informed that all he could hope for was "frequent visits" by British warships. His "requisition" for supplies for a 500-man local military force was rejected. Douglas was curtly told that the Russians were hardly likely to attack any place so unimportant as Fort Victoria. Colonel Mundy of the War Office, in his minute on Douglas' requisition for military supplies, cynically observed that the HBC was trying to transfer to the British government the cost of defending its

[6] PRO, WO1/551, pp. 871-74.

establishment from the neighbouring Indian tribes. Then he rubbed salt in the wound by adding:

Practically considered the empire at large has no such interest in the maintenance and support of this outlying settlement (even supposing it to be seriously threatened.) [7]

Another notation recorded that Captain Colquhoun Grant, back from Vancouver Island, had given an opinion that the Russian force at Sitka was more likely to fear an attack than to launch one. [8]

That Russian force up at Sitka had not been left out of account by Douglas but, like Grant, he did not regard it as dangerous. In fact Governor Douglas viewed this Russian war as a golden opportunity to move north and, by force of arms, to add Alaska to the British Empire. Probably it was for this purpose that he chiefly wanted the muskets, rifles, artillery, munitions and supplies for his proposed force of five hundred men. Towards the end of his letter of May 16th to the Duke of Newcastle, Douglas wrote:

... a very serious injury might be inflicted on Russia by taking possession of all their settlements on the American coast, north of Queen Charlotte Islands, they are all upon the sea board, and accessible to shipping. Their defences are on a scale merely calculated to cope with savages, and could not be maintained against a regular force of 500 men. [9]

Newcastle's reply was chilling. No doubt Alaska could be taken over with comparative ease, but it was not the policy of Her Majesty's government to seek any territorial gains in this war with Russia.

Instead of sending forces to take Alaska, the British joined with the French in a disastrous attack on the Siberian naval base of Petropavlovsk. During the course of this operation the British admiral, giving way to despair, committed suicide, and finally the French and British warships had to sail away, leaving the base still firmly held by the Russians. Early in October of this year H.M.S. *President*, H.M.S. *Pique*, and H.M.S. *Virago* arrived in Esquimalt after the Petropavlovsk debacle, partly for supplies and partly for much-needed

[7] PRO, WO1/551, p. 148.

[8] *Ibid.*, p. 156.

[9] *Ibid.*, p. 146.

hospital care for their wounded. But there was no hospital in Victoria — a fact which led to a hurried decision by the Admiralty to establish a naval hospital at Esquimalt in readiness for the next such emergency. The building of this hospital was the first step in the creation of an increasingly important Esquimalt naval base.

With the wisdom of retrospect, we can see that Whitehall, instead of authorizing the HBC to enter into a compact of neutrality with the Russian American Company for the duration of the Crimean War, should have agreed to Douglas' proposed expedition against Alaska. Had the warships so ineffectually used at Petropavlovsk directed their guns against the weak Alaskan establishments, with landing parties made up of Douglas' five hundred HBC Scots, French-Canadians and Indians, the campaign could hardly have failed. And since Russia had by now largely lost interest in her North American territories and soon would be trying to sell them to either Britain or the United States, she would probably have been ready to hand them over in perpetuity to Britain in the treaty she signed after her defeat.

*   *   *

This year saw an immigrant train heading south-westerly across southern British Columbia. The HBC, possibly as a means of getting rid of some of the more disaffected of the métis around the Red River Colony, had engaged James Sinclair (who had taken Red River immigrants to Oregon in 1841) to recruit a second party and conduct them to Fort Walla Walla, one of the faltering posts which the Company still maintained within what was now American territory. Sinclair's Cree guide led them into British Columbia through Kananaskis Pass, the first white men to use this route. But his choice was almost disastrous. The party got lost, plodded through three feet of snow this October, and took thirty days to get through the Rockies whereas in 1841, using the Whiteman Pass, Sinclair had got his people through in just ten days. No further expeditions of this sort were attempted by the HBC, and Sinclair himself was killed in 1856 in one of the endemic Indian wars in Washington Territory.

*   *   *

Much more important than the passage of these transients across the south-eastern corner of our province was the arrival this year of the men and women who were to be the true founders of Nanaimo. With growing awareness of the extent of the coalfields adjacent to Winthuysen Inlet, the HBC decided to bring out from England some experienced coal-miners, along with their wives and families. The recruiting centre was at the Brierley Hill Colliery in Staffordshire. After some twenty-three miners had been enlisted in the Company's service, they and their families were transported to London and embarked on the *Princess Royal.* The latter was a fine new ship replacing the unwieldy old *Norman Morison* and her journey out from Britain was a relatively fast one, taking only a little less than six months. Nevertheless, the chronicle of that voyage is "a gloomy history of death, misery and dissatisfaction."[10] There was an unconscionable number of deaths, especially among the children, the body of one baby being merely thrown overboard with no more ceremony than if it had been a dead cat.[11]

At last the *Princess Royal,* having fought her way through a winter gale in the Strait of Juan de Fuca, put into Esquimalt harbour with her one hundred and twenty passengers, seventy-five of whom (headed by George Robinson, designated as manager and superintendent of the HBC's coal mine and brickworks at Nanaimo) were speedily transferred to the steamer *Beaver* and the schooner *Recovery* for the short voyage to Nanaimo, or Colvile Town as it was more frequently known. Here things were in a state of comparative readiness for their coming. The previous year two expert French-Canadian axemen, Leon Labine and Jean Baptiste Fortier, had built a sturdy bastion for their protection from the "Sne-ny-mo" Indians. Seven dwelling houses, built of logs, had been erected and another three were being constructed.

According to Nanaimo tradition, when the *Princess Royal* party came ashore at Pioneer Rock, about eleven o'clock on the morning of November 27th, a sudden shaft of sunshine broke through the gray clouds which had, until that moment, shrouded the sky.

[10] Barrie H. E. Goult, "First and Last Days of the 'Princess Royal' ", *BCHQ* 3 (1939) : 17.

[11] *Ibid.,* p. 19.

One last item must not go unrecorded — the building, at the foot of Victoria's Portage Inlet, of Craigflower School, now the oldest surviving schoolhouse in British Columbia. Among the Victoria-bound passengers on the *Princess Royal* was a Mr. Clark, en route to become schoolmaster at Craigflower. Even as the *Princess Royal* was on the last stretch of her journey to Vancouver Island, work was proceeding, though a little erratically, on the building of Craigflower School. Robert Melrose noted in his diary:

September: Sa. 23 School-house frame erected, whole company in general notoriously drunk.[12]

[12] *BCHQ* 3:206.

1855

Douglas orders a census — Adam Horne comes upon an Indian massacre — And finds a way across Vancouver Island — The strange death of Paul Fraser.

In 1854 Governor Douglas ordered that, on the last day of the year, an official census be taken of the entire white population of Vancouver Island. This census was conducted with meticulous thoroughness and, in July of 1855, the results were submitted to the Secretary of the Hudson's Bay Company in London. The carefully drawn up tables exhibited a method and thoroughness that would delight the heart of the most demanding statistician. Not only was the population tabulated both according to place of residence and age, but every house, shop, outhouse, church, school, sawmill, flourmill and threshing mill was enumerated. Each farm had its acreage (both of improved and unimproved land) recorded, also the cash value of the property and of its equipment, the number of its horses, milch cows, working oxen, other cattle, sheep, swine and poultry. Similarly each farm had its produce for the year listed: wheat, oats, peas, barley, wool, potatoes, cheese, butter, turnips, and tares (vetch). Published by W. Kaye Lamb in the *British Columbia Historical Quarterly*,[1] these tables are of major historical significance, giving us for the first time a detailed, authoritative statement of the progress of colonization on Vancouver Island. (On the mainland there was, of course, as yet no colonization, only the few fur-trading establishments of the HBC.)

The evidence yielded by this census is interesting and at times surprising. Of the total white population of 774 souls, almost half were children who had not yet reached the age of twenty. The main

[1] *BCHQ* 4 (1940):51-58.

centre of population was of course the "town" of Victoria, with 79 dwelling houses and a population of 232. The second largest centre of population was Nanaimo with 42 dwelling houses and a population of 151. Most of the rest of the population was to be found on farms in the Victoria district, with the four farms which the HBC's subsidiary, the Puget's Sound Agricultural Company, maintained in the Esquimalt area sustaining a white population of 154.

*　　*　　*

Not every event that we would like to include in this chronicle can be precisely dated. However, according to the veteran HBC man Adam Horne, it was "in 1855 or thereabouts" that he made a brief but highly dangerous trip across Vancouver Island from the mouth of the Qualicum River to the shores of Barkley Sound. Summoned to Victoria by Roderick Finlayson, he was informed that the HBC believed that an Indian trail crossed the Island in this area and he was to take six men, proceed up the Qualicum River, and endeavour to find if any such trail did exist.

A few days later, camping overnight near the mouth of the Qualicum, Horne's men were alarmed to see in the early morning a fleet of northern canoes already heading up the river. Keeping carefully concealed in the safety of the forest edge, they soon saw dense clouds of smoke arising from the banks of the Qualicum. Finally about noon the northern canoes began leaving the river for the open sea. In each canoe Indians, standing, proudly brandished decapitated heads by the hair. Having given the northern Indians several hours to travel a good distance southwards, Horne and his men got their canoe from its place of concealment into the water, reloaded it, and poled their way up the Qualicum River to where smoke was still rising. Later Horne recalled the scene that greeted them when they went ashore:

What had evidently been a rancherie was now a blackened heap of burning timbers. Naked bodies could be seen here and there, but not a living being was in sight. Our interpreter called out several times that if there was any person living to come out — that we were friends, and would do them no harm. He got no answer, except the echoes from the surrounding hills, and he then walked over to where the lifeless bodies were lying. Horror of horrors! Every trunk was headless and fearfully mutilated.[2]

At length an old Iroquois engagé (one of the HBC's hired hands) put his ear to the ground and, hearing the slightest of sounds, led them to where an old Indian woman, dying of her wounds, cowered beneath the roots of a riverside maple. During her last minutes of life, she told them that the murderers were Haidas, intent on avenging one of their number who had been slain while attempting to abduct a girl belonging to the Cape Mudge band. The Haidas, striking while the Qualicums were still asleep, had spared only two women and six children whom they had seized as slaves.

The extermination of the Qualicums posed a serious problem for Horne since he had counted upon them to show him the alleged trail leading to the west coast of Vancouver Island. Depressed by what they had just seen, some of his men favoured abandoning the expedition. Horne, however, had them paddle some distance up coast, cache supplies for their return to Victoria, and hide their canoe. They then circled through the forest in search of the anticipated trail, which they soon found. Setting out, they reached the shore of a lake (Horne Lake), everywhere marked with the tracks of wapiti, deer, wolves and bear. Pushing on, they reached the point where the tortuous trail commenced the ascent of the last mountains separating them from the Pacific. On the morrow they reached the summit, cached some more of their goods, and made a precipitous descent to saltwater.

Scarcely had they arrived when Indians, most of whom had never before seen white men, sent flights of arrows winging towards them. Despite this hostile reception Adam Horne, with his usual imperturbability, managed at last to enter into negotiations, giving mirrors, knives, biscuits and, to the chief, a Hudson's Bay blanket. The peace thus obtained was a brief and fragile one, ending as soon as the HBC party started on their return journey, taking with them a Songhees slave boy whom they had ransomed at the price of two HBC blankets. Moving swiftly, Horne's party managed to shake off their pursuers and retraced their route to the scene of annihilation near

---

[2] W. W. Walkem, *Stories of Early British Columbia* (Vancouver, 1914), p. 42.

the mouth of the Qualicum River. No single survivor had returned to bury the dead, whose bodies had been partly devoured by wild animals. Back in Victoria a few days later, Horne could inform Finlayson that the supposed cross-Island trail did indeed exist, but that entering into trade with the Indians in the Alberni district would prove a ticklish business.

*   *   *

Not all the threats faced by HBC officers were posed by the Indians, for death could come at the hands of their own men. Such may have been the case with Chief Trader Paul Fraser when he came to a not unfitting end this summer. As mentioned earlier, New Caledonia at this period provided an unhappy exception to the usual HBC practice of fair and honourable dealing. One of the more ruffianly officers of the Company in New Caledonia was Paul Fraser, who had taken over command of Fort Kamloops. Indulging his vile temper, Fraser early this year so beat Falardeau, one of his engagés at Kamloops, that the man died two days later. An Iroquois servant of the Company was planing boards to make a coffin for Fraser's victim when the Chief Trader saw what he was doing. "Rough, unplaned boards are good enough for that rascal!" shouted Fraser. The Iroquois retorted, "Hehm! when you die you may not have even rough boards to be buried in!"[3]

Such was the background when, this July, Fraser and Chief Trader Manson were taking the annual brigade over the route between Tulameen and Fort Hope. Upon arrival at an accustomed camping place on Manson Mountain, the invariable HBC practice was followed and the officers' tent was raised before the men set about making their own bivouacs. Manson and Fraser were sitting inside their tent when there was a sudden crash. A tree being felled by one of the engagés had come down upon the little tent, barely missing Manson and inflicting upon Fraser injuries from which he died an hour later. The interesting and unanswerable question is whether Fraser was killed by accident or design. Accident is possible, but a little unlikely. An experienced woodsman can leave a tender-

---

[3] Morice, *History of the Northern Interior*, pp. 275-76.

foot open-mouthed at the precision with which he can drop a tree precisely where he wants it. Manson being as unpopular as Fraser with their men, no tears would have been shed if the tree, possibly skilfully and deliberately brought down on their tent, had killed both the Chief Traders. As it was, the warning addressed to Fraser several months earlier was fulfilled. He was put uncoffined into a shallow grave scrabbled in the rocky mountainside and heaped over with stones. If a projected plan is carried out to make a hiking trail along this stretch of the old brigade route, future years will see many a trail-walker passing by Paul Fraser's lonely grave, rediscovered in 1935.

Fraser was unfortunate in not living longer, for 1855 was to prove the most prosperous year experienced by the Hudson's Bay Company since its merger with the North West Company back in 1821. When all the returns were in for "Outfit 1855", a Chief Trader's share of the net profits was found to be £872 10s. 1d., a very impressive sum indeed in the values of that day.[4]

*   *   *

This year the Hudson's Bay Company appointed its third chaplain to serve on the Pacific coast. The decision to send him out was rather a brave one in view of the Company's earlier unhappy experiences, first with the Rev. Mr. Beaver[5] and then with the Rev. Mr. Staines. This time, however, the Company was fortunate in its choice. The Rev. Edward Cridge was apparently the curate of a London parish, with some experience as a schoolmaster, when the HBC offered him the post made vacant by Staines' death. After anxious consultation with his fiancée, Mary Winnell, Cridge accepted the offer. They were married on 14 September 1854 and within a week sailed for Vancouver Island aboard the *Marquis of Bute*, arriving at Fort Victoria on April 1st of this year. Cridge proved the ideal man, whose exemplary piety did not keep him from thoroughly enjoying Governor Douglas' riding parties. Both Cridge and his wife were to live in Victoria into the twentieth century.

[4] For a table of the returns realized by the "Wintering Partners" between 1821 and the reorganization of 1871, see PABC, MS. A/B/15/1.

[5] See *British Columbia Chronicle, 1778-1846*, pp. 301-04.

The Royal Navy was very much in evidence this year. Smarting from their shameful defeat of the previous year, the French and British sent an augmented fleet to make a second assault upon Petropavlovsk. Converging there at the end of May, the allies were amazed to find the fortress abandoned except for a few American traders, one of whom observed to the British commander, "I guess ye're rather late, Admiral."[6] The Russians, under contingency instructions from St. Petersburg, had evacuated the fort after the wreck of the frigate which was to have reinforced them. Frustrated, the would-be attackers steamed away. Some of the British warships — H.M.S. *Monarch*, H.M.S. *President*, H.M.S. *Dido* and H.M.S. *Brisk* — later put in at Esquimalt. Here they found, awaiting expected casualties, the "Crimea Huts", hospital buildings which Governor Douglas had erected in accordance with directions from the Admiralty. On August 1st, to entertain officers off the British warships, Governor Douglas held a ball to which he invited also the officers of the U.S. Survey Ship *Active*, which happened to be visiting at the time. Philip Johnson of the *Active* noted in his journal that some of the ladies were quite pretty, the food and drink copious, and Douglas decidedly formidable: "The Governor looks all over and acts exactly what he is. He is quite tall and well made and Pomposity itself."[7]

One of the officers aboard H.M.S. *Brisk* was later, as Admiral Sir Cyprian Bridge, to include in his published reminiscences an interesting account of Esquimalt and Victoria as he had known them back in 1855:

On entering the snug harbour of Esquimalt we could see only one house, the residence of the magistrate or judge, on our port hand as we came in, and three neatly-built wooden huts on the opposite shore. These had just been put up to serve as hospitals for casualties occurring at Vladivostock [*sic*].

Vancouver's Island was then under the Hudson Bay Company, whose governor lived near Fort Victoria, the site of what is now the capital. Esquimalt as a settlement did not exist. What afterwards became the

---

[6] J. M. Tronson, *Personal Narrative* ..., p. 94 — quoted by Barry M. Gough, *The Royal Navy and the Northwest Coast of North America, 1810-1914* (Vancouver, 1971), p. 125.

[7] Quoted in Franz Stenzel, *James Madison Alden* (Fort Worth, 1975), p. 42.

dockyard was an island which at low water one could reach by wading. There were three or four farms but not one of these was visible from the anchorage.

There was a road from the harbour to Fort Victoria, on nearing which a river had to be crossed by a substantial wooden bridge. Close to the bridge, on the side farthest from the fort, was an Indian town, known as King Freezy's town, which consisted of several long wooden sheds or lodges. . . .

The fort stood on ground rather like an English common, a nearly level area studded with bushes. As we walked towards it we were joined by a troop of young Indians, all of whose faces were daubed with bright red paint. They each had on a striped cotton shirt but no other clothes. They were made to stop at a respectful distance from the gateway of the fort, as no Indian was allowed inside except under strict precautions. The officers in the fort were very hospitable, and showed us much civility.[8]

*   *   *

Our chronicle for this year must not omit one event which, though it occurred in American territory just a few miles south of the international boundary, foreshadowed coming events in British Columbia. A. C. Anderson has the story for us:

It was in 1855, when Mr. Angus McDonald, whom I had left in charge of Fort Colvile on my departure in 1851, wrote down to Fort Vancouver, stating that one of his men, while employed hauling firewood, had, almost undesignedly, amused himself by washing out a pannikin of gravel on the beach near Colvile. Some particles of gold appeared — enough, however to excite curiosity and invite further research — explorers went out; and, at the Mouth of the Pend'Oreille River, close by the Boundary line, diggings which were moderately productive were discovered.[9]

The gold fever spread. In October Donald McLean, who had taken over at Fort Kamloops, reported:

Gold is abundant at Colville, and I suspect that many, if not all, of our men will be off in that direction before long.[10]

[8] *Some Recollections* (London, 1918), pp. 121-22.

[9] *History of the Northwest Coast*, p. 53.

[10] Morice, *op. cit.*, p. 284.

Actually the search for gold would not remain south of the boundary, and when it extended northwards it would have results infinitely more important than the desertion of some engagés from Fort Kamloops.

1856

An expedition against the Cowichans — The first legislative assembly meets at Victoria — Gold is found on Thompson River.

Adam Horne, having the previous year discovered the Indian trail linking Qualicum with Alberni, was now given the unenviable job of using it to open trade with the truculent and suspicious Indians of Barkley Sound. Horne has left no account of the two expeditions which he made this year, but a record of them was entered into the HBC's Nanaimo Journal. The entry for May 10th notes the departure of Horne with a party of six and instructions "not to proceed further than the high mountain situated a little beyond the large lake in the interior, but if the interior tribe be peaceable he may proceed to Alberni Canal."[1] Another entry eight days later notes the return of Horne, who had pushed through to the seaboard and obtained some beaver and marten skins. Horne's second expedition left Nanaimo on September 10th. The Nanaimo Journal entry for September 20th triumphantly declares:

Mr. Horne returned after a successful expedition across the island, bringing with him numerous skins, and accompanied by seaboard Indians of the tribe See-shaad.[2]

Not all dealings with the Vancouver Island Indians proceeded as satisfactorily as those undertaken by Adam Horne. The turbulent Cowichan Indians caused renewed trouble this year, one of them assaulting and maiming a certain Thomas Williams. At once the sacred principle was invoked that an Indian must never be permitted to attack a white man without condign punishment. The trouble in this case was that the Cowichan tribe, which dominated

[1] Capt. John T. Walbran, *British Columbia Coast Names, 1592-1906* (Ottawa, 1909), p. 250.
[2] *Loc. cit.*

south-eastern Vancouver Island, provided sanctuary for the culprit. That tribe could put into the field, or rather infiltrate through the forests, a formidable fighting force. Under the circumstances, Governor Douglas requested help from the Royal Navy and, accompanied by H.M.S. *Trincomalee*, set out for the Cowichan country aboard the HBC steamer *Otter*. His report on this expedition, addressed to the Rt. Hon. Henry Labouchere, Secretary of State for the Colonies, is worth reproducing in its entirety since it gives so clear a picture of Douglas' spirit, methods and policies:

Victoria, Vancouvers Island
6th September 1856.

Sir,

I have to announce for the information of Her Majesty's Government my return this day, from "Cowegin", with the expeditionary force placed at my disposal by Rear Admiral Bruce for service in the Cowegin Country.

We succeeded after much trouble in securing the person of the Indian, who lately attempted to take the life of Thomas Williams, the Natives themselves having been prevailed upon to seize and deliver him into our hands.

He was tried before a special Court convened on the spot and was found guilty of "maiming Thomas Williams with intent to murder," an offence which the Statute 1st Victoria Cap 83 Section 2 considers felony and provides that the offender should suffer death.

He was accordingly sentenced to be hanged and the sentence was carried into effect, near the spot where the crime was committed, in the presence of his Tribe upon whose minds, the solemnity of the proceedings, and the execution of the criminal were calculated to make a deep impression.

The Cowegin Tribe can bring into the field about 1400 Warriors but nearly 1000 of these were engaged upon an expedition to Fraser's River, when we entered their Country. About 400 Warriors still remained in the Valley, nevertheless no attempt was made, except a feeble effort by some of his personal friends, to rescue the prisoner or to resist the operation of the law.

The Troops marched some distance into the Cowegin Valley, through thick bush and almost impenetrable forest. Knowing that a mere physical force demonstration would never accomplish the apprehension of the culprit I offered friendship and protection to all the natives except the culprit, and such as aided him or were found opposing the ends of Justice. That announcement had the desired effect of securing the neutrality of the greater part of the Tribe who were present, and after we had taken possession of three of their largest Villages the surrender of the culprit followed.

The expeditionary force was composed of about 400 of Her Majesty's Seamen and Marines under Commander Mathew Connolly and 18 Victoria Voltigeurs commanded by Mr. McDonald of the Hudson's Bay Company's service.

My own personal staff consisted of Mr. Joseph McKay and Mr. Richard Golledge, also of the Hudson's Bay Company's service, and those active and zealous officers were always near me, in every danger.

In marching through the Thickets of the Cowegin Valley the Victoria Voltigeurs were, with my own personal Staff thrown well in advance of the Seamen and Marines formed in single file, to scour the Woods, and guard against surprise, as I could not fail to bear in mind the repeated disasters, which last Winter befel the American Army while marching through the Jungle against an enemy much inferior in point of numbers and spirit to the Tribes we had to encounter.

I hope I may be permitted to recommend that very talented and active officer Commander Mathew Connolly to Her Majesty's Government for promotion, as I should really be wanting in justice to his extraordinary merit were I to refrain from urging this request as a personal favor to me.

I may also remark for the information of Her Majesty's Government that not a single casualty befel the expeditionary force during its brief campaign, nor was a single Indian, the criminal excepted personally injured, while their property was carefully respected.

The expedition remained at Cowegin two days after the execution of the offender, to re-establish friendly relations with the Cowegin Tribe, and we succeeded in that object, to my entire satisfaction.

I greatly admired the beauty and fertility of the Cowegin Valley, which contains probably not less than 200,000 acres of arable land. I shall however address you on that subject in a future communication.

Trusting that my proceedings on this occasion may meet with the approbation of Her Majesty's Government,

I have etc.

(signed) JAMES DOUGLAS
Governor[3]

*   *   *

In the mid-nineteenth century the British government, in its administration of its colonies, was firmly attached to the principle of

---

[3] PRO, ADM 1/5678. Commander Connolly's own report on the expedition, to Admiral Bruce, will be found in ADM 1/5672.

elected legislatures. On February 28th this year, London informed Governor Douglas that rule by himself and an appointed Legislative Council was not good enough, and he would have to introduce an elected assembly. Poor Douglas was sorely disturbed by these orders. For much of his life a backwoods fur-trader, he knew little of the niceties of electoral law or of parliamentary procedures. Nevertheless, with the assistance of his Council, he gamely set about meeting the wishes of Whitehall. Since London's proposed electoral qualification, ownership of twenty acres of land, would have disenfranchised nearly everybody living in Victoria, Douglas liberalized the property requirement and gave the vote to every freeholder owning property worth £300. Four electoral districts were set up, and the following representatives were returned:

Sooke:	John Muir
Esquimalt:	Dr. J. S. Helmcken
	Thomas J. Skinner
Victoria:	Capt. E. E. Langford
	J. D. Pemberton
	James Yates
Nanaimo:	Capt. C. E. Stuart

On August 12th the new assembly, the first elected legislative body in British North America west of Upper Canada, was sworn in by Chief Justice Cameron, and Dr. Helmcken was elected as Speaker. Only one complication marred the inauguration: Captain Langford and Captain Stuart were found to lack the required qualifications. Chief Trader J. W. McKay and Dr. John F. Kennedy were elected in their stead.[4]

The first meetings of the new legislature were held in Fort Victoria's Bachelors' Hall. Dr. Helmcken has preserved the scene for us:

The "House of Assembly" Hall was a room therein about twenty feet in length by about a dozen in breadth, lined with upright plank unpainted, unadorned, save perhaps with a few "cedar mats" to cover fissures. . . . In the centre stood a large dilapidated rectangular stove, its sides made of iron sheet, beautifully and picturesquely bulging. At the

4 Blakey Smith, *Helmcken Reminiscences*, p. 333.

end was a wooden home manufactured table, upon which stood a hundred paged ledger, an inkstand, pens, and a small supply of "foolscap," but without a "mace". . . . Around the Speaker's table stood half a dozen very ordinary wooden chairs, for the use of the members, and at a respectful distance a couple of benches, without backs for the audience. This furniture really belonged to Bachelors' Hall, and therefore the "House of Assembly" and country were not put to any unnecessary expense. At the end of the year the accounts indicated that this august body had cost about twenty-five dollars, which occasioned some ironical remarks from the London *Times*.

No Chaplain, no prayers, no "Sergeant-at-Arms," no reporters, no nothing to add grace and dignity to the floor, which could not boast either of carpet or cleanliness; whatever existed of the latter depended on "Dick," the Indian boy, who attended on the Bachelors.[5]

Helmcken also left us vivid little thumbnail sketches of the half dozen legislators over whom he presided as Speaker:

Mr. James Yates, radical, growler, cantankerous yet earnest, who hated the Governor and the Hudson's Bay Co., although he had come out in their service. Thos. Skinner, a genial gentleman, a sort of liberal conservative, Bailiff of the Puget Sound Company's farm at Esquimalt. He liked the smell of the fox and to follow the hounds; but preferred this to being the fox. Jos. Pemberton, Surveyor General, who always endeavoured to induce both sides to agree! in medio tutissima his motto. Jos. McKay, lively and active, who knew everything and everybody. The patriarchal Muir, one of the led, who had been in the Hudson's Bay service at the coal mines at Fort Rupert — who said Aye or Nay when present. Dr. Kennedy, who voted; and last, J. S. Helmcken . . . innocent and ignorant of "politics", a London sparrow, too fond of nonsense and cigars.[6]

The new Assembly was purely consultative, though it did show considerable spirit in questioning the Governor about the details of his policies and practices. One very important power it did possess — that of voting or withholding supplies.

Generally the new body was regarded with more amusement than respect. The joke lay in the minute size of the electorate. Chief Factor John Work, writing to his old acquaintance Edward Ermatinger, had caustic comments to make upon "7 members chosen by

---

[5] *Ibid.*, pp. 333-34.

[6] *Ibid.*, p. 334.

about 40 voters".[7] As Dr. Ormsby has noted, even in London there were officials who had opined "the establishment of [the] representative system under the circumstances of the Island wd be little better than a parody".[8] Nevertheless, democracy of a sort had come to Vancouver Island.

Governor Douglas' forebodings about the Assembly proved unjustified. It did at times put him on his mettle but it never really made trouble for him. He was fortunate with the Council also — Captain Cooper, the robust and argumentative anti-HBC member whom Governor Blanshard had appointed, decided to head back to England and so resigned his Council seat.

*　　*　　*

There were interesting developments on the mainland. The wars raging between the Indians and the Americans were making Fort Colvile increasingly isolated and insecure. To play safe, the Company this year ordered the construction of a new post, Fort Shepherd, like Colvile on the Columbia River but far enough to the north to lie just within British territory and also to be accessible by an all-Briitsh route from Fort Langley.

In April of this year Governor Douglas, writing to London, reported "a discovery of much importance",[9] the finding of gold on the Columbia River north of the 49th parallel. Very soon afterwards gold was found on the Thompson River, close to its junction with the Nicoamen. Four years later Douglas was to enter into his journal a brief account of the latter event:

Gold was first found on Thompson's River by an Indian ¼ of a mile below Niconim [sic]. He is since dead. The Indian was taking a drink out of the river. Having no vessel he was quaffing from the stream when he perceived a shining pebble which he picked up and it proved to be gold. The whole tribe forthwith began to collect the glittering metal.[10]

[7] Oregon Historical Society transcript, *MS. 319.*

[8] *British Columbia: A History*, p. 122.

[9] Douglas to Labouchere, 16 April 1856. Great Britain, Parliament, *Correspondence Relative to the Discovery of Gold in the Fraser's River District*, London, 1858 (Command Paper 2398).

[10] *Diary* 14 Sept. 1860. PABC B/20/1858.

The amounts subsequently found were not large and Chief Trader McLean at Kamloops declined to buy them, protesting he had no means of measuring such small quantities. Douglas in Victoria reacted with greater awareness, and told McLean to acquire all the gold he could. Apparently Douglas supplied McLean with spoons (presumably heavy iron ones) for the Indians to use in prying gold nuggets out of rocky crevices.

On July 30th Douglas wrote to Captain W. H. McNeill at Fort Simpson:

Gold has been found near Thompson's River, and it is supposed the streams in that district will prove extremely productive. We are now engaged exploring the country extensively.[11]

Douglas' expectations did not go unrealized. On October 29th he was able to inform the British Colonial Secretary, Labouchere:

From the successful result of experiments made in washing gold from the sands of the tributary streams of Fraser's River there is reason to suppose that the gold region is extensive. . . . [12]

[11] HBCA B.226/b/12, fo.94d.
[12] Great Britain, Parliament, *Correspondence Relative to Gold in Fraser's River District*, p. 6.

1857

Amateur Theatricals — Goldseekers from the United States — Douglas extends his governorship to the British mainland — Captains Prevost and Richards — The San Juan Islands, British or American?

This January the gentlemen at Fort Victoria amused themselves by putting on Sheridan's *The Rivals*. Perhaps other plays had been part of earlier New Year festivities at the Fort, but this production is the earliest of which we have any knowledge. A neatly handwritten playbill survives to give us the names of the cast:

Annual Amateur Theatricals
Vancouver's Island
Wednesday Jany 14th 1857

THE RIVALS
(By Richard Brinsley Sheridan)

Dramatis Personae

Sir Anthony Absolute	Mr. J. W. McKay
Capt. Absolute	Mr. McDonald
Acres	Mr. Farquhar
Sir Lucius O'Trigger	Mr. Pemberton
Fag	Mr. Pearse
David	Mr. Barr
Thomas	Capt. Swanson
Mrs Malaprop	Mr. Margary
Lydia Languish	Mr. Newton
Lucy	Mr. Gollidge

Boy, Servants, &c.

Scene — City of Bath

Vivat Regina[1]

[1] PABC, S/C/AM1.

95

The production was accompanied by a specially penned prologue in which the cast regretted their delay in staging the production, which no doubt was originally intended for New Year's. Their excuse was that the diversity of their professional duties had kept them from getting together earlier:

> To have met you earlier was our intent,
> But graver matters happen'd to prevent.
> The Baronet,[A] the shop was bobbing round,
> And selling tea and sugar by the pound.
> Who can extract a Captain[B] from a store,
> Deep in details of outfit fifty four?
> Instead of steering coaches with his whip
> Thomas[C] was thinking where he'd steer his ship.
> Instead of sauntering in white and plush
> Fag's[D] calves were active in the bush.
> O'Trigger,[E] too, in happier pursuit
> Paced lines and measured to prevent dispute.
> Oh! Longer letters met false Lucy's[F] eyes
> And dull the books o'er which Miss Languish[G] sighes.
> Even our prompter[H] at old Cadb'ro Bay
> Look'd down on Acres in another way.

[A — Chief Trader McKay had charge of the Hudson's Bay Company sales at the fort.

B — McDonald, a clerk in the Company's service.

C — Capt. Swanson served in the Maritime Department.

D — B. W. Pearse was the assistant to the Colonial Surveyor.

E — J. D. Pemberton was the Colonial Surveyor.

F — R. Golledge was secretary to Governor Douglas.

G — William Newton was bookkeeper for Capt. Langford, the bailiff of the Esquimalt farm.

H — Leigh, who has been identified as the prompter, was apparently employed on the Cadboro Bay farm.]

No doubt the old mess-hall at Fort Victoria was swept with laughter as the play built up to its crowning comic moment, Bob Acres' duel, but we must leave this scene for more serious matters.

*   *   *

Actively encouraged by the Hudson's Bay Company which was equipping them with shovels, picks and pans, the Indians were finding more and more gold in the area around the confluence of the Fraser and Thompson Rivers. Unfortunately word of their discoveries was gradually percolating down into American territory. This year a few American miners moved north of the international boundary. The Indians, angered at seeing these white men coming for the gold which they regarded as their own inheritance, and superstitiously believing their presence would drive the salmon from the rivers, decided to keep the newcomers out of the gold areas. Their decision elicited from Douglas a comment that "I cannot help admiring the wisdom and foresight of the Indians."[2] Writing this July to Labouchere, the British Colonial Secretary, Douglas informed him:

A new element of difficulty in exploring the gold country has been interposed through the opposition of the native Indian tribes of Thompson's River, who have lately taken the high-handed, though probably not unwise course, of expelling all the parties of gold diggers, composed chiefly of persons from the American territories, who had forced an entrance into their country.[3]

By November, Douglas was taking a more serious view of the situation. There appeared to be looming a real prospect of war between the Indians and those Americans who were intent upon getting into the British gold areas. Writing to Chief Trader McLean at Kamloops, Douglas urged him to do everything he could both to restrain the Indians and to discourage the Americans.[4] What was really needed, however, was direct government action before the situation got out of hand. Unfortunately, even though the mainland north of the 49th parallel had been given to Britain by the Treaty of Washington, London had not yet set up any government for the area. The officers of the Hudson's Bay Company's little fur trade forts on the British mainland were totally without governmental authority. No person or body existed with legal powers to impose law and order, supervise mining claims, or attend to any of the other problems that were now beginning to loom up.

[2] Douglas to Sir George Simpson, 17 July 1857. HBCA, B.226/b/13.

[3] Great Britain, Parliament, *Correspondence Relative to Gold in Fraser's River District*, p. 7.

[4] HBCA, B.226/b/15.

At this point James Douglas showed his mettle. Although the Queen's commission had made him governor only of Vancouver Island, on December 28th of this year, lacking time to confer with London but acting as the nearest properly constituted British authority, Douglas on his own responsibility assumed jurisdiction over the mainland. This day he issued a proclamation declaring that any person removing from the districts of Fraser River and of Thompson River any gold, metal, or ore "without having been duly authorized in that behalf by Her Majesty's Colonial Government, will be prosecuted, both criminally and civilly, as the law allows."[5] He followed this up on the morrow with regulations requiring gold miners to pay the Crown a fee of ten shillings a month, payable in advance. British government had come to the mainland.

*   *   *

Douglas had done what he could to establish control. One danger remained. No official surveys had yet established exactly where the international boundary ran, and no official markers warned settlers or miners when they had crossed the 49th parallel and were in the domains of Queen Victoria. Fortunately both the British and the Americans had recently appointed boundary commissions to attend to this very matter. In June of this year Captain James C. Prevost, the British Commissioner for the Maritime Boundary, had arrived with his ship, H.M.S. *Satellite*. Prevost had been in these parts previously, in 1851 when serving aboard H.M.S. *Portland*, and in 1853 and 1854 while commanding H.M.S. *Virago*. These visits had left the deeply religious Prevost convinced that only Christianity could save the Indians from degeneration and barbarity. Accordingly, with the Admiralty's permission, he had brought out with him this year, aboard the *Satellite*, a young Anglican lay missionary, William Duncan, a man destined to hold an important place in British Columbia's early history. Writing from Esquimalt to the Secretary of the Church Missionary Society, in October this year, Prevost expatiated on the continuing need for missionary endeavour among the Indians:

[5] Great Britain, *Correspondence Relative to Gold*, p. 9.

I firmly believe they require a teaching of the Spirit to direct them. Their unbridled passions this year have known no bounds. I could enumerate no less than 70 and 80 cold blooded murders committed amongst themselves in the year 1857. Not a month ago Lt. Gooch of this ship [the *Satellite*], while exploring this island, passed through a village (Nitinat) where 17 heads were exposed on poles as trophies and to dry.[6]

(Incidentally, we tend to forget how superficial as yet was the white man's penetration into much of British Columbia. Prevost was told by a friend just returned from exploring Howe Sound that he "discovered a tribe of Indians who had never seen a white man since the year Vancouver visited them in 1793."[7])

Prevost's concern for the welfare of the Indians was deep and abiding. Years later, as Admiral Prevost, retired, he would personally visit the Anglican missions on the northern British Columbia coast. Perhaps Nature had intended that Prevost should be a missionary himself. Most certainly this highly religious Victorian evangelical was the wrong man to serve on the Boundary Commission — "a veritable old woman, unfit to cope with the American side"[8] as far as opinion in Victoria was concerned. This estimate was concurred in by a naval colleague who wrote, "I fear Captain Prevost of the *Satellite* is not the man to cope with a keen yankee lot such as are opposed to him. . . ."[9]

The point at issue between Prevost and the Americans was the course to be followed by the boundary once it left the 49th parallel and threaded its way through the Strait of Georgia to the Strait of Juan de Fuca. A stronger man than Prevost might have secured American acceptance of Rosario Strait, that clear and obvious channel which was normally used by shipping passing through the Gulf Islands. Prevost, however, had been able to win nothing from Archibald Campbell, the wily, evasive, and highly political American commissioner who unyieldingly insisted that the boundary pass through Haro Strait, depriving Britain entirely of the San Juan

---

[6] Prevost to Venn, 17 Oct. 1857. Archives of the Church Missionary Society, C C2/o1-13.

[7] Prevost to Venn, 12 Aug. 1857. Archives of the C.M.S., C C2/o1-13.

[8] Blakey Smith, *Helmcken Reminiscences*, p. 167.

[9] F. W. Richards' letter of 27 Aug. 1858. Sir Frederick Richards, "Pages & Papers", *Naval Review* [c.1932], p. 123.

San Juan Boundary Dispute

.... Line Claimed by Britain

———— Possible Compromise

— · — · — Line Claimed by U.S. and Eventually
Awarded by German Kaiser in 1872.

0   5   10   15   20

SCALE IN MILES

Islands. In fact, as a manoeuvre to win British acceptance of Haro Strait, Campbell at times made the preposterous claim that the boundary should follow the 49th parallel up to the shores of Vancouver Island, near today's Ladysmith, thence southwards hugging the Vancouver Island coastline to Haro Strait — thus giving to the United States Galiano, Mayne, Saturna, Salt Spring and the Pender Islands, and leaving only Sidney and James Islands to the British.[10]

Such was the situation when, on November 10th, the Royal Navy's survey ship *Plumper* entered Esquimalt harbour, her assignment being to spend some years in making a far more detailed and accurate survey of the shores of Vancouver Island and the lower mainland than Captain Vancouver had been able to provide more than sixty years before. The captain of H.M.S. *Plumper* was Captain George H. Richards, rather a small man physically but a mass of energy, shrewdness and humour, as strong as Prevost was weak. He read over the Campbell-Prevost correspondence and was contemptuous of Campbell's case, finding "he has not one single argument whereon to rest his claim."[11] On the other hand, Richards formed a very high opinion of Lieut. Parke of the United States Corps of Topographical Engineers, whom he found "an officer of superior talent, of frank and conciliatory manner, and gentlemanly bearing."[12] If the boundary issue had been left to Richards and Parke a compromise would probably have routed the boundary down the "Middle Passage" between San Juan Islands on the west and Orcas and Lopez Islands on the east, and a world of future trouble have been escaped. Unfortunately Campbell and Prevost between them had got things so deadlocked that the matter of the boundary through the Strait of Georgia had to be referred to the two home governments while work proceeded with marking the mainland boundary along the 49th parallel.

In consequence of the maritime boundary stalemate, Richards

---

[10] Richards to Capt. Washington, 11 Oct. 1858. *Letter Book: Correspondence to the Hydrographer of the Navy 1859-62*, p. 90. (In private possession.) For a map prepared by the American Boundary Commission showing this line as a possible boundary, see U.S. Archives, Map Record Group 76, Series 73, Misc.

[11] *Letter Book*, p. 39.

[12] *Letter Book*, p. 36.

turned to his major task, charting the western coasts of British North America. A routine was developed whereby from March to November the *Plumper* was usually at sea despatching parties in small boats to do the work inshore. From November until March the *Plumper* was at her base in Esquimalt, where a drafting office was set up in one of the "Crimea huts". Here the observations of the preceding field season were converted into charts for forwarding to England. All too often for Captain Richards' liking, Governor Douglas requisitioned him and his ship for special duties, chiefly in policing the Indians, but year by year the survey steadily proceeded. The work accelerated after January 1861 when Richards and his surveying officers transferred from the *Plumper* to H.M.S. *Hecate*, a larger, more commodious and powerful paddlewheel sloop.

In 1863 Richards sailed home to England with the *Hecate*. The notable reputation that he had achieved in China, South America, New Zealand and the Arctic had been enhanced during the five arduous years when, aided by young officers whom he had inspired with his own devotion to the work, he had surveyed the Gulf of Georgia (which he renamed the Strait of Georgia), its various archipelagos, the entire coastline of Vancouver Island, the Fraser River up to Fort Langley, Burrard Inlet, Howe Sound, Jervis Inlet, Bute Inlet, Victoria, Esquimalt and Nanaimo harbours. Awaiting him in England was the ultimate professional recognition of appointment as the Hydrographer of the Navy. As such he subsequently was given the rank of rear-admiral. After his retirement he became Sir George Richards.

Following Richards' departure his former second-in-command, Daniel Pender, with the famous old *Beaver* now converted into a survey ship, laboured for years more, carrying the survey right up to the northern limit of British sovereignty at 54°40'. Finally, in the Hydrographic Office in England, a clerk was able to take a pen and, at the end of the abstract of letters received from Pender, to write in red: "Survey of British Columbia closed 11 Jan. 1871."[13] Today British Columbia's coast is studded with Pender Harbour, Pender Hill, North and South Pender Islands, Pender Point and Pender

[13] Hydrographic Office, Taunton, Somerset, *S-Book: Abstract of Letters Received 1867-1884*, p. 112.

Rock, not to mention Mount Pender and Vancouver's Pender Street. These honours were all fully merited. When Pender arrived in Esquimalt Harbour aboard H.M.S. *Plumper* in 1857, he could hardly have imagined he would spend the next thirteen years amid the tides, storms and fogs and occasional sunshine of the British Columbia coast.

1858

BRITISH COLUMBIA'S WONDERFUL YEAR

Negroes seek freedom on Vancouver Island — Americans hunt for gold on the bars of the Fraser River — Royal Engineers — British Boundary Commission and the Sumas mosquitoes — Harrison-Lillooet Trail — Steamboats on the Fraser — Reinhart's Okanagan journey — "The Fraser Canyon War" — Royal Navy strengthens the Governor's hand — Mr. Nugent, "Special Agent of the United States" — A new crown colony — Sir Edward Bulwer Lytton, its foster father — Inauguration of British Columbia.

The Romans had a term for such a year as this — *annus mirabilis*, "the wonderful year." If 1849 was California's *annus mirabilis*, just as surely 1858 was British Columbia's, and for exactly the same reason — a great gold rush. Sometimes one wonders why British Columbia's "Fifty-eighters" are not as famous as California's "Forty-niners." The answer may be that "Fifty-eighter" is just too awkward on the tongue. Certainly we have never had a song like "Clementine" with its renowned "miner, forty-niner".

Consider the pattern of the year! 1858 began with Victoria a sleepy little village with less than 300 white inhabitants. At times, this summer, it had as many as 6000 immigrants housed in a city of tents close to the old fort. At the end of 1858 Victoria was a town with a stable population of over 3000,[1] and two competing newspapers. During the year over 30,000 white gold-miners[2] flooded into

---

[1] The figures both for the initial population and that at the end of the year are those of the correspondent of the London *Times* writing on the spot. *Times*, 19 Jan. 1859, p. 6. (Despatch dated 11 Nov. 1858.)

[2] D. Sage, "Gold Rush Days on the Fraser River", *Pacific North West Quarterly* 44 (1953): 161, finds that the figures in the *Prices Current and Ship-*

British Columbia. By mid-November of this year these miners, by the estimate of the Hudson's Bay Company, had obtained by their labours 106,000 ounces of gold.[3] For this the Company paid a standard price of $16 an ounce, making the gold worth over $1,600,000. But a dollar in those days had a purchasing value far beyond that of the anaemic dollar of today, possibly being worth as much as twenty-five times a modern dollar.[4] Accepting very tentatively some such equivalence, the gold produced in British Columbia in 1858 would have been worth something like $40,000,000 in modern values. In fact, since much of the gold that was taken out of the country, especially by the Chinese, never passed through regular banking channels, the total value may have approached $50,000,000 in today's money.

What triggered the gold rush of 1858? As we have noted, in the two previous years word of the discoveries around the junction of the Thompson and Fraser Rivers had gradually spread southward through Washington and Oregon, but what is commonly alleged as the cause of the sudden rush was Governor Douglas' shipment of some 800 ounces of gold to the San Francisco mint in February of this year. News of the gold received from "British America" spread through California like wildfire. The days were past in the Golden State when a prospector in the Sierras could pick up one-pound nuggets lying on the earth's surface. Few if any gold-bearing bars were still to be washed on unstaked streams. Large companies had

---

ping List (San Francisco) when totalled show 25,728 miners left for the Fraser River between April 30 and November 30. This does not include the *Commodore*'s first party. Moreover, other miners came from Oregon and Washington by way of Puget Sound, and some others from the goldfields of Australia and New Zealand (Otago).

[3] Douglas to Simpson, 11 Dec. 1858. HBCA, B.226/b/15. The San Francisco *Bulletin*, 21 Dec. 1858, p. 1, estimated "an aggregate of $1,000,000 taken out of the Fraser River in the last season." The Victoria *Gazette* (19 April 1859) placed the total value of the gold received by the HBC and San Francisco as $1,494,211.

[4] Determining the value of the dollar in 1858 in terms of modern values is a difficult task. The cost of living in the gold areas was ruinously expensive because goods had to be brought long distances and were often in short supply. The lucky miners were those who, when they left the country, had a sizeable amount of gold to take back home where prices were much lower and a dollar a day was the standard wage.

bought up the rich claims and brought in expensive machinery to work them. Many a miner found himself no longer a free soul but a hired hand, working for wages deep in some cold dank tunnel. For Californians the Fraser River promised a return to the halcyon days of '49.

March saw the year's first miners from the States heading for the new goldfields. Their logical route should have been the inland one, long used by the Hudson's Bay Company fur brigades — up the Columbia River to the Okanagan River and Lake, and finally to the South Thompson River near Kamloops, and then west to the known gold area centering around the junction of the Fraser and Thompson. But a merciless war was being waged between the United States Army and the Indians in the interior of Washington Territory, making it extremely dangerous for any prospectors to use the Okanagan route. The safer way was to travel by sea from San Francisco to Victoria (or to Port Townsend or Bellingham Bay, both within the United States but very close to the British boundary), and from thence to proceed up the Fraser to the gold areas. Of these three bases, Victoria proved by far the most popular. The citizens of Victoria first learned of the coming rush on April 25th, when the steamer *Commodore* arrived with some four hundred goldseekers, the vanguard of the army to follow.

*   *   *

But here we must digress briefly and speak of another group of passengers who landed from the *Commodore*, a little party which had come to British territory in quest not of gold but of something more precious — freedom and dignity in their daily lives. Dr. Helmcken in his *Reminiscences* recalled how, when the *Commodore* anchored, there emerged from her:

> ... black emigrants, from "the land of the free and the home of the *slave*." These, "like the pilgrim fathers of old" kneeling on the ground, prayed and blessed it as the true land of freedom and their future home. They called for blessings on the flag that floated above the fort. . . . [5]

Although California was not one of the "slave states", it had dealt

---

[5] Blakey Smith, *Helmcken Reminiscences*, p. 338.

harshly with its black population. Hardly had California attained
statehood when it ruled that no Negro could give evidence in court
against a white man, and that any fugitive from a slave state must
be returned to his place of servitude. In January and February of
1858 bills were introduced in the California state legislature foreshadowing further injustices — any Negro whose master was merely
"sojourning" in California must remain his slave, and the immigration even of free Negroes must cease. In the light of these bills and
still more threatening ones, the coloured congregation of the Zion
Methodist Episcopal Church of San Francisco convened on April
14th to debate emigration either to Mexico or Vancouver Island.
Five days later they decided to send an advance party of sixty-five
persons to Vancouver Island aboard the *Commodore*.

The Negroes who landed at Fort Victoria this April were members
of respectable coloured families, and they were welcomed by the
Rev. Mr. Cridge. From Governor Douglas they received a categori-
cal assurance that, at the end of seven years' residence, they could
become British subjects able to vote, serve on juries, and exercise all
the other rights enjoyed by those bearing allegiance to Queen
Victoria. In May, glowing reports from Vancouver Island having
been received in San Francisco, the rest of the congregation prepared
to follow their brothers and sisters to the British territory. Probably
about four hundred came in all.[6] They proved good settlers. Today
only a few descendants, living chiefly on Salt Spring Island, preserve
something of their identity. The rest have long since been assimilated
totally into our population.

It was the ill-fortune of these Negro immigrants to arrive more or
less simultaneously with thousands of American goldseekers who had
no use for "niggers". Douglas, who had appointed several of the
Negroes to Victoria's police force, found it advisable, in the face of
American hostility, to discharge them after two months.[7] The next
few years saw various rebuffs and insults. When the growing city
acquired a volunteer fire brigade its members, predominantly American, refused to accept Negro members. When the dark-skinned

---

[6] F. W. Howay, "The Negro Immigration into Vancouver Island in 1858",
BCHQ 3 (1939):113.

[7] D. W. Higgins, *The Passing of a Race* (Toronto, 1905), pp. 165-66.

newcomers went to the theatre, American roughnecks, supporters of Jim Crow segregation, emptied flour bags upon them. One of the Americans had the audacity to write an open letter to the Rev. Mr. Cridge objecting to him permitting blacks to be present in his congregation:

... The sexton has repeatedly insulted our people, by crowding negro men into the same seats with white and respectable ladies. ...

The negro has his proper place among created beings. To make him our equal, he must submit to being skinned, renovated, "born anew", or any other process of change to make him white.[8]

Appalled, Mr. Cridge sent his own letter to the *Gazette*, totally repudiating such unchristian sentiments.

*   *   *

Let us return to our major theme — the gold rush. Ship followed ship with more Californians bent on "making a pile" on the Fraser. As "Fraser fever" swept California, farmers abandoned their crops in the fields, miners left prosperous claims, business after business closed its doors, and houses which had sold for $500 were offered for $100. Every available ship, no matter how unseaworthy, put out from San Francisco and headed north, its decks black with passengers jammed aboard without any consideration for safety or sanitation. During the first half of June seven sailing ships and four steamers left San Francisco with fortune-hunters heading to the Fraser. One of the small steamers carried 1000 passengers, and another 1200. On July 8th two California steamers, the *Orizaba* and the *Cortez*, arrived more or less simultaneously at Victoria and landed 2800 passengers.[9]

Once ashore, the miners wanted to get to the Fraser River as soon as possible. Unfortunately for these early arrivals, there were no ships to take them up the Fraser, apart from the occasional HBC boat going to Fort Langley. Some parties of miners bought Indian canoes, dangerously unstable for inexperienced whites. But there were not enough dugouts for thousands of men and so, in the spring of this

[8] Letter of Henry Sharpstone. Victoria *Gazette*, 24 Aug. 1858.

[9] Victoria *Gazette*, 10 July 1858.

year, the tent-town around Victoria rang with the sound of hammers as the migrants built their own boats to take them across the Strait of Georgia and up the Fraser. Most of these were awkward little craft, "coffin-shaped" according to one description. Too often that epithet was prophetic. Nobody will ever know how many men drowned when these little boats came to grief in sudden storms. As they threaded their way through Active Pass, and camped overnight at Miners Bay on Mayne Island, many had only the dimmest idea of where they would find the mouth of the Fraser. One sloop containing twelve miners mistook the entrance to Burrard Inlet for the mouth of the Fraser, had their vessel looted, and were themselves massacred by the Indians.

One joyful discovery awaited these first-comers when they travelled up the Fraser River beyond Fort Hope. They did not, after all, have to make the appallingly difficult journey to the river's confluence with the Thompson before they got into the gold area. Gold was waiting for them up and down the length of the Fraser Canyon in gravel bars which sometimes reached out into the river but more often lay parallel with the shore. The first to be discovered was Hill's Bar, south of Yale. One of Hill's partners has left an account of this momentous discovery:

... we camped for lunch on a bar about ten miles from Hope to cook lunch, and while doing so one of our party noticed particles of gold in the moss that was growing on the rocks. He got a pan and washed a pan of this moss and got a good prospect, and after our gastric wants were satisfied we all prospected the bar and found it a rich bar in gold. With our crude mode of working with rockers we made on an average fifty dollars per day to the man. We named this bar in honor to the man that washed the first pan of moss, Hill's Bar.[10]

They had struck probably the richest bar on the entire river. But there were plenty of others, starting below Hope and extending upstream far above the Fraser Canyon — a few names survive on our maps, but most of them are now forgotten. The names of these bars reflect the predominantly American background of the miners of '58: Boston Bar, Puget Sound Bar, Sacramento Bar, Union Bar,

[10] "The Discovery of Hill's Bar in 1858", *BCHQ* 3 (1939):218.

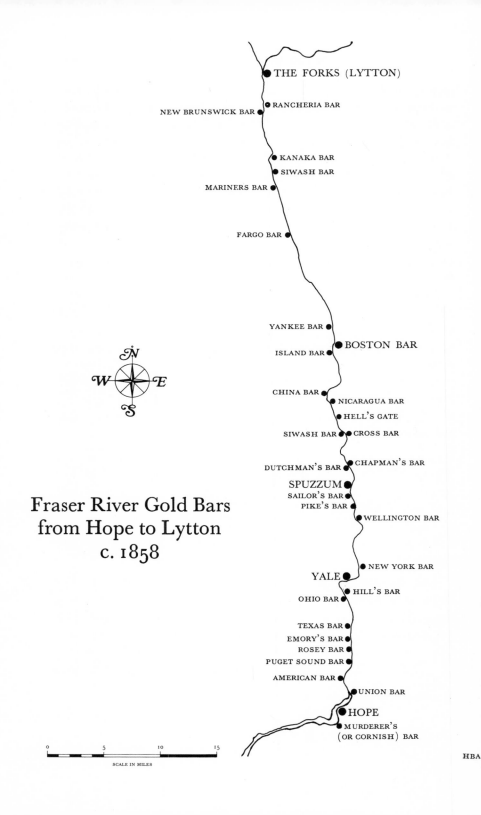

THE FORKS (LYTTON)

RANCHERIA BAR

NEW BRUNSWICK BAR

KANAKA BAR

SIWASH BAR

MARINERS BAR

FARGO BAR

YANKEE BAR

BOSTON BAR

ISLAND BAR

CHINA BAR

NICARAGUA BAR

HELL'S GATE

SIWASH BAR   CROSS BAR

DUTCHMAN'S BAR   CHAPMAN'S BAR

SPUZZUM

SAILOR'S BAR

PIKE'S BAR

WELLINGTON BAR

NEW YORK BAR

YALE

HILL'S BAR

OHIO BAR

TEXAS BAR

EMORY'S BAR

ROSEY BAR

PUGET SOUND BAR

AMERICAN BAR

UNION BAR

HOPE

MURDERER'S
(OR CORNISH) BAR

Fraser River Gold Bars
from Hope to Lytton
c. 1858

N
W   E
S

0   5   10   15

SCALE IN MILES

HBA

Santa Clara Bar, American Bar, Texas Bar, New York Bar, Ohio Bar and Washington Bar. But there were men of many other races and nationalities among the miners, and so we find China Bar, Kanaka Bar, Dutch Bar, Cornish Bar, and even Canada Bar.

Late in May Governor Douglas decided to cross to the mainland and see what was happening on the Fraser. After reaching Fort Langley aboard the HBC's steamer *Otter*, he and his party proceeded upstream in Indian canoes, escorted by Captain Prevost and six bluejackets in one of H.M.S. *Satellite*'s boats. At Hill's Bar he found a potentially dangerous situation:

> On the arrival of our party at "Hill's Bar", the white miners were in a state of great alarm on account of a serious affray which had just occurred with the native Indians, who mustered under arms in a tumultuous manner, and threatened to make a clean sweep of the whole body of miners assembled there.
>
> The quarrel arose out of a series of provocations on both sides, and from the jealousy of the savages, who naturally feel annoyed at the large quantities of gold taken from their country by the white miners.
>
> I lectured them soundly about their conduct on that occasion, and took the leader in the affray, an Indian highly connected in their way, and of great influence, resolution, and energy of character, into the Government service, and found him exceedingly useful in settling other Indian difficulties.
>
> I also spoke with great plainness of speech to the white miners, who were nearly all foreigners, representing almost every nation in Europe. I refused to grant them any rights of occupation to the soil, and told them distinctly that Her Majesty's Government ignored their very existence in that part of the country, which was not open for the purposes of settlement, and they were permitted to remain there merely on sufferance; that no abuses would be tolerated; and that the laws would protect the rights of the Indian, no less than those of the white man.[11]

This was brave talk by Douglas, with his six naval ratings and handful of Hudson's Bay Company men, but he knew he would have to have more force than this in the future. He was lucky in that H.M.S. *Satellite* and H.M.S. *Plumper* were available, but they were

[11] Great Britain, Parliament, *Papers Relative to the Affairs of British Columbia and Further Papers Relative to the Affairs of British Columbia*, Command Papers 2476, 2578, 2724 and 2952 (hereafter referred to as *B.C. Papers*), 4 parts (London, 1859-1862), I: 16.

clearly not sufficient for the crises that might lie ahead. Already, on May 8th, Douglas had appealed to the Colonial Secretary in London for naval reinforcements. On May 12th, hoping to expedite matters, he had written directly to Rear-Admiral R. L. Baynes, the British Commander-in-Chief, Pacific, urging that, since foreigners were "crowding into the British Possessions with reckless precipitation" and their sympathies were decidedly "anti-British",[12] the admiral should send him more warships.

In his moment of urgent need Governor Douglas did not look to the Royal Navy alone for assistance in heading off troubles which could lead to an American takeover. He asked London to furnish him with troops. The latter plea did not go unheeded. On July 30th of this year Sir Edward Bulwer Lytton, the new Colonial Secretary, wrote to Douglas that a contingent of Royal Engineers would soon be en route for service on the British mainland, which was to be set up as a new Crown Colony distinct from Vancouver Island. As Lytton saw things, these Royal Engineers would serve three purposes. First, they would carry out a program of public works, laying out townsites, making surveys, and aiding in the construction of roads; second, they would serve as a defence force, but in a manner less likely to provoke the Americans than the despatch of infantry, cavalry or artillery; and finally, they would help to create a British tone, offsetting the Americanism of the miners.[13]

The Royal Engineers promised in July by Lytton could hardly reach British Columbia until the end of the year, but meanwhile Governor Douglas had an interim accession of strength. On July 12th H.M.S. *Havannah* arrived at Esquimalt, carrying sixty-five Royal Engineers and their officers, members of the British Boundary Commission assigned to work with American colleagues in determining just where the 49th parallel ran from the Rockies to the Pacific. Normally their time and energy would go into the boundary survey

---

[12] PRO, ADM 1/5696.

[13] This last reason is generally overlooked but Lytton, writing to Colonel Moody who commanded the Engineers, noted, " . . . I anticipate no small advantage towards stamping our native idiosyncrasies on a Colony which may comprise so many foreigners, and promoting a high social standard of civilization, from the fact that yourself and your brother officers are amongst its practical founders. . . . " (Lytton to Moody, 29 Oct. 1858.) *B.C. Papers*, I : 75.

but, should an emergency suddenly arise, they would be available to help Douglas maintain peace and order.

The officers of the British Commission to determine the mainland boundary were bright and energetic young men. In command was Major (soon to be Lieut.-Col.) J. S. Hawkins, the British Land Boundary Commissioner. For his secretary and adjutant he had Lieut. Charles Wilson, R.E. Also with him were two astronomers, Captains Haig and Darrah; Dr. Bauerman, geologist, and Dr. Lyall, surgeon and naturalist. Finally there was the magnificently bearded John Keast Lord, veterinarian and naturalist. Drawing on his experiences with the Boundary Commission, Lord would publish in 1866 his two-volume *The Naturalist in Vancouver Island and British Columbia*, to be followed the next year by *At Home in the Wilderness*, one of the most interesting and readable of all the books relating to our early history.

Lord was not the only author among the group; young Lieut. Wilson kept a lively diary, though this was not to appear in print for over a century. An interesting passage in Wilson's diary, dated July 13th of this year, gives his first impressions of Victoria. They will surprise those who keep the old stereotype of Victoria as a quiet English cathedral town somehow magically transferred to the West Coast. In 1858 Victoria had more in common with the American Wild West. Wrote Wilson:

Vancouver Island itself is most beautiful, but turned quite upside down by the gold discovery, a regular San Francisco in 49. You are hardly safe without arms & even with them, when you have to walk along paths across which gentlemen with a brace of revolvers each are settling their differences; the whiz of revolver bullets round you goes on all day & if anyone gets shot of course it's his own fault; however I like the excitement very much & never felt better in my life.[14]

The same aura of melodrama surrounded Victoria for Wilson's colleague, the veterinarian Lord:

... in all directions were canvas tents, from the white strip stretched over a ridge-pole, and pegged to the ground (affording just room

[14] *Mapping the Frontier: Charles Wilson's Diary of the Survey of the 49th Parallel, 1858-1862, While Secretary of the British Boundary Commission*, ed. George F. G. Stanley (Toronto, 1970), p. 25.

enough for two to crawl in and sleep), to the great canvas store, a blaze
of light, redolent of cigars, smashes, cobblers, and cocktails. The rattle
of the dice-box, the droning invitation of the keepers of the monte-
tables, the discordant sounds of badly-played instruments, angry words,
oaths too terrible to name, roystering songs with noisy refrains, were all
signs significant of the golden talisman that met me on every side, as I
elbowed my way amidst the unkempt throng, that were waiting means
of conveyance to take them to the auriferous bars of the far-famed
Fraser River.[15]

The not so peaceful life of Victoria was soon exchanged by the
sappers and their officers for the rigours of work in the field when,
starting at Semiahmoo Bay and moving east, they checked with the
Americans the line of the boundary. Late July found them working
in the vicinity of Sumas Lake, learning about one of the terrors of
pioneer British Columbia life — the mosquitoes. Lord has left a vivid
account of the sufferings of the Royal Engineers:

Night and day the hum of these blood-thirsty tyrants was incessant; we
ate them, drank them, breathed them; the thickest leather clothing
scarcely protected one against their lancets. With trousers tied tightly
round the ankle, and coat sleeves round the wrist, the head enveloped
in a gauze bag, hands in gloves, and feet in shooting-boots, we lived
and slept, or rather tried to do so. Lighting huge fires, fumigating our
tents, trying every expedient we could think of, was all in vain, the
mosquitoes seemed happy in a smoke that would have stifled anything
else that was mortal; and, what was worse, they increased in number
daily.

Eating or drinking, attired as we were, required an immense amount
of ingenuity, first dexterously to raise the net, and then deftly throw
the wished-for morsel into the mouth; the slightest bungle or delay in
restoring the covering, and a torrent of mosquitoes gained admittance,
causing insufferable agonies.

Human endurance has its limits; the most patient get rebellious at
being flayed alive. It was utterly impossible to work or write, one's
entire time being occupied in slapping, stamping, grumbling, and
savagely slaughtering mosquitoes. The human face divine rapidly
assumed an irregularity of outline, far from consonant with the strict
lines of beauty; each one looked as though he had gone in for a fight
and lost it. The unfortunate mules and horses, driven mad, raced about

[15] John Keast Lord, *The Naturalist in Vancouver Island and British Columbia*
(London, 1866), I:37.

wildly, dashing into the lake, out again, then trying the shelter of the willow-trees, and rolling in the grass in very agony; but all was of no avail; go where they would, do what they would, their persecutors stuck to them in swarms. The dogs, howling piteously, wandered up and down restless and wretched, until, guided by a wise instinct, they dug holes in the earth as a *dernier ressort*; then, backing in, lay with their heads at the entrance, shaking their ears, and snapping angrily at the ravening legions, anxious and ready for immediate assault.

To endure any longer such ceaseless persecution was impossible; officers and men began to show symptoms of fever, the result of want of sleep, and irritation arising from mosquito bites. To withdraw into the hills and abandon the work until winter was the only alternative. We were fairly vanquished — the labour of a hundred men and as many mules and horses put to an end by tiny flies.[16]

The Sumas mosquitoes had routed the Royal Engineers! Lord's account should not be dismissed as comic hyperbole. Today Sumas Lake, once a natural flood plain of the lower Fraser, has been diked and drained. Sprays are used with telling effect on the remaining ponds and streams, but still the Fraser Valley mosquitoes manage to supply the newspapers with a few items every summer.

The same high water which had brought on the Sumas mosquitoes had created a different problem for the miners upriver in the Fraser Canyon. The freshets having brought down a tremendous amount of water, the gold bars had disappeared under a turgid torrent. Over a month would pass before the bars would begin to reappear. Unable to work, hundreds of the miners headed back to Victoria. Many were practically destitute. Without government help some would starve.

These unemployed miners were only one of Douglas' problems. He knew that, if the Interior goldfields were really to be exploited, the trails which led to them would have to be improved, and ultimately a wagon road would have to be provided. As things stood, the cost of getting provisions to the "diggings" was enormous. A barrel of flour which cost $16 at Bellingham Bay cost $25 at Fort Langley, $36 at Hope and $100 at Sailors Bar. Prices went even higher when the flour, after being packed over the rudimentary trails

[16] John Keast Lord, *At Home in the Wilderness: What to do There and How to do It. A Handbook for Travellers and Emigrants*, 3rd ed. (London, 1876), pp. 275-77.

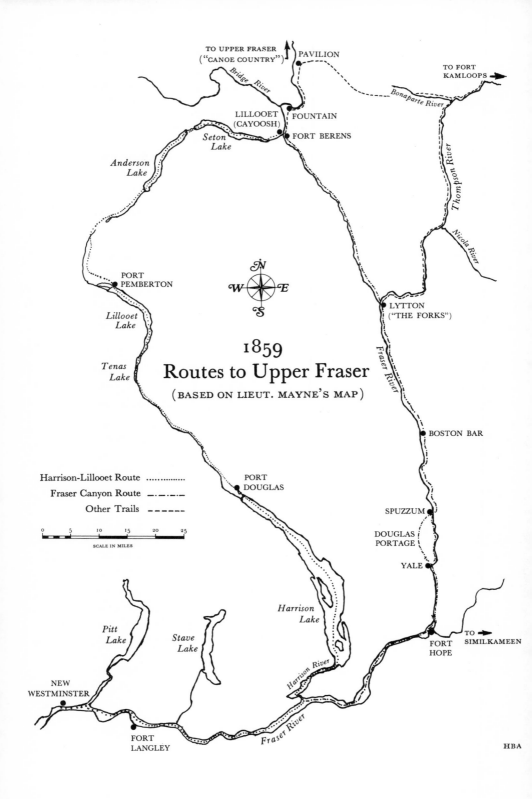

TO UPPER FRASER
("CANOE COUNTRY")

PAVILION

TO FORT KAMLOOPS

Bridge River

Bonaparte River

LILLOOET
(CAYOOSH)

FOUNTAIN

FORT BERENS

Seton Lake

Thompson River

Anderson Lake

Nicola River

PORT PEMBERTON

LYTTON
("THE FORKS")

Lillooet Lake

Fraser River

Tenas Lake

1859
Routes to Upper Fraser
(BASED ON LIEUT. MAYNE'S MAP)

BOSTON BAR

Harrison-Lillooet Route ....

Fraser Canyon Route —·—·—

Other Trails — — — —

PORT DOUGLAS

SPUZZUM

DOUGLAS PORTAGE

YALE

0   5   10   15   20   25
SCALE IN MILES

Harrison Lake

Pitt Lake

Stave Lake

TO SIMILKAMEEN

FORT HOPE

NEW WESTMINSTER

Harrison River

FORT LANGLEY

Fraser River

HBA

of the upper Fraser Canyon, arrived at "The Forks" (Lytton) for transportation even farther upstream.

*   *   *

On 17 July 1858 the Victoria *Gazette* carried banner headlines:

VERY IMPORTANT INTELLIGENCE

NEW ROUTE DISCOVERED

TO THE

UPPER FRAZER RIVER

Reading the paper, miners learned what the Hudson's Bay Company had long known — that a route existed to the upper country, one which by-passed the terrible terrain of the Fraser Canyon by going up Harrison River and Harrison Lake, following the course of Lillooet River and Lake, and Anderson and Seton Lakes, finally rejoining the Fraser at Lillooet.

Douglas swiftly decided both to improve communications with the Interior and to provide relief for the unemployed miners by setting them to work constructing a mule trail, four feet wide, along the portages of the Harrison-Lillooet route. Some five hundred men signed up for the road work, the understanding being that the government would provide them with transportation, equipment and food while they contributed their labour without charge, and put down a deposit of $25, refundable in goods if their conduct proved satisfactory. The whole operation was placed under the direction of A. C. Anderson, who had travelled over the route in 1846, and the men were organized into companies of twenty-five, each serving under a "captain" of their own choice.

Work began late in July when the *Umatilla*, on an initial reconnaissance, became the first steamboat to reach the upper end of Harrison Lake. Here the *Umatilla*'s passengers found some thirty miners who had already arrived in a whaleboat. By August the project was well under way and by mid-September the trail was through to Lillooet Lake. Here a blockhouse had been erected. Later that month three hundred men were hacking out a mule trail between Lillooet Lake and Anderson Lake. Along the short portage from Anderson Lake to Seton Lake an enterprising American entrepreneur, Dozier, constructed a wagon road, apparently meaning to enrich himself with the tolls to be paid by those using it. The last stretch of the road, from Seton Lake to Cayoosh or Lillooet, presented few problems. By the end of October the new route was deemed complete and Governor Douglas proudly reported to London:

I have the satisfaction of announcing that the great work of the season, the route by Harrison's River to a point on Fraser's River, beyond the mountains, about eight miles below the upper fountain [Fountain] is now completed. . . . [17]

In December the Victoria *Gazette* ran an enthusiastic story about the Harrison-Lillooet route:

Good boats are running on all the lakes, while farms have been taken up at many favorable locations, and numerous houses of public entertainment are opened all along its line.[18]

The *Gazette* estimated that, in consequence of the new route, goods could be transported from Port Douglas at the head of Harrison Lake to Lillooet at a cost of only 18 cents a pound, whereas use of the appalling Fraser Canyon trails entailed a charge of 46½ cents a pound for anything transported from Yale to Lytton.[19]

Actually Governor Douglas at first overestimated what had been achieved by the Harrison-Lillooet trail builders. The veteran Hudson's Bay Company officer J. W. McKay, inspecting the work, grimly reported to Douglas: "The bridges constructed by the roadmakers are in general too low, most of them will be swept away during the next freshets."[20] Moreover, to save time and expense, the construction gangs had repeatedly routed the trail along dry creek beds. All these stretches would become impassable when the spring run-off filled the beds with raging torrents. Moreover, imperfect and unsatisfactory though the route was, it had proved extremely expensive, swallowing up some £14,000, more than half of the slender revenues available to Douglas.

[17] Douglas to Lytton, 9 Nov. 1858. *B.C. Papers*, II:29.
[18] Victoria *Gazette*, 18 Dec. 1858.
[19] *Gazette*, 26 Oct. 1858.
[20] *B.C. Papers*, II:31.

Aware of the enormous expenditures which would confront him in the coming years, Douglas made an eloquent plea for financial assistance from Britain:

> To accomplish that great object of opening up a very inaccessible country for settlement, by the formation of roads and bridges immediately and pressingly wanted; to provide public buildings for the residence of the officers of the Crown, for the use of the Judiciary, for offices of record; and, in short, to create a great social organization, with all its civil, judicial, and military establishments, in a wilderness of forest and mountain, is a herculean task, even with all the appliances of wealth and skill, and it must necessarily involve, in the first place, a large expenditure, much beyond the means of the country to defray. . . . My own opinion of the matter is that Parliament should at once grant the sum of £200,000, either as a free gift or a loan to be repaid hereafter, in order to give the new colony a fair start in a manner becoming the great nation of whose empire it forms a part.[21]

The eloquence was in vain. Lytton, the Colonial Secretary, crisply replied: "I am fully satisfied that Parliament would regard with great disfavour any proposal of a gift or loan to the extent you suggest."[22]

Lacking financial help from the homeland, Douglas had to continue to rely upon those various levies which, still lacking authority from Whitehall, he had instituted on his own responsibility. He had designated Victoria as the only port of entry for the gold-fields, and at the newly-opened Victoria Customs House levied a ten per cent ad valorem duty on all imported goods destined for the mainland. (Vancouver Island itself remained duty free.) Moreover, every trader doing business on the Fraser was required to pay $7.50 a month for a trading licence. The most comprehensive of Douglas' measures, however, was the $5 licence (payable annually) which every miner had to buy before entering the Fraser.

*   *   *

By the summer of 1858 things had changed greatly from those early spring days when so many miners had had no choice but to

---

[21] B.C. Papers, II:10.

[22] B.C. Papers, II:75.

cross the Strait of Georgia in Indian dugouts or boats of their own construction. Enterprising American skippers had brought their paddlewheelers north and were regularly plying up and down the Fraser. Great was the excitement on June 6th when the sidewheeler *Surprise* became the first steamer to journey up the river all the way to Fort Hope. A correspondent of the San Francisco *Bulletin*, himself en route by canoe from Langley to Hope, has left a vivid account of meeting the *Surprise* on the last lap of her historic voyage:

After supper and a smoke, watches being settled [against Indian attack] etc., we got under the blankets and were talking, when one of the party exclaimed that he heard the sound of paddle-wheels. In an instant we were on our feet and listening. There was no doubting it. As the steamer neared us with her lights shining out in the darkness, our camp was in about as excited a state as could be imagined. Along she came until abreast our fire, when the anchor dropped and in two minutes I was aboard the *Surprise*, whilst the party ashore were saluting her with guns and revolvers. . . .

She had left Fort Langley at 7½ P.M., and had made twenty miles in two hours, the current running about six knots against her. The next morning, the 6th, at 3½ A.M., she went ahead, and at 2 P.M. arrived at Fort Hope.[23]

From this time on, miners who were ready to pay the $20 fare could travel in comfort from Victoria to Fort Hope aboard the *Surprise*. The comfort was only relative however — if the steamer got caught in a bad current the passengers were put ashore and told to get hauling on the tow ropes.

Shortly after the *Surprise* inaugurated her service, a competitor appeared on the river, the little *Sea Bird*. Alas for the *Sea Bird*! On her second trip downstream she grounded on Seabird Island a few miles below Hope. Her people escaped with the exception of her Negro cook, who was robbed by the Indians and so badly injured that he subsequently died in the naval hospital at Esquimalt.

The captain of the *Surprise* would have dearly loved to take his ship even farther up the river to Yale but the *Surprise*, being a sidewheeler, simply could not muster the power needed to overcome the swifter currents above Hope. On July 21st, however, the stern-

---

[23] San Francisco *Bulletin*, 19 June 1858, p. 2.

wheeler *Umatilla* managed to become the first steamboat to travel right up to the gateway of the Fraser Canyon. The voyage must have been an alarming one, with the boat throwing up smoke and sparks from her tall stack, while her decks seemed to heave like the sides of a volcano. Somehow the boiler did not explode and, to hurrahs and fusillades of gunfire, the doughty *Umatilla* tied up — the first steamer to Yale. However, the adventure was deemed too dangerous to repeat and Yale had to wait a considerable period before more powerful sternwheelers established the little town as indeed the "head of navigation" on the lower Fraser.

*   *   *

Douglas attached great importance to the permits which he required the miners, British as well as foreign, to purchase. By the very act of purchase, aliens were forced to acknowledge British sovereignty. To insure that the miners obtained their licences, Douglas kept guardships, usually H.M.S. *Satellite* at the entrance and the HBC's *Recovery* farther upstream, watching the traffic going up the Fraser River. A third watch was maintained for a while by a party of marines stationed at Fort Langley with the *Satellite*'s launch. Probably they were to keep some sort of surveillance over the mouth of the Chilliwack (now Vedder) River, for here the Whatcom Trail joined the riverside trail along the Fraser. This Whatcom Trail, which led overland from Bellingham Bay, was ardently promoted by the American merchants there, who wanted to see their Whatcom supplant Victoria as the gateway to the Fraser gold area. Their chief argument was that their trail eliminated the dangers of having to cross the Strait of Georgia and enter the Fraser, trusting to small boats or Indian dugouts. This argument lost its cogency once steamboats began playing between Victoria and Fort Hope. As a countermove the Whatcom merchants had Captain DeLacy build an extension of the Whatcom Trail. This followed a tortuous route, via Cultus Lake, Chilliwack Lake, and the Skagit River, finally linking up with the HBC brigade route by its Horseguards Camp, north of the present Hope-Princeton Highway. Once on the HBC trail, goldseekers would have a clear route — via Otter Lake, Nicola Lake, and Fort Kamloops — to the Fraser's rich "upper country". And they would get there without having to face the terrible Fraser Canyon. Unfortunately, however, this later Whatcom Trail proved too long and too difficult ever to win acceptance.

It was the special responsibility of the purser of any steamer sailing for the Fraser to see that all the miners on board had their licences. Usually there was no trouble. On one occasion, however, the *Surprise*'s purser found that fifty of his passengers (mostly bellicose Irishmen) flatly refused to purchase licences. It so happened that off Point Roberts H.M.S. *Satellite* ordered the *Surprise* to come alongside, and sent aboard a party of marines to check the licences, man by man. When the recalcitrant miners once more refused to pay, they were quietly informed that either they would purchase their mining licences forthwith, or be put ashore to fare as best they could in the wilderness. They paid.

*   *   *

We have noted three main ways of getting to the goldfields: the Harrison-Lillooet route, the Fraser River route, and the Okanagan route from the United States. The first of these, being under construction, was little used this year. The second, up the Fraser Canyon, was very difficult, especially the "Big Canyon" stretch from Spuzzum to near Boston Bar. Agile Indians could backpack supplies through the Big Canyon for the miners on the bars along the way, but a correspondent for the San Francisco *Bulletin* who travelled the route this summer has vividly described the dangers confronting the traveller:

Catching at branches to check oneself, sliding down the smooth surface of some rock . . . jumping from one rock to another, one minute sixty feet above the water, creeping around a place, with just about foothold for a sparrow, with the pleasant prospect of a mill race underneath. . . . [24]

Obviously horses could not possibly traverse this part of the Fraser Canyon, and had to use a detour. Setting out from Fort Yale, the

[24] San Francisco *Bulletin*, 6 Sept. 1858, p. 2. For another account of the terrors of this route see R. C. Mayne, *Four Years in British Columbia and Vancouver Island* (London, 1862), p. 106.

packtrains for a while avoided the lower canyon by following the Douglas Portage which led up the next valley westward from the river and rejoined the Fraser near Spuzzum. Here, in return for a yearly rental of $600 to the government, Harrison P. Eayres operated a toll ferry across the river, close to the present Alexandra Bridge. Once across the river the packtrains, instead of venturing into the Big Canyon followed for a while that original brigade route used by the Hudson's Bay Company in 1848 and 1849. This took them to the Anderson River which they followed back to the Fraser, rejoining the river and the canyon trail at the Indian village of Quayome, near Boston Bar. From here the terrain was not too bad, with a number of flats; but then came the endless zig-zagging as they went "up top", ascending Jackass Mountain and making the long descent on the other side. Much of this narrow trail used appallingly steep gradients, and curved along nerve-chilling cliffs. During the summer of '58 this packtrain trail was gradually improved, largely through the volunteer labour of miners waiting for a drop in the river level to permit resumption of work on their inundated claims, but also partly through miners who, by subscription, hired some of their fellows to improve particularly bad or threatening sections. Governor Douglas also supplied some modest funds, spared from the Harrison-Lillooet project, for the upkeep and improvement of this trail. During the winter, the mule trail with its higher altitude was often closed by snow.

But what of the third of the goldfield routes, that via the Okanagan? As mentioned earlier, Indian wars in Washington Territory had made travel through this area extremely hazardous until the boundary line had been crossed and the miners were safely in British territory. Nevertheless strong parties, generally numbering at least 160 men and organized along quasi-military lines, did manage to get through. Among those who made the journey without losing either scalp or head was one Herman Francis Reinhart, whose account is perhaps the most vivid and detailed left by any of the goldseekers of 1858. The following excerpt begins with Reinhart's company finally crossing into British territory about the beginning of July:

For a few days we traveled along with great care, constantly on the lookout for an Indian attack. We crossed several nice streams and fine looking farming and grazing land, and got to the British line. Here about a hundred Californians out of our train concluded to go a different route, by way of the S[i]m[i]lk[a]meen, then on to Fort Hope, down low on the Fraser River. We tried to talk them out of going that way, but no, they were not afraid of Indians, and could travel where they wished to for all the Indians in British America. They were mostly from Northern California. . . .

In a few days we got to O[kanogan] Lake. Our advance guards saw some Indians just leaving their camp and cross the lake in canoes for fear of us. The boys saw a couple of their dogs at their old camp ground, and shot them down, and they saw some old huts where the Indians had stored a lot of berries for the winter, blackberries and nuts, fifty or a hundred bushels. They helped themselfs to the berries and nuts, filling several sacks to take along, and the balance they just emptied into the lake, destroying them so that the Indians should not have them for provision for winter. I, and a great many others, expressed their opinion that it was very imprudent and uncalled for, and no doubt the Indians would retaliate. But they only laughed and thought it great fun to kill their dogs and destroy and rob them of their provisions. Most everyone but those who had done it disapproved of the whole affair.

The next night we camped on the bank of Lake O[kanogan], which is about 150 miles long and from one to six miles wide. Next morning a man named White, of Company B, could not find his horse. Some of his friends helped hunt for it, but as the train went on the men were coming down the hill, and someone fired a shot at White, and some men above him on the hill saw some Indians trying to cut White off from his companions. The men called to White to go down as the Indians were after him. So they gave up the horse, and did not look any more, for the train had already started on.

We traveled along the lake all day and camped on the banks at night. Every morning after we left camp some Indians would come across the lake in canoes and look over our camp grounds to look if we had left or thrown away anything (sometimes we threw away old clothes, hats, shoes, shirts or old blankets or crusts of bread or meat, and they would come and get them after we left). . . . That morning the advance guard planned to punish the Indians if they should come to camp as usual after we left. So right after breakfast some 25 men concealed themselves in a gulch close to camp, and the train went on as usual. We were passing along a high trail close to the lake and we soon saw three or four canoes start to come across from the other side, with seven or eight Indians in each canoe, to go to our camping place. I had gone with the train some one and one fourth to one and one half miles, when we heard some shooting. I stopped to listen and counted over fifty shots.

In the course of half an hour our advance guard that had formed the ambush came up to us and related how they were all lying down in the gulch, to be out of sight, and they got to talking to each other and forgot about the Indians to be ambushed, and they were surprised as well as the Indians, for the Indians had landed and were coming towards camp right to where the white men lay concealed. They had no idea of danger from the whites, so some whites happened to raise up to see if the Indians had landed yet, when behold! the Indians were within eight or ten feet from him, and they did not see the whites till they all raised and made a rush for the Indians with their guns and pistols all ready to shoot. As soon as the Indians saw the whites, they were so frightened that some turned back and ran towards their boat, some fell down on their knees and begged for [them] not to shoot, as they had no arms at all, and they threw up their hands and arms to show that they had nothing. But the whites all commenced to fire and shoot at them, and ran out to the lake after those who were getting in their canoes, and kept on shooting till the few that got into the [canoes] got out of reach of their guns and rifles. And lots jumped into the lake was shot in the water before they could swim out of reach of their murderers — for they were nothing else, for it was a great slaughter or massacre of what was killed, for they never made an effort to resist or fired a shot, either gun, pistol, or bow and arrows, and the men were not touched, no more than if they had shot at birds or fish. It was a brutal affair, but the perpetrators of the outrage thought they were heroes, and were victors in some well-fought battle. The Indians were completely dumbfounded to see a lot of armed men when they expected no one, and ran toward their canoes to get away, and the Indians knelt down and begged for life, saying they were friends. There must have been 10 or 12 killed and that many wounded, for very few got away unhurt. Some must have got drowned, and as I said before, it was like killing chickens or dogs or hogs, and a deed Californians should ever be ashamed of, without counting the after-consequence.

We traveled on, but many of us expected some revengeful attack. We could hear Indians, nights, and saw smoke and signals of lights and smoke on every hill and in every direction to each other in the mountains some forty or fifty miles away. About a week after the Indian slaughter, in the night (the guard had seen Indian tracks in the evening close to camp) the guard brought in two Indians. A mass meeting was called and the Indians were questioned by an interpreter. They were friendly Shuswa[p] Lake, British Columbia, Indians on their way to Colville, in Washington Territory (one of their wives lived there) and with the permission of the old chief Nick at the Fort Kamloops or

Thompson, on Shuswa[p] Lake. He was on the way to visit his wife; they had walked into camp without fear or evil intention. They said they had been at the Hudson Bay store at Fort Thompson, and old Nick's tribe were friends to the English, French and Scotch living there, trapping, and many were married to Indian squaws. At first our men were for taking them out and shooting them right off for spies, expecting we would be attacked, but they kept denying [it], and [said] they were good peaceable Indians.... At last we came to the conclusion to take them back with us as prisoners to Shuswa[p] Lake, and took their arms from them and always kept guard over them.

One morning Company F (Dancing Bill's) took leave and went ahead. They said we did not travel fast enough for them. Next day a part of the French company started on ahead. They thought they would do better by not traveling with the bloodthirsty Americans. They understood the Indians better than us, and by their intermarriage with the Indians, expected the Indians on and around Thompson River would favor them with what they knew of the locality of the gold.

Some new discoveries had been made north of the Canoe Country, at or above the forks of Fraser River. Sidolia, the Italian, wanted me to go; he still had all three of our horses. I told him to go on, and after I got to Fraser River, I could come up to where he was. Next night the French company had only gained about one and a half miles, and after they had camped an old Frenchman that had traveled with us a day or two in the Cascade Mountains ... had left a partner in our train, Company B, and he concluded to come back to his partner, stay all night, and catch up to the balance of his company early in the morning before they packed up, and then go on with them again. So at break of day he started ahead to catch up to the part of the French company he was going with, but after going about half way the Indians intercepted him and killed and shot him through the head, three or four shots, and his body was all shot full of holes. They stripped him and rolled him out of the trail into a gulch alongside of the trail. He had a shotgun; they took that, and no one, it seems, heard the firing at either ours or his camp. We started after breakfast and some of our advance guard saw the blood in the road, and Indian footprints or tracks, came to look close and followed the blood. A few yards below, they found the body, still quite warm; he could not have been dead twenty minutes. So the train stopped and we loaded his body, naked, across a riding saddle, and some men led the horse, and others held on the body, went on over the point of the hill where he was killed.

When we saw the body, we knew the old Frenchman and sent some horseback men ahead to hurry and stop the French train or company to bury their man. It took us three or four miles to catch up to where they had stopped, and we all stopped and dug a grave and buried him. He was perfectly helpless and harmless.

We kept on till we came to Fort Thompson. The Indians kept on the hills and making smoke signals all night, and kept speaking to each other in their own language. Our two prisoners said they were O[kanogan] Lake Indians, and had been following us ever since the slaughter of the Indians at the Lake. They had killed the old Frenchman and were trying to get the Indians on Thompson River to help them kill us all, but the Indians around the Fort were a sort of civilized, and under old Nicholas, and he was a good Catholic, and Capt. Mc[Lea]n of the Hudson Bay Company Fort was his friend. The friendly Indians were all Catholics and had priests at the fort.

The next day at noon we camped right opposite the fort. There were lots of houses, the first we had seen after leaving Fort O[kanogan]. It made us feel more cheerful and more like civilization, and here the French company parted from us. We kept down the Thompson River to [Kamloops] Lake, where we had to cross over with rafts and canoes, and swim the horses and mules. Some would have to be held up by the heads from out of the canoes. It was a wide, rough place to cross. Some ten or twelve head of horses were drowned and strangled by not being held up properly at the crossing of the lake.

Old Nicholas the head chief of the Indians around that country, came to see us about the two prisoners we had brought back from Lake O[kanogan]. He was an old man about 65 or 70 years old, wore a stove pipe hat and citizen's clothes, and had a lot of medals of good character and official vouchers of good conduct for many years. He was quite angry and said he was surprised to see 300 men take two Indian prisoners and bring them back two or three hundred miles because we thought they were spies, and it was mighty little in us and did not show great bravery. And about the O[kanogan] Lake massacre, that it was brutal, and he could not think much of the Bostons, or Americans, that would do the like. Some of our boys were awful ashamed and some angry to hear an old man tell them so many truths, and some were mad enough to kill him for his boldness in his expressions to us all. But it was a fact none could deny, and Maj. Robertson [Robinson] let the two prisoners go. I think some of the men gave them some clothing and provisions, with some money to satisfy them for their loss of time and trouble.[25]

The callous attitude towards the Indians shown by so many of Reinhart's comrades was exhibited also by the miners, predominantly

[25] *The Golden Frontier: The Recollections of Herman Francis Reinhart 1851-1869*, ed. D. B. Nunis Jr. (Austin, 1962), pp. 125-29. Reprinted by permission of the University of Texas Press.

American, working the bars in the Fraser Canyon. When these intruders first arrived, the Indians very understandably maintained that, since the land was theirs, the whites should pay them for the claims that they worked and for the gold that they extracted. The Indians found their arguments totally ignored and for a while, in an atmosphere of mutual hostility, the Indians and the whites worked on the same bars, with the Indians occasionally infuriating the whites by calmly helping themselves to piles of auriferous gravel dug up by the latter, and then extracting the gold themselves. But the odds changed as more and more miners arrived, wearing their uniform of slouch hats, shirts of heavy gray flannel or red serge, corduroy trousers with legs tucked inside high boots. The Americans among the newcomers generally wore a cartridge belt and a pair of revolvers slung around the waist. Gaining confidence with numbers, the miners drove the Indians from the bars. Even the Chinese were expelled from China Bar, and an attempt was made to keep all Chinese from travelling beyond New York Bar, a few miles above Yale.

The Indians reacted bitterly against exclusion from the gold bars. Ugly situations arose. Miners found themselves being made to pay more and more outrageous prices for the use of the Indians' canoes. Occasionally, after they had paid and embarked, they were seized and robbed. Indians would appear in force at a gold bar, shoulder their way into the cabins and help themselves to whatever took their fancy. The Indians' hatred mounted when the whites started molesting their women. Killings began, with arrows and bullets seeking their victims. The natives dwelling in the Fraser Canyon, known as the "Couteau" or "Knife" Indians, turned also to their traditional practice of decapitating their enemies. The stripped headless corpses of white miners came floating down the Fraser, along with the bodies of numerous miners drowned in canoe accidents in the treacherous waters.

Capt. Snider took out of the water at Yale ten dead whites; at Deadman's Bend on the opposite shore they took out nineteen, and the Hudson's Bay Company at Hope took out thirty-two. . . . Some of the corpses found their way to the ocean.[26]

[26] Walkem, *Stories of Early B.C.*, pp. 58-59, giving the reminiscences of Ned Stout, a pioneer miner of '58.

In mid-August, reduced to panic, the miners on the various up-stream bars hurriedly cached their supplies and equipment, then fled to Yale. Increasing excitement marked the arrival of each new band of refugees at Yale, or the spectacle of yet another headless white body coming downstream. Ignoring the British authorities, the miners (led chiefly by Californians) started organizing entirely illegal military units rejoicing in such titles as the "Whatcom Company" and the "Pike Guards" (named presumably not for the seventeenth century weapon but for General Zebulon Pike, the American frontiersman and soldier who had died in the War of 1812 leading an American attack on York, now Toronto). At great personal peril, a few Indian chiefs appeared at Yale and tried to negotiate. One of them, Suseechus, was saved from lynching by the timely arrival of the Justice of the Peace from Hill's Bar, who with some difficulty took him into protective custody. Ovid Allard, in charge of the HBC post at Yale, managed to persuade the mob that two old Indian chiefs from a rancherie seven miles above Yale were "good Indians" and these were allowed to depart with white flags to fly above their village to save it from the coming destruction.

At last, headed by such characters as "Captain" Rouse formerly of the Texas Rangers, "Captain" Snyder and "Captain" Graham, the avengers started moving up the Canyon. The Indians fought to save themselves, but the onslaught of the whites was merciless:

Detached parties of Indians often hemmed us in, skulking behind low bushes, while occasionally some of them would send a chance musket ball whistling across the rocks with savage interest [intent?]. Our arsenal consisted of twelve double-barrelled shotguns and six Kentucky rifles, and several large horse pistols. We lost a man nearly every day; Jack McLennan was one of these, and at Slaughter Bar we lost six of our comrades. This Slaughter Bar was between Boston Bar and Jackass Mountain. Opposite Keefers we made an attack on their caches which contained all their dried salmon and berry cakes, and burned the rancherie as well. When we arrived at Ten-Mile Creek the Indians tried to head us off, but we set fire to the bush about 2 o'clock at night and retired into the darkness. The light of our bush fire exposed the Indians who were lying waiting for us on the opposite bank, and they were all killed off by the fire of the heavy Kentucky rifles.[27]

[27] Walkem, *Stories of Early B.C.*, p. 58.

The Indian population of the Canyon was not large — the correspondent of the San Francisco *Bulletin*, accompanying the white heroes, placed it at not more than five hundred. Against such odds the natives stood no chance, especially when the miners decided to starve them into surrender by denying them all access to the river, thus cutting them off from the salmon runs which provided them with their staple food for the coming year. Faced with hopeless odds, the Indians abandoned the struggle.

As the miners straggled back to their diggings, they often found their cached provisions and equipment missing — whether taken by the Indians or the undisciplined expeditionary companies, nobody could say.

Meanwhile, what of Governor Douglas back in Victoria? The feared explosion had come and he was still without any naval reinforcements from Admiral Baynes, or any troops except the Boundary Commission's small detachments of sappers strung out along the 49th parallel. Moving swiftly, Douglas assembled a force of sorts and, on August 30th, set out for Yale accompanied by 20 Royal Marines under an officer from H.M.S. *Satellite* and 15 Royal Engineers. Accompanying the party was Donald Fraser, correspondent of the London *Times*. To Fraser's despatches we owe our very detailed knowledge of the expedition's adventures. At Fort Langley Douglas' party was met by Chief Trader Yale with an account of what he, personally, had endured from the Americans. Reported Fraser:

The gentleman in charge complained of the Yankees having been very intrusive, impertinent, and lawless when they first came up the river in force, and when they fancied they were beyond control of the authorities. They invaded his cornfields, ate the green peas, stole the oats, tore down the fences for firewood, and misconducted themselves in other ways. How strange that the natural coarseness, the bad manners, and the vulgarity of this people will cling to them wherever they go! For my own part, I take this to be an illustration of the effect of bad Government upon national manners and morals. A stop must be put to these unseemly and brutal displays of their customs in this country. Our own self-respect calls for their repression. If these people don't know the practice of decency, they must be taught it; and if they don't choose to learn it, they must go back to their own country, where they

can indulge their propensities. I, of course, allude to the "Hoosier" class
— the great Yankee "unwashed," and do not include in my denuncia-
tion any American who deserves the epithet of gentleman.[28]

Resuming their journey, the Britishers found a short distance above
Hope a notable example of the Yankees being "very intrusive,
impertinent". Posted on one of the bars was a sign naming it "54
deg. 40". The British angrily pulled up the placard and threw it in
the river. More serious were the complaints which they were beginning to hear from the Indians. Describing a halt at what the
Americans had named "Fort Union", Fraser noted:

The Governor is engaged endeavouring to trace the murders committed
on the river. The information received goes to implicate white men.
Indians complain that the whites abuse them sadly, take their squaws
away, shoot their children, and take their salmon by force.[29]

At Emory Bar, Governor Douglas was confronted by miners
wanting a judicial decision from him — they had discovered that
above high water mark there were "dry diggings", levels where the
Fraser had deposited its gold millenia earlier, before it had cut its
channel down to its present level. The question was: if a man had a
claim on a bar, with its twenty-five foot frontage, how far back did
the claim extend into the dry diggings above the bank?

The opening of the case was quiet enough, drawled out in measured
tones with a Yankee twang of great power; but the statement of facts of
the first speaker was "demurred" to by a defendant in the outer ring of
the circle. The demurrer was taken up by a third man before it could
be discussed. A fourth and a fifth came into the arena, and they all set
to tooth and nail. . . . One quoted Californian laws, another Australian,
and a third the "law of all creation". . . . The Governor endured it all
like a stoic.[30]

Two stops beyond Emory Bar, Douglas was once more approached
by wronged Indians:

A village orator appeals to the Governor for relief against the miners,
who are intruding upon the Indian domain. The poor creatures! They

---

[28] *The Times*, 30 Nov. 1858, p. 4.

[29] *The Times*, 1 Dec. 1858, p. 10.

[30] *The Times*, 24 Dec. 1858, p. 7.

were very modest in their demand. They only asked for a small spot to draw up their canoes, and to dry their fish upon, to be exempted from mining. Their request was granted by the Governor, and the boundaries marked by the sub-commissioner.[31]

At last, on September 13th, Governor Douglas and his escort arrived at Yale, the trouble centre. Here, during the following week, he pursued his investigation of the "Fraser Canyon War."

Yale had acquired an unholy reputation in 1858. D. W. Higgins, living there at the time of Douglas' September visit, later recalled vividly the Yale that he had known:

A city of tents and shacks, stores, barrooms and gambling houses. The one street crowded from morning till night with a surging mass of jostling humanity of all sorts and conditions. Miners, prospectors, traders, gamblers and painted ladies mingled in the throng.[32]

In every saloon a faro-bank or a three-card-monte table was in full swing, and the hells were crowded to suffocation. A worse set of cutthroats and all-round scoundrels than those who flocked to Yale from all parts of the world never assembled anywhere. Decent people feared to go out after dark. Night assaults and robberies, varied by an occasional cold-blooded murder or a daylight theft, were common occurrences. Crime in every form stalked boldly through the town unchecked and unpunished. The good element was numerically large; but it was dominated and terrorized by those whose trade it was to bully, beat, rob and slay.[33]

Higgins' description may sound melodramatic, but it is supported by Fraser's account in *The Times*. After recording the arrival of Douglas and his escort, he wrote of Yale:

We found the place and its "surroundings", as an American termed the neighbourhood, so filthy and unsavoury — so exactly like its inhabitants, in short, that we could not pitch our tents in or near it; so we shot across the river, shook the dust of this modern Sodom from off our feet, and camped on a clean sandspit on the opposite side. . . . [34]

A grim-faced Douglas set about his investigations. No doubt that

[31] *Loc. cit.*

[32] *The Mystic Spring and Other Tales of Western Life* (New York, [1908]), p. 215.

[33] *Ibid.*, p. 31.

[34] *The Times*, 25 Dec. 1858, p. 7.

horseshoe-shaped mark, which was notorious as the symbol of his anger, appeared again and again on his forehead. The miners, it was plain, had proceeded with outrageous illegality against the lives and property of the natives. Light was thrown on a variety of episodes, not least the famous night battle of August 21st in which, supposedly, the American Whatcom Company had valiantly stood off a night attack by the "Injuns" at the cost of the lives of two of their officers, "Captain" Graham and "Lieutenant" Shaw. Under examination the sad truth became apparent. There never had been any night attack by the Indians. A noise in the night had awakened a sleeping sentry, and his outcry had thrown the entire camp into panic. Men had blazed away with their guns into the darkness. One of their shots had killed Shaw. As for the hapless commander Graham, leaping to his feet in the dark, he had fumbled with his revolver and contrived to kill himself.

On September 20th, having completed his investigation and satisfied himself that the peace was no longer in danger, Douglas started back to Victoria. From there, on October 12th, he wrote a report to Lytton, the Colonial Secretary, in London. Discreetly he said hardly a word about the recent American-Indian "war" fought on British soil. He did mention that there had been much unrest, which he attributed to the excessive use of liquor. He noted that he had enjoined moderation in its use by the whites, and had prohibited its sale to the Indians. Further to moderate the consumption of "rotgut", he had set up for the saloons a licensing system which would cost them six hundred dollars each. At Hope he had found a number of persons wanting to settle on the land. He had ordered townsites laid out both at Hope and Yale and had arranged for the provisional occupancy of land, pending the establishment of a duly constituted government which could issue land titles. While making sure that his report would contain nothing to flutter the dovecotes in Whitehall, Douglas did allow himself one dry piece of understatement:

We found a large assemblage of people at Fort Yale, expecting our arrival, with some anxiety in order to ascertain the views of Her Majesty's Government.[35]

[35] PRO, ADM 1/5721.

He mentioned that, in order to assure better governance for Yale, he had appointed a chief of police and five constables.

This last measure of Douglas' seems to have amused Donald Fraser, who reported in *The Times* that, if the Fraser miners were to be reduced to good order and obedience to the law, 250 police would be needed at Hope, another 250 at Yale, and a third 250 at Fort Dallas, the newly-opened HBC post close to where the Thompson joined the Fraser at The Forks. He opined that the 750 police would need to be supported by "three or four" gunboats on the river.[36]

As it happened, there was already en route to British Columbia a man who would do as much as 750 policemen and four gunboats in instilling respect for the law into the violent mining camps. His name was Matthew Baillie Begbie. He was a highly civilized English gentleman, indomitable in spirit, totally incisive in mind and manner, who carried with him an appointment as "Judge of British Columbia." In that colony he would win for himself two titles — one would be "Sir Matthew Begbie", the other (less deserved) "The Hanging Judge."

Five days after Douglas sent to Sir Edward Bulwer Lytton his report on the Fraser Canyon troubles, he received a definitive reply to his earlier appeals for additional naval support. It took the form of H.M.S. *Ganges*, the flagship of Rear-Admiral Baynes which arrived at Esquimalt with the admiral himself on board. As far as European naval warfare was concerned, the *Ganges* was an interesting anachronism, the last sailing ship-of-the-line that the Royal Navy would ever commission for service abroad. But she carried 84 guns and more than 700 bluejackets and marines. Douglas welcomed her with profound relief.

*   *   *

The fear which had been haunting Douglas all along, of course, was that the thousands of American miners on the Fraser would attempt to annex the territory to the United States. That danger would probably become acute only if the government of the

[36] *The Times*, 25 Dec. 1858, p. 7.

United States began to give annexation some measure of official, even if covert, support. Accordingly it was with no great happiness that Douglas this autumn received at Victoria Mr. John Nugent, the newly-arrived "Special Agent of the United States", charged with looking after American interests north of the 49th parallel. Especially in view of Nugent's well-known prejudice against the English, there could be a sinister parallel between his mission and that of Thomas Oliver Larkin, the confidential American agent at Monterey who had conspired with the American residents to take California from Mexico. Two days after Nugent's arrival, the Victoria *Gazette* noted, "a large number of Mr. Nugent's old California friends, and American residents here, called upon him at his hotel".[37] About a week after the Special Agent's arrival, the San Francisco *Herald* significantly remarked:

American interests in New Caledonia now far exceed those of British residents, insomuch as numbers are concerned, and the enormous increase in the value of property in Vancouver Island is entirely due to American immigration; the presence of an American war vessel of suitable force, such as the frigate Merrimac, would, therefore, be a desirable feature in the neighborhood of Victoria.[38]

It did not take Nugent long to find ways of creating trouble. Since there were no trained British lawyers in Victoria other than the acting Attorney-General, all men placed on trial, be they British, French, German, American or of any other nationality, had to conduct their own defence with whatever help they could get from their friends. Nugent saw an opportunity and struck:

The undersigned, Special Agent of the United States, has the honor to state to His Excellency Governor Douglas, that he is informed there are six American citizens now in the prison of the fort, awaiting trial on various charges: that these persons are denied the benefit of counsel, for the reason that no member of the American bar is permitted to practise in the courts of this colony. . . . [39]

Then Nugent made his demand: that American lawyers be allowed

[37] *Gazette*, 22 Sept. 1858.

[38] Reprinted in *Gazette*, 28 Sept. 1858.

[39] Nugent to Douglas, 6 Oct. 1858, PABC D/A/Un3N.

to defend American prisoners. Such a course would have been a totally unacceptable infringement upon the British system of justice, as well as giving American prisoners a privilege not available for any other defendants. Governor Douglas refused, and Mr. Nugent became angry. He was also mortified when he found that at least one of the Americans he was championing was, in fact, a British national. In late October Nugent travelled to Yale to consult with the dissatisfied Americans there. When he returned to Victoria he found that a furious Douglas would no longer communicate directly with him, but only through letters sent over the signature of his secretary. This gubernatorial freeze elicited a letter from Nugent in which he made the nasty thrust that he was prepared to overlook the affront since presumably Douglas was not sufficiently acquainted with diplomatic protocol to realize how very incorrect his behaviour had been. Fortunately at this point Nugent returned permanently to the United States. On November 13th he addressed a parting message to all the Americans resident on Vancouver Island and the mainland. Its final paragraph read:

It is unnecessary for me to make any further or more pointed application of this declaration to the circumstances of American citizens in these Colonies. Their own intelligence and prudence will enable them so to guard their conduct that they shall never forfeit that provident and fatherly care and protection which it promises, and which the Government of the United States has both the ability and the will to exercise over all its children, in whatever part of the world they may be.

JOHN NUGENT
Special Agent of the United States[40]

Actually Nugent's conduct had proved offensive to many of the Americans he had come to "protect", and he had split the American community into two factions. After his departure, in "cards" published in the *Gazette*, 45 Americans endorsed Nugent's position and 95 repudiated it.

*   *   *

In a way it was splendid timing that took Nugent off the scene at this point. It meant he could not be present, like a malicious witch

[40] *Gazette*, 16 Nov. 1858.

breathing maledictions in a fairy tale, at the actual birth of British Columbia at Fort Langley on November 19th.

Word of the gold rush to the Fraser River had scarcely reached London when it was realized that a properly constituted government would have to be provided for the area. Since Douglas had already, on his own initiative, extended his authority from Vancouver Island to the mainland, it might have seemed logical simply to expand the boundaries of the existing Crown Colony to include the mainland. On the other hand, the mainland goldfields had brought a population and problems very different from those of Vancouver Island. Accordingly the British government decided to establish the mainland as a separate Crown Colony with a government of its own. On 8 July 1858 a bill was introduced in the British House of Commons to provide a government for "New Caledonia." After all, of the two original Hudson's Bay Company departments west of the Rockies, the richer Columbia had been largely lost to the Americans, and it seemed logical to name the new colony after the survivor, New Caledonia. Somewhere along the legislative route with the new bill, however, somebody recalled that a cluster of French islands in the South Pacific was already known as New Caledonia. A troublesome duplication of the name should be avoided. Lytton wrote to Queen Victoria about the problem — perhaps Her Majesty had some name she would like to apply to the new colony. Back came the royal reply:

The only name which is given to the whole territory in every map the Queen has consulted is 'Columbia,' but as there exists a Columbia in South America, and the citizens of the United States call their country also Columbia, at least in poetry, 'British Columbia' might be, in the Queen's opinion, the best name.[41]

BRITISH COLUMBIA! It had a fine resonant ring. Moreover, it had a special historical aptness. It preserved the name of the empire lost to the Americans, and at the same time it served as a reminder that a portion of it had been saved, to grow and mature in another tradition. On August 2nd, royal assent was given to "An Act to Provide for the Government of British Columbia."

---

[41] The full text of this letter was printed by F. W. Howay in *British Columbia: From the Earliest Times to the Present* (Vancouver, 1914), II:49.

Since the Colonial Secretary, Sir Edward Bulwer Lytton, played a very special role in the inception of British Columbia, he merits particular note in any chronicle of this colony. An English aristocrat born of a family with a reputation for eccentric brilliance, Lytton was a man of distinct personal charm, sophistication and urbanity. He possessed diverse and notable talents. At Cambridge he had won the Chancellor's Medal for English poetry, and at the age of twenty-four he had published his first novel. (Today he is chiefly remembered for *The Last Days of Pompeii* and *The Last of the Barons*.) He was a dramatist also, and *The Cambridge History of English Literature* still characterizes his *Richelieu* and *The Lady of Lyons* as "theatrical classics". Lytton was, in short, a highly creative person, and his spirit of creativity found a special outlet in bringing into being British Columbia.

His plans for the new colony were comprehensive and imaginative. It was his idea to secure a sizeable contingent of **Royal Engineers** to map and survey, build roads, and determine the site of the capital city. Nobody but the best would do for British Columbia: the Royal Engineers he sent out were not to be just one of the forty regular companies constituting the force, but picked volunteers carefully chosen for their variety of skills. Lytton's intense personal interest in his new creation, British Columbia, is shown by the fact that when Captain Parsons sailed with the first advance party of Royal Engineers, the elegant Lytton came aboard their ship, the *La Plata*, off Cowes and, addressing him and his twenty men, declared:

The enterprise before you is indeed glorious. Ages hence industry and commerce will crowd the roads that you will have made; travellers from all nations will halt on the bridges which you will have first flung over solitary rivers, and gaze on gardens and cornfields that you will have first carved from the wilderness; Christian races will dwell in the cities of which you will map the sites and lay the foundations. You go not as the enemies, but as the benefactors of the land you visit, and children unborn will, I believe, bless the hour when Queen Victoria sent forth her sappers and miners to found a second England on the shores of the Pacific.[42]

[42] Victor A. G. R. Bulwer-Lytton, *The Life of Edward, First Lord Lytton* (London, 1913), II:293.

For the officer to command the entire force being sent out to British Columbia, Lytton went to the top and got Colonel Richard C. Moody, who had been in command of the Royal Engineers stationed in Scotland, and had recently won admiration for his planned restoration of Edinburgh Castle.

Lytton showed the same care in recruiting the cadre which would found British Columbia's civil service. Of Judge Begbie something has already been said. For the command of British Columbia's colonial constabulary Lytton obtained Chartres Brew, whom he described as:

... the most experienced and trustworthy man I could select amongst the Irish Constabulary (a body of men peculiarly distinguished for efficiency)....[43]

Throughout the latter part of this year and on into the next, Lytton was on the lookout for good men for British Columbia. And, with useful help from his Parliamentary Under-Secretary, he found them, men such as George H. Cary, Attorney-General; Captain W. D. Gosset, Colonial Treasurer; and W. O. Hamley, Collector of Customs. For the very top job there could be only one choice: James Douglas, who now would be Governor both of Vancouver Island and British Columbia, with two administrations serving under him. But one essential condition would have to be met: Douglas must sever his connection with the Hudson's Bay Company to prevent any conflict of interest. In October Douglas submitted his resignation from the HBC's service and the next year he was succeeded in the HBC's western management by his son-in-law, A. G. Dallas.

The great moment of the birth of British Columbia came, as every school child in B.C. ought to know but does not, at Fort Langley on 19 November 1858. Apparently only one reporter was present to cover that historic event, a correspondent from the Victoria *Gazette*. We reproduce in its entirety his historic despatch, as it appeared on the first page of the *Gazette*'s issue of November 25th:

[43] Lytton to Douglas, 16 Oct. 1858. *B.C. Papers*, I:70.

LETTER FROM NEW FORT LANGLEY

Installation of the Government of British Columbia.

New Fort Langley, 20 Nov. 1858.

Editors Gazette: — Yesterday, the birthday of British Columbia, was ushere'd in by a steady rain, which continued perseveringly throughout the whole day, and in a great measure marred the solemnity of the proclamation of the Colony. His Excellency Gov. Douglas, with a suite comprising Rear Admiral Baynes, (commanding the naval forces on the Pacific station), Mr. Cameron, the respected Chief Justice of Vancouver Island, Mr. Begbie, the newly appointed Judge of British Columbia, Mr. Lira, and others, proceeded on board H.M. ship Satellite, Capt. Prevost, on Wednesday morning, by the Canal de Haro to Point Roberts, where His Excellency remained during the night. On Thursday morning His Excellency and suite were conveyed by the Hudson Bay Company's screw steamer Otter to the Company's steam-ship Beaver, which was lying moored within the mouth of Fraser river. Both vessels then proceeded in company as far as Old Fort Langley, where the Otter disembarked a party of eighteen sappers under the command of Capt. Parsons, who immediately embarked on the Recovery revenue cutter, joining the command of Capt. Grant, R.E., who had previously reached this spot with a party of the same corps. Both these gallant officers have recently arrived from England with small parties of men under their command. The Beaver then proceeded with His Excellency aboard to New Fort Langley, where preparations were made for the ceremonial of the following day.

On Friday morning, the 19th inst., His Excellency accompanied by his suite, and received by a guard of honor commanded by Capt. Grant, disembarked on the wet, loamy bank under the Fort, and the procession proceeded up the steep bank which leads to the palisade. Arrived there, a salute of eighteen guns commenced pealing from the Beaver, awakening all the echoes of the opposite mountains. In another moment the flag of Britain was floating, or, to speak the truth, dripping over the principal entrance. Owing to the unpropitious state of the weather, the meeting which was intended to have been held in the open air, was convened in the large room at the principal building. About 100 persons were present.

The ceremonies were commenced by His Excellency addressing Mr. Begbie, and delivering to him Her Majesty's commission as Judge in the Colony of British Columbia. Mr. Begbie then took the oath of allegiance, and the usual oaths on taking office, and then, addressing His Excellency, took up Her Majesty's Commission appointing the Governor, and proceeded to read it at length. Mr. Begbie then administered to Governor Douglas the usual oaths of office, viz.: allegiance, abjuration, &c. His Excellency being thus duly appointed and sworn in, proceeded to issue the Proclamations of the same date, (19th instant) viz.: one proclaiming the Act; a second indemnifying all the officers of the Government from any irregularities which may have been committed in the interval before the proclamation of the Act; and a third proclaiming English Law to be the Law of the Colony. The reading of these was preceded by His Excellency's Proclamation of the 3d inst, setting forth the Revocation by Her Majesty of all the exclusive privileges of the Hudson Bay Company. The proceedings then terminated. On leaving the Fort, which His Excellency did not finally do until to-day, another salute of 17 guns was fired from the battlements, with even a grander effect than the salute of the previous day.

On leaving the river side, in front of the town, a number of the inhabitants were assembled with whom His Excellency entered into conversation previous to embarking on board the Beaver, and by whom he was loudly cheered in very good style as he was on his way to the steamer.

Viator.

The ceremony at Fort Langley marked the end as well as the beginning of an era. The British government had decided to abrogate the Hudson's Bay Company's trading monopoly with the Indians on the mainland, and also the Company's lease of Vancouver Island (though legal technicalities would delay this "resumption" of Vancouver Island until 1867). As noted in the *Gazette*'s report, the very first proclamation read by the new Governor, within minutes of his installation, ended the special privileges that the Hudson's Bay Company had enjoyed within British Columbia.

California miners who had arrived filled with the old Oregonian propagandistic lies about the cruel, grasping inhumanity of the Hudson's Bay Company had learned differently. They had found its officers, if not enthusiastic about their presence, fair and humane. Not that the even-handedness of the HBC did not cause the occasional shock. When American miners, bent on reserving the gold bars for whites, refused to let newly-arrived Orientals disembark at Hope, they were cowed by Chief Trader McLean who, having rallied the local Indians to his support, with drawn revolver forced the Americans to let the Chinese come ashore.

A revelation concerning the Company came when a number of

the traders who had come up from the United States tried to get the HBC to join them in hoisting the price of flour to unconscionable heights so that they could all make a vast profit. The HBC steadfastly refused to profiteer at the expense of the miners. Dr. Helmcken noted the episode in his memoirs:

Flour once fell short and the merchants wanted to corner the whole, but the HBCo would not join and at the command of Chief Factor i.e. Governor Douglas the HBCo went on selling at the usual rates, but only in comparatively small quantities to individuals, for which they received much praise from the consumers.[44]

An American miner noted one of the consequences:

Thus the schemes to extort money from the miners were frustrated, and the speculators suddenly became wholesale dealers in flour, without any chance of realizing an expected enormous profit.[45]

There was another consequence. The story spread throughout the mining camps. James Douglas, Governor of British Columbia, would consistently have the respect and gratitude of the miners.

That the Colonial Office appreciated Douglas' achievements was indicated late in November, when he was appointed a Companion of the Most Honourable Order of the Bath. That Douglas himself placed a high value on his services to the British Empire was indicated by his request for the extremely generous salary of £5000 per annum as governor of both British Columbia and Vancouver Island. He must have been very disappointed when Lytton replied that Her Majesty's government could not offer Douglas more than £1800.[46] Lytton softened the blow somewhat by saying that Douglas could award himself a supplement out of government revenues if they could stand the strain. In the end Douglas secured a total of £3000 per annum for himself.

*   *   *

New settlements were suddenly coming into existence. At Fort Langley there was a sale of building lots in the proposed British

[44] Blakey Smith, *Helmcken Reminiscences*, p. 159.
[45] Wm. Downie, *Hunting for Gold* (San Francisco, 1893), p. 201.
[46] *B.C. Papers*, II: 1 & 73.

Columbia capital of "Derby" (on the site of Old Fort Langley).
The townsite of Lytton was laid out. Port Douglas arose where the
steamboats ended their run up Harrison Lake. Port Douglas finds
an early mention this November in the estimate Governor Douglas
made of the mining population along the Fraser River. This reads:

From Cornish Bar to Fort Yale	4,000
Fort Yale	1,300
Fort Hope	500
From Fort Yale to Lytton	300
Lytton	900
From Lytton to the Fountain	3,000
Port Douglas and Harrison's River	600
Total	10,600[47]

Event after event clamours for inclusion in our chronicle. One of
these was the hiring by the Royal Navy[48] of six Indians as axemen
to clear sites for survey markers for H.M.S. *Plumper* — as Captain
Richards observed, one Indian could clear as many trees in a day as
a bluejacket could in a week.[49] A continuing worry for the Navy was
the number of desertions by seamen who wanted to make a fortune
in the goldfields. To cut down on such desertions, Governor Douglas
for a while followed the practice, begun during the gold rush in
Australia, of using colonial funds to double naval wages.

For Victoria this was a notable year for "firsts". The city had its
first and only local gold rush when Peter Leech found a minor showing at nearby Goldstream. Within the little town we have the founding of the first school for girls, St. Ann's Academy; the construction
of the first brick building; the publication of the first book, *Rules of
Practice . . . in the Supreme Court of Civil Justice*, followed by a
collection of government proclamations and Waddington's *The
Fraser Mines Vindicated*. The first steamer to be built in these parts,
the sidewheeler *Caledonia*, was launched this year. Victoria, moreover, had its first fatal duel, with "Liverpool Jack" killing a young
Englishman. And this year Victoria acquired its first uniformed

---

[47] *B.C. Papers*, II:29.

[48] PRO, ADM 1/5694, Y. 96.

[49] Richards to Hydrographer of the Navy, 15 March 1858. *Letter Book*, p. 57.

police force. Much of the work of the latter arose out of Governor Douglas' proclamation of September 6th, which strictly prohibited the sale or gift of liquor to Indians. Near Beacon Hill, already a recreational area, the newly-formed Victoria Cricket Club had its first match, against a team from H.M.S. *Satellite*.

Of all the things which were new this year, perhaps the most welcome to the Victorians was their first bit of paved road. The streets of Victoria had become notorious either as centres for dust storms in dry weather, or as quagmires in the wet months. After heavy rains, drays sank up to their hubs and horses up to their bellies on Wharf Street. Report had it that one Victoria merchant, wanting to get a message to a second merchant on the opposite side of the mass of mud which was the "street", hired an Indian to use his bow and arrow to get the message across. Certainly everybody felt like giving a cheer when, this October, Victoria acquired its first short stretch of pavement, a small portion of Yates Street "being paved on the MacAdam system."[50] Civilization was on its way, if one measures it by such things.

[50] *Gazette*, 20 Oct. 1858.

1859

"Ned McGowan's War" — *Colonel Moody ends the trouble* — *Founding of Queenborough* alias *New Westminster* — *Methodist missionaries from Canada* — *Early newspapers* — *Amor De Cosmos* — *Northern Indians descend on Victoria* — *Wealth of the Fraser gold bars* — *Similkameen and Rock Creek* — *Explorations of William Downie* — *Judge Begbie on circuit* — *Lieut. Mayne and Chief Lolo* — *"The Pig War"* — *General Harney frustrated.*

The new year began with Victoria in the midst of its first economic depression. Thousands of miners who had worked on the Fraser bars had retreated to California, there to winter in comfort while icy blasts and heavy snows descended upon their abandoned camps. Some Victorians maintained that the goldhunters would return with the spring but others, who had moved north from San Francisco and had opened stores for the gold rush trade, went around looking glum.

One event gave stimulus at least to the social life of the town. This was the arrival, on Christmas Day 1858, of Colonel Richard Clement Moody, R.E., accompanied by his wife and family. The Colonel had come via Panama ahead of the main body of his troops, to see how the advance parties were getting on with their job and to lay out a program of work for the rest once they had completed their long voyage around Cape Horn. On 4 January 1859 Moody was sworn in as Lieutenant-Governor and Commissioner of Lands and Public Works for British Columbia. The next day he was off to war, "Ned McGowan's War", a strangely serio-comical episode in the history of British Columbia, but one which has perhaps been treated too lightly in the past.

Edward McGowan was a smooth, well-educated, dangerous man.

The Vigilance Committee, which for the safety of the citizenry had conducted a number of hangings after the collapse of law and order in San Francisco, wanted McGowan in connection with several killings. Arriving in Yale in September 1858, McGowan had promptly administered a severe beating to a former member of the San Francisco Vigilance Committee. Withdrawing to Hill's Bar, which now became his stronghold, he announced that he would not allow himself to be taken to answer for this beating.[1]

McGowan, as already suggested, was very different in appearance and manner from the traditional western "bad man". He was a criminal with charisma, and inspired remarkable loyalty in the gang of Californians, many of them old associates, who helped him to dominate Hill's Bar. True, there was a duly appointed Justice of the Peace, George Perrier, but he was a poor thing ready to carry out the bidding of the dangerous McGowan.

The Justice of the Peace at Yale was a man totally different in character from Perrier but almost equally unfitted for his position. He was P. B. Whannell, who styled himself "Captain Whannell", falsely claiming to have held the Queen's commission in Australia before he had left Melbourne with another man's wife. He was a big, blustering, arrogant man with a tremendous sense of his own importance.

"Ned McGowan's War" began, in a sense, on Christmas Day 1858 at Yale, when two of McGowan's Hill's Bar men assaulted a Negro named Dixon. It took a very brave Negro to file charges against white men and, when Dixon proceeded to do so, Whannell took him into protective custody. The assailants, Burns and Farrell, having headed back to Hill's Bar, Whannell sent his brother justice there warrants for their arrest. Perrier, as soon as he had taken Burns and Farrell into custody, should have returned them to Yale. However (almost certainly at McGowan's direction) he refused to expose them to the rigours of Whannell's justice, and announced that he would hear the charges himself. Forthwith he sent his constable to Yale to ask that the Negro plaintiff be turned over to him and brought to Hill's Bar for examination. Whannell was furious at

[1] San Francisco *Bulletin*, 25 Sept. 1858, p. 3.

Perrier's invasion of his jurisdiction. Dixon, he knew, would be in danger of lynching if he were sent to Hill's Bar. Instead of acceding, he gave peremptory orders to Perrier's constable to bring Burns and Farrell back from their sanctuary. Perrier's constable refused to do so, and Whannell in a burst of fury imprisoned him.

At this point McGowan decided to teach a lesson to the unco-operative J.P. at Yale. He put it to Perrier that Whannell had shown contempt for the Hill's Bar court by arresting its constable, and should be arrested for his contumely. When Perrier weakly protested that, since he had lost his constable, he had no one to serve a warrant on Whannell, Ned McGowan had a ready solution. Let Perrier swear in him and some of his cronies as special constables and they would attend to the business. The oaths were administered and, armed to the teeth, the new constables started for Yale and there seized Whannell. We can quote from McGowan's own reminiscences for an account of what happened upon his triumphant return to Hill's Bar:

When we arrived at the bar, Judge Perrier at once opened his court, and I produced the body of the prisoner and made a return on the back of the warrant, and my functions as a "constable" ceased. The Judge then invited me on the bench alongside of him, where I sat all the time while the trial was in progress.

We put the constable of the bar on the stand, and several other witnesses, to prove the "contempt". He [Whannell] made no defense; which was the only sane act I ever knew him to be guilty of. Judge Perrier made him stand up, and gave him a pretty sharp lecture about his tyrannous and illegal acts, and then sentenced him to pay a fine of fifty dollars, and costs, and to stand committed till the sentence be complied with. His friend, Dr. Fifer [a Yale physician] paid the fine and costs, and Judge Wannel [*sic*] was released from custody.

The court and its friends then adjourned to Paddy Martin's "dead-fall", and put up the fifty dollars and costs for "drinks all round".[2]

If McGowan and his cronies thought they had successfully begun a process of intimidation which would make Whannell as responsive as Perrier to their wishes, they had made a serious miscalculation. Whannell upon his release despatched to Governor Douglas an account of the outrage to which he had been subjected. Receipt of

[2] Edward McGowan, "Reminiscences", *Argonaut*, 1 June 1878, p. 10.

Whannell's report resulted in Colonel Moody and Judge Begbie being sent to Yale.

Pausing en route to Fort Langley, Colonel Moody picked up Captain Grant and twenty-two sappers who had been building barracks in the vicinity. With them, he and Judge Begbie boarded the steamer *Enterprise* and headed upriver to Hope. It was a bitterly cold January, with plenty of ice in the river, and for several days the *Enterprise* sat frozen in the stream, powerless to proceed. Finally Moody, Begbie, and the little group of Royal Engineers landed at Hope. Here the Colonel paused while he considered fresh reports from Yale.

Meanwhile reinforcements were being rushed to Colonel Moody's support since, it was feared, he might be confronted with a general American insurrection. Up the Fraser to Fort Langley came the survey ship H.M.S. *Plumper*, with bluejackets and marines hurriedly drawn from the larger warship *Satellite*. But even the *Plumper* drew too much water to proceed to Hope, and no river steamer was to be found at Langley. The only solution apparently was to embark the naval party in Indian canoes — but no canoe was large enough to carry the piece of light artillery which was the backbone of its strength. In this quandary the naval force was kept at Fort Langley until instructions could be received from Moody. The messenger sent to the Colonel was a singularly attractive and gifted young officer off the *Plumper*, Lieut. R. C. Mayne. A few years later, in his book *Four Years in British Columbia and Vancouver Island*, Mayne recalled how, in company with a Hudson's Bay Company officer, he made that journey by canoe up the ice-strewn Fraser. For their crew Chief Trader Yale had chosen five Indians and four half-breeds; he had "harangued" them on the importance of their mission and had presented them with bright ribbons of red, blue and yellow. These they proudly attached as streamers to their caps. Off before noon, the party stopped at five o'clock for supper, and then they paddled all through the night:

If the journey by day was strange and somewhat exciting, how much more so did it become when night set in! Wet, cold, and tired, we rolled ourselves up in the rugs, and in time fell into a broken sleep, lulled by the monotonous rap of the paddles against the gunwale of the canoe, the rippling sound of the water against its sides, the song of the men now rising loud and shrill, now sinking into a low drowsy hum.[3]

All singing ceased whenever the voyageurs undertook the risky manoeuvre of taking the canoe across the river to where weaker currents could be found for a while along the opposite shore. At four o'clock in the morning they landed, snatched two hours sleep, and breakfasted. By seven-thirty they were back on the river, fighting the current and dodging the ice floes.

On the second day on the river they passed the *Enterprise* and learned that because of her trouble with the ice the Colonel had lost time and was still at Hope. Mayne's party pushed on. Then, when darkness was beginning to fall, disaster struck. Three miles short of Hope they wrecked their canoe on a rock at Murderer's Bar.[4] Contemplating the wreckage, Mayne and his companions realized there was only one thing to do. Taking to the riverside trail, three or four feet deep in snow, they walked the last stretch into Hope. Soon Mayne and his companion were inside the fort, seated by a warm fire in the presence of Colonel Moody, Captain Grant, Judge Begbie and the local HBC officers.

Moody decided that he did not require at this time the naval expeditionary force that was waiting orders at Langley. He had given much thought to the ticklish decisions awaiting him at Yale and had decided to go there unescorted, even by his original small guard of Royal Engineers. In a letter to a friend he subsequently explained his reasoning:

I there [at Hope] left the soldiers, determining to go alone up the River to the scene of disturbance, & to quell it all quietly, if it were possible — I had great confidence in myself & always consider Soldiers as the very last dire necessity — Their presence also often exasperates. ... We [Moody, Begbie and Mayne] stopped at some of the Mining Bars, I conversed in a friendly way with all, asked about their prospects, wished them well & so on, scarcely alluded to the disturbances above & in fact acted in a manner to subdue all excitement & to allow informa-

---

[3] P. 62.

[4] So named for a murder committed there. Governor Douglas regarded the name with distaste and ordered it changed to Cornish Bar, but the old name persisted.

tion to go forward that I was coming up in this quiet peaceable way. Ned McGowan, I discovered afterwards had his scouts out and exact intelligence of all my movements fr the very first.[5]

It was fortunate that Moody proceeded in this manner, because McGowan had already decided what he would do if he found himself confronted by a fire-eating colonel bent on using troops against him:

We had arranged a plan, in case of a collision with the troops, to take Fort Yale and then go down the river and capture Fort Hope (they were only trading posts called forts), and retreat with our plunder across the country into Washington Territory — only twenty miles distant. This would, we supposed, bring on the fight and put an end to the long agony and public clamor — through the press of the country — that our boundary line must be "fifty-four forty or fight".[6]

McGowan's plan was not empty braggadocio. Many of his men were veterans of the Mexican-American War. McGowan's aide, Major Dolan, was in Moody's words "a *real* major", not just one of the numerous Yanks whose pals had conferred military titles upon them. Moody was very impressed by the way in which McGowan's force had exploited the natural defenses of Hill's Bar.

Persuaded that Colonel Moody did not seek a bloody confrontation, McGowan let him come unopposed to Yale. According to Moody:

On arriving at Fort Yale in the eveng [of January 15th], the River Bank was crowded, & McGowan was in the crowd, & the Hill's Bar (the rebels) men were nearly all there (this I learnt there). They gave me a Salute, firing off their loaded Revolvers over my head. . . . I stood up, and raised my cap & thanked them in the Queen's name for their loyal reception of me — It struck the right cord [*sic*], & I was answered by 3 long loud cheers — I passed down their ranks, saying something friendly right & left. . . . [7]

---

[5] W. E. Ireland, ed., "First Impressions: Letter of Colonel Richard Clement Moody, R.E., to Arthur Blackwood, 1 February 1859", *BCHQ* 15 (1951): 96-97.
   For an important series of documents relating to "Ned McGowan's War", see F. W. Howay, *The Early History of the Fraser River Mines*, Archives of B.C., Memoir 6 (Victoria, 1926).

[6] McGowan, "Reminiscences", *Argonaut*, 8 June 1878, p. 10.

[7] Moody to Blackwood, 1 Feb. 1859. *BCHQ* 15:97.

The next day was Sunday and in the courthouse at Yale Colonel Moody conducted divine service according to the liturgy of the Church of England:

It was the 1st time in B. Columbia that the Liturgy of our Church was read. The first time that we know of that people had assembled together for Public Prayer of any kind in the Colony. — To *me* God in His mercy granted this privilege. The room was crowded full of Hill's Bar men as well as others, old grey bearded men, young eager eyed men, stern middle aged men, of all nations knelt with me before the throne of Grace. My heart was in the utterance I gave to the beautiful prayers of our Liturgy. When it was concluded, I gave them a few words in wʰ I must have expressed my affection for them, & I prayed God to bless them & to prosper them in all their labours.[8]

Following the service, Perrier was informed that Governor Douglas had removed him from his position of Justice of the Peace at Hill's Bar. Possibly irritation at losing so useful a tool had something to do with an assault that McGowan launched that afternoon upon Dr. Fifer, who had belonged to the Vigilance Committee which had driven McGowan from San Francisco. The attack on Dr. Fifer, made within a hundred yards of Moody, alerted the Colonel to the precariousness of his situation. He decided that before starting his real business, the investigation of the recent events at Yale, he had better have some troops on hand. Accordingly, when dark fell, Mayne slipped downstream in a small canoe and, arriving at Hope, delivered orders to Captain Grant which brought him and his Royal Engineers to Yale by the next morning. Continuing down the river to Langley, Mayne delivered Colonel Moody's instructions to the marines and bluejackets there to start for Hope so as to be closer to the scene of possible conflict.

On Monday, January 17th, strengthened by the arrival of the little company of Royal Engineers, Moody and Begbie visited Hill's Bar and commenced their investigation. The next day saw several hundred of McGowan's men holding a meeting to which Colonel Moody and Judge Begbie found themselves suddenly and unexpectedly invited. The meeting opened with three cheers for Governor Douglas. Then an address was read for the benefit of Moody and

[8] *Ibid.*, pp. 101-102.

Begbie in which praises for British justice and declarations of support for the government of British Columbia were mixed with vehement charges against Whannell, Perrier's rival on the bench. At Moody's insistence the more outrageous epithets were removed from the address, though he still declined to answer it. Finally the meeting broke up incongruously, with the lawless Californians, now on their best behaviour, giving three cheers for Queen Victoria.

The next day Judge Begbie held court. To minimize tension, Moody had placed his troops out of sight, on the outskirts of Yale. He was amused by the irony that inside the courthouse, surrounded by heavily armed miners, he and Begbie were the only two persons not carrying guns. The first case to be heard dealt with McGowan's attack a few days earlier on Dr. Fifer. McGowan pleaded guilty, made "a very clever & very gentlemanly speech", and received the heaviest fine that Begbie could impose. Next came the more serious matter of the attack on the magistrate at Yale, with all its circumstances, including what Moody subsequently termed the "bold, insane, reckless zeal, & utter ignorance of Captn Whannel".[9] But here McGowan proved invulnerable. As Begbie swiftly recognized, there was no way of getting around McGowan's astute move of having acted with his henchmen as sworn constables following the instructions of Justice of the Peace Perrier. The charges against them had to be dismissed.

Now that the crisis was over, Ned McGowan and his gang could not do enough for the British authorities. Moody and Begbie, as well as Mayne, (who had arrived with a party of marines), were invited over to Hill's Bar. Moody's health would not let him attend (he was suffering the consequences of "excessive cold, the daily wet feet, cold up to my knees in snow and sludge, sleeping on all manner of things") but Begbie and Mayne attended. Mayne has left his recollections of the occasion:

... upon Hill's Bar being visited by Mr. Begbie (the Chief Justice) and myself, he [McGowan] conducted us over the diggings, washed some "dirt" to show us the process, and invited us to a collation in his hut, where we drank champagne with some twelve or fifteen of his Californian mining friends. And, whatever opinion the Vigilance Committee

9 *Ibid.*, p. 101.

of San Francisco might entertain of these gentlemen, I, speaking as I found them, can only say that, all things considered, I have rarely lunched with a better-spoken, pleasanter party.[10]

Ned McGowan's War was over. Moody and his Royal Engineers started back to Fort Langley, leaving the recently arrived Inspector of Police, Chartres Brew, and a party of Royal Marines to keep an eye on the situation at Yale for a bit longer.

Actually the whole exercise had been most useful and instructive for Colonel Moody. He had received his first introduction to the new mainland colony of British Columbia, to the Fraser River, and the gold-miners. He had had an opportunity to look at Derby (on the site of the original Fort Langley) which Governor Douglas, without waiting for the Colonel's arrival from England, had already decided to make the capital of British Columbia. Lots had been sold there, and construction started on a barracks for the Royal Engineers. Douglas had chosen this site using such old Hudson's Bay Company criteria as accessibility by water and availability of good arable land. Colonel Moody, however, looking at the site through the eyes of a professional soldier who might have to defend it against a possible American takeover of the gold colony, was appalled by Douglas' choice. Not a single natural feature rendered the location defensible. Since it was on the south shore of the Fraser, the Americans would have to cross only a few miles of level country to get to it. On the other hand, while travelling up the river, Colonel Moody had seen what he considered an ideal site on the north side. Close to the river's mouth, this site consisted of sloping ground where New Westminster's federal penitentiary now stands. Nearby was Mary Hill, ideal for a citadel whose guns would guard the capital and keep the Americans from crossing the Fraser. Except for the stands of immense trees which would have to be cleared away, the site was superb. Moody became lyrical as he contemplated it:

Viewed fr the Gulf of Georgia across the meadows on entering the Frazer, the far distant giant mountains forming a dark background — the City wd appear throned Queen-like & shining in the glory of the midday sun. The comparison is so obvious that afterwards all hands on board the Plumper, & indeed everyone joins in thinking the appropriate name wd be "Queenborough".[11]

Back in Victoria, Moody presented Douglas with the case against Derby and that for Queenborough. Douglas saw the military sense of it all, and agreed that Queenborough should be the place. He insisted, however, that the name would have to be "Queensborough", while Moody held out for his beloved "Queenborough". Deadlock resulted. Nevertheless, on February 14th Douglas issued a proclamation declaring:

It is intended with all dispatch to lay out and settle the site of a City to be the Capital of British Columbia, on the right or North bank of Fraser River.[12]

Those who had bought lots at Derby would be able to return them to the Crown and apply their cost to lots at the new site for the capital.

*   *   *

Aware of the value of her new gold colony of British Columbia and alerted to the dangers of an American take-over of the territory, Britain had done more to strengthen Douglas' position militarily than to send out Colonel Moody with his Royal Engineers and to keep Admiral Baynes and his flagship with the other warships at Esquimalt. Opportunely, Britain had just ended hostilities in China with the capture of Canton. Here, free for action elsewhere, was the First Brigade of the Royal Marines. Accordingly, in mid-November of 1858, the brigade's commanding officer was instructed to choose from volunteers 6 officers and 158 men to constitute two companies for service in British Columbia.[13] These were taken aboard H.M.S. *Tribune* which, along with H.M.S. *Pylades*, was being transferred from the China Station to augment the British naval force based at Esquimalt. In mid-February of 1859 the two ships arrived at Vancouver Island and the "supernumerary marines" were landed. Ap-

[11] Moody to Blackwood, *BCHQ* 15:93.

[12] *Gazette*, 17 Feb. 1859.

[13] PRO, ADM. 1/5703.

parently they were set to work assisting the Royal Engineers until such time as they might be needed against an enemy.[14]

On April 12th of this year, the main body of Moody's Royal Engineers arrived at Esquimalt aboard the sailing ship *Thames City*: 4 officers and 118 N.C.O.s and men, along with 31 women and 34 children. A few late arrivals in June, including 2 non-commissioned officers from the Royal Artillery and 2 from the Fifteenth Hussars,[15] brought Colonel Moody's force up to its final strength of 165 men.

Douglas could at last regard his military position with some equanimity. If the Americans returned in force this spring and some sort of annexationist insurrection broke out in the gold camps, he would not be helpless. Besides Colonel Moody's Royal Engineers and another 65 Royal Engineers attached to the Boundary Commission, he now had 164 Royal Marines from China, plus whatever additional marines or landing parties of bluejackets he could secure from the ships under Admiral Baynes' command. In a real emergency he could probably muster at least four hundred professionally trained troops. Such a force was not a large one compared with the three regiments that the Americans had in Washington Territory, primarily for war with their Indians, but it was not inconsiderable.

Space does not permit us here to trace the events of the *Thames City*'s long six-month voyage from Britain to Vancouver Island via Cape Horn. Considerable ingenuity was shown in killing the tedium of the long weeks. A brass band supplied concerts, an amateur theatrical company offered its productions, dances and parties were arranged, and a ship's newspaper, edited by Second-Corporal Sinnett assisted by Lieut. Palmer, was produced in manuscript each week. The paper, known by the resounding title of *The Emigrant Soldiers' Gazette and Cape Horn Chronicle*,[16] was read every Saturday to the assembled company by Capt. H. R. Luard, the commanding officer.

---

[14] It is a little odd that, while so much has been written about Colonel Moody's Royal Engineers, hardly any work has been done on the larger force of Royal Marines commanded by Captains Magin and Bazalgette.

[15] Lillian Cope, *Colonel Moody and the Royal Engineers in British Columbia* (M.A. Thesis, UBC), pp. 37-38.

[16] This has twice been printed in very limited editions. The second, and more available, was that produced in Victoria in 1907 by the King's Printer, Lt.-Col. Richard Wolfenden, himself a corporal in the original corps.

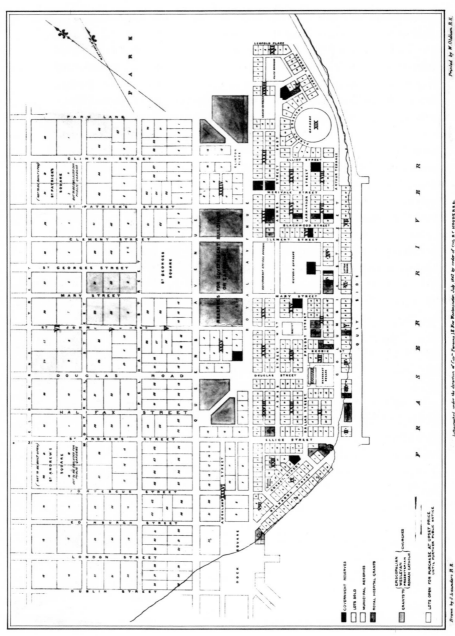

Royal Engineers' Plan for New Westminster

Drawn by J. Saunders R.E.

Lithographed under the direction of Cap.ⁿ Parsons R.E. New Westminster July 1862 by order of Col. R.^t MOODY R.E.

SCALE FROM INCHES TO A MILE

Printed by W. Oldham R.E.

Upon their arrival at Esquimalt, the group was soon transferred to the mainland. Here Royal Marines[17] had been assigned to clear the site of the new capital for British Columbia, and the advance parties of the Royal Engineers were already building a camp for the corps, a short distance to the east of the city-to-be. While housed temporarily aboard the HBC schooner *Recovery*, the Royal Engineers built at Sapperton their barracks, complete with married quarters, storehouses and offices, and embellished the grounds with flower beds. On the cleared townsite of Queenborough-Queensborough various public buildings were erected this year — a customs house, a treasury building, a survey office, and a magistrate's office. Meanwhile the decision about a name for the new capital had been referred to no less august an arbitrator than Her Majesty Queen Victoria. Rejecting both Moody's Queenborough and Douglas' Queensborough, she ruled that the capital of this new Britain rising in the west should be — NEW WESTMINSTER!

*   *   *

Mention of the proclamation of New Westminster's change of name occurs in a letter of August 5th, written by the Rev. Edward White, the Methodist minister there.[18] Since the arrival of the Methodist clergy is one of the significant events of this year, some account must be given of their mission. The original initiative had come from the Wesleyan Missionary Committee in England, which late in 1858 had raised £500 to enable the Toronto-based Wesleyan Methodist Church of Canada to send to the Pacific coast clergymen to minister to the miners and convert the Indians. On February 10th the chosen band arrived at Victoria: Dr. Ephraim Evans, the superintendent; the Rev. Edward White, the Rev. Arthur Browning, the Rev. Ebenezer Robson, and their wives. They were greeted by an ardent co-religionist, Brother John T. Pidwell, who had a large house ready for them. On Sunday, February 13th, the missionaries conducted their first service, using the courtroom of the newly-constructed police barracks. Four days later, the Hudson's Bay

17 Gough, p. 145.
18 *Christian Guardian*, 14 Sept. 1859, p. 146.

Company having offered a free passage on the *Labouchere*, the Rev. Mr. Browning left to take up his post at Nanaimo, where a number of the Staffordshire miners had a Methodist background. Upon arrival at Nanaimo, Browning found that the local school-master, a somewhat exceptional man named Cornelius Bryant, was already holding services there. Bryant himself would become an ordained Methodist minister, and a notable figure in the early history of that church.[19]

On March 2nd, leaving White to hold the base in Victoria, Dr. Evans with Robson and Pidwell started on a reconnaissance up the Fraser River. At Fort Langley they were able to raise, by subscrip-tion, enough money (or gold dust, since money was rarely used) to purchase a canoe which they proudly named "Wesleyan". Unable to afford an Indian guide, they started for Hope without one, despite the warning that they would "be capsized two or three times and drowned once". Nevertheless, Robson's skill as a canoeist brought them safely to Hope. In later years Robson was to recall:

At Hope, Yale, and the mining bars from Murderer's Bar to the famed Hill Bar, I visited the miners in their cabins and preached to all who would listen the glorious Gospel of Christ, often paddling alone, in my little canoe *Wesleyan,* through Hell Gate, and over Emory's Bar and other "riffles" which mark the course of the turbulent Fraser in that region.[20]

Leaving Robson at his future base at Hope, Evans and Pidwell went on to Yale. Dr. Evans was appalled by what he saw there. True, the miners desisted from working on their diggings on Sunday, but they used the day of rest to come to Yale to do their shopping. For the shops and saloons, Sunday was the busiest day of the week. A shocked Dr. Evans reported, "There is a fearful amount of Sabbath dese-cration."[21]

Back at Victoria after this trip, Dr. Evans sent White to take up his post at the hamlet shortly to be named New Westminster. White held his first service here on April 2nd, under a large tree. His

---

[19] *v.* Patricia M. Johnson, "Teacher and Preacher: Cornelius Bryant", *Beaver* (Winter 1961), pp. 34-39.

[20] *How Methodism Came to British Columbia* [1904], p. 9.

[21] *Christian Guardian,* 8 June 1859, p. 90.

congregation consisted of fifty assorted males, and the sole female resident. He did better a few Sundays later when Colonel Moody had him preach at a church parade at Sapperton, attended by two hundred men.

Life settled down to a routine with each of the four Canadian clergymen at his post, preaching to pathetically small congregations, while bravely pushing ahead with plans to build churches and parsonages. Melodramatic incidents occurred along the way. Browning reports one which happened while he was visiting Dr. Evans in Victoria:

Had word, the morning of my coming here, of a fight being in progress, between two tribes of Northern Indians staying here. Ran over and found it a regular battle, the bullets whistling right merrily, as they flew on their mission of death. Knowing the parties engaged, and talking a little of their language, I went in their midst. The Doctor soon arrived, and passed up and down among them, unconscious of fear. The field of battle lay in a square, from two fronts of which musketeers were busily firing, and having their volleys returned. A row of tents at two distinct distances, and occupied by the two tribes, sent out also, many a bullet toward each other. The Police Commissioner had failed to restore order. . . . Many bodies lay around, and the excitement among the savages was intense. I never saw men so changed. The Doctor persevered, and, after a while, we managed to bring the two chiefs together, and taking their hands in my own, I adroitly joined them together, and immediately proclaimed a truce. For two hours I went from house to house, enforcing the disarming process, and by the grace of God, succeeded. We found seven killed on the spot, and many wounded very badly.[22]

To Browning's amazement, he felt less fear while ending this battle than he had experienced a year earlier back in Ontario, when local hoodlums were preparing to attack a Methodist camp meeting.

Before we leave the pious Methodists to their moral earnestness, good works, and singularly disappointing rewards, we must note one thing. Their frequent reports, printed in Toronto in *The Christian Guardian*, were read in many a sombre Ontario farmhouse. The repeated mention of fortunes to be made either by mining the goldfields, or by cultivating crops in the rich valley bottoms, did not go

---

[22] *Christian Guardian*, 6 July 1859, p. 106.

unheeded, and gradually a stream not of Americans but of Canadians began to come out to British Columbia. Some of them exercised the privilege extended to all British subjects, under a new land policy, of pre-empting 160 acres of land upon payment of a two-dollar registration fee.[23]

*   *   *

Governor Douglas was consistently a good friend to the Methodists just as he was to the clergy of other churches, and he found time to help them amid all his problems and worries. Not the least of the latter was his trouble with the press. The earliest newspaper on Vancouver Island, as previously noted, was *The Victoria Gazette*, which first appeared in June 1858. This was a good, moderate journal, respectful towards the government and as such foredoomed to live only a couple of years. It was soon joined by a French language paper, *Le Courier de la Nouvelle Caledonie*, which went through a few editions, under the ownership of the colourful Count Paul de Garro, before disappearing from the face of the earth. Then, on 11 December 1858, the first issue of *The British Colonist* appeared, and Douglas' troubles began.

The editor of the *Colonist* was a brilliant eccentric, born in Nova Scotia where he had been christened William Alexander Smith. Moving out to California he became not a gold-miner, but one who picked up gold by photographing the miners. In 1854, by an act of the California state legislature, he changed his name to "Amor De Cosmos", a bastard mixture of Latin, French and Greek which he mistranslated as "Lover of the World". It was a curiously inapposite name for a waspish man with a venomous pen, one who at times verged on paranoia. De Cosmos' particular target was Governor Douglas and his advisers. To De Cosmos it was shameful that the colony of Vancouver Island did not have the responsible government which Britain had granted her more populous and longer-established colonies in eastern British North America. He totally ignored the

[23] This privilege applied only to unsurveyed Crown lands, apart from areas set aside for proposed townsites, mining areas and Indian reserves. Pre-emptors were given a guarantee that, after the land had been surveyed, they could buy it at a price not exceeding 10 shillings an acre (actually the price was fixed at 4s.2d. per acre). *B.C. Papers*, III:91-92.

manifest ability with which Douglas was handling the multitudinous problems brought on by the gold rush on the mainland. He equally ignored the patent fact that Vancouver Island, with its highly transient population and lack of financial stability, was not yet ready for democratic self-government. He ignored also the fact that Douglas, having to find men that he could rely on, must inevitably turn for assistance to the small group of Hudson's Bay Company officers, both retired and active, with whom he had long been associated and who were highly experienced in the ways of the country. To Amor De Cosmos, Douglas' counsellors, some of them related to him by marriage, were a "Family Compact", and Douglas a tyrant.

In his first edition of the *Colonist*, De Cosmos threw down the gauntlet in a succinct review of the Governor's career to date:

Unfortunately for these colonies Gov. Douglas was not equal to the occasion. He wanted to serve his country with honor, and at the same time preserve the grasping interests of the Hudson's Bay Company inviolate. In trying to serve two masters he was unsuccessful as a statesman. His administration was never marked by those broad and comprehensive views of government, which were necessary to the times and to the foundation of a great colony. It appeared sordid; it was exclusive and anti-British; and belonged to a past age. A wily diplomacy shrouded all.[24]

This was mild compared with what De Cosmos printed in his second edition, when he declared Douglas' government was characterized by "toadyism, consanguinity, and incompetency, compounded with white-washed Englishmen and renegade Yankees."[25]

Douglas, autocratic by temperament and training, was the last man to know how to cope with De Cosmos' demagoguery. Goaded beyond reason, he issued this March a proclamation invoking a series of archaic British statutes and prohibiting De Cosmos from publishing his paper unless he posted a bond of £600. That sum, he knew, lay far beyond the editor's means. The next day the *Colonist* failed to publish. But De Cosmos was not without his friends and champions, while Douglas, of course, had not been faultless in his administration. Some of De Cosmos' articles had touched on legitimate

[24] *Colonist*, 11 Dec. 1858.
[25] *Colonist*, 18 Dec. 1858.

grievances. The consequence was mounting public indignation against Douglas' violation of freedom of the press. A public meeting was held at which the necessary funds were raised for the required bond, and publication resumed. Nevertheless De Cosmos, after the posting of that bond, was a bit more circumspect about what he printed in the *Colonist*. A year later, on the anniversary of his triumph, De Cosmos rejoiced at how, unexpectedly, the *Colonist* had survived when:

> ... the conspirators against liberty, Gov. Douglas, Donald Fraser (the London Times' correspondent), W. A. G. Young, Chief Justices Cameron and Begbie, Police Commissioner Pemberton, and other such tyrannical nabobs were congratulating themselves on the suppression of a small newspaper whose only strength lay in the unvarnished truths it told of an unscrupulous oligarchy.[26]

If Douglas let the gadfly De Cosmos bother him unduly, he can be excused. He already had problems and vexations enough without having to endure the slings and arrows of the *Colonist*. A continuing problem was posed by the Indians. Douglas consistently viewed them with understanding and sympathy, and they responded by giving him their respect. But, all the same, they could cause him plenty of headaches. Early this year there was trouble with the Nitinat Indians, who had seized the American brig *Swiss Boy* when she put into Nitinat Sound to wait out a storm at sea. After a couple of days in captivity, the captain and crew made their way to Victoria. Captain Prevost was sent upcoast with H.M.S. *Satellite* to arrest George, the Nitinat chief, and to bring to Victoria the ship with her cargo of lumber — but he found that the Indians had made off with everything portable.

At Victoria itself there was constant Indian trouble. It was bad enough when Douglas had to deal only with the local Songhees. Their thieving and drunken assaults produced repeated demands in the local press that the entire tribe be expelled from the area. Douglas withstood these demands. The situation became worse during the early spring with the arrival of flotillas of canoes filled with northern Indians. In mid-March the Haidas caused so much trouble that

---

[26] *Colonist*, 12 April 1860.

some three or four hundred of them were ordered into their canoes and towed up to Johnstone Strait by H.M.S. *Tribune*. The Royal Navy rendered this service not out of any great sympathy for the Haidas, but simply to encourage them to be on their way and to see that they did not attack any of the smaller tribes living along the first stretch of their homeward journey. The measure seems to have been quite ineffective for fresh canoeloads continued to arrive. Captain Richards regarded the whole exercise as rather pointless, observing:

It would be easy to blockade them at the entrance of Johnston's Strait — and send them back — but the Governor I suppose is well versed in Indian diplomacy, and prefers letting them arrive at Victoria and using his own persuasive powers to induce them to return. There can be no doubt but that the greatest caution is necessary in dealing with these savages; from want of this the Americans are at deadly strife with them, and from the observance of it, we King George men as we are termed are safe everywhere.[27]

In mid-April, when the Police Commissioner ordered a count of all the northern Indians camped around Fort Victoria, the return read:

TRIBE	HUTS	INDIANS
Hyder [Haida]	32	405
Simpsian [Tsimpsean]	34	574
Stikkeen [Stikine]	17	223
Duncash	9	111
Bella Bella	11	126
Charcheena	4	62
Cawquald [Kwakiutl?]	4	44
Total	111	1545

The *Gazette*, publishing these figures at the end of the month,[28] stated that, by actual count, another 690 northerners had arrived since the taking of the census. If one includes an estimated local population of about 600 Songhees, some 3000 Indians were wandering around Victoria, doing some trading, prostituting their women, waylaying drunken sailors meandering along the road to Esquimalt,

[27] Richards to Capt. Washington, 24 March 1859, *Letter Book*. The *Gazette*, 10 March 1859, incorrectly reported H.M.S. *Plumper* would be towing the 40 Haida canoes north.

[28] *Gazette*, 28 April 1859.

and terrorizing white women who found Indians wandering around their houses when their menfolk were off at their labours.

*   *   *

Despite these problems right on the threshold of Victoria, where Douglas customarily resided, his main concern this year was not with Vancouver Island but with his second colony, burgeoning British Columbia. The dire prognostications of the pessimists had proved groundless and a great many miners did return from California to the goldfields this spring. And a host of newcomers arrived to try their luck on the Fraser for the first time. By the end of the previous year the miners had been working all the way from the bars south of Yale, where the gold dust was as fine as flour, to beyond "The Forks" (now the site of a hamlet called "Lytton") where the gold was in larger flakes, and still farther north to Alexandria. This year the prospectors pushed up the Fraser beyond Alexandria and fanned out along auriferous tributaries flowing from the eastward. By the end of 1859 we have miners finding gold at Horsefly River, and on Rip Van Winkle Bar on today's Van Winkle Creek. "General" Joel Palmer reported to an Oregonian newspaper that he had learnt of miners finding gold as far distant as the forks of the Quesnel River: "On this river and its two forks are, perhaps, the richest gold mines yet discovered in British Columbia."[29] And gold was being found elsewhere besides on the Fraser and its tributaries. Sergeant Compton, serving with the United States Boundary Commission, discovered gold where the Similkameen crossed the newly-defined border — he and the soldiers with him set about panning the gold as long as they could keep their secret. Then in October, farther east in the Boundary country, a Canadian named Adam Beam found gold on Rock Creek, and still another rush was under way. These new gold areas aroused excitement, but their yields were modest compared with the wealth pouring forth from the Fraser diggings and those on its newly-prospected tributaries.

What was life like for those who went up the Fraser? A great many prospectors, arriving at the wrong season when the bars were

[29] *Oregon Statesman* (Salem, Oregon), 14 Feb. 1860, p. 1.

under water, used up their meagre supplies but gained nothing. Others arriving when the season was right found all the known gold bars fully staked, discovered no new ones, and suffered appallingly. Lieut. Wilson, R.E., noted in his diary for September 16th this year:

Many poor fellows, sons of gentlemen, are nearly dying of starvation out here; one I met whilst down the river, who had been in the army, without a penny in his pocket, fishing for his dinner; it made me feel quite melancholy to see him.[30]

Even those making good returns led a hard, lonely life. This summer a versifier at Emory Bar wrote a doleful "Miners' Song on Frazer River". It begins:

> Where mighty waters foam and boil,
>   And rushing torrents roar,
> In Frazer River's northern soil,
>   Lies hid the golden ore.
>
> *Chorus*
>
> Far from home, far from home,
>   On Frazer River's shore,
> We labor hard, so does our bard,
>   To dig the golden ore.
>
> Far, far from home we miners roam,
>   We feel its joys no more;
> These we have sold for shining gold
>   On Frazer River's shore.
>
>   . . .   .
>
> In cabins rude, our daily food
>   Is quickly counted o'er;
> Beans, bread, salt meat, is all we eat —
>   And the cold earth is our floor.[31]

The matter of food was crucial. The farther inland the miners went, the more fantastic its price became. Little wonder! The "grub" all had to be carried (sometimes for hundreds of miles) on the backs of packtrain animals or, where mule trails were impossible, borne by

[30] *Mapping the Frontier*, p. 72.
[31] *Hutchings' California Magazine* 4 (1859): 108.

Indian packers. Everywhere the cry went up for a wagon road to link the goldfields with the seacoast.

Douglas heard the clamour and understood it. He had already, at a very substantial cost, put through the Harrison-Lillooet trail. Perhaps this should be rebuilt and widened to provide the needed wagon road. But, before embarking on this costly venture, Douglas wanted to satisfy himself that there was not some more direct and feasible route for a wagon road from saltwater to the gold areas on the upper Fraser.

The previous year he had sent Chief Trader J. W. McKay and a veteran Californian miner, William Downie, to explore the area between Pemberton and Howe Sound. If a road could be put through that way, it would greatly shorten the old route from Pemberton to the sea via Lillooet Lake, the Lillooet River valley, Harrison Lake and River, and the Fraser River. Thus McKay and Downie became the first white men to pass by Alta Lake, now dotted with recreation housing, and Whistler Mountain with its hordes of skiers. Successfully they followed the Cheakamus River down to the sea. McKay and Downie reported that a practicable Pemberton-Howe Sound route existed but concluded that, since so much work had already gone into the Pemberton-Harrison route, it would be best to stay with it.

This year, while Downie was upcoast prospecting for gold, Douglas had him also looking for a route inland from the head of either Jervis Inlet or Bute Inlet. After submitting a largely negative report, Downie went off on an unsuccessful expedition to find gold in the Queen Charlottes. The latter venture having failed, he embarked on one of the more notable exploring expeditions in the history of British Columbia. Leaving Fort Simpson on the last day of August, he entered the Skeena River and travelled up it, prospecting as he went. A little beyond the junction of the Skeena and the Bulkley Rivers, by today's Hazelton, Downie stopped and, close to Hagwilget Canyon, posted the following strangely prophetic sign:

> NOTICE — September 22, 1859. — I have this day located and claimed this pass, as the route of the Great Canadian and Pacific Railroad.[32]

---

[32] Downie, *Hunting for Gold*, p. 225.

Today the Canadian National Railway runs along this route.

From here Downie travelled overland across the great bend made by the upper Skeena and Babine Rivers and so reached Babine Lake. Travelling up Babine Lake he met, to his amazement, a white man. He was Gavin Hamilton of the Hudson's Bay Company, en route to purchase dried fish from the Skeena Indians. After travelling about seventy miles up Babine Lake, Downie made a portage to Stuart Lake. Here he ran into trouble:

> Arrived at Stuart's Lake, we found no means of crossing, no Indians to direct us, and no food to sustain us; nor had we any shot to enable us to kill ducks. We camped here three nights without food, sleeping the greater part of the time to stifle our hunger.[33]

At last one of the party found the wreck of an old Indian canoe, "split to pieces". Downie lashed logs to it and, in a last desperate move, started down the lake on that frail raft. Soon a wind came up. The resulting waves were breaking over the decrepit craft and its wretched occupants when a kindly Indian came to their rescue, took them into his lodge, fed them and took them to Fort St. James. From there it was a simple matter to follow the brigade route via Stuart River and the Nechako to Fort George and then travel swiftly down the Fraser until the gold area was reached. Downie had demonstrated that it was possible to get to the gold areas by way of the mouth of the Skeena. Douglas was enthusiastic about this discovery but, in fact, the distances were prohibitively long and this never became an access route to the Fraser goldfields.

For lack then of any thing better for a potential wagon road, Douglas was stuck with his Harrison-Lillooet route. Among those who travelled over it this spring and summer and submitted reports on it were Judge Begbie, Lieut. Mayne, R.N., and Lieut. Palmer, R.E. On March 28th of this year Begbie, using the precarious Fraser Canyon route, set out from Yale to travel the first assize circuit in British Columbia's interior. Since snow had closed the high trail which alone was usable for mules and horses, the Judge, Mr. Nicol the High Sheriff, and Mr. Bushby the Registrar and Assize Clerk, had to clamber on foot the length of the Fraser Canyon, with their

---

[33] *B.C. Papers* III:73.

Indian carriers, in order to reach Lytton. Begbie reported that from Yale to Quayome (Boston Bar) the route had been impassable for any animal except a man, a dog, or a goat. He and his companions had at times depended as much upon their hands as their feet. From Lytton, Begbie and his court officers travelled as far north as Fountain, then returned south to Lillooet. Here he was confronted with Indians and whites hurling charges and recriminations against each other. The whites were of course principally American but included a variety of nationalities. Among them Begbie could not find twelve British subjects. Thus he had to abandon his project to convene a grand jury to investigate the causes of friction. The Lillooet Indians made a very good impression on Begbie:

My impression of the Indian population is that they have far more natural intelligence, honesty, and good manners than the lowest class, say the agricultural and mining population, of any European country I ever visited, England included.[34]

From Lillooet Begbie travelled to the coast by the Lillooet-Harrison route. Passing two hot springs, he named them St. Agnes' Well and St. Alice's Well. (The latter is now the Harrison Hot Springs spa.) At the end of his journey, Begbie informed Governor Douglas that more bridges were needed on the Lillooet-Harrison route, and he characterized part of the trail as "a narrow, rocky, precipitous goat path". Still, he felt that the portage trails between the lakes could be rebuilt as wagon roads.

Next to report to Douglas was Lieut. R. C. Mayne, that spirited young naval lieutenant whom we last met accompanying Colonel Moody during Ned McGowan's War. This May, Douglas sent Mayne on an extended reconnaissance which took him up the Fraser Canyon and along the Thompson River, then over to Fort Kamloops by way of Nicola River and Lake. On his return, journeying by way of Kamloops Lake, Cache Creek, Bonaparte River, Hat Creek, Marble Canyon and Pavilion Lake, Mayne rejoined the

[34] *B.C. Papers* III:21. Begbie's efforts in describing and mapping the country through which he passed were not appreciated by the Royal Engineers. Lieut. Palmer described him as the "Arch Enemy", and went on to say: "I'm spiteful, but I can't help it. He has no business to be mapping when there are R.E.'s in the country." (*BCHQ* 11 (1947):198).

Fraser near Fountain, continued south along that river to Lillooet, and then travelled to the Coast via the Lillooet-Harrison route. Mayne's trip was a valuable one which yielded the best map so far made of the country over which he had travelled. It also provided him with colourful material when, on his return to England, he came to write his book, *Four Years in British Columbia and Vancouver Island*. Thus, at Kamloops he had an opportunity to meet the famous Shuswap chief Jean-Baptiste Lolo, generally nicknamed "St. Paul":

His face was a very fine one, although sickness and pain had worn it away terribly. His eyes were black, piercing, and restless; his cheekbones high, and the lips, naturally thin and close, had that white, compressed look which tells so surely of constant suffering.[35]

When Mayne remarked that Lolo, in his decayed health, must find it hard to rule over his people,

...he heard me with a grim smile, and for answer turned back his pillow, where a loaded gun and a naked sword lay ready to his hand.[36]

The invalid Lolo showed, in fact, unexpected reserves of strength. Rising from his bed, he mounted his horse, and accompanied Mayne on a ride to see the view from the top of a neighbouring mountain, which was forthwith named Mt. St. Paul in honour of the old chief. Moreover, Lolo insisted on accompanying Mayne on the next lap of his journey, that from Kamloops to Pavilion.

In his report to Governor Douglas, Mayne noted that regular packtrains were using the Harrison-Lillooet route, that boats were plying the lakes which formed parts of its course, and that a large restaurant had been built at the south end of Anderson Lake "for the entertainment of the muleteers".[37] He said little about the quality of the trail.

For a thorough report on the Harrison-Lillooet route, and its potentialities should a wagon route alternate with the water links, Douglas had to depend upon Lieut. H. Spencer Palmer of the Royal

---

[35] Mayne, *Four Years in B.C. & V.I.*, p. 119.
[36] *Ibid.*, p. 120.
[37] *B.C. Papers* III:33-37.

Engineers. In a detailed report submitted in July this year, Palmer gave a professional's appraisal of the work done in 1858. Port Douglas and Port Pemberton, key transshipment centres, had been built on quite unsuitable sites. The trail, again and again, simply would not do. Comments occurred such as:

> On this portion of the route the same general defects exist as on the first part, viz: —
> A bad line of trail both in general direction and in detail.
> Precipitous ascents and descents.
> Indifferent bridges and corduroys.
> A stony and irregular trail.[38]

True, several of the major bridges had been well constructed and Dozier's mile and a half of wagon road linking Seton and Anderson Lakes was conceded to be "very fair". But all this was minor. Palmer made it clear that construction of a wagon road would entail extensive rerouting, expensive blasting and a great deal of improving of the grades.

Douglas must have looked grim when he finished reading Palmer's report. Still, a wagon road would simply have to be put through. In fact already Colonel Moody, for the government, had signed a contract with Messrs. William Holmes and Walter Thomson to work, under the direction of the Royal Engineers, on a wagon road not less than twenty feet wide which would link the lakes which studded the Harrison-Lillooet route. The contractors were to be paid $200 for each mile of construction — partly in cash, partly in provisions, and partly in land grants.[39] To obtain the required cash payments Douglas would have to depend in good measure on an unpopular "mule tax".

The Royal Engineers were concerned with other roads and trails this year. Burrard Inlet, Colonel Moody realized, would probably become a major harbour for ships unwilling to come up to New Westminster because of the navigational hazard of the sandheads at the entrance to the Fraser. Accordingly Lieut. Blake, one of the Royal Marines from China, was asked to find a route connecting

---

[38] *B.C. Papers* III:42.
[39] For this contract, see PABC, E/B/H73.1.

the capital with the inlet. It was not easy country to traverse, but after a few arduous days Blake emerged on top of Burnaby Mountain where Simon Fraser University now looks down on Burrard Inlet and Indian Arm. This same year, using a rather different route, the Royal Engineers built a trail linking their camp at Sapperton with the head of Burrard Inlet at Port Moody. Subsequently this was widened for wagons and named the North Road.

*   *   *

The summer of this year saw a major confrontation between the British and the Americans: the so-called "Pig War". It all came about because of that ambiguity in the Treaty of Washington's provision that the Anglo-American boundary should follow "the middle of the channel which [south of the 49th parallel] separates the continent from Vancouver's Island". The drafters of the treaty had not known that there were three such channels. The most important of these proved to be Rosario Strait and a map published in 1848 by authority of the U.S. Senate duly showed the new boundary as passing down the centre of Rosario Strait.[40] As this line gave Britain the San Juan Islands, the Americans after second thoughts claimed the boundary should instead follow through Haro Strait, the first of the channels to be discovered and named. Thus the San Juan Archipelago would belong to the United States. Accordingly, after the Hudson's Bay Company founded a sheep ranch on San Juan Island in 1853, the Americans responded by appointing the first of a series of Deputy Collectors of Customs for the San Juans. These officers generally fled the islands in the face of Indian threats. Occasionally they were reduced to the humiliation of seeking safety at the HBC farm, where the Company's usual good relations with the tribes continued to prevail.

Such was the situation when in 1858-59 a few Americans, disappointed in their ventures in the Fraser goldfields, became squatters, establishing small farms on the islands. One of these men, Lyman

[40] PRO, FO925/1382. *Copy of Section of Map of Oregon and Upper California from the Surveys of John Charles Fremont and Other Authorities.* Drawn by Charles Preuss under the order of the Senate of the United States, Washington City, 1848.

Cutler, built a shack this April, planted a garden, and surrounded it with an inadequate fence, all in the middle of the HBC's best sheep run. Among its livestock, the Company had a fine black breeding boar which soon found its way through Cutler's ill-constructed fence and began rooting out his young potatoes. On June 15th, during one of these porcine raids, the furious Cutler shot the offending pig. Realizing the trouble that he had started, Cutler offered to recompense the Hudson's Bay Company with a pig of his own.

It so happened that San Juan Island provided Victorians with a favourite picnic site and at this juncture a holidaying party arrived from Victoria aboard the *Beaver*. Among the party was A. G. Dallas, the senior HBC man on the coast. According to Dallas, once he learned of the slaughter of the pig, he gave Cutler a severe rebuke and warning. According to the Americans, he told Cutler he must either pay $100 in compensation, or be taken to Victoria to stand trial. In any event, during the next few days the Americans persuaded themselves that the British were persecuting an American on American soil. Cutler filed a complaint before Paul K. Hubbs, the U.S. Deputy Collector, a man later well known to Dr. Helmcken, who characterized him as "one of the men so common in frontier life — a rowdy — ignorant hoodlum — who thought an American ought to be boastful and a bully — and he acted as such."[41] Hubbs drafted a report about the British action anent the pig, addressed the missive to his superior in the U.S. Customs Service, set off to deliver it, and en route arrived at Fort Bellingham where he told the militant Captain Pickett, U.S. Army, of Cutler's humiliating experience. Pickett informed Hubbs that he was expecting a visit within a few days from General William S. Harney, the recently-appointed officer commanding the Department of Oregon, and he declared that he would tell the General of the happenings on San Juan Island.

Enter now the villain of the piece: the bellicose, short-tempered Harney. In earlier years Harney had served in an Indian war in Florida, where he had perpetrated atrocities. In the American assault on Mexico he had been chief of cavalry under General Win-

---

[41] Blakey Smith, *Helmcken Reminiscences*, p. 164.

field Scott, but had proved so insubordinate that Scott had relieved him of his command. After Mexico had been crushed, Harney went back to Indian fighting, this time along the River Platte. Transferred to Utah for the hostilities with the Mormons, he was about to hang Brigham Young and the rest of the "apostles" when he was removed from his command. Then came his transfer to Oregon.

Harney was an extremist of the "Fifty-four forty or fight" breed. After arriving at Fort Bellingham and learning of the petty disturbance at San Juan, he may well have decided that here was a way of picking a war with Britain, one in which, aided by an insurrection of the thousands of Americans north of the boundary, he might win the Fraser goldfields for the United States and the American presidency for himself.[42] On July 8th Harney arrived at Victoria to see the enemy whom he would shortly confront. Governor Douglas extended to him the usual courtesies, complete with an artillery salute and a complimentary dinner. This same day Harney dashed off a despatch to General Scott, now Commander-in-Chief of the U.S. Army. This despatch declared:

The population of British Columbia is largely American and foreigners; comparatively few persons from the British Isles emigrate to this region. The English cannot·colonize successfully so near our people; they are too exacting. This, with the pressing necessities of our commerce on this coast, will induce them to yield, eventually, Vancouver's Island to our government. It is as important to the Pacific States as Cuba is to those on the Atlantic.[43]

Hoping to hasten these anticipated developments, Harney proceeded to San Juan Island. Here Harney told Hubbs to draw up a petition asking for military protection from the Indians, to collect all the signatures he could, and to send the document to him at his base.

Two or three weeks later, on the evening of 26 July 1859, when Hubbs was snoozing in his cabin on San Juan Island, there was a knocking on his door. At the threshold, in full uniform, stood a sergeant of the United States Army with news that, under General Harney's orders, Captain Pickett with about sixty soldiers from Fort

---

[42] For mention of Harney's political ambitions, see David Richardson, *Pig War Islands* (Eastsound, Washington, 1971), p. 83.

[43] Quoted by Richardson, *op. cit.*, p. 55.

Bellingham was taking possession of the island to protect American sovereignty. Hastening to the beach, Hubbs pointed out a suitable camping area for the soldiers aboard the steamer *Massachusetts* at anchor out in the bay.

July 27th saw two developments. The American troops landed — and H.M.S. *Satellite* put ashore Major John de Courcy, who raised the British flag and read his commission appointing him stipendiary magistrate with jurisdiction over San Juan. The next day H.M.S. *Tribune*, 31 guns, arrived on the scene with Governor Douglas' instructions to prevent any more American landings and to get the troops already on the island evacuated. Two days later C. J. Griffin, the manager of the HBC farm, formally asked Captain Pickett to remove his troops from British territory. Pickett refused, and the battle line was drawn. Fortunately Captain Hornby of the *Tribune*, bent on avoiding a crisis if at all possible, decided not to use force at this juncture, even though, with his numerically larger force and heavy guns, he could have easily annihilated Pickett and his men. On August 1st, H.M.S. *Satellite* joined H.M.S. *Tribune* at San Juan Island. Despite British warnings, the *Massachusetts*, back with American reinforcements, began to unload another company of troops and a few howitzers. Then, just as the British were about to open fire, H.M.S. *Plumper* arrived from Victoria with very important news: at a meeting of the Legislative Council of Vancouver Island, Captain Michael de Courcy, the Senior Naval Officer at Esquimalt, had prevailed against the bellicose Governor Douglas. Hostilities were not to be commenced despite the American provocation. Pickett was a brave, even a reckless officer. In the American Civil War he would win fame by leading "Pickett's Charge" at the Battle of Gettysburg. Nevertheless, unaware of the British decision to withhold fire, he was far from happy at finding himself confronted by the overwhelming force of the Royal Navy. To General Harney he sent a despatch declaring he and his men would be a mere "mouthful" for the British.

On August 5th Admiral Baynes arrived at Esquimalt with his flagship, H.M.S. *Ganges*. He immediately approved of the course taken by Captains Hornby and de Courcy in denying Harney the war that he so obviously wanted. Baynes pointed out that matters must proceed through the proper channels — issues concerning war or peace must be decided in London. London, once informed, got in touch with Washington. The American president, it transpired, had no more desire for war than the British prime minister. President Buchanan hastily sent General Scott out to the Pacific to take charge of the situation. Scott relieved Harney of his command and an agreement was reached under which both Britain and the United States would maintain a garrison, limited to a hundred men, on the disputed island. Governor Douglas, who still believed that the Yankees should have been forced off the island, made difficulties but finally, on 21 March 1860, Captain George Bazalgette of the Royal Marine Light Infantry landed with marines at Garrison Bay, while ten miles away an equal American force remained at Griffin Bay. And here the two contingents remained until 1872 when the matter was referred to the German Kaiser for arbitration. He turned the matter over to three German judges who, by a split decision, gave the San Juans to the United States.

*   *   *

This chronicle for 1859 should perhaps end with the high excitement which attended the Pig War. But many, many other events of the year have gone unmentioned. Let us briefly note a few of the more historic, bizarre, and amusing:

January saw the founding of the Victoria Philharmonic Society. At a large and enthusiastic meeting Judge Begbie was elected president and John Bayley conductor.

February saw some Anglo-American tension when Governor Douglas refused to have a salute fired to honour the birthday of that notorious rebel, George Washington. His action provoked a furious letter, signed "An American, Thank God", in the *Colonist*. A dinner was held at which the toast to Washington was defiantly proposed before that to the Queen. At an inconclusive public meeting, a debate was held concerning the merits of seeking annexation by the U.S.A.

A happier development this month saw the beginnings of the Royal Victoria Hospital (later the Royal Jubilee Hospital). A provisional committee, acting in response to an initiative from Governor Douglas, appealed for subscribers to finance the venture.

March saw the officers of the army and navy uniting for a festive occasion. Lieut. Wilson, R.E., has preserved a record of it for us:

March 15th.   We gave a ball to the fair ladies here; two of the Men-of-War, the *Satellite* & *Plumper*, with ourselves, determined to join together & give a grand ball to the ladies of Vancouver Island.
... The ladies were nicely dressed & some of them danced very well, though they would look much better if they would only learn to wear their crinoline properly. It is most lamentable to see the objects they make of themselves, some of the hoops being quite oval, whilst others had only one hoop rather high up, the remainder of the dress hanging down perpendicularly.... After the ball we had to escort most of the young ladies home for you must know that there are very few vehicles in this country & most of the progression is on foot. I conveyed some ladies home who lived about a mile out of the town. You would have laughed to have seen us at that time of night floundering through the mud, the ladies with their ball dresses tied up round their waists & long boots on.[44]

April saw the palisades of old Fort Victoria being torn down. The ladies of the surrounding settlement had complained that, when they dressed up in their hoop skirts to go shopping at the Hudson's Bay Company store in the fort, "the small wickets do not suit our expanding dresses". They had also tartly observed that they disliked having to ask the porter to open the great main gate to let them in. So the ladies triumphed where the Indians had failed, and the walls of Fort Victoria came tumbling down.

This same month saw Douglas writing to Sir Edward Bulwer Lytton about a problem of growing urgency:

The want of an Assay Office in the Colony is felt as a public inconvenience, and is no doubt highly detrimental to the commercial interests of the country. There being at present no means here of ascertaining the true commercial value of gold dust, the merchant to save himself from loss will only purchase it at a low rate, which the miner will not accept, or the gold dust is retained in the merchant's hands in deposit, until samples of it are sent and tested at San Francisco. Hundreds of

---

[44] *Mapping the Frontier*, p. 45.

miners worn out with the expense and delay so occasioned, fly in disgust with their gold to San Francisco.[45]

Lytton saw the cogency of Douglas' case; the Master of the Mint in England was consulted and, before the year ended, an Assay Office had been established in New Westminster.

May saw Douglas' relations with A. G. Dallas, a son-in-law and his successor as the head of the Hudson's Bay Company's affairs west of the Rockies, becoming a little less cordial. Dallas was annoyed that Douglas had declared Beacon Hill a public park. According to Dallas, the land with which Douglas had been so generous belonged to the HBC.

The 24th of May was the Queen's birthday, and was marked at Victoria by festivities in the newly-created Beacon Hill Park. New Westminster celebrated the great day at the Royal Engineers' camp. There the Royal Engineers paraded, H.M.S. *Plumper*, anchored in the Fraser, fired a royal salute, and Colonel Moody made a speech. A sports meet was held, with a bluejacket winning the prize at the top of the greasy pole. "The soldiers' wives and children were entertained with tea and cake, kindly provided by Mrs. Moody." Amor De Cosmos, reporting all this in his *British Colonist*, could not resist appending a nasty note:

HISTORICAL — Queen's birth-day, May 24, 1859, Lieut. Gov. Moody and lady cheered by the people at Queenborough.
　　Gov. Douglas, without his lady, at Beacon Hill Races, Victoria, almost unnoticed.[46]

June saw British Columbia's first lumber strike when the axemen working for the British Boundary Commission struck for higher wages.

July saw Douglas with his usual prescience noting that one of the mainland's greatest natural resources was "an almost unlimited amount of water power".

[45] Douglas to Lytton, 8 April 1859. *B.C. Papers* III:2.
[46] *Colonist*, 30 May 1859.

The great event of this month was the completion of the first parliament buildings at Victoria, the famous "birdcages" which remained in use until the 1890s. Their design offered clever Mr. De Cosmos an opportunity to display his wit:

No one with any pride of country would ever invite a stranger to examine our colonial buildings, except to show the way in which the Imperial treasury was attacked, during the existence of the Comic Colonies. A traveller placed suddenly among the buildings would consider that he was surrounded by a farm house, with an outhouse on each side, and a blacksmith shop and two barns in the rear. When he examined the gingerbread brick-finish — the want of style, order, or proportion in the architecture, he would assert that the proprietor and architect had been to town once in their lives, and had seen a town clock, and had bought a picture of a Chinese house, and that from these had been formed the plan of the six structures, now being constructed across James' Bay, at an expense of $90,000 when all is included.[47]

To give access to the new government buildings, a bridge had just been built where the esplanade in front of the Empress Hotel carries today's traffic. Fill had not yet reclaimed the site on which the Empress itself so confidently stands.

August saw increasing friction between Vancouver Island and her sister colony, British Columbia. The people of British Columbia resented Mr. Justice Begbie having his residence in Victoria, though the atmosphere was more genteel there than in raw little New Westminster. The Victorians, for their part, were annoyed that their hospital and their prison were having to accept patients and prisoners from the mainland.

September saw the Duke of Newcastle, who in June had succeeded Lytton as Colonial Secretary, sending a peremptory letter to Douglas, the consequence of continued British Columbia complaints about the non-residency of their principal civil servants:

It is stated that the Judge, the Colonial Secretary, his assistant, the Attorney-general, and the Treasurer, are all at present residing in Vancouver's Island.

[47] *Colonist*, 20 July 1859.

This state of things must be put an end to at once and the gentlemen in question must be warned that they must repair with the least practicable delay to the scene of their duties, or, if they decline to do so, must at once resign their situations.[48]

Douglas did not let the ducal letter make him change his course. After waiting a few months he smoothly replied that since he himself, as governor of both the colonies, had his seat in Victoria he needed to have British Columbia's Colonial Secretary and Attorney-General there with him for purposes of constant consultation. He added that it probably benefited B.C. to have its Treasurer in Victoria.[49] As a sop to His Grace, he reported that Begbie was preparing to take up permanent residence in British Columbia, something that Begbie failed to do.

There were other developments this September. On the 17th the invaluable Lieut. Palmer of the Royal Engineers set off from Fort Hope, by horseback, on an overland reconnaissance to Fort Colvile on the Columbia. For the first stretch, following the HBC brigade route as far as Tulameen, he had the company of Judge Begbie and his registrar, who were travelling on foot to Kamloops where assizes were to be held. Continuing eastward, the young lieutenant noted that military posts should be established at Keremeos and in the Okanagan Valley. Actually none were ever constructed along the frontier.

When Lieut. Palmer was only a few miles from Fort Colvile he had the unexpected pleasure of meeting another British army officer, Captain John Palliser. Since 1857, Palliser's "British North American Exploring Expedition" had been actively assessing the resources of the western prairies and looking for passes through the Rocky Mountains. Palliser and his men had made various excursions into British Columbia, and had agreed to converge on Fort Colvile in Washington Territory and travel home via Portland, Oregon. Palliser himself arrived at the Colvile rendezvous via Kootenay Lake and Kootenay River, reaching the Columbia at the site of modern Castlegar. Travelling down the Columbia, he stopped briefly at Fort

---

[48] Newcastle to Douglas, 5 Sept. 1859. *B.C. Papers* III:101.
[49] Douglas to Newcastle, 26 Jan. 1860. *B.C. Papers* III:95.

Shepherd, the Hudson's Bay Company's replacement for Fort Colvile, which now lay in American territory. Since there was actually some doubt as to whether or not Fort Shepherd had been built sufficiently to the north to be in British territory, Palliser took his own observations and found the new fort was just three-quarters of a mile within British Columbia.

While I was observing, a circle of Scotchmen, Americans, and Indians, surrounded me, anxiously awaiting my decision as to whether the [local gold] diggings were in the American territory or not; strange to say the Americans were quite as much pleased at my pronouncing in favour of Her Majesty, as the Scotchmen; and the Indians began cheering for King George.[50]

A wintry voyage down the Columbia ended for Palliser when his schooner got caught in the ice below Walla Walla. Realizing that his original plan was no longer feasible, Palliser headed for Victoria instead of Portland. Back in British territory, he joined a couple of other officers in giving a great ball at Victoria, visited Colonel Moody and his Royal Engineers at New Westminster, and then with his companion the geologist James Hector left for England via San Francisco and Panama.

October saw the Attorney-General of the two colonies, G. H. Cary, being arrested at Victoria as he stepped off the New Westminster boat. The charge was accepting a challenge to a duel, sent to him by the lawyer D. Babington Ring, who had also denounced him as a coward in the local press. Appearing before the local magistrate, Pemberton, the Attorney-General received his choice of posting a £500 bond to keep the peace or spending twelve months in jail. Angrily denouncing the proceedings as illegal, the Attorney-General opted for jail, but remained there very briefly.

November saw the Anglican parson at Hope announcing the establishment of the "Fort Hope Reading Room and Library". Books available ranged from the Waverley novels in twenty-four volumes

[50] Irene M. Spry, ed., *The Papers of The Palliser Expedition 1857-1860*, Champlain Society 44 (Toronto, 1968), pp. 478-79.

to *Bennett's Poultry Book*, and from "Youatt on Cattle" to Long-fellow's poems. Newspapers included, besides those published in the twin colonies, the *Illustrated London News*, *Punch*, the *Athenaeum*, the *New York Tribune*, and the *Alta California Bulletin*.

December saw the Royal Engineers celebrating Christmas at Sapperton. The sappers who had been cutting trails and building wharves were given a few days respite from their labours and on Christmas Eve, each with a candle in his hand, went carol singing around the new town. Christmas Day, under the pious Colonel Moody, saw only religious services, no festivities. On Boxing Day the non-commissioned officers, who at their own expense had built a small theatre, invited most of the inhabitants of New Westminster to a dance there. The next day the officers entertained guests at a grand dinner at their mess.

This same month A. G. Dallas, in Victoria, wrote to the Governor and Committee of the Hudson's Bay Company in London:

The fur trade will, I believe, soon become not worth carrying on at many of our posts, and I wish now simply to lay before the Governor and Committee the existing prospects for a commercial business in this colony.[51]

The first step was being taken in a process which would make most of today's British Columbians aware of the Hudson's Bay Company, alias "The Bay", merely as a chain of first-rate department stores.

*   *   *

Looking over our little calendar of monthly highlights, we note that it has been devoted almost entirely to respectable persons of the middle class. But what of disreputable persons of the lower class? Surely they should not be ignored! And so, to close this account of a memorable year, we print the following from the *Colonist* of 15 June 1859:

[51] HBCA, B. 226/b/19.

VICTORIA POLICE COURT

Before Justice Pemberton

Monday, June 13th.

A man in miner's costume, mysteriously to himself, lost his equilibrium, and was and was [*sic*] found in the gutter, last night, by one of the "blues" [police]. The "stone jug" brought him to his senses, and a fine to the court lightened his purse.

PATRICK, too fond of the "mountain dew" of Erin, and a frequenter of the dock, obtained leave of his Worship to occupy a small retreat, for seven days, to allow the vapor to disperse.

A French Canadian, who had been trying his hand with Paddy's weapon, a "sprig of shillelah" on the head of one [of] his countrymen, healed the wounds with a silver plaster.

JAMES MEAD, who has been sojourning in Victoria for a few days, felt pugilistically inclined, on Saturday night last; the liquor he had imbibed was distilled from malt, not from honey, from which the delicious liquor called *mead* is made. For his ignorance he had to pay forfeit.

SHOOTING CATTLE. — An express arrived while Court was sitting from Mr. McKenzie's Farm, with information that two fine bullocks had been shot and nearly the whole of the carcasses taken off. His worship immediately sent officers in pursuit.

Tuesday, June 14th

Indian No. 1, brought up for stealing from the tent of a man named Davis, a coat and $40, and making a clean sweep of boots, coffee, bacon, pots, &c. Deferred for further evidence.

Indian No. 2, was employed by a party who had just come down the river, to assist in carrying his blankets &c., to a tent. White-man paid red-skin for his labor, but the instinct of the Indian led him to a bush where he watched the egress of the parties from the tent and adopting the white-man's practice of "appropriation" took off the blankets and other moveables. Case adjourned.

Selling Whiskey to Indians: Officers Tease and Smith brought up a party this morning who were accused of selling whiskey to Indians. From information received they planted themselves in ambush. The informants (Indians) went forward to negotiate for a *whole barrel*, but the vender smelt a rat, and agreed to deliver it near the church at a certain hour, when the Argus-eyed detectives might be supposed to be under the influence of Morpheus. By the ingenuity of counsel the defendant proved an abili; but a summons was forthwith issued for his better half, who it seems transacted the affair. The case comes on again tomorrow.

Deserters: Eight man-o'-war's-men belonging to the ships now lying at Esquimalt, were handed over by the police authorities this morning, to a file of Marine Artillery and conveyed on board a barge to be taken to their respective ships. They had been in the woods since Sunday, without food. The party who had promised to procure a boat [to take them to the American shore] deceived them.

1860

The first Anglican Bishop of British Columbia — Unusual election tactics in Victoria — Indians evicted from Alberni sawmill site — Gold discovered in Cariboo — A boy's adventure on the Hope-Similkameen trail — The "Rock Creek War" — Governor Douglas' tour — A changing population — Achievements of the Royal Engineers — Gunboats Forward *and* Grappler *permanently stationed at Esquimalt — A pioneer geologist — More Indian troubles at Victoria — "Captain John" slain in Victoria jail.*

The year opened with the arrival on January 6th of the Rt. Rev. George Hills, the Church of England's first Bishop of British Columbia.[1] Consecrated in Westminster Abbey the previous February, he was the very model of an Anglican prelate, devout but not unworldly, with formidable energies and extended vision, a bishop who combined a commanding ecclesiastical presence with an appreciative eye for a good horse. His new diocese had been splendidly endowed by the very wealthy Miss Angela Burdett-Coutts. Whereas the Methodists had started with a gift of £500 from their English brethren, Bishop Hills began with £15,000 from Miss Coutts.

Arriving at Victoria, Bishop Hills found seven ordained Anglican clergy already in Vancouver Island and British Columbia: the Rev. Edward Cridge, the former Hudson's Bay Company chaplain at Fort Victoria; the Rev. W. Burton Crickmer, at Fort Langley but soon to move to Yale; three missionaries sent out by the Society for the Propagation of the Gospel (the Rev. Richard Dowson, the Rev. James Gamage, and the Rev. A. St.D. F. Pringle); and finally two other clergymen who had been recruited by himself but had arrived

---

[1] Frank A. Peake, *The Anglican Church in British Columbia* (Vancouver, 1959), p. 19.

ahead of him — the Rev. R. J. Dundas and the Rev. John Sheepshanks. A few months later they were joined by two further recruits
enlisted by the Bishop and paid for out of the diocese's munificent
endowment: the Rev. A. C. Garrett and the Rev. R. L. Lowe.[2]

Spring saw the new bishop visiting the mainland colony where,
on May 22nd, he laid the cornerstone for Holy Trinity Church at
New Westminster. Then he started inland. At Hope he celebrated
Holy Communion in the presence of Governor Douglas and Judge
Begbie. Then he went on to Yale, where he was depressed to find
only three communicants. Journeying on via Lytton to Lillooet, he
paused for a few days at the latter settlement to preach to the
Indians. His companion, the Rev. John Sheepshanks, has left us an
amusing account of the ecclesiastical return journey through the
Fraser Canyon:

> First came the tall, grave, dignified Bishop. So tall was he, and so
> long of limb, that riding on a big horse, if he dropped his whip on the
> ground, he could pick it up while still in the saddle.
>
> Next came the young presbyter [Sheepshanks], his chaplain, by no
> means so correct in his appearance, in wide-awake, serge coat, clerical
> tie — which he never abandoned — corduroy trousers, and hob-nailed
> boots.
>
> Next came "the faithful William," the Bishop's servant, not much
> relishing the rough work of missionary travel, and the cavalcade wound
> up with two packed horses, and the packer.[3]

At times His Lordship's "English clerical ideas of propriety" were a
little offended, not least by his cheerful chaplain's habit of whistling
popular songs while they were on the trail. He reproved the young
man, saying that such conduct might indeed be termed "unclerical".
Thereafter Sheepshanks did his whistling while taking a walk by
himself after mealtime. Finally their trip ended, with Sheepshanks
returning to his parish at New Westminster, and the Bishop returning to Victoria where Christ Church, the modest edifice begun by
Staines and completed by Cridge, served as his cathedral.

* * *

[2] *Ibid.*, p. 28.

[3] D. Wallace Duthie, ed., *A Bishop in the Rough* (London, 1909), p. 45.

The arrival from England of Bishop Hills received less attention than might have been expected because Victoria at that time was in the midst of an exciting election campaign. Victoria was a two-seat riding and everybody could see that there would be a close race between G. H. Cary, the Attorney-General (and the "Establishment" candidate) ; Selim Franklin, an independent; and Amor De Cosmos, editor of the *Colonist*, running on a reform ticket.

An amusing episode marked the nomination meeting:

Mr. Cary, though first in the field as a candidate, and first nominated at the hustings, refused to speak until after Mr. De Cosmos, and showed a most refined taste as well as excellent breeding, in calling out "Smith!" "Amor!" "Cupid!". Lawyer-like he wished to obtain by clever manoeuvre *the last word*.[4]

Possibly De Cosmos would have got elected had not the Attorney-General resorted to a remarkable tactic. Satisfied that Victoria's Negro immigrants were against De Cosmos, he ruled that, since the U.S. Supreme Court had declared that slaves could not be American citizens, eighteen of the coloured community had never held citizenship in any other country and therefore could be immediately recognized as British subjects, even though they had been in the colony something less than two years, not the seven years required before an alien could become naturalized. The tactic worked. The election results were:

Cary	137
Franklin	106
De Cosmos	91

Cary and Franklin were declared elected.

In August Amor De Cosmos tried to get elected in a by-election held for the Esquimalt riding. The "Establishment" candidate here was George Tomline Gordon, the Colonial Treasurer, and De Cosmos was the only other nominee. This time the Attorney-General had a new trick to play. Cary noted that, although De Cosmos had been born a British subject in Nova Scotia under the plain name of William Smith, while in the United States he had changed his name to Amor De Cosmos. But was a Californian change of name valid in

---

4 *Colonist*, 7 Jan. 1860.

22. Colonel Richard Clement
Moody, R.E.

23. Chief Justice
Sir Matthew Baillie Begbie

24. The Rt. Rev. George Hills,
Bishop of British Columbia

25. Amor De Cosmos

26. The Royal Engineers' Camp, Sapperton

27. View of New Westminster in the 1860s

28. Hyack Volunteer Fire Brigade, New Westminster

29. Coal Workings and Bastion at Nanaimo

30. The Town of Hope

31. View of Yale

British territory? Ostensibly to save De Cosmos from any possible disqualification due to election under his Californian name, the Attorney-General ruled that on election day, at the open poll, De Cosmos' supporters must declare their vote to be for "Smith, commonly known as De Cosmos". Election day came. Man by man the tiny electorate of Esquimalt arose and called out either "Gordon" or "Smith, commonly known as De Cosmos". The voting seemed completed, with Gordon in receipt of 11 votes and Smith, commonly known as De Cosmos, having 10, when, at the last moment, the "liberals" dragged to the meeting one bashful citizen, sympathetic to their cause but shy of declaring his vote. Asked by the Sheriff for his vote, the young man in his agitation cried out "De Cosmos". A groan went up from those who had brought him. Calmly the sheriff made his return:

Gordon	11
Smith, commonly known as De Cosmos	10
De Cosmos	1

and declared Gordon elected.[5]

The general election in January had produced a cruel but not unamusing hoax. Captain Langford, manager of the Esquimalt Farm at Colwood maintained by the HBC's subsidiary the Puget's Sound Agricultural Company, had become well-known both for his aversion to work and his inclination to entertain lavishly at the Company's expense. Somebody, not impossibly Judge Begbie, as a New Year's Day joke, got the government printer to run off placards carrying an announcement, ostensibly by Langford, declaring his candidacy in the coming election. The placards with their message went up all over town. They made wonderful reading:

To the Electors of Victoria.

Gentlemen,

Some injudicious person, assuming my name, has put forward in answer to your requisition, a long winded and spiteful address, containing many things which I, of course, should not like to have repeated, among other things, His Excellency's complaint that he was without any intelligent assistance, when I was at his elbow; a statement that I

5 *Colonist*, 14 Aug. 1860.

required a full discussion of the whole subject of Taxation, before I could form any opinion in reference to it; and other matters showing a shallowness of comprehension and an envious disposition, which I really ought to be ashamed of.

The easiest way for you, gentlemen, to judge of my merits, is to make a short statement of what I am, and what I have done.

I came here about eight years ago, the hired servant of the Puget Sound Company, for the wages of about Six Dollars a week, and my board and lodging; the privileges of board and lodging were also extended to my wife and family, in consideration of the Company's having the benefit of their labor on the Farm of which I was to have the charge.

I was brought out here at the expense of the Company: I was placed on the Farm I now occupy, bought by the Company, stocked by the Company, improved by labor supplied by the Company entirely. In fact, I have not been put to penny expense since my arrival in the Colony. The boots I wear, and the mutton I and my family and guests eat, have been wholly supplied at the expense of the Company; and I flatter myself that the Colonial reputation for hospitality, as displayed by me at the expense of the Company, has not been allowed to fall into disrepute. I have given large entertainments, kept riding horses, and other means of amusement for myself and my guests: in fact I may say, that I and they, have eaten, driven, and ridden the Company for several years, and a very useful animal it has proved, though its ears, gentlemen, are rather long.

All this time I was and am the Farm-Bailiff of the Puget Sound Company, at wages of £60, ($300,) per annum, and board, a position I value much too highly to vacate until I shall be kicked out of it. I have refused to render any account, any intelligible account, of my stewardship: in fact I had kept no accounts, that I, or anybody else, could make head or tail of. When requested to give satisfactory explanations, I told my owners pretty squarely, that they should have no satisfaction except that usual among gentlemen; and as I knew nobody would call me out and pistol me, I commenced a system of abuse with which you are doubtless tolerably well acquainted; at the same time currying popularity with my farm servants, by letting them eat and drink, play or work, just as they liked, which I could do cheap, as the Company pays for all.

I am sorry to say, however, gentlemen, that although pretty jolly just now, I have not been careful enough to keep a qualification for myself for the House of Assembly, although I have run my owners many thousands of pounds in debt. However, I hope to bnlly [sic] them out of their property entirely, — "improve" them out of their land. How I propose to do this, seeing that all the land, capital, stock, and labor, has been provided by them, is a secret. In the meantime, if I should not be fortunate enough to nail a qualification before the Election, I shall do as I did before, hand in a protest against the grinding, despotic tyrany, which requires a qualification at all, notwithstanding Runnymead and Rule Britannia: The House, I doubt not, will allow me to sit, and I shall be too happy to serve you as I have served my present employers. I have the honor to be, gentlemen,

Your most obedient

E. E. Longford [sic][6]

Captain Langford was a proud man. He took the humiliation to heart and sought redress by going to law. The result was disastrous. Chief Justice Cameron ruled that Langford must pay £90 costs for a non-suit. Langford being unable to pay, a bailiff seized his household effects. In July a despairing Langford appealed to Governor Douglas, declaring that he had only:

... attempted to seek redress for a cowardly and infamous attack on my *private* character dragging the names of my Wife & daughters before the public and attempting to stigmatize our poverty as a crime.[7]

Apparently Douglas did not intervene, and the Langfords left the colony for good on 12 January 1861.

*   *   *

In April 1860 there arrived in Victoria a newcomer who was destined to play a significant role in British Columbia's early history, both as an Indian agent and commissioner and as our first agent-general in London. He was Gilbert Malcolm Sproat, sent by the London firm of Anderson and Company to establish a sawmill on Vancouver Island. In August, with two armed vessels the *Woodpecker* and the *Meg Merrilies* and fifty men, Sproat arrived at the head of Alberni Inlet to establish his mill in the area where Mac-Millan Bloedel now have their enormous wood products operation. Unfortunately Sproat found the site occupied by an Indian summer encampment and so he informed the local chief that he would have

---

[6] Sydney G. Pettit, "The Trials of E. E. Langford", *BCHQ* 17 (1953):21-22 & plate facing p. 17. (Also PABC, E/B/L26.)

[7] PABC, C/AA/10/L26.

to move his people "as we had bought all the surrounding land from the Queen of England, and wished to occupy the site for a particular purpose." The chief did not see why the land which belonged to his band should be sold to the newcomers by the Queen of England and, in order to avoid trouble, Sproat agreed to buy the land once more, this time from the Indians in return for trade goods worth some £20. Despite acceptance of this payment the Alberni Indians, instead of moving their village, proceeded to erect barricades around it, to bring out guns and pikes, and to cover their faces with black war paint. Sproat then pointed out that, since he had cannon on his boats, the natives were hardly likely to defeat him in any battle. Aware of the devastation that the white man could inflict with his great guns, the Indians then moved to another camping place, no great distance off. A few days later Sproat called on the leaders of the Albernis in their new home. Later, in his book *Scenes and Studies of Savage Life,* Sproat would include an account of the ensuing interview.

"Chiefs of the Seshahts," said I on entering, "are you well; are your women in health; are your children hearty; do your people get plenty of fish and fruits?"

"Yes," answered an old man, "our families are well, our people have plenty of food; but how long this will last we know not. We see your ships, and hear things that make our hearts grow faint. They say that more King-George-men will soon be here, and will take our land, our firewood, our fishing grounds; that we shall be placed on a little spot, and shall have to do everything according to the fancies of the King-George-men."

"Do you believe all this?" I asked.

"We want your information," said the speaker.

"Then," answered I, "it is true that more King-George-men (as they call the English) are coming: they will soon be here; but your land will be bought at a fair price."

"We do not wish to sell our land nor our water; let your friends stay in their own country."

To which I rejoined: "My great chief, the high chief of the King-George-men, seeing that you do not work your land, orders that you shall sell it. It is of no use to you. The trees you do not need; you will fish and hunt as you do now, and collect firewood, planks for your houses, and cedar for your canoes. The white man will give you work, and buy your fish and oil."

"Ah, but we don't care to do as the white men wish."

"Whether or not," said I, "the white men will come. All your people know that they are your superiors; they make the things which you value. You cannot make muskets, blankets, or bread. The white men will teach your children to read printing, and to be like themselves."

"We do not want the white man. He steals what we have. We wish to live as we are."[8]

*   *   *

The founding of the Alberni sawmill, a large one cutting 18,000 feet of lumber a day and employing some seventy white men, was only part of the accelerating growth of the lumbering industry at this period. Agriculture was on the increase also, though the number of new farms being cleared was not impressive. But despite these developments, the economies of both Vancouver Island and British Columbia continued to rest upon a single commodity — gold. True, there were fewer miners than in the days of "Fraser Fever", and the white miners had largely abandoned to Chinese and Indians the Fraser Canyon bars which were considered pretty much worked out. Consequently, of the twenty-four business firms formerly active at Hope, only three survived this spring. The centre of activity had moved to the "upper country" extending from Fort Alexandria eastward to Quesnel Forks. Here there was no lack of gold — not the fine "flour gold" dust of the lower Fraser but heavy flakes and even nuggets.

This year a new name was heard: CARIBOO! The vanguard of miners had reached Cariboo Lake and were striking it very rich on the creeks flowing into it. On September 11th, under a caption "The Cariboo Diggings", the *Colonist* carried a story that read in part:

The Cariboo Country

Lays from thirty to sixty miles above the [Quesnel] Forks, in a north east direction, and comprises a portion of the country drained by the waters of the North Fork. Twenty-five miles up the North Fork, there is a lake four miles in length; one mile above again, one twelve miles long. Into these lakes from the north, some five streams empty, two of which have been prospected and found to be rich. The two prospected have been manned [named?] Harvey's and Keethley's Creeks.

[8] G. M. Sproat, *Scenes and Studies of Savage Life* (London, 1868), pp. 3-4.

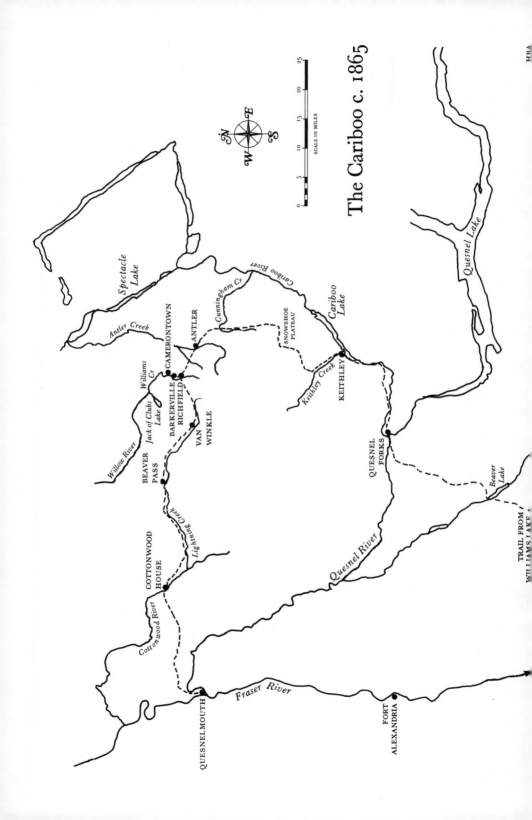

The Cariboo c. 1865

SCALE IN MILES

HBA

Spectacle Lake

Antler Creek

Cunningham Cr

Cariboo River

CAMERONTOWN

ANTLER

Williams Cr

SNOWSHOE PLATEAU

BARKERVILLE
RICHFIELD

Jack of Clubs Lake

Keithley Creek

Cariboo Lake

Beaver River

VAN WINKLE

KEITHLEY

Willow River

BEAVER PASS

QUESNEL FORKS

COTTONWOOD HOUSE

Lightning Creek

Beaver Lake

Cottonwood River

Quesnel River

TRAIL FROM WILLIAMS LAKE

QUESNELMOUTH

Fraser River

FORT ALEXANDRIA

Quesnel Lake

$400 PER DAY TO THE HAND!

On Harvey's Creek men are making from eight dollars to $50 per day to the hand, and in some cases, much more. Harvey & Co. (five men) four days ago, cleaned up and found they had made $2,100 for six days' work, of as pretty gold as ever came out of the ground.[9]

The *Colonist* went on to report that on the Sebastopol claim on Keithley Creek seventy buckets of "dirt" had yielded $140, a very handsome return indeed in terms of the values of the day.

The newly-staked Cariboo creeks, the Quesnel River and its tributaries, the Horsefly diggings, the older ones on the upper Fraser and in the Fraser Canyon, were not the only sources for the torrent of gold that poured out of British Columbia this year. Hundreds of men were at work along the Similkameen River, whipsawing rough planks, constructing flumes, sluicing out the gold from the bars. It was a hard life in a world in which boys quickly became men. Thus we have the story of young Willie Gray:

When I was 13 years old we moved to British Columbia. This was in 1858. I began working with canoes and bateaux on the Fraser river. A good many people got drowned on the Fraser river, as it is a dangerous stream, but father used to say that danger was all in a day's work, and one must take what comes. . . .

In the summer of 1860 we crossed the mountains to the Similkameen river to prospect for gold. We found gold on the south fork. Father built two rockers, and for the next two months we kept busy. At the end of that time our supplies were running very short. I was 13 [15?] years old, and father decided I was old enough to assume responsibility, so he sent me to Fort Hope to secure supplies. There was only an Indian trail, but I knew the general direction. I had to ford streams and cross rivers, but I had learned to swim when I was 8 years old, so that didn't bother me. As we were short of provisions, I only took two sandwiches, thinking I could make the 140 miles within two days. I had a good riding horse, and I was going to ride from daylight to dark. I had not gone over 20 miles when a rather hard character in that country called "Big Jim" met me in the trail. He stopped me and said, "Have you got anything to eat?" I told him I only had two sandwiches. He said, "I haven't had anything to eat for two days. Hand me those sandwiches." I looked at him and concluded it was safest to give him the sandwiches. He bolted them down, and grumbled because I had no more. He was

[9] *Colonist*, 11 Sept. 1860.

on his way out to Fort Hope, but his horse was almost worn out. I wanted to go by, but he wouldn't let me. He said, "Oh, no you don't — we will stay together for company. Your horse is a good deal fresher than mine, and I may need him."

As we made our way across a high cliff, his horse lost its balance and fell, striking the rocks more than 200 feet below. He made me get off my horse and mounted mine. We rode and tied[10] from there on in to Fort Hope. It took us four and a half days, and all we had to eat during that time was a foolhen that he knocked down. My clothes were almost torn to shreds.

When I got home, I went in the back door. My mother saw me. She raised her hands above her head and said, "Oh, Willie, what has happened to your father?" I told her my father was all right, but I was nearly starved. I secured two horses and loaded them with bacon and beans, rice and other supplies, and started back for our camp. When some prospectors in town learned that we were making $10 a day to the man, they followed me to our camp.[11]

Let us leave Willie Gray and those who followed him to the Similkameen, and move eastward to the Rock Creek diggings, discovered the previous year but only now being really worked. This summer the *Colonist* ran a triumphant article with the headline:

THE BEST NEWS YET
ROCK CREEK A SUCCESS

From $20 to $100 per day to the hand[12]

Rock Creek presented a very ticklish problem for Governor Douglas. The new diggings were only two or three miles north of the international boundary and prospectors flooded in from the United States. The merchants who supplied the miners' needs brought in their stock from south of the line, totally ignoring the customs duties payable at the border — not that there was any official there to

---

10 "Ride and tie" was a procedure used when there were two men with only one horse. One man started riding down the trail, the other following behind on foot. When the first man had travelled a certain distance he dismounted, tied the horse to a tree, and continued on foot. When the second man reached the tethered horse he mounted it and rode on until he overtook the first man, when again the first man got the horse for the next stretch, and so the procedure continued for the duration of the journey.

11 Fred Lockley, "Reminiscences of Capt. W. P. Gray", *Quarterly of Oregon Historical Society* 14 (1913):324-26.

12 *Colonist*, 14 Aug. 1860.

32.   A Way-side House — Arrival of Miners

33.   A Way-side House at Midnight

34. Tenas Lake (Little Lillooet Lake) on the Harrison-Lillooet Route

35. Lillooet

36.   Miner's Cabin, Williams Creek, Cariboo

37.   Bill Phinney working at Old Caledonia Mine, Cariboo

38. Rafting through the Grand Canyon of the Fraser

39. Lord Milton and Dr. Cheadle with guides

collect them! Governor Douglas promptly decided on one thing — the newcomers at Rock Creek would have to take out British Columbia mining licences, that minimal recognition of British sovereignty upon which he always insisted. Accordingly, the Governor appointed Peter O'Reilly gold commissioner and despatched him to Rock Creek. The miners, resentful that the gold lay in that "darned English country", flatly refused either to take out mining licences or to file their claims with O'Reilly. When they passed from snarling verbal abuse to hurling stones, O'Reilly retreated to the coast and reported to Governor Douglas. News of the "Rock Creek War" reached Douglas in Victoria just when His Excellency was preparing to make a tour on the mainland. Plainly he would have to extend his itinerary to Rock Creek and attend to the trouble there.

On August 28th Douglas left Victoria. Sticking to his original plans, he boarded the steamer *Colonel Moody* at New Westminster, leaving it at Port Douglas at the head of Harrison Lake. Rock Creek would come later in the tour.

Douglas had a special reason for wanting to inspect the way between Port Douglas and Lillooet. Following his decision to convert into wagon roads those horse trails which linked the water sections of this route, he had set the Royal Engineers, assisted by Royal Marines and civilian labourers, to commence the necessary road-building. Now he wanted to see how the work was progressing. Journeying north from Port Douglas, he found that the Royal Engineers had completed their wagon road for most of the twenty-eight miles to Tenas or Little Lillooet Lake. Five and a half miles in a rowboat, and an additional mile and a half over the excellent Decker's Portage, brought him to Lillooet Lake. Here a little steamboat, identified variously as the *Marsella*, *Marzella*, *Marzelle* or *Martzell*, took him the sixteen miles up to Port Pemberton. Having travelled some thirty-four miles farther via the Birkenhead ("Mosquito") Portage to Anderson Lake, Douglas estimated that it would cost about $450 a mile to use the expensive Royal Engineers to replace this trail with a wagon road. Douglas made the sixteen miles down Anderson Lake aboard the new steamer *Lady of the Lake*. He then walked the mile and a half to Seton Lake. Here he found the steamer *Champion* laid up for repairs and had to use a small boat to complete his final sixteen or so miles of water travel. The Governor soon covered the last three miles by land to Cayoosh, otherwise known as Lillooet. Here on September 9th he read the church service, complacently noting in his journal, "Congregation large. Very orderly & Attentive".[13]

After several days at Lillooet, partly spent in reassuring the Indians that, unlike their brothers in the United States, they would not be expelled from their traditional lands, Governor Douglas travelled to Lytton. He here authorized the expenditure of £100 to open up a trail linking Lytton with the Bonaparte River, by Hat Creek. Then, after journeying a short distance up the Thompson, Governor Douglas followed the Nicola River to Nicola Lake, finding the country en route "sweetly pretty". From Nicola Lake the Governor travelled south to the newly-established settlement at Vermilion Forks. To this he gave the name of "Princetown", (now Princeton) in honour of H.R.H. the Prince of Wales, who was currently visiting the eastern colony of Canada.

Finally came the crucial trip to Rock Creek and its turbulent American miners who had driven out His Excellency's gold commissioner. Passing Keremeos and not failing to spot the good land there, he continued to Osoyoos Lake, visiting a British Boundary Commission camp along the way. Then it was up over Anarchist Mountain, and along a winding track amid the hills and glens of the boundary country until he descended into the hot valley where the Rock Creek miners were at work. In his diary for September 25th Douglas curtly noted: "Visited the town this morning, spoke to the miners and returned to camp."[14] For a more detailed account we may turn to an eyewitness, Robert Stevenson.[15] According to Stevenson, Douglas came into the camp wearing his full official uniform,

[13] The above account of Douglas' journey from Port Douglas is based upon that he gives in his despatch to the Duke of Newcastle, dated 9 October 1860 (*B.C. Papers* IV:22-26), supplemented by that in Douglas' journal kept during the trip, now in the Provincial Archives of British Columbia (MS. B 20 1858, a somewhat miscellaneous item containing entries up to the summer of 1861). There are a number of minor inconsistencies between the two accounts. The distances given are those cited by Douglas.

[14] For this diary, see fn. 13 above.

[15] Walkem, *Stories of Early B.C.*, pp. 255-56.

accompanied by Cox, his new gold commissioner for the area, and Arthur Bushby, a clerk. Earlier the miners had refused to meet with Douglas, but now some three hundred assembled. First His Excellency offered them some good news — a wagon road would be put through from Hope, and the Kettle River would be bridged. But then he had a warning: either they would comply with the British law or he would visit them again, this time with five hundred marines. At the end of his speech Douglas asked his audience to wait inside the unfinished saloon which had been their meeting-place until he could get to the door and shake each man by the hand as he left. At this gesture, the miners burst into applause and the Rock Creek War was over.

On his return journey to Hope via Princeton, Douglas met Edgar Dewdney, who was just completing the government's new Dewdney Trail linking Hope with Princeton. This was "a good hard trail, without making any ascent or descent of consequence".[16] Douglas discussed with Dewdney the cost of converting his trail into a wagon road.

In October, His Excellency was back in Victoria. Here he was once more able to devote himself to such local duties as visiting the jail, ordering the confiscation of all the prisoners' novels, and sternly directing that the inmates be permitted only works "of a strictly religious or instructive character".[17]

*   *   *

The Rock Creek War was not the only incident that threatened trouble with the Americans this year. Late in January, Lieut. McKibben, U.S. Army, marched across the boundary, entered Fort Langley with a sergeant's guard, seized two men (apparently American deserters) and marched them back to the U.S. Army post at Semiahmoo. Speculation was that General Harney, the villain in the San Juan melodrama and still in command during an unsuccess-

---

[16] This description comes from a letter from Dallas to Angus Macdonald at Fort Colvile, 10 Oct. 1860, describing his recent passage over the Dewdney Trail, and noting that the rigours of the old brigade route over Manson Mountain are now a thing of the past. HBCA, B.226/b/19.

[17] "Won't Let Them Read Novels", *Colonist*, 24 March 1860.

ful appeal to Washington to countermand his dismissal, had sent up Lieut. McKibben for one last try at provoking war with Britain.

British Columbian anger over the McKibben incident was matched this September by American wrath over a decision handed down by Chief Justice Cameron of Vancouver Island. The centre of this particular storm was a mulatto slave, named Charles, owned by Major James Tilton of Olympia, Washington Territory. Charles had learned that there was no slavery up in the British territory, and decided to escape to the land of the free. Accordingly, he stowed away aboard the American ship *Eliza Anderson* on one of her regular runs from Olympia to Victoria. Unfortunately for him, he was discovered while the ship was still at sea and was locked in a cabin, to remain a prisoner until the ship returned to Olympia and his master could reclaim him. Somehow, while the *Eliza Anderson* was at Victoria, word got around about the boy locked up on board. A delegation from the Negro community called on Cary, the Attorney-General, who promptly issued a writ of Habeas Corpus to Sheriff Harris, ordering him to bring Charles before the Supreme Court of Vancouver Island where the legality of his imprisonment could be put to the test. The Sheriff boarded the *Eliza Anderson* and, after a little trouble, came ashore with the boy.

Appearing in person as counsel for Charles, Attorney-General Cary first declared that, since the *Eliza Anderson* was indubitably in a British port, a British sheriff had every right to go aboard and take into his custody the young Negro. In any event, as a consequence of Sheriff Harris' action, Charles had been brought ashore, and was at this very moment on British soil. Then Cary played his trump card: in 1772 Lord Mansfield in a famous decision had ruled that, slavery being repugnant to British law, any slave became a free man once he touched British soil. Captain Fleming also present in court denounced the whole proceedings as illegal under international law, but Chief Justice Cameron held otherwise, and ordered Charles set free. The Olympia *Pioneer and Democrat*, when it learned of Chief Justice Cameron's decision, devoted two and a half columns to an editorial attacking it.[18]

[18] For a fuller treatment of the Charles Case, see Robie L. Reid, "How One Slave Became Free", *BCHQ* 6 (1942):251-56.

When July 4th came around this year and the British population in Victoria and New Westminster braced themselves for the usual American volleys of gunfire and rhetoric, they found that the day passed off singularly quietly. Suddenly they realized that the American element had perceptibly dwindled. Taking the place of the Yankees were an increasing number of settlers and miners from Ontario and Britain, as well as a notable influx of Chinese. Writing from New Westminster on this same July 4th, the Rev. Edward White noted the mounting flow of Oriental immigration:

The Chinese are still coming into the Colony in great numbers. Within the last two weeks over 700 have arrived, and others are on the way. Some come from California, but the greater portion come direct from China. . . . Leading Chinese merchants say that we shall have 50,000 from their country in British Columbia before two years are passed.[19]

Suddenly a new prospect loomed. British Columbia might be saved from the Americans only to be lost to the Chinese!

New Westminster was prospering this year, and the Rev. Mr. White, apart from ominously noting the Chinese influx, could find plenty to encourage him. New arrivals from Canada West (Ontario) were beginning to impart a Canadian tone to New Westminster, exhibiting "liberality of sentiment and generosity of heart".[20] The newcomers, accustomed to responsible government in the colonies down East, did not take kindly to Douglas' "despotism". They were considerably heartened in their fight for "liberal government" when, on July 16th, New Westminster became the first incorporated city in British Columbia and so achieved some degree of representative government. Victorians might jeer at New Westminster with its half-cleared streets as the "City of Stumps", but the little town was growing quickly. More and more government offices were being opened, including the Treasury Department which had lingered as long as possible outside the colony in the more comfortable world of Victoria. Moreover for the first time goods were being unloaded at the wharves at New Westminster, brought in by ships which had

---

[19] *Christian Guardian*, 15 Aug. 1860, p. 129.

[20] Letter of Rev. A. Browning. *Christian Guardian*, 23 May 1860, p. 82.

sailed directly from San Francisco, thus eliminating costly transshipment at Victoria. A couple of months after New Westminster's
incorporation, the Rev. Mr. White succinctly described the scope of
the "city":

We have ten stores, (one of them a large wholesale establishment,)
eight saloons, five hotels and other boarding houses, one blacksmith,
one watchmaker, one shoemaker, one tinsmith, one bakery, and two
butcher shops; 3 carpenter shops, one law office, and two real estate
d[itt]o. We have a custom house, treasury and essay [sic] buildings, a
court house and jail, and a post office. We have about twenty private
residences, and as many tents and shanties.[21]

White placed New Westminster's population at about 250, plus a
"floating" element. He did not include as part of New Westminster
the neighbouring village of Sapperton where, dominated by the large
house built for Colonel Moody, the Royal Engineers had their base.

*   *   *

Relations between Colonel Moody and Governor Douglas deterio-
rated this year. Upon his arrival Colonel Moody had been sworn in
as Lieutenant-Governor of British Columbia, and had everywhere
been spoken of as the Lieutenant-Governor. The title no doubt was
dear to Moody who, having formerly been Governor of the Falkland
Islands, undoubtedly entertained ambitions of becoming Governor
of British Columbia at some future date when Douglas might revert
to being the governor only of Vancouver Island. Certainly Douglas
during the early months of 1859 was meticulous in referring to
Moody as the "Lieutenant-Governor". But then Lytton, in a despatch to Douglas, pointed out that use of this title was improper
since Moody held merely a *dormant* commission as lieutenant-
governor, one which would come into effect only in the event of
Douglas' own death or disability. Once Douglas received this message, his whole tone towards Moody changed. He saw himself as
dealing, not with a colleague of importance approaching his own,
but with a subordinate whose influence in England was less than he
had imagined. Moody's position became much more difficult, and

---

[21] *Christian Guardian*, 31 Oct. 1860, p. 174.

he was prevented from developing any comprehensive plans for the use of his men. Douglas, around the middle of this year in fact, largely took over direction of the road-building program for the mainland colony. Before criticizing the Governor, one should remember that Douglas knew the country much better than the Colonel did, and had some justifiable impatience with the Royal Engineers when they wasted time in needless perfectionism, such as wanting to build an English-style canal, complete with a lock, to join Harrison Lake to the Fraser River. As Captain Richards of the Royal Navy noted in his private journal, Colonel Moody wanted to concentrate on "a Town & Military establishments" and failed to realize that roads were British Columbia's prime need.

As we have noted, the Royal Engineers put in a lot of work this year on the Harrison-Lillooet route, but Douglas was also interested in improving the Fraser Canyon route. At the beginning of the year he appropriated $300 to have a trail cut around the face of Jackass Mountain, so that the packers would not have to take their mules all the way over the summit. And he decided to eliminate the Douglas Portage by building a new pack trail, one which would skirt the Fraser, to link Yale with Spuzzum, where a ferry took travellers to the other side of the river. The latter work was contracted out to two civilians, Powers and McRoberts, but Douglas brought in Royal Engineers, under Sergeant-Major Cann, to blast a way around rocky bluffs which, descending sharply to the river above Yale, were a major obstacle to the contractors.

Douglas also used Royal Engineers this year to determine the feasibility of building a wagon road from the coast to Yale, one that would at the same time open up the rich agricultural lands in the Fraser Valley, particularly those in the Sumas-Chilliwack area. Colonel Moody, on his own initiative, set up military reserves for the future protection of New Westminster and Burrard Inlet. Interestingly, on two of these, today's Stanley Park and the site of the University of British Columbia, pieces of artillery were actually installed during World War II to give at least token defence to the city of Vancouver.

*   *   *

And what of the Royal Engineers' sister service, the Royal Navy? There was much coming and going of frigates, survey ships and gunboats this year, with Rear-Admiral Baynes and his flagship H.M.S. *Ganges* much of the time at the Esquimalt base. The earliest musical composition known to have been written in British Columbia, "The Vancouver Island Waltz", was written by one Horne, apparently the flagship's bandmaster.[22] The Admiralty had, by now, decided that Vancouver Island and British Columbia needed a small permanent naval force. Accordingly, two little gunboats, the *Forward* and the *Grappler*, had been specially outfitted for service on this coast, and they arrived at Esquimalt this July, convoyed from England by H.M.S. *Termagant*. The *Termagant*, having seen her charges safely to their destination, was sent on a cruise through the Gulf Islands to Burrard Inlet. Unfortunately, while travelling through Active Pass at reduced speed in the wake of the slower *Plumper*, she got caught in the tiderips there. Scraping against the rocky shore, she ripped off her copper sheathing, gouged holes in her planking, and got free with four trees entangled in her rigging.[23] A navy diver tried to repair her at Nanaimo, but could not attend to the job properly. Still leaking rather badly, H.M.S. *Termagant* headed for the nearest drydock, that at San Francisco.

The two gunboats, each with its pair of cannon and crew of forty men, were almost immediately set about their duties, chiefly those of policing the unruly Indians along the coast. H.M.S. *Forward* under Lieut. Robson seems to have seen the more action. In August she steamed up the Fraser after a Chinaman had laid a complaint that he had been robbed by an Indian. The thief having been given up by the chief, quick punishment was administered according to the Navy's own ruthless code — the Indian, without the benefit of appearance before a magistrate, was stripped to the waist, lashed to a grating, and given thirty-six strokes of the lash. Later the *Forward* was despatched to Cape Mudge where the Yucultas, over-confident in the strength of their fortified village, refused to return stolen

---

[22] For the score see PABC, S/M/H78.

[23] For an account of this misadventure, and the *Termagant*'s cruise generally, see the journal kept by John C. Sabben, apparently one of her midshipmen. PABC, E/B/Sa 1.

property until the *Forward*'s guns were levelled against the stockades and several of the defenders killed.

Other naval occasions may be noted. At the end of July H.M.S. *Satellite*, which had proved so invaluable during the crises of 1858 and 1859, sailed for home. The crews of all the other warships at Esquimalt manned their rigging and cheered her as she put to sea. At the end of the year a new survey ship, H.M.S. *Hecate*, arrived from England. It had not taken Captain Richards long to find that the *Plumper* was far from suitable for the work assigned to her. She was small and cramped (484 tons), underpowered with her auxiliary engines capable of only about 6½ knots an hour. So ill-lit was her interior that during the winter months there was not enough light for the drafting which had to be done, and shore quarters had to be used in one of the "Crimea huts" at Esquimalt. Finally, at the end of 1859 Richards wrote to the Hydrographer of the Navy, pointed out *Plumper*'s many disadvantages (including her inability to hold her own against the 8-knot tides off parts of Vancouver Island), and frankly asked if he could not be given a replacement, preferably a paddle sloop of the *Hecate* class.[24] And now, on 23 December 1860, almost a year to the day of his sending of this letter, Richards had the pleasure of seeing H.M.S. *Hecate* (860 tons) herself arrive in Esquimalt harbour. Joyfully Richards and his officers moved aboard her. Lieut. Mayne found that his new cabin was as large as the messroom on the *Plumper*. Finally the *Plumper*, with her old crew but with the officers who had brought out the *Hecate* from England, sailed for home.

One unusual service was rendered by the Royal Navy this year. Many of the miners who came to the goldfields had picked up a fair bit of non-academic geology but so far, except for Bauerman, who was working with the British Boundary Commission, hardly any work had been done by a trained geologist in either colony. It happened that Dr. Charles Forbes, the surgeon on H.M.S. *Topaze*, had a considerable amount of geological knowledge. Accordingly, Governor Douglas borrowed him this summer to make a survey of the formations from the mouth of Harrison River to the 28 Mile

[24] Richards to Capt. Washington, 21 Dec. 1859. *Letter Book.*

House on the Lillooet trail. Starting from Port Douglas with "three Spaniards [Mexicans?]" and "4 intelligent Siwashes [Indians]",[25] Forbes surveyed the upper part of Harrison Lake, noting with particular interest the effigy of Shay, the Indian spirit "presiding over the Siwash Meteorological department", who determined when the wind should blow and the rain should fall. Later, Forbes worked along the newly-completed wagon road north from Port Douglas to Little Lillooet Lake, where the recent blasting done by the Royal Engineers gave him an excellent opportunity to study the rocks and strata. In October he submitted a report to Douglas full of learned mention of "dense blue trap bedded and jointed", "erupted Plutonic rock of a granitic character forced through trap" and "metamorphic clay slate highly charged with oxide of Iron."[26] Perhaps in British Columbia, the home of so many geologists, Dr. Forbes does deserve to be better known because of this early reconnaissance.

*   *   *

Victoria did not prosper greatly this year, though her population was gradually growing. The arrival of two yachts added some local interest. One was the little twenty-ton cutter *Templar* brought around the Horn as deck cargo by the somewhat eccentric Captain C. E. Barrett-Lennard, who put her in the water at Victoria and took her on a cruise around Vancouver Island, proudly flying the burgee of the Thames Yacht Club and doing some trading for furs along the way.[27] The other was the schooner *Emma Rooke* which arrived from Hawaii, still an independent kingdom, bearing Prince Lot Kamehameha (brother of the King), the Hon. M. Kekuanoa (governor of Oahu), two other members of the House of Nobles, and Josiah C. Spalding, A.D.C. to the Prince. They stayed for a week at the French Hotel before sailing for California.

[25] Until well into the present century "Siwash", probably a corruption of the French "sauvage", was a standard word to apply to an Indian.

[26] Forbes' report to Douglas is among the manuscripts of the Metropolitan Toronto Central Library. We are indebted to the Library for letting us use it. A similar but not identical report appears in *B.C. Papers* IV:32-40.

[27] For details see Barrett-Lennard, *Travels in British Columbia with the Narrative of a Yacht Voyage round Vancouver's Island* (London, 1862).

Victoria's cultural amenities were increasing. Occasionally touring companies of actors from San Francisco would play the city. The *Colonist*'s drama critic does not seem to have been unduly demanding:

COLONIAL THEATRE — We were glad to observe a good house last evening at the Colonial Theatre. Victor Hugo's great drama of "Lucretia Borgia" was rendered in a manner that seemed to afford the audience much satisfaction — judging from the frequent applause. Miss Lulu's Lucretia was very much admired. . . . The dance by Miss [Lulu] Sweet, was very chaste and beautiful, and was well worth the price of admission. The song by Mr. Oliver was the best we have yet had the pleasure of listening to on the stage of the Colonial. The evening's entertainment closed with the "Dead Shot" — a laughable farce, which afforded much amusement to the audience.[28]

Miss Lulu Sweet, as a matter of fact, was the belle of the season. Ever more eulogistic notices in the Victoria press attended her performances. Hardened miners down from the "diggings" and callow midshipmen off the warships rose to give her standing ovations. When her company played at New Westminster, the grave and pious Colonel Moody, perhaps impressed by the chastity of her dancing, named in her honour Lulu Island in the estuary of the Fraser River.

*   *   *

But life at Victoria was not all a round of balls and parties, receptions for Hawaiian royalty, concerts by the Philharmonic Society and plays at the Colonial Theatre. Victoria still had a major problem provided by the Indians. This year once more the northern Indians descended upon the island capital in their thousands. Many camped close to the Esquimalt Road, with Roderick Finlayson's farm being a favourite site. An outcry rose that the government must expel all these "savages" from the vicinity of Victoria, but Governor Douglas, who was always a friend to the Indians, would not agree. If outraged by expulsion from Victoria, the Indians might retaliate with attacks on Nanaimo, Fort Rupert or Fort Simpson. Late in June, however, after a Haida chief had had his slave murder a

[28] *Colonist*, 23 Oct. 1860.

Tongass chief, Douglas ordered all the northern Indians to move to specially designated sites, carefully chosen so that no tribe would be in proximity to any other tribe with which they were at enmity. To cow the northerners into making this change of quarters, Admiral Baynes paraded his red-coated marines on Beacon Hill. The Haidas, perhaps the proudest of the tribes, showed their annoyance the next day by opening fire on the schooner *Royal Charlie* as she sailed through the narrow entrance to Victoria harbour. Nobody was hurt, but the captain and passengers did not enjoy the experience. Together they signed a letter of complaint to Magistrate Pemberton. Pemberton had at his disposal a small police force, no doubt impressive enough in their blue uniforms but hardly sufficient in number to cope with hundreds of Haidas. When Pemberton pointed out this rather obvious fact to Governor Douglas, Douglas appealed to Admiral Baynes for help. The Admiral promptly sealed off the entrance to Victoria harbour with a couple of boats from H.M.S. *Ganges* and landed a hundred marines. The Haida encampment was searched and "about a hundred muskets, with some revolvers and knives" were seized and taken to the police station. It was at this point, after the disarming of the Haidas, that on July 2nd their chief "Captain John" and his brother were killed.

Captain John was a truly remarkable man. Aged about forty-five, of splendid physical appearance, with a fine black glossy moustache, he was noted for his urbanity and poise in his dealings with the whites. Born in Alaska, he may have had some Russian blood in him. As a young man he had shipped aboard an American vessel, where he acquired his name of "Captain John", mastered English, and became well acquainted with the ports between Alaska and Mexico. Returning to his old home, he married a Haida woman and set up as a medicine man of sorts. During his year and a half on the American vessel, he had learned something of the treatment for measles and, when that disease swept through the Haidas, won such a reputation and made so much wealth effecting cures that he became their principal chief. Captain John was the Haida who had precipitated the recent trouble by ordering the killing of the Tongass chief because of a minor incident. Following the slaying, he had remained within his lodge, surrounded by a guard of trusted warriors.

The natural inclination of the Tongass braves after the murder of their chief was to attack Captain John in his stronghold and secure revenge by slaying him. Governor Douglas, however, made it plain to the Tongass Indians that under no circumstances would he permit any attacks of this kind. The Governor announced, instead, that if either the Tongass Indians or the Haidas felt at any time that they had suffered wrong, they were to turn to the white man's law for justice. The Tongass leaders decided to take Douglas at his word. Going to the Victoria police station, they lodged a complaint, and a warrant was issued for the arrest of Captain John and his brother for the murder of their chief.

They must have been brave men who served the warrants on the Haida chiefs. Somehow or other, the two were taken into custody and brought into the Victoria police station. Here the magistrate informed them that they would be locked up overnight. They were led through an adjacent prison yard and into the prison, where a jailer named Crowley commenced the customary search before locking up the new prisoners. Just at that moment Captain John spoke quickly to his brother, and the two Haidas, simultaneously drawing knives, attacked Crowley. A police officer hurled himself upon Captain John in time to save the jailer, though he sustained a slight wound himself. Crowley managed to get an arm up in time to ward off a blow which Captain John's brother directed at his heart. Blood streamed down his badly wounded arm. Wild disorder prevailed. Policemen drew their guns, and when their shooting stopped both Captain John and his brother lay dead.[29]

The effect on the Haidas was terrifying. Giving way to wild excitement, they swore instant revenge on the white settlers around Victoria. A mounted messenger raced to warn the Saanich farmers. When the alarm reached Uplands Farm at Cadboro Bay seventeen white men, women and children gathered up blankets and wraps and fled deep into a wooded ravine, hoping to escape detection when the Haidas came to burn and loot and kill.[30] Fortunately for them

[29] For the Admiralty file on the naval assistance given the civil authorities during the Tongass-Haida crises, see PRO, ADM.1/5736, Pt. II. For a detailed report on the killings at the jail, see *Colonist*, 3 July 1860.

[30] Edgar Fawcett, *Some Reminiscences of Old Victoria* (Toronto, 1912), p. 90.

and the other settlers, the Haidas never appeared. They had decided to head for home.

By now Douglas had had enough of the incessant brawls and killings of the Indians. Though he still refused to order their expulsion, he set up a new regime. With Admiral Baynes' cooperation, a picket boat was stationed at the entrance to Victoria harbour. The lieutenant commanding it had strict orders to stop and search every Indian canoe coming in from the sea, to seize any arms in the possession of the newcomers, and to issue receipts which would enable them to pick these up again at the police station upon departure. Only two weaknesses flawed this scheme. The first one, sardonically noted by the *Colonist*, was that there was little point in disarming Indians when, upon landing at Victoria, they could immediately go to the HBC store and buy new guns. The second was that the Indians soon learned to time their arrival for midnight, to go ashore and cache their arms in the dark, return to their canoes, and in the morning make their official arrival, blandly presenting themselves to the blue-jackets for inspection. Once ashore, they of course hastened to secure their hidden arms. Still, gun control of a sort had been instituted.

*   *   *

We must not close our chronicle for this year without noting one of the most significant proclamations that Governor Douglas issued during 1860 for his mainland colony of British Columbia. Anxious to secure a stable agricultural basis for the gold colony, Douglas had decided to change the regulations governing land tenure since these had done more to inhibit than encourage prospective farmers. Accordingly, on January 12th, His Excellency proclaimed remarkably attractive new regulations. Any British subject, or any foreigner who had sworn allegiance to the Queen, could go wherever he wished in the colony (apart from townsites, auriferous areas, or Indian settlements and reserves) and by planting four stakes at the corners of a rectangular block of land, not exceeding 160 acres, could "pre-empt" it. All that was required was that he should file a rough description of the land and its location with a magistrate and pay an eight shilling registration fee. Then, when the area was finally

surveyed and offered for public sale, he would be given the first
opportunity to purchase it, at a price not exceeding ten shillings an
acre, providing he could produce a certificate from the nearest
magistrate declaring that, as pre-emptor, he had made permanent
improvements to the land to the value of ten shillings per acre.
Douglas was aware, of course, that many farmers and ranchers
would want tracts larger than 160 acres. He therefore included a
provision that at the sales of surveyed Crown lands, a pre-emptor
could buy, for that price not exceeding ten shillings per acre, not only
his own pre-empted 160 acres but an unlimited amount of adjacent
acreage, provided that he did not infringe upon lands already
appropriated.[31]

On the face of it, this was a thoroughly sensible and far-sighted
measure, calculated to get a stable population on the land, to
increase agricultural production, and to speed up the colonization of
the country. Yet the following year Douglas bitterly noted, "The
Pre-emption Law has been strangely misrepresented and perverted
to the purposes of speculation."[32] The sad fact was that the intervening months had seen spectacular land-grabbing, especially by Douglas' own subordinates from the Attorney-General down. Just about
everybody seems to have been involved, securing from obliging
magistrates certificates for non-existent improvements and in various
other ways abusing the scheme. It was one of the most profitable
things in British Columbia, especially after the upset price of Crown
land had been reduced from 10s. to 4s.2d. Colonel Moody, normally
a high-minded gentleman, was able as Commissioner of Lands to
secure for himself almost two thousand acres in the vicinity of New
Westminster. However, attacked by the press, Moody in August
1861 offered to sell his rural lands to active settlers.

*   *   *

In September of this year, at the age of seventy-three but still
active as the head of the Hudson's Bay Company operations in North

[31] For the text of Douglas' new land law, see *B.C. Papers* III:91-92.
[32] PABC, B 20 1858, p. 86.

America, Sir George Simpson died at Hudson's Bay House, Lachine, close to Montreal. Ten days earlier he had had the honour of receiving there the Prince of Wales. A whole age seemed to have passed since 1828 when a young clerk named James Douglas had welcomed him to Fort St. James.

1861

More gold finds in Cariboo — Fantastic wealth — Cariboo Wagon Road is begun — Bella Coola and Bute Inlet routes — Judge Begbie's "Bowie Knife Address" — Hazards of steamboat travel on the Fraser — Indian troubles — "Battle of Cape Mudge" — The Victoria Rifle Volunteers — Indian policemen — Death of Lieut. Robson — An embezzling Colonial Treasurer — Douglas plans to invade the United States.

One of Governor Douglas' promises when ending the Rock Creek War had been that a wagon road would be built from Hope to Similkameen, and then on to Rock Creek. This year Captain Grant, R.E., with eighty sappers and ninety civilians, opened a new route beyond Skagit Bluffs to Princeton, while three other parties under Royal Engineer NCOs prepared to widen the Dewdney Trail between Hope and Skagit Bluffs (see map p. 14). But work on this wagon road was abandoned after word came of gold discoveries in the Cariboo so incredibly rich as to make insignificant the gold finds in the Similkameen country and on Rock Creek. All British Columbia's road building must now be devoted to opening up the new El Dorado far to the north.

Much had been happening in the Cariboo country. Late the previous year a small party of prospectors, starting out from Keithley Creek, had crossed the Snowshoe Plateau and descended into the valley of Antler Creek. Here they struck it rich; sometimes a single pan would yield $75 or even $100 worth of gold. And on the surface of the bedrock the miners found rich pockets of "sunburn gold", brownish in colour. When the discoverers of Antler Creek returned to Keithley for supplies, one or another of them talked too much and the secret was out. The result was an incredible mid-winter gold rush over the snow, five or six feet deep, to get claims staked along Antler Creek. In March 1861 when P. H. Nind became the first gold commissioner to visit Antler Creek, he found John Rose and Ben MacDonald, two of the original discoverers, living in a log cabin, and all the rest of the miners inhabiting burrows in the snow. By summer, however, Antler was a town with sixty houses, not to mention Beedy's store, and the inevitable saloons and gambling houses. Meanwhile the prospecting frontier moved onwards. This year four other famous gold creeks were discovered and worked — Williams Creek, Lowhee Creek, Grouse Creek and Lightning Creek.

A tremendous breakthrough occurred this summer at Williams Creek. The gold there had been found in a blue clay stratum approximately nine feet below the surface, but one day at the claim of Abbott and Jourdain, while Jourdain was off obtaining provisions, Abbott decided to dig beneath the blue clay. He did so and, when his partner arrived after two days' absence, Abbott showed him fifty ounces of nuggets from the new lower zone. From that point on the yield of various of the claims became fantastic. The "companies" of miners began counting their take in pounds of gold, not ounces. Victoria could scarcely believe the figures when the gold was shipped out in the autumn. In mid-October the *Otter* docked in Victoria with gold worth $250,000 from the Abbott-Jourdain company. A few days later the *Caledonia* arrived with gold worth $240,000. On one of her trips from the Fraser in mid-November, the *Otter* carried $300,000 worth of gold. At the end of the year the *Colonist* compiled the following figures for gold shipped to San Francisco via Victoria in the preceding twelve months:

Per Wells, Fargo & Co.	$1,339,895
Per McDonald & Co.	296,975
	$1,636,870[1]

This would equal something like forty million dollars in modern values. Moreover, it was notorious that at least as much gold was being taken out of British Columbia totally unreported as was handled by the two Victoria banking houses. Donald Fraser, correspondent for the London *Times*, estimated that this year, in the whole of British Columbia, some 5000 miners took out gold worth

---

[1] *Colonist*, 10 Jan. 1862.

$6,791,409[2] but his figures, which would represent more than $150,000,000 in modern values, are suspect.

One name is curiously absent from the newspaper accounts of the gold shipments — that of the Hudson's Bay Company. This is the more strange in that the Company with its establishments at Kamloops, Alexandria and today's Prince George, with its intimate knowledge of the country, and with its close connections with the Indians, should have been making much more profit by sending out parties to get gold instead of furs. However, in a startling display of deliberate blindness, the HBC chose to ignore the bonanza at its doorstep. On August 27th of this year a letter of instructions to Peter Ogden, in charge of New Caledonia, which included all the Cariboo gold area, declared:

You will urge on the Gentlemen in charge of posts in New Caledonia that they are not to have anything to do with mining operations, on the Company's account, but simply to attend to their duties as fur traders, which will be found the more profitable business in the long run.[3]

Thus, amid fantastic riches, the HBC quietly mouldered away, its profits steadily declining.

Commenting on the extraordinary wealth of the new gold area, Lieut. Wilson, secretary of the British Boundary Commission, noted in his diary for November 29th:

The accounts of the gold discoveries at Cariboo are perfectly fabulous and at the same time quite true. Large fortunes have been made in a few weeks, from £6000 to £10,000 earned in a month or six weeks; many instances have occurred of £90 worth of gold being washed out of a tin pan full of earth. Old miners say they never saw anything like it in the best days of California in 49 and 50. Cariboo is a dreadful place to get at, however, right up in the mountains . . . and inaccessible for 7 or 8 months out of the year from snow.[4]

Cariboo was indeed a terrible place to get at. And the miners, every time they crossed another plateau or ridge and dipped down into another valley, found themselves at the end of an ever more

---

[2] *Times*, 6 Feb. 1862, p. 10.

[3] HBCA, B.226/b/22.

[4] *Mapping the Frontier*, pp. 166-67.

seriously over-extended supply line. Their provisions had to be brought into Victoria, taken by steamer up the lower Fraser, somehow sent up to Lillooet and on to Williams Lake, packed in via Quesnel Forks and Keithley to Antler, then over to a new settlement named Richfield on Williams Creek, and from there taken to the claims staked on a score of creeks. (Later of course the main route was via Quesnel, Cottonwood House, Van Winkle and on to Barkerville.) When bad rains or snow made the trails impassable, the miners at the end of this long tenuous supply line could be faced with famine.

Governor Douglas carefully appraised the situation. The Royal Engineers had at last got the Harrison-Lillooet route in good shape. Stage coaches would soon be using the road linking Port Douglas and Lillooet Lake and boats, chiefly steamers, ran the lengths of Lillooet, Anderson and Seton Lakes, between which were suitable portage facilities. A good road ran from the east end of Seton Lake to Lillooet. The trouble was that no less than seven transshipments of freight were necessary, making the route slow and expensive.

What was really needed was a route by which freight, once it had been unloaded at Yale from the Victoria or New Westminster steamer, could be put into a wagon which would take it straight through to the Cariboo goldfields. Accordingly, Governor Douglas decided to build the Great Cariboo Wagon Road to link the head of navigation at Yale with Richfield on Williams Creek. Forthwith a detachment of Royal Engineers started a preliminary survey for a wagon route through the Fraser Canyon's most difficult stretch, that between Yale and Boston Bar. The upper Fraser Canyon above Boston Bar posed fewer problems, and this September the Rev. Arthur Browning at Hope was able to report "a waggon road is about commencing from Boston Bar to most probably William's Lake."[5]

*   *   *

While plans proceeded for the new wagon road through the Fraser Canyon, men were still hoping for a more direct route which would run almost straight east from the Pacific Coast to the Cariboo

[5] *Christian Guardian*, 4 Dec. 1861, p. 192.

diggings. One possibility was the route that Sir Alexander Mackenzie had followed in 1793 across the Chilcotin Plateau and out at
Bella Coola. In 1860 a similar but more southerly route from Fort
Alexandria to Bella Coola was followed by Colin McKenzie. On May
24th of this year Ranald Macdonald and John Barnston left Alexandria with three men and followed Colin McKenzie's route out to
Bella Coola and back. On his return to Alexandria on July 10th,
Barnston reported to Mr. P. Nind, gold commissioner for Cariboo,
that it would be quite feasible for a trail to be put through for use a
year hence. But Douglas realized that a pack trail would no longer
suffice — only a wagon road could meet the needs of Cariboo.
(Many many years would pass before a road would finally be built
up the tremendous ascent from the Pacific at Bella Coola to the
Chilcotin Plateau to the east.)

Competing with the suggested Bella Coola route was one, ardently
championed by Victorian merchants, which would start from the
head of Bute Inlet and, following the Homathko River north through
the Coast Mountains, would finally emerge on the Chilcotin Plateau.
The only trouble was that the Homathko route through the Coast
Range was even more of a road-builder's nightmare than the Fraser
Canyon. But Victorians did not want to be told anything of the sort.
For them it was enough that the Bute Inlet route would by-pass
New Westminster and establish, once and for all, the pre-eminence
of Victoria. Moreover, plenty of Victorians had been speculating on
Bute Inlet lands, sending up their value remarkably. When William
Downie, who had first-hand knowledge of Bute Inlet and realized its
disadvantages, addressed a Victoria public meeting on the subject,
he got an emphatic response from his audience:

No sooner had my hearers understood from my remarks that I could
not recommend Bute Inlet, when it seems that one and all took it for
granted that I was in some kind of a collusion with the Westminster
people to squash the big land schemes of Bute Inlet. Yells went up in
different parts of the audience, such as "Put him out!" "What's he
talking about?" "Bully for you!" And then various articles were thrown
across the hall, breaking sundry lamps in their route towards myself,
who had certainly become the central point of interest.[6]

[6] *Hunting for Gold*, pp. 265-66.

After Downie's address a group of Victorians headed by Alfred Waddington, unready to surrender their dream, sent the well-known surveyor Robert Homfray with a party of six to make a fresh report on the Bute Inlet route. After enduring "the greatest suffering and privation" due to the loss of their canoe and most of their provisions, Homfray's party managed to reach a point which the Indians assured them was only a five days' journey from Alexandria. Homfray's report, received in mid-December, was hailed by the *Colonist* as satisfactory.[7] But Downie was to be proved right. Though the Bute Inlet project was kept alive for years by Victorians, and interest in it revived when the Canadian Pacific Railway was looking for a western terminus, to this day no road has reached Bute Inlet from the Interior.

*   *   *

If bringing in supplies was a major concern for the Cariboo miners, so was the safe sending out of their gold. To meet the latter problem, Governor Douglas instituted a gold escort. Unfortunately, since no compensation was paid for gold lost while in the care of the escort, few miners chose to trust their treasure to it. Rather, they kept it hidden under the floor of their cabins, buried under the roots of trees, or even carried it with them daily to and from their shafts, finally bringing it down to the Coast in person. This latter course had its own risks: there were tales of miners heading back to the Coast who had been robbed of their precious dust and nuggets. More would have been robbed had it not been for the endeavours of the local magistrates and the small but active colonial constabulary, backed by the formidable Judge Begbie. Tall (six foot four), with his long black cloak swirling behind him, eyes of a special brightness gleaming between the stylish rake of a "wide-awake" hat and the carefully trimmed lines of his Van Dyke beard, Begbie was a commanding figure. When Begbie held court, even in the remotest settlement, he wore the robes and wig of an English judge, and when he pronounced the death sentence he put on the traditional black cap.

[7] *Colonist*, 21 Dec. 1861.

This year Begbie's assize circuit took him both to Quesnel Forks and Antler Creek. Probably this was the year he made his "Bowie Knife Speech" at Williams Lake. A crowd of miners had gathered here at the trial of an American charged with assault with a bowie knife (a heavy sheath knife with a long single-edged blade). Summing up the case and passing judgment, Begbie said:

Prisoner, I am glad to see that your case has drawn together, in this temporary court of justice, so many of your compatriots. I am given to understand that the mining class of the western states look upon liberty as a condition of life which gives them the right to defy the laws of their country, and to govern it according to their wishes by the might of the bowie knife and Colt's revolver. You, prisoner, are a good representative of that class, and I am told that there are many more of your kidney within the sound of my voice.

Let me define for those who have come from the United States what our laws look upon as liberty. It is laid down very clearly so that no person can make any mistake as to its meaning. "Liberty is the power of doing what is allowed by law. When you go beyond that you indulge in license." I have been appointed a judge to interpret the law, and to see that the law is carried out. We have a law which prohibits the use of bowie knives, pistols and other offensive weapons, and in those countries over which the British flag flies there is no necessity for carrying or using offensive weapons, and let me tell those who are in court that in the course of my duty I will punish most severely all those who, coming into this British colony, make use of such deadly weapons. Prisoner, the jury have very properly found you guilty of this wanton and cowardly attack. You will spend three years in a place of confinement to be determined on, and in giving you this sentence I feel that I have been very lenient with you.[8]

It was a violent era by British North American if not American standards. This year when Adam Beam, or Bean, quarrelled with John Wadley over a claim on Mission Creek in the Okanagan, they decided to settle it by a duel. The manner of proceeding was somewhat unorthodox, with Beam using a six-shooter and Wadley a double-barrelled shotgun. The distance was thirty yards. Wadley missed with both barrels, but one of Beam's six shots creased Wadley's scalp and three went through the rim of his hat. These men at least gave each other a fair chance. Less fortunate was

8 Walkem, *Stories of Early B.C.*, pp. 33-34.

popular little Dr. Fifer who was murdered in cold blood at Yale this year. The killer was hanged on a gallows raised above his victim's grave.

*   *   *

Yale was growing in importance. More powerful sternwheelers were increasingly able to get all the way up the Fraser to the little town which was truly becoming the head of navigation on the river. Still, there were plenty of risks, not only from running aground or hitting snags, but from building up too great pressure in the boiler when a sternwheeler was attempting the final stretch upstream. This April, disaster overtook the *Fort Yale* as she fought her way over the riffle at Union Bar, two and a half miles above Hope. With a tremendous blast her boiler exploded. Four of those aboard her were killed and two were listed as missing. Among the dead was her captain, S. B. Jamieson. Four months later his brothers, Archibald and James Baird Jamieson, were killed when another boiler explosion ripped apart the *Cariboo* as she was pulling out of Victoria harbour on a night run to New Westminster. Among other *Cariboo* victims was Count Paul de Garro, whom we noted as the owner of the short-lived *Le Courier de la Nouvelle Caledonie*.

*   *   *

An historic newspaper, the *British Columbian*, published its first issues this year. Under the energetic editorship of John Robson, this took the place of the ailing *New Westminster Times*, the first newspaper on the mainland. John Robson was a brother of the Methodist minister Ebenezer Robson, and he shared the latter's moral earnestness. Moreover, like his brother editor Amor De Cosmos in Victoria, Robson was an ardent champion of "liberalism" in politics. The first issue of the *British Columbian*, that of 13 February 1861, spelt out Robson's position without any ambiguity:

... the BRITISH COLUMBIAN has been brought into existence for the express purpose of advocating certain measures. ...

The cardinal measures which we shall advocate are a RESIDENT GOVERNOR, and RESPONSIBLE GOVERNMENT, or, in other words, REPRESENTATIVE INSTITUTIONS similar to those at present existing in the Eastern British Provinces and Australia.

Governor Douglas was to have his benign authoritarianism challenged in British Columbia just as it had been on Vancouver Island.

March 23rd was a great day for New Westminster, for it saw Captain Richards bring H.M.S. *Hecate* to anchor opposite the youthful capital. The *Hecate* was by far the largest ship ever to have sailed up to the city. Her arrival gave the lie to those Victorians who maintained that the sandheads of the Fraser were as effective a barrier to navigation as the notorious bar at the mouth of the Columbia River and that consequently New Westminster could never become a real seaport. Using buoys to mark a safe channel through the sandheads, Captain Richards declared that ships could come up to New Westminster with perfect safety. Gleefully the citizens of the Royal City contemplated the eclipse of Victoria as a port of transshipment, with the supplies for the goldfields coming to New Westminster directly from Britain and California. The citizens of New Westminster wanted to honour Captain Richards with a testimonial banquet, but this he modestly declined though he did accept a complimentary address. Despite Richards' assurances, not all skippers were ready to bring their ships into the Fraser. For improved communication with ships, especially warships, which preferred anchoring in English Bay to entering either the Fraser River or Burrard Inlet, a trail was completed this year linking False Creek with New Westminster.

*   *   *

Various other events of this year may be noted in a simple calendar.

January saw Victoria rejoicing. In mid-December the little gunboat *Forward* had gone to the aid of the Peruvian brigantine *Florencia*, stranded in Nootka Sound. Weeks had passed with no further word of the gunboat, and both H.M.S. *Hecate* and H.M.S. *Plumper* put to sea in an anxious search for her. But now, on January 15th, after she had been given up for lost, the *Forward* steamed into Victoria harbour loaded with survivors not from the *Florencia*, who had already been rescued, but from the American brig *Consort*. Boiler troubles and wild easterly gales had repeatedly delayed the gunboat, and she had been forced at last to steam around the northern end of Vancouver Island and return along the protected eastern shore of the island. Victoria rejoiced to see the gallant Lieut. Robson and his crew thus come back from the dead.

February saw that restless globetrotter Lady Franklin, widow of the lost Arctic explorer, arrive in Victoria with her niece and companion, Miss Sophia Cracroft. On the morning of her arrival, she attracted much attention when she promenaded Yates Street,[9] accompanied by Captain Richards of H.M.S. *Hecate*, who had played an active part in the search for her husband. The two ladies were quickly immersed in receiving and returning social calls. Bishop Hills was very much in evidence and made an excellent impression, which was fortunate since Miss Angela Burdett-Coutts, the munificent benefactor of Hills' diocese, had asked Lady Franklin to let her know how the work of the Church of England was progressing under his direction. One day the ladies visited the school for Indian children conducted by the Rev. A. C. Garrett. In a letter home, Sophia Cracroft described the scene in the classroom:

They are seated in separate tribes, the 2 larger divisions being occupied by the Hydah & the Sang soo [Songhees] tribes, who are hostile to each other. Stray children of other tribes were on the small benches, the upper ones of which have a desk before them for writing. They were all decently dressed, & many of the girls were wrapped in gay plaid shawls given them for good conduct; some, both boys and girls, were huddled up in the usual fashion, in a dirty blanket, others wore a gay kind of wrapper made by themselves of red & blue cloth ornamented with rows of mother of pearl buttons, with pretty effect. We often see them in the streets here. Some wore rings of silver in their lips, ears & noses; and most of the bigger girls had bracelets of silver. One had 6 or 8 on one arm. They were very much cleaner than we had any idea of expecting — even their lanky hair had evidently been combed, though it was somewhat of a fuzzy crop and hung over their foreheads. In spite of partial concealment the "Flat head" distortion [of the skull in infancy] was more or less visible in most of them. It was more observable in the tallest girl than in anyone I have ever seen.[10]

[9] *Colonist*, 23 Feb. 1861.

[10] Dorothy Blakey Smith, ed., *Lady Franklin Visits the Pacific Northwest*, PABC Memoir XI (Victoria, 1974), pp. 19-20.

Governor Douglas' wife, ill at ease in white company, was something of a recluse. She did, however, issue one of her rare invitations
to Lady Franklin and Miss Cracroft, who in her journal-letter for
February 28th reported:

> We were engaged today to take luncheon with the Governor's wife
> Mrs. Douglas, in place of paying her a formal visit. Have I explained
> that her mother was an Indian woman, & that she keeps very much
> (far too much) in the background; indeed it is only lately that she has
> been persuaded to see visitors, partly because she speaks English with
> some difficulty; the usual language being either the Indian or Canadian
> French w^h is a corrupt dialect.[11]

From Victoria, Lady Franklin and her niece travelled up to Yale
where the miners gave her a rousing welcome and named the
entrance to the Fraser Canyon "Lady Franklin Pass". The name did
not endure, though we still have Lady Franklin Rock in the river
there.

March saw Lady Franklin and Miss Cracroft preparing to leave
Victoria. One of the last social occasions was a "Pic-Nic" at Craigflower arranged by local officials of the Hudson's Bay Company. The
day was beautiful and sunny as the ladies stepped into a large canoe
manned by French-Canadian voyageurs, wearing their traditional
colourful attire. Paddling to the beat of old voyageur songs, the men
bore them under the bridge where Victoria harbour narrows to the
Gorge. Enthusiastic admirers above greeted them with "three rousing, hearty British cheers". At Craigflower the ladies partook of a
collation provided by their hosts.

April saw the coming of a new admiral and new flagship — Rear-
Admiral Sir Richard Maitland and H.M.S. *Bacchante*. Normally a
cordial relationship existed between Victoria and the Royal Navy,
but this was hardly maintained after Maitland arrived. Admiral
Maitland was a rigid martinet, and his flagship a most unhappy one.
Deserters began fleeing the *Bacchante* almost as soon as she arrived
in Esquimalt, headed by Lieut. Byam, R.N., who, deserting in style,

---

[11] *Ibid.*, pp. 22-23.

booked a passage to San Francisco on the mail steamer *Cortez*. At one point twenty of the flagship's men, including warrant officers, headed *en masse* across the Strait of Juan de Fuca to find sanctuary on American soil. Maitland's flag-lieutenant, unsuccessfully pursuing them, almost got drowned. Bent on maintaining tight discipline, Maitland had offending bluejackets serve time with the common convicts in the Victoria chain gang, a proceeding which elicited public sympathy for the seamen and indignation against the admiral.

This month the usual influx of Victoria-bound northern Indians began. In a strongly-worded editorial the *Colonist* declared, not for the first time, its feelings about these migrants:

Every year since 1858, the town and country around Victoria has been overrun by Russian, Queen Charlotte's Island, Fort Rupert, Fort Simpson, and Northwest Coast Indians. On their passage down and up they have been a perpetual source of terror to the settlers on Salt Spring Island and Nanaimo. . . . In the rural districts around Victoria, they have slain the cattle of our farmers with impunity; and in some cases, caused families to move into the town for protection. When congregated in Victoria, the murderous crew have set all laws at defiance. . . . Their midnight broils, and infernal war-hoop [*sic*], has made night hideous. . . . their feuds have rendered the road to Esquimalt dangerous; and some even of these savage robbers, like accomplished foot-pads, have attacked and interrupted the travel to and from Esquimalt; whilst the whizzing stray bullets have wounded and disabled men at our wharves. . . . the women have rendered the whole outskirts of the town a perfect brothel. Vagrancy, filth, disease, drunkenness, larceny, maiming, murder, prostitution, in a multiplied form, are the invariable results of an annual visit from the Northern Tribes. The only thing we receive in return for these monstrous crimes are a few, very few furs, and some whistles, pipes, or trifles carved out of carbonised slate and occasionally a day's labor from the vagrants.

. . . .

We ask, in the name of humanity, Christianity, and civilization, shall these things be continued? . . . We unhesitatingly declare for stopping the immigration, and for stopping it in time. Not one should be allowed south of Cape Mudge. The advance guard numbering some four hundred souls have already arrived, and thousands more will soon follow in their wake. A gunboat should be sent up Johnson's [*sic*] Straits at once, to warn the tribes against coming here.[12]

12 *Colonist*, 18 April 1861.

May saw real trouble with the Indians, the so-called "Battle of Cape Mudge". Some four hundred Haidas travelling homewards in thirty canoes had landed on Salt Spring Island, where they looted a storehouse and defied the settlers. A messenger had been sent posthaste to Victoria, and the gunboat *Forward* started in pursuit of the marauders, catching up with them where they were camped in a cove close to Cape Mudge. When the gunboat came into view the Haidas, having covered their faces with their traditional black war paint, refused an order to send their tyees (chiefs) aboard, and jeered at the Navy's "Tenass [small] boat". Lieut. Robson replied by firing his cannon over the heads of the Haidas, but their only response was a crackling burst of musket and rifle fire. The *Forward* raised her rifle-plates to protect her crew, then once more opened fire with her cannon, this time demolishing many of the Haidas' canoes. Meanwhile the *Forward*'s riflemen kept up a telling fire. These tactics broke the fighting spirit of the Haidas, who fled into the forest, abandoning their surviving canoes and property. A little later a canoe brought out to the ship "Captain Jefferson", one of the Haida chiefs. He was told that all the tyees must present themselves. When they did, they were held as prisoners, or rather as hostages, and the Haidas on the shore were ordered to come out to the *Forward* and hand over all their guns. Once the Haidas had been safely disarmed, a landing party went ashore and began a three hours' search of the Indian encampment:

A number of stolen articles were seized — consisting of saws, hammers, planes, plane-irons, a quadrant, a writing-desk with the owner's name, a quantity of silks and cotton, together with a number of other articles "too numerous to mention." . . . There were found with them a number of articles they could not, possibly, have known the use of, such, for instance, as theodolites and hydrometers, which were, no doubt, plundered from some unfortunate craft that has fallen in their way.[13]

The Indians were found to have suffered four killed and several mortally wounded. One bluejacket had been wounded in the leg.

After two chiefs and three other Indians had been taken aboard the *Forward* to stand trial in Nanaimo or Victoria for possession of

[13] *Colonist,* 22 May 1861.

stolen property, the little gunboat's mission was completed. But at this point a somewhat paradoxical situation developed. The Haidas' enemies, the Yucultas, had been watching the battle with relish, officiously offering to fight as allies of the British. Now the disarmed Haidas faced annihilation. Robson, however, did the decent thing and gave them back their rifles and muskets so that they could fight off any Yuculta attack and safely reach their homes in the Queen Charlotte Islands.

June saw Governor Douglas, in his speech from the throne, calling for the raising of a local militia. Later this month some 130 men enrolled in a unit known first as either "The Vancouver Island Rifle Volunteers" or as "The Victoria Volunteer Regiment of Rifles", but finally called "The Victoria Rifle Volunteers". Neither this nor a company raised in Nanaimo this year was the first militia unit to be established in the British colonies on the Pacific Coast. That distinction went to a group of Negro immigrants of 1858 who, possibly as a result of pique at being excluded from the all-white volunteer fire brigade, went to Governor Douglas and, apparently in April 1860,[14] got his permission to form a volunteer regiment. This force bore the title of "The Victoria Pioneer Rifle Corps" but was soon known to everybody around Victoria as "The African Rifles". When the members of the African Rifles learned of the formation of the white militia unit, they sent word that, since in any future war they would almost certainly be under the command of the lieutenant-colonel commanding the Victoria Rifle Volunteers, they would like to have some voice in his selection. A spirited reply was returned: neither a white company in Nanaimo nor a black company in Victoria could have any part in this decision.[15]

Organization of the all-white Victoria Rifle Volunteers proceeded apace, officers were elected, and dark green uniforms with black facings and braid were ordered from England. The chain gang was set to clearing a parade ground for the unit. Drills were held, and in August an artillery company was raised to complement the infantry.

---

[14] S. W. Jackman, "The Victoria Pioneer Rifle Corps, British Columbia, 1860-1866", *Journal of the Society for Army Historical Research* 39 (1961):41-43.

[15] *Colonist*, 4 July 1861.

Several reasons accounted for this sudden burst of military activity. Indian scares certainly were partly responsible, but more important was the outbreak in April of the American Civil War. Everyone was aware that Britain might well intervene on the side of the South, in which case Vancouver Island and British Columbia might expect a Northern attack.

Significantly, this same month the *Colonist*, approving the move to form a Canadian confederation in eastern British North America, expressed the hope that the Pacific colonies could become "an integral portion of a confederacy numbering four millions of inhabitants."[16]

July saw a tidy little coup by four Indian members of the Victoria Police Force: "Sir Robert Peel", "Canary", Edensah (Edensaw?) and Winnets. Carefully they arranged for two "klootchmen" (Indian women) to go to a ravine where John Wemyss, a suspected seller of illicit liquor, had his house. No sooner had Wemyss taken the women's money than the four policemen beat on his door with their truncheons and, in the Queen's name, ordered him to admit them to his premises. Many Indians regarded with anger the whiskey-sellers who were proving the ruin of their race. When the four constables started for the prison with Wemyss, a crowd of other Indians attacked their prisoner so violently that Wemyss was shortly "about the worst-used specimen of humanity that has ever been taken to jail in this town." The *Colonist*, reporting the episode, headed the item "BRAVO! INDIAN POLICEMEN".[17]

August saw misfortune overtake H.M.S. *Hecate*. Early on the morning of the 19th, in dense fog off the entrance to the Strait of Juan de Fuca, she ran on two small rocks off Neah Bay. A roller dropped her heavily on the rocks, so damaging her that she had to head for repairs to the nearest drydock — that of the U.S. Navy at Mare Island, California. The incident helped to emphasize the Royal Navy's need for a properly equipped naval dockyard of its own at Esquimalt.

[16] *Colonist*, 14 June 1861.
[17] *Colonist*, 30 July 1861.

September saw old John Tod, retired from the Hudson's Bay Company's service and living comfortably in his modest house on Oak Bay, still writing to Edward Ermatinger, who forty years earlier had been a fellow clerk in the service of the great Company. Tod's sight was failing now, but his mind was as sharp as ever, and he still wrote cogently to his orthodox friend, urging him to abandon "the old rotten timbers of ancestorial faith", and asking his opinion of the newly published and highly controversial *Essays and Reviews*. Tod's love of music was as intense as when he had entertained himself and his Indian girl with his lonely flute at Fort McLeod. Recently a tune which Ermatinger had composed and "pricked" for him back around 1820 had been arranged for Tod by the Victoria Philharmonic Society:

... those gentlemen are so very Kind, whenever I pay them a visit, as I sometimes do in an evening, as to gratify my ears by performing the same. . . . [18]

A group of old HBC factors and traders formed a select society in Victoria. Thus Tod in a subsequent letter mentioned:

Our old friends Work & Yale are both well — the latter and I were talking of You the other day — like myself having spent the greater portion of his life in Seclusion, he seems at times much at a loss, on getting into Company.[19]

With a strange sense of wonderment Tod recalled the "vast Solitudes of former days" occupied now by "not less than ten or twelve thousand inhabitants".

October saw the death of the "Czar of Salt Spring Island", a poor lunatic surveyor named Rowe, who had built himself a hut on that pleasant island and issued a proclamation declaring himself Czar. Wandering about with two revolvers and a double-barrelled shotgun, he threatened all who approached his retreat. Periodically he posted proclamations commanding his "faithful subjects" to perform various absurd duties. The settlers shrugged their shoulders — as if they had

[18] Tod to Ermatinger, 27 July 1861. PAC, *Ermatinger Papers*.
[19] Letter of 1 Sept. 1861, *Ermatinger Papers*.

not enough troubles with Indians without this madman coming to pester them! But now in October, while the poor Czar was away from his empire, some Cowichans murdered him at Saanich and took his gun and blankets.

November provided Victoria with the pomp and panoply of a naval funeral. Out for a ride, Lieut. Charles Robson of the *Forward* had been thrown when a sheep wandered between his horse's legs. His injuries proved fatal. On November 7th his remains were borne from Esquimalt aboard the *Forward*'s sister gunboat, *Grappler*, escorted by five boats from other Royal Navy ships. At the HBC wharf the officers, sailors and marines were landed. The procession was formed which was to escort the coffin to the little cemetery placed English-style next to Christ Church. First, marched a company of marines gorgeous in scarlet; second, the band of H.M.S. *Topaze* playing the dead march; then, drawn by sailors, came the gun-carriage bearing Robson's coffin beneath a Union Jack, with his cocked hat and sword on top. There followed as mourners eight of his principal civilian friends. Behind them marched the entire ship's company from the *Forward*. After them walked the officers of H.M.S. *Forward* and the captains and other officers of H.M.S. *Topaze* and H.M.S. *Hecate*. Last came His Excellency the Governor. As the long procession wound its way up Church Hill, some five hundred citizens fell into line behind it. The Rev. Mr. Dundas read the austere and beautiful Anglican service for the burial of the dead. Back in England Mrs. Robson went about the routine of a Victorian lady, ignorant she was now not a wife but a widow. At the end of the service a party of marines fired the customary triple volley over the grave. Then the entire company, perhaps fifteen hundred in number, turned away. It was the grandest funeral Victoria had ever seen.

Among those present was probably a young lad named Edgar Fawcett. Late in life he wrote a curiously random book entitled *Some Reminiscences of Old Victoria*. In it he recalled how as a boy he had "a great weakness for funerals" and "naturally liked the naval funerals best" because of all their display. He gave some macabre details:

The state of Victoria's streets at that time was such that it required a
deal of power to propel any vehicle, and especially was this the case with
Quadra Street. I have often seen a funeral come to a dead standstill
and the hearse dug out of the mud. . . .

We will suppose the hearse has been dug out, and in the cemetery
near the grave, in many cases men might be seen bailing out the grave,
one below and one on top. . . . And I have known when it was necessary
to hold the coffin down in the water with shovels or have a man get
down and stand on the coffin until enough soil was thrown on it to keep
it down.[20]

December saw the *Colonist* running a campaign to close Victoria's
"Dance Houses", where Cariboo miners, down from their claims for
the winter, found the solace of female company. These houses were
of course little more than brothels:

They are not only public nuisances, but they are destructive to the
good order and morals of those who frequent them, and corrupt the
minds of the younger members of the community. The Police Magistrate
has remarked from the bench that the houses were opened for the
amusement of the miners, and at their request. . . . It is a misnomer to
call them "places of amusement". They are sinks of iniquity and
pollution.[21]

All of which provoked a pseudononymous letter-writer to ask the
editor which he thought was better, to maintain a couple of sinks of
pollution or to close them and turn the whole town into a general
cesspool with the girls soliciting on the streets.

On December 23rd old John Tod, sitting down to write once more
to Edward Ermatinger, had to break the sad news that their old
friend Chief Factor Work was dead. Tod had been a constant visitor
seeking to comfort the dying man. His note was brief indeed:

I have just returned home from the house of Mourning where lays
the body of our departed friend Work — the enclosed will explain all
— Feeling so completely jaded & worn out from the want of sleep these
many nights past I am quite unable to say more at this time.[22]

The enclosure was the *Colonist* obituary, headed "Death of Hon.

[20] Pp. 130-31.
[21] *Colonist*, 20 Dec. 1861.
[22] Tod to Ermatinger, 23 Dec. 1861, *Ermatinger Papers*.

John Work",[23] which reviewed his career from his entry into the service of the Hudson's Bay Company in 1814 to his death while a member of the Legislative Council of Vancouver Island.

Christmas Day of this year was a very happy occasion for the Rev. Robert Christopher Lundin Brown, M.A., first rector of the Anglican parish at Lillooet. Upon his arrival from England this clerical gentleman had been taken aback to find:

Often without a servant, he would have to light his fire, sweep his floor, cook his dinner, and, worst of all, thereafter cleanse the dishes.[24]

The white miners to whom he had been sent to minister were plainly not interested in religion, having come to British Columbia to find gold, not God. Fortunately Brown found an ally in the local magistrate who recruited a committee to build a little church. On Christmas Day this year the first services were held in the new building. The whites came to the morning service and the Indians, soon to have a church of their own, came to that in the afternoon. Thereafter Brown found it difficult to muster congregations, but he had a strategy which worked fairly well. Shortly before Sunday evensong, the Rev. Mr. Brown called around at the billiard parlour and invited the miners congregated there to come up to the service.

On such occasions the saloon-keeper would say, "Wall, boys, here's the parson come again to ask you to go to church." The answer often was to this effect, "Wall, I guess some of us 'ull give him a call tonight." Accordingly, perhaps during the general confession, would be heard the welcome clatter of half a hundred feet approaching the sacred building.[25]

Brown was sorely distressed by the moral turpitude of the flock which only half-condescended to accept him as their shepherd. He was upset when he found that one of his few regular attendants was a notorious gambler who "kept a squaw-dance establishment". One Sunday, Brown launched forth on a stern sermon against "the pre-

[23] *Colonist*, 23 Dec. 1861.

[24] R. C. Lundin Brown, *British Columbia. The Indians and Settlers at Lillooet. Appeal for Missionaries* (London, 1870), p. 5.

[25] *Ibid.*, pp. 5-6.

vailing vice, concubinage with native females". The next Sunday not a single person came to his service. When he next went around to recruit a congregation he got some plain speaking from the miners, who strongly resented his denunciations and hell-fire. A chorus greeted him, "Church is played out!" One miner told him, "You may lead those men, you needn't attempt to frighten or drive them." Another treated the rector to a parable: "You may hammer away at a lump of ice and only make its surface rougher; whereas you will melt it at once by the application of a little warm water."[26] Brown had learned an important lesson.

This December brought a major surprise and shock to Victoria. In October Mr. John D'Ewes, the Postmaster-General, had decamped with all the money he could lay his hands on. About the same time Captain Nagle, the Harbour Master, was suspended and his accounts found to be £100 short. Now, on December 23rd, came the culminating shock: Captain G. T. Gordon, the Colonial Treasurer, was arrested at his home on a charge of embezzlement. Taken to prison, he escaped a few months later, reappearing in the safety of the United States.

Presumably what had launched an investigation into Gordon's handling of public funds was an urgent, confidential message of warning from the Duke of Newcastle, Secretary of State for the Colonies. Addressed to Douglas, it read:

Dear Sir,
    Immediately upon my return to England from North America I saw in the Gazette the name of "Tomline Gordon" as Treasurer of British Columbia or Vancouver's Island, I do not at this moment recollect which. The appointment had been confirmed during my absence.
    I am bound to tell you that this person resided for some years in my neighbourhood and was obliged to leave the Country in consequence of his seduction of his friend's wife under circumstances of peculiar aggravation. It then was discovered that he had for years carried on a complete system of fraud and swindling.
    I fear he may be led into some serious fraud upon the Colonial Revenue and the sooner you can get rid of him the better for all concerned.

[26] *Ibid.*, p. 6.

You should at once though without making any unnecessary stir have an examination of the accounts.

I am,
Yours very truly,
NEWCASTLE[27]

The year ended with Governor Douglas writing to the Duke of Newcastle suggesting an invasion of the United States. Douglas had been moved to this project by word of the Trent Affair. Early in November, Captain Wilkes,[28] commanding U.S.S. *San Jacinto*, had violated international law by boarding the British steamer *Trent* on the high seas, and forcibly removing Mason and Siddell, two emissaries of the Confederate States who were travelling to Europe. This incident brought Britain and the Northern States to the very brink of war. Douglas thought it to be an excellent time to go over the brink and, at this moment when the United States was immobilized by civil war, to take over not only the disputed San Juan Islands but the whole territory north of the Columbia which had been extorted from Britain in 1846. Douglas was confident of victory:

With Puget Sound, and the line of the Columbia River in our hands, we should hold the only navigable outlets of the country — command its trade, and soon compel it to submit to Her Majesty's Rule.[29]

Heady irredentist visions swirled through Douglas' mind. Once more he saw the Union Jack flying at the mouth of the Columbia.

It might have happened. At one point only a slight modification in the wording of a crucial message to the American government, a change made at the instigation of Prince Albert, averted the anticipated war. As it was, Douglas found himself in receipt of orders to observe the strictest neutrality during the American Civil War.

[27] Newcastle to Douglas, 31 Dec. 1860, *Newcastle Papers* (on deposit at the University of Nottingham).

[28] This was the same Wilkes who commanded the United States Exploring Expedition which visited the Pacific North-west in 1841. See *British Columbia Chronicle, 1778-1846*, pp. 330-31 and p. 349.

[29] Douglas to Newcastle, private, 28 Dec. 1861. PABC, Vancouver Island, Governor Douglas Despatches, 1859-61. Quoted, Ormsby, *British Columbia: A History*, p. 186.

1862

British Columbia's severe winter — The Cariboo Gold Rush — The "Overlanders" — Billy Barker strikes it rich — Wealth and destitution in the goldfields — James Thomson's letters home — Road-building — Cariboo camels — The Bentinck Arm Company and the Bute Inlet Company — Smallpox — Stikine a "humbug" — Esquimalt becomes a fortified naval base — The brideship Tynemouth *— The Bank of British Columbia — Begbie vs. Robson — The three greenhorns pre-empt "The Brickmakers' Claim" — William Duncan founds Metlakatla.*

The New Year ushered in one of the severest winters ever recorded in British Columbia. At New Westminster patches of ice began to drift down the Fraser and gradually the frost froze these together into great floes. Carried up and down by the flood and ebb of the tide, they made a continual clashing night and day as they struck against each other. Finally the river froze completely. An enterprising American surprised the Indians by putting on skates and skimming along the ice at an amazing speed. "Hockey sticks were cut from the forest, and the male portion of the population, officials, parsons, store-keepers, woodmen, and Indians, were engaged in this exciting game upon the broad river." The ice grew thicker and thicker, and after a while cattle and even carts travelled up and down the Fraser. For eight entire weeks the ice was so thick that no steamer could break its way through to New Westminster and the little capital was completely cut off from the world. Those from outside who simply had to get through to New Westminster or to the road to the Interior arranged to be landed on the shores of Burrard Inlet or Semiahmoo Bay, and travelled overland from there.

One of the persons who played hockey on the frozen Fraser was the Rev. John Sheepshanks, rector of Holy Trinity Church at New Westminster. Later he would return to England and in time become Lord Bishop of Norwich. In *A Bishop in the Rough*, compiled by one of his clergy using excerpts from Sheepshanks' diaries, we find a vivid description of this incredible winter:

My blind fell down the other morning, and I fastened it up again by driving a nail in with my sponge. I cannot easily comb my hair, for it is frozen together. . . .

All the bed-clothes near my mouth are stiff with ice. When one proceeds to breakfast, the cups and saucers are stuck hard to the cupboard. The bread is frozen, and must be put in the oven before it can be eaten. The ink is solid, and in the evening the camphine will not burn.[1]

Gradually the weather became less arctic and ships could once more sail between Victoria and New Westminster. However, according to the not always reliable recollections of old Jason Allard, as late as mid-April the steamer *Flying Dutchman* had to use explosives to blast a passage through the ice at Union Bar above Hope.

*   *   *

There was reason enough for the *Flying Dutchman* to try to get through to Yale even though the ice was still in the river. Thousands of men were impatient to get to the Cariboo goldfields, for this was the year of the great Cariboo Rush, comparable only with the Fraser River Rush of 1858. Even in the latter part of 1861 it was apparent to everyone that this new rush was in the making. Victoria was already half-depopulated as many men quit their jobs or closed their shops and headed for the nugget-rich creeks of Cariboo. With news of Cariboo's gold being trumpeted around the world by the newspapers, an influx from outside was inevitable. And the inevitable occurred in 1862. Thousands upon thousands came. Many arrived from Britain where Donald Fraser's despatches in the *Times* had reported the enormously rich finds in Cariboo, with never a word

---

[1] Pp. 57-58. In 1971 the present writers, eager to peruse the original diaries which Duthie had merely excerpted, made contact with a daughter of Bishop Sheepshanks but only to receive sad news: the movers had lost the crate containing the diaries when the Bishop, entering retirement, left the Palace.

about the ventures which brought only disappointment. Typical roseate passages by Fraser read:

> It is common to meet men who have sums varying from $5,000 to $10,000; and this evening ... three men arrived from Fraser River who made $80,000 between them in six weeks.[2]

A miner writes that his gains far surpass anything ever produced in California, and cites the fact of $1,700 having been dug *out of two crevices* in the rock *less than three feet under the surface*. In fact, the explanation of the enormous yields is, as I before stated, the large, solid, nuggety character of the gold and its proximity to the surface. Men who had never mined before, tradesmen, mechanics, and labourers new to the work, did just as well as the old practised miner.[3]

As to the mining prospects, they are as clear as the sun at noon. *Every able man who chooses to work will make money.*[4]

Hundreds of Englishmen thronged to steamship agencies to book passage to Panama en route to the new El Dorado. Soon the steamers from Panama to Victoria were overloaded with almost twice their authorized number of passengers. Since working-class Englishmen and Scots could rarely raise the expensive fare from Britain, the hopeful novice British gold-miners mostly had a middle-class background. Some came from what the Victorians called "good families" — like that of Clement Francis Cornwall, aged twenty-six, and Henry Pennant Cornwall, aged twenty-four, sons of the Reverend A. G. Cornwall, rector of Newington Bagpath-cum-Owlpen and Beverstone-cum-Kingscote, Chaplain-in-Ordinary to Queen Victoria.[5] (Actually the Cornwall brothers' visit to the goldfields proved brief, and they started ranching at Ashcroft Manor named after the family home, Ashcroft House in Gloucestershire. One day the elder brother would become Lieutenant-Governor of the Province of British Columbia.)

To the far reaches of Queen Victoria's great empire went the tidings of the wealth to be found in the Crown Colony of British

---

[2] *Times*, 11 Dec. 1861, p. 8.

[3] *Times*, 5 Feb. 1862, p. 10.

[4] *Times*, 6 Feb. 1862, p. 10.

[5] E. P. Johnson, "The Early Years of Ashcroft Manor", *BC Studies* 5 (Summer 1970) :3.

Columbia. Australians began to arrive, and in June ships from New Zealand brought over two hundred gold-miners from the Otago fields.

No other settled part of the British Empire was closer to British Columbia than Canada West (Ontario). In an unguarded moment the Rev. Edward White, at New Westminster, anxious to see good Ontario Methodists settle in British Columbia, had written to the *Christian Guardian*, published in Toronto:

The bags of [gold] *dust* which are now coming down, confound and strike dum[b] every person who has dared to call Fraser River gold mines a *humbug*. If I had time and space I would fill sheets with the reports of lucky ones. I could give you a long list of those who went up last spring with hardly enough to pay their expenses to Cariboo, and are now returning with from $5,000 to $20,000 each.

... for good and wise men who will come here for Christ's sake, and will "stand up for Jesus" after they get here, there is an open door, a wide field for usefulness, a rich harvest of this world's goods, and a glorious immortality. Why should the children of this world have all the gold and political power, and all the rich lands of this far colony?[6]

Why indeed, when the gold to be found in a few weeks in the Cariboo could buy a good farm in the Niagara peninsula? Thousands of young men began scraping together the money to travel to Cariboo via New York and Panama or, more adventurously, to strike overland.

*   *   *

And so we come to the famous (perhaps too famous) "Overlanders of 1862" who figure so prominently in the simplified British Columbia history popular in some quarters. The Overlanders of 1862 were not the first settlers to travel to the Pacific Coast by a British overland route. We have commented earlier on the two Red River parties brought out by James Sinclair in 1841 and 1854. Moreover, in 1859 no less than three Canadian parties[7] made the overland trip to the Fraser River diggings, two using southern passes and the Kootenay plains, the third coming through Tête Jaune

[6] *Christian Guardian*, 4 Dec. 1861, p. 192.
[7] M. S. Wade, *The Overlanders of '62*, PABC Memoir IX (Victoria, 1931), p. 9.

Cache. No records survive of their journeys, with their inevitable misadventures and hardships. Had we their stories we might find that these contained episodes eclipsing any of the difficulties of the thoroughly documented overland migrations of 1862.

The Overlanders of 1862 must not be thought of as a single cohesive unit, initiated under central direction. What happened was that, in various areas in the two Canadas, men joined together to journey overland to the Cariboo. Many of these parties converged either at the railhead at St. Paul, Minnesota, or at Fort Garry. On July 5th the following companies were camped together near Fort Garry:

Queenston Company	24 men
St. Thomas Company	21 men
Ogdensburgh, N.Y. Company	7 men
Whitby Company	6 men
Scarborough Company	5 men
Chatham Company	3 men
Ottawa Company	8 men
Huntingdon Company	21 men
Montreal Company	7 men
London Company	5 men
Toronto Company	7 men
Acton Company	6 men
Waterloo Company	6 men
Goderich Company	5 men

131 men[8]

This does not quite complete the tally, however, for at the Red River settlement three more men joined the migrants. One of them, August Schubert, was accompanied by his wife Catherine (who refused to stay behind), and their three small children, ranging in age between six and three.[9]

A decision having been reached to amalgamate the companies, Thomas R. McMicking was elected as "Captain" and a set of rules was adopted. Then the immigrants started their long train of Red River carts creaking across the plains, drawn by oxen. By the time

[8] *Ibid.*, p. 51.
[9] *Ibid.*, p. 53.

McMicking reached Fort Edmonton his followers had swollen to 150 in all. Here some of the migrants, deceived by a false report of gold to be found east of the Rockies, decided to turn aside. On July 28th and 29th, the constituent companies, now down to 125 individuals, resumed their journey to the Cariboo. Their carts they had left behind them as unsuitable for the country ahead. In their place they had a packtrain of 140 horses, mules and oxen, each with a load of from 150 to 250 pounds. To see them through the Rockies they had an expert guide, André Cardinal, who on August 27th brought them, without the loss of a single person, to Tête Jaune Cache. Here, in the lush pastures close to the headwaters of the Fraser, the horses and cattle were able to recoup.

Probably the migrants had thought that once they were over the Rockies they would have only a fairly short and easy journey to the Cariboo. Certainly such a misconception had been rather widely circulated by the eastern press. In fact, it was only after the travellers had crossed the Rockies that they met their real difficulties and dangers. To the Overlanders' shock they found that the Shuswap Indians whom they met at Tête Jaune Cache had never heard of Cariboo, much less were able to indicate the way thither. The best the Indians could do was to point out a trail leading to the North Thompson River. After much discussion, McMicking's followers decided to separate. Most of the companies were resolved to build canoes and rafts and start down the Fraser, which they knew must in time bring them to Quesnel, the gateway to the Cariboo. A minority decided to take the horses, along with most of the cattle, and head south for the North Thompson River and Fort Kamloops.

On September 2nd this second party, consisting of 36 persons and 130 cattle and horses, set forth. Soon they reached the junction of the Albreda and North Thompson Rivers, but their trail had been gradually petering out, and an increasing amount of time and effort was being spent slashing a trail for the livestock. At Slaughter Camp a key decision was reached: the cattle would have to be butchered and, while rafts and canoes were being built, the meat "jerked"[10] for future use. Then the entire body started down the North Thompson.

[10] A method of preserving meat by cutting it into thin lean strips which are dried in the sun or by the heat of fires.

For a few days Heaven kept a special watch over the random little craft as they rushed down the unknown river, travelling at what seemed the speed of a railway express. Again and again they narrowly avoided being wrecked on log jams. Then suddenly the travellers were confronted by Murchison Rapids, which culminate in Hell's Gate Canyon, "a more appalling death-trap than the canyon of the same name on the Fraser River above Yale".[11] The leading raft had no time to pull ashore. Down it went into the rapids and was wrecked in midstream. One man was drowned, but two others clung to a rock until they were rescued by companions in a canoe. The weather had turned to a mixture of rain and snow and the party, after abandoning their craft, spent three miserable days portaging nine miles to the calm water below Hell's Gate. Here new rafts were built. Some of these came to grief in other rapids lower down the river, and their occupants were forced to walk the last stretch along the river bank. Others managed to bring their rafts safely all the way to Kamloops. On October 11th the first overlanders reached the fort, hungry and ragged. Few of them had many of their belongings left. On the 13th the Schuberts' raft arrived. Tradition says that it was the very next day that Mrs. Schubert gave birth to a daughter. Named Rose, she was the first white child born in the Interior of British Columbia.

Let us leave the Thompson River party enjoying the care and hospitality of kindly J. W. McKay, the Hudson's Bay Company's Chief Trader at Fort Kamloops, and turn to their comrades from whom they had parted at Tête Jaune Cache. The latter had abandoned any idea of travelling as a group under a single commander. As soon as each company had its rafts or canoes ready, it launched them and started careering down the upper Fraser. The Shuswap Indians, seeing them embarking, murmured "Poor white men no more!" They knew that only a few days' travel would bring the newcomers to the terrors of the Grand Rapids. The first canoe to hit the Grand Rapids, that of the Toronto company, was wrecked almost immediately. The Goderich company's canoe was lost in the Grand Rapids also, and this time a man was drowned. Somehow

[11] Wade, *Overlanders of '62*, p. 113.

the rafts (including the giant one, measuring 85 feet by 22 feet, of the Huntingdon party) got through intact. Further hazards lay ahead, but on September 8th the Queenston raft, one week after leaving Tête Jaune Cache, became the first to reach Fort George (Prince George). Chief Trader William Charles was absent, but his assistant immediately did all he could for one of the party who was seriously ill. Ironically, having reached this haven, the sick man died that evening.

On September 8th, depressed by the two deaths, the survivors resumed their voyage downstream. Somehow they safely passed the great dangers of the Fort George and Cottonwood canyons, and the whitewater of China Rapids, as well as the lesser dangers of log jams, snags, "sweepers", gravel bars, cross currents and eddies. On September 11th the Queenston and Huntingdon rafts arrived at their destination, Quesnel. Here they were joined on October 4th by the Symington party. As dark was falling on October 13th, a fourth and final party of Overlanders, the Redgrave company, pulled in at Quesnel. These last had an eerie story to tell. On September 30th, in the Grand Rapids, they had lost a man named Carpenter. Before entering the rapids, he had made the final entry in his diary. It read:

Arrived this day at the cañon at 10 a.m., and drowned running the canoe down; God keep my poor wife![12]

And what of the men now that they had reached Quesnel and were within easy reach of Williams Creek, the heart of the gold country? They found Quesnel, now that the 1862 season was nearing its end, full of disillusioned, half-destitute men who told them that the Cariboo was a fraud, a "humbug" to use the slang of the day. They declared that the men from the East would be ill-advised to continue on to the goldfields and there to risk death from starvation. A few persisted, however, in pushing on to the goldfields where one, James Wattie, did indeed finally make a fortune. Most of the Overlanders, however, were so tired and discouraged that, on the

---

[12] See *British Columbian* 12 Aug. 1863; also Wade, p. 136. For a slightly different wording and a more circumstantial account of the incident, see Margaret McNaughton, *Overland to Cariboo* (Toronto, 1896), pp. 97-98.

very threshold of the Cariboo, that lure which had brought them across the continent, they turned their backs upon it and made for New Westminster or Victoria. They were fortunate that they could earn enough through roadwork or casual jobs to keep themselves alive until they reached the Pacific Coast.

Some of the Overlanders lost little time in heading back to Canada once they had raised enough money to buy tickets that would get them to New York via Panama. Others stayed on and made satisfactory lives for themselves in the new country. Among those who prospered in British Columbia were John Fannin, first curator of the Provincial Museum; John Andrew Mara, M.P.; Alexander Leslie Fortune, the first settler in the North Okanagan; and Robert Burns McMicking, a future general manager of the B.C. Telephone Company.

*   *   *

On the whole those who by-passed the Cariboo goldfields were well advised to do so. But the Cariboo was not, as the Jeremiahs said, a "humbug" — far from it. Admittedly, simple panning on the creeks which were not yet fully staked would yield little gold. But there were real fortunes for those companies of miners who had pooled their resources and dug deep shafts, through heavy over-burden, to reach the ancient auriferous creek or river beds many feet below. Gold would continue to pour from such mines. In mid-June this year Thomas Elwyn, the new gold commissioner, arriving at Williams Creek when the season had barely started, reported to the Colonial Secretary in Victoria that sensational returns were already coming in:

The yield of Gold on this creek [Williams] is something almost incredible, and rich claims have risen to three times their market value of last winter. . . . Cunningham & Company have been working their claims for the past six weeks, and for the last thirty days have been taking out Gold at the rate of three thousand dollars every twenty four hours. . . . Mess[rs.] Steel & Cº have been engaged for the last ten days in making a flume but during the previous three weeks their claims yielded two hundred ounces a day. These figures are so startling that I should be afraid to put them on paper, in a report for His Excellency's information were I not on the spot and *know* them to be the exact truth.[13]

Information from other sources bears out the Elwyn report. Steele & Company, freed from work on their flume, made $2500 (something like $60,000 today) in half a day. The famous Diller Claim paid $20,000 in a single day. And this year an adjacent mine yielded the richest pan of gold ever washed in the Cariboo. J. C. Bryant, the finder, tells the story:

One day when I was cleaning up the bedrock in the mine where I was superintendent, I got to a place where I dug off a piece of the bedrock. It was soft and came off like cheese with the shovel. Right under this place, in a little hole, not much bigger than a gold pan, I saw what I took to be solid gold. I obtained a gold pan, cleaned it out, and then washed what I took out. Then I went to the shaft and washed out a bucket, and shouted up to the windlass man on top: "Run over to the cabin and see if Kelly is there. If he is tell him I want to speak to him." Kelly came to the top of the shaft and I called up to him, "I'm going to send you up a prospect." I dumped what I had into the bucket and sent it up.

Men at that time were very plentiful in Cariboo, and were always wandering round looking for work, and watching everything in the washing line. There were quite a number in the shaft house when my prospect went up. I called up to Kelly to dump it into a gold pan and I would come up and weigh it. Well, I went up and weighed it. There were 96 ounces [worth $16 per ounce] and seven dollars in it, or a total of $1,543. This was about the biggest pan of dirt that was ever taken out in the Cariboo.[14]

Best remembered of all those who struck it rich in Cariboo this year was a curious little Cornishman turned sailor, who had deserted his ship and headed for the Cariboo. Bow-legged, and with a bushy black-grey beard, Billy Barker was decidedly an original. Entering a saloon, he liked to go into a little song and dance routine, chanting:

> I'm English Bill,
> Never work, an' never will.
> Get away girls,
> Or I'll tousle your curls.

[13] PABC, Colonial Correspondence, F525/10.
[14] Walkem, *Stories of Early B.C.*, p. 147.

When Billy and the six other Englishmen who made up his "company" arrived at Williams Creek, he found the known gold-bearing stretch above the canyon had all been staked by others. That there was no gold below the canyon was a matter of common knowledge. Billy however went to take a look for himself. He found an outcropping of rock and reasoned that, if the creek had once run in that direction, it would have been deflected by the rock and have deposited much of its gold there. So, while the old hands laughed at the fool Englishmen, Billy staked a claim by that ancient rimrock. He and his partners began digging through centuries of detritus: gravel, boulders, and whatever else had come down over the centuries. Ten feet down they went and no gold. Twenty, thirty feet and still no gold. Forty and fifty feet and still nothing. Above the canyon gold lay at no great depth below the surface and people shook their heads at the craziness of going to such depths, especially since it was common knowledge that Billy and his men were running out of money, even though Judge Begbie had given them some help. But finally, fifty-two feet down, Billy and his friends struck gravel rich, amazingly rich, with gold. The Anglican Bishop, the Rt. Rev. George Hills, was visiting the Cariboo this summer. In his diary he made an entry:

When lead struck on Barker's claim, about August 21st, all went on spree for several days, except one Englishman, well brought up.[15]

They had occasion for celebration. According to unofficial estimates, Billy and his partners took out $600,000 in gold. Needless to say, a host of miners hurriedly staked the land adjacent to the Barker claim, and to their shanties was given, fittingly, the name of "Barkerville".

*   *   *

How did it happen, then, that here in this El Dorado with its Dillers, Bryants and Barkers, thousands of unemployed men drifted around for a few weeks, then left declaring that a pack of lies had been told them about the wealth to be won in Cariboo?

[15] Quoted by Louis LeBourdais, "Billy Barker of Barkerville", *BCHQ* 1 (1937): 165. See LeBourdais' article for the sad story of how reckless generosity and a foolish marriage stripped Billy of his wealth within a few years.

There were various explanations. Most of those joining in the Gold Rush of 1862 had pathetically naive ideas about how easily they would become rich. A few days' travel, they had thought, would bring them to the gold district. There they would take their pans out of their packs and at once begin washing the rich gravel. Then, at the end of a few weeks, each with a heavy bag of gold, they would head home. Illustrative of this naiveté was a letter from Ontario received by the Methodist minister at Hope. The writer wanted the Rev. Mr. Browning to tell him how he should time his trip so as to arrive "ten days before the crush", and he made it clear that he must be back home in Ontario nine months after his departure, with at least two thousand dollars profit made on his trip.[16]

A great many of the newcomers arrived much too early for the season. Today, tourists wishing to visit the Provincial Government's restoration of Barkerville, the principal Cariboo gold town, are disconcerted to learn that, because of the high altitude, the road is closed by snow until well into June. In 1862 those who knew the Cariboo regarded July 1st as the real beginning of the season there. But some participants in this year's gold rush arrived in Victoria as early as February. Here they spent expensive months, waiting either in the hotels or in a new tent town which quickly sprang up around the town. By mid-April the Fraser was sufficiently clear of ice for the first steamer to head upriver. Logically, it should have carried nothing but provisions, both for the men who were now running low on food after wintering in the Cariboo, and for the horde of treasure-hunters already chafing to be off to the goldfields. As it was, the boat made the voyage laden with so many passengers that it could carry only half its usual freight. When, after weeks of backpacking or leading recalcitrant packhorses or mules over appalling trails, the greenhorns arrived on the banks of Williams Creek, Antler Creek, Lightning Creek and the rest, they found these streams had already been fully staked, and the surrounding country was still covered with deep snow — and within a few weeks they had exhausted their provisions and slender capital. Returning to the coast, they met other parties coming up and assured them that Cariboo was a humbug.

---

[16] *Christian Guardian*, 2 July 1862, p. 106.

Many of those they encountered, already worn out with clambering up and slithering down precipitous muddy trails, over ridge after ridge, turned around and headed back with them.

Typical of those who met returning pessimists was young Doug Bogart, who started out from Victoria late in May. Using the Harrison-Lillooet route, he and his party required a month to get to the forks of the Quesnel; " . . . before we reached there however we met men by the hundreds going down saying Cariboo was played out." Resolutely pushing on, Bogart's party reached Keithley Creek, began panning on the spot, and could not find a trace of gold. They went on to another creek, apparently reaching it about nightfall:

. . . the next morning got up and could see men standing in groups all around not working as you would expect making money as they were led to believe they could, but where one man had work hundreds were idle. . . . [17]

A few days later Bogart and his friends had "seen the Cariboo was no place for us" and decided to head back. "I did feel mad to think that we had to walk five or six hundred miles, and then be fooled." On the trip down they consoled themselves at night around the campfire by singing such sad ditties as "Sad was the day we went away a-hunting of the gold", and another which began:

> We did not find it was a sell
> Until we got to Forks of Quesnell.
> Look away to Cariboo.

Perhaps it was by some other campfire that a disillusioned bard intoned the following verses:

> Five hundred miles to travel where none but mosses grew
> To cheer the weary pilgrim on the road to Cariboo,
> With savages all round them and tigers [cougars] in full view
> Those were the kinds of comforts on the road to Cariboo.
> For every man who makes his pile, there thousands are that rue
> The day they left their happy homes for the mines of Cariboo. [18]

[17] Ontario Provincial Archives, Toronto, MSS. Misc. Coll. 1862.

[18] A copy of these verses, with no indication of their authorship, is to be found in the typescript *Letter Book of John Evans: The Welsh Mining Adventure in Cariboo, 1862-64*, UBC Special Collections.

Swept by the bitterness of his discontent, Bogart closed his eyes to what was around him and declared there were not fifty acres of arable land in all British Columbia. Other more prescient immigrants, also disappointed in the Cariboo goldfields, took out land and established large ranches where they would make, if not a fortune, at least a competence.

A young Englishman, Harry Guillod, arriving at Lightning Creek in August, could congratulate himself that he had hit the season right. Unfortunately, like so many others before him, he found that the proven gold creeks were fully staked, with some of the staking done by speculators who had tricked the gold commissioner into letting them have as many as six claims instead of the single one to which they were entitled. Two courses of action were open to Guillod and his companions: they could go out into the wilderness and prospect for a new place to stake (though the likely areas had been well covered), or they could buy an existing claim. Since many of the claims had already been proved sterile, claim-buying was not for tenderfeet but for experienced miners who could look at a stream and, from intuition based on long experience, could sense the course that it must have followed millenia ago. Such men could sometimes deduce where a known gold stratum or "channel" might be tapped. Guillod and his companions decided to buy a claim, partly on the strong advice of an apparently disinterested bystander who advised them that they were getting in on a good thing. Only later did they discover that their counsellor had been paid ten dollars by the seller to give them this advice. Later, writing up a journal of his trip, Guillod noted:

Monday Augt 25th I called it Black Monday, because we signed the agreement which put us in possession of our claim.[19]

Their purses lighter by $500, Guillod, his brother and friend, started examining their claim. They found that they had acquired a shaft twenty feet deep, filled with water. For a fortnight they tried to get the shaft dry, only to find that their pumps were not sufficiently powerful. On September 18th they closed down the operation for

[19] Dorothy Blakey Smith, ed., "Harry Guillod's Journal of a Trip to Cariboo, 1862", *BCHQ* 19 (1955):216.

the year, taking out the flume, and putting away their boards, troughs, sluice boxes, picks and shovels. Guillod was not entirely discouraged, even though he had a terrible time getting back to the Coast, having lost one shoe. The sole of the remaining shoe he used as a sort of sandal for one foot, while out of its upper he fashioned a sandal for the other. He returned to the Cariboo the following year. Apparently he was more successful this time, but he had learned that if one obtained gold one was winning against heavy odds:

... now and then a man comes down with thirty or forty pounds of gold dust; while a thousand return without a cent. ... [20]

Another who trudged the endless miles to Cariboo this summer was one James Thomson, a sturdy Scot aged about forty. In the early 1850s Thomson had made a tidy sum in the California gold-fields. With this he bought in 1854 a farm in Canada West, bringing to it his nineteen-year-old bride. The years passed and children were born to them. Thomson brought out his destitute old father from Scotland to share their home. With the contracts he had obtained for nearby railway and canal construction, Thomson was prospering. But the construction ended and an economic depression struck the Canadas. Left to make his livelihood off the poor land around today's Cardinal, Ontario, Thomson realized too late the wisdom of those who had urged him to spend his California savings on a smaller but more fertile farm in the land to the west. Confronted with poverty, and with a wife, children and his old father dependent upon him, James Thomson remembered how once he had prospered in California. Now there were new gold discoveries in the West, in a place called British Columbia. Perhaps, with his experience, he could gloriously revive his fortunes in Cariboo. In April of this year, with his brother-in-law Anson and half a dozen other men from his district, Thomson left for New York and the long journey by way of Panama to the new El Dorado.

On July 27th James Thomson wrote to his wife Mary from Williams Lake. Things had not gone well since he had written to her

20 *Ibid.*, p. 219.

last from Victoria. Their troubles had begun once they got off the steamboat which had brought them from New Westminster to Yale:

We had 600 lbs of provisions on board the Boat, expecting to get it packed from Yale but when we got there the mules were all engaged. So we each took what we could carry, sold the balance and started on foot for a journey of 380 miles. We travelled 13 miles that afternoon and 22 miles the next day which brought us to Boston Bar. Here they had commenced work making a waggon road which is intended to run from Yale to the mines. As it was still early in the season to go to the mines the roads bad and provisions scarce and dear, we concluded it was better for some of us to remain. Accordingly Anson, James McIlmoyl, Irvine Raney and Smith from Mountain hired with the contractor for one month while Picken, Thos Harbottle and myself should go on to Cariboo and prospect.

I find that I have not paper enough to give you an account of my journey. Three weeks travel brought us to Forks of Quesnell (322 miles from Yale). We went 60 miles beyond the *Forks* to Antler and Williams Creek where some of the richest diggings are but did not succeed in finding any gold. We dug several holes, but like hundreds of others were unsuccessful. The ground is nearly all taken up and holes being dug but only a few claims are paying and they are very rich, which has given rise to the excitement about Cariboo. Every one seems to be convinced that this country has been greatly misrepresented both as an agricultural and a mining country. No doubt new discoveries will be made and much gold found but this season provisions will be so dear that very few will be able to stay long enough to prospect thoroughly. When we were at Antler Creek, Flour, Beans, sugar, Salt & Rice were each one dollar per lb. Fresh Beef 50 cents & Bacon $1.25 6/3 and at Williams Creek a quarter of a dollar was added to the price of each. Just think of Two hundred & fifty dollars for a Barrel of Flour and everything else in proportion. We could not stand it long.

When we left the Boys the ageement was that at the end of a month they should come on after us and we would meet them at Forks at Quesnelle a month after we got there. Accordingly we returned to that place and found Anson & Irvine waiting for us. The five started to come but when they had travelled three days they met so many returning with bad news about the mines that they concluded to turn back and go to work again and sent Joe and Anson on to meet us. When we met we concluded that it was no use trying to prospect any more at present, but go down where provisions were cheaper and work at any thing we could get to do. Accordingly we left the Forks a week past on Thursday and got here on Saturday night, staid over Sunday and on

Monday morning took a job of building a clay oven for Mr Davidson proprietor of a Farm, Store & Tavern. He is newly settled here and is doing business in a large tent. Is now preparing to build a house and we will furnish the Lumber & Shingles. . . . The weather here very warm at present and we are very much pestered with mosquitos and flies. In Cariboo it is quite cold, rain almost every day, on the morning of 3rd July there was several inches of Snow on our tent and we walked over old snow six feet deep.

With heartfull respects for all I am ever,

Your Devoted Companion

James Thompson

Reading the cool formality of the closing to this letter, some persons might suspect that James and Mary were not a very loving couple. No deduction could be more mistaken. Enclosed with the letter just quoted was another, a more private one for the wife:

Mary my Beloved Companion, I have written you quite a long letter. It may be that you will have to read some of it to enquiring friends. I would now wish to have a little talk between ourselves. Oh Mary were you by my side I have much that I would like to say. Mary I have thought of you more, prayed for you more, and if possible loved you more this summer than ever before. Volumes would not contain all the thoughts I have of Home and the loved ones there. Mary I often wish that I had more of your courage and energy and resignation to battle with the disappointments of life. I sometimes wonder how I ever came to leave a kind and affectionate wife and all that the heart of man could desire of a family to sojourn in this land. But then the thought comes up that we were poor, that you had to deny yourself many of the comforts of life that a little money would have secured, and then I think of my poor old Father toiling and labouring when he ought to be enjoying the evening of his days in ease and comfort. Then I pray God to strengthen my arm and encourage my heart and bless my exertions to procure the means to make you comfortable. . . .

What troubles me most is how you are to put in the long cold winter in that old house. Could you do anything by papering to make it warmer? Could *Aunty* paper her house to keep out the wind some? I hope to be able to send you some money perhaps by Christmas to help you to rig up for winter. Try to get warm clothing for all.

I suppose the children have forgotten all about Pa. Tell them I have not forgotten them. I have got a Bible lesson for them to learn, I hope to hear them repeat it yet. Oh if God would enable one to return and hear Minnie repeat that verse I would be a happy man. It is the 2nd verse of the 4th chapter of Micah (ommitting the first and the last clause, get down to paths. May God bless all, and bring us to that land, where *farewells* are unknown.[21]

J.T.

Actually James Thomson got home sooner than he had expected when he wrote to Mary from Williams Lake. On December 30th of this year, in a final entry in his diary, he noted that he was near Ogdensburg, New York, and should be home on the morrow. It must have been a blissful New Year's Day in 1863 with James Thomson reunited with Mary and their children, back from that dangerous and distant land where so many who sought gold disappeared forever.

What of James Thomson thereafter? He never went back to Cariboo. But the financial competency which it had denied him he obtained as a bookkeeper for the Edwardsburgh Starch Company which had built its factory close to the Thomson farm.

*   *   *

Perhaps because of involvement in their Civil War at home, comparatively few Americans joined in this Gold Rush of 1862. The newcomers were in the main from Canada[22] and Britain. The result was that after 1862 the American element in British Columbia became less important.

We noted earlier that many of the destitute men coming back from the Cariboo found work on the road. It was their one piece of good fortune that this year Governor Douglas' tremendous road-building program got well under way. The Royal Engineers had already surveyed the route for the wagon road right through the Fraser Canyon from Yale to Lytton and beyond. Now, while the Royal Engineers themselves were building the difficult six-mile stretch

---

[21] R. A. Preston, ed., *For Friends at Home: A Scottish Emigrant's Letters from Canada, California and the Cariboo, 1844-64* (Montreal, 1974), pp. 298-305. The Bible text for the children to learn reads: "Come, and let us go up to the mountain of the Lord, and to the house of the God of Jacob, and he will teach us of his ways, and we will walk in his paths."

[22] According to the New York *Scottish American*, quoted in the *Christian Guardian*, 17 Sept. 1862, p. 5, "the number of Canadians in Cariboo is almost as great as that of the people of all other nationalities combined."

from Yale to Pike's Riffle (near Spuzzum), contracts were let to civilians to build the rest under the supervision of the military. J. W. Trutch contracted to build the road from Pike's Riffle to Chapman's Bar and on to Boston Bar, and Thomas Spence to continue the road from Boston Bar to Lytton. Messrs. Oppenheimer, Lewis and Moberly were awarded a contract to build the road beyond Lytton, along the Thompson River to Cook's Ferry (today's Spences Bridge), and then over to Cache Creek and northwards to Lac La Hache where it would join another road which that notable entrepreneur Gustavus Blin Wright was building from Lillooet to Soda Creek, just north of Williams Lake. At Soda Creek, Wright had men building a steamer which would take passengers and freight up the navigable stretch of the Fraser extending to Alexandria and Quesnel.

Financing this tremendous project was not easy. True, Governor Douglas could count upon mounting government funds. As Dr. Ormsby has noted:

... the colony's revenues from customs duties, tolls, miners' licences and the sale of lands were increasing with each month. The time had come when the Colony could well afford to borrow money. He [Douglas] applied to the Bank of British Columbia for a loan of £50,000.[23]

But even so, more money was needed than Douglas could raise. The solution was to let the contractors make a speculation out of these roads, putting up a fair amount of the money themselves in return for the right to collect tolls along the completed roads. Thus Gustavus Blin Wright was promised that, once he completed the wagon road from Lillooet to Soda Creek, he would be authorized to collect for five years a toll of one cent per pound on goods and twenty-five cents per head of stock.[24]

For a project of this dimension, Wright would require about eight hundred men, providing invaluable employment for destitute gold miners. Even more men would be needed to construct the wagon road up the Fraser and Thompson canyons and on to Clinton. On April 4th of this year a large advertisement appeared in the *Colonist*:

[23] Ormsby, *British Columbia: A History*, p. 185.
[24] *Colonist*, 7 April 1862.

The Great Cariboo Wagon Road

In April 1862 a young Englishman, Frederick Dally, landed at Esquimalt, and shortly thereafter opened a photographic studio in Victoria. The hundreds of Dally photographs which still survive constitute our greatest photographic archive for colonial British Columbia.

In 1867 and again in 1868, Dally made photographic expeditions up to the Cariboo. With the help of the following Dally pictures and a little imagination, readers can make the journey up the Cariboo Road of colonial days.

Generally one's journey commenced at New Westminster, with a river steamer taking one up the Fraser River to the head of navigation at Yale. At Yale one reached the beginning of the Cariboo Road.

Fraser River sternwheeler at Emory Bar, near Yale

40. Barnard's Stage at Yale

41. Alexandra Bridge, Fraser Canyon

42. Seventeen Mile Bluff, Fraser Canyon

43. Boothroyd's Hostelry, north of Boston Bar

44. The Cariboo Road at Jackass Mountain

45. View of Lytton

46. Spence's Bridge, Thompson River

47. Cariboo Road at the Great Bluff, Thompson River

48. Approaching Cache Creek

49. Clinton Hotel

50. Soda Creek, showing Colonial Hotel and river steamer

51. Quesnelmouth

52.   Barkerville, the main street, before the fire of 1868

53.   Barkerville, the Hotel de France

1000 Laborers Wanted
To Work on the Great Trunk Wagon Road from Yale
to Cariboo

Wages will be paid in cash on the Road.
Sub-contracts will be let in large and small sections.
For further particulars apply to Charles Oppenheimer, at Yale or
Lytton, or to Thomas B. Lewis and Walter Moberly, on the Road.

C. OPPENHEIMER & CO.

Travellers heading to and from Cariboo this year, either along the old trails or the newly-constructed stretches of wagon road, received a shock which must have made some wonder if they were suffering from *delirium tremens*. Swaying along the trail towards them came camels! A number of these had earlier been imported into California as pack animals; and Messrs. Adam Heffley, Henry Ingram and Frank Laumeister, knowing as much, had imported twenty or so of the beasts to pack on stretches of the Harrison-Lillooet route. Since each animal could carry 500-600 pounds (much more than a mule) and could live off country where mules required expensive feed, the enterprise had seemed a sound one. Unfortunately the swampy and stony stretches alike of the British Columbia trails proved so hard on the camels' feet, and their strange pungent smell caused so much panic among the packhorses that after a while these strangely exotic animals were taken off the trails. The last survivor died at Westwold around 1905.

*   *   *

While the great work force was pushing through the Cariboo Wagon Road (and incidentally improving the future prospects of New Westminster), the merchants in Victoria, fearful of eclipse by the mainland capital, rallied to the support of the Bute Inlet Company and the Bentinck Arm Company. These, they were confident, would find shorter more feasible routes to the Cariboo which would divert trade through Victoria. Neither company was financed by the government; each, however, was authorized to attempt construction of a road from saltwater to the Cariboo and, once such a road had been built, to charge for five years tolls of $1\frac{1}{2}$ cents a pound for freight and fifty cents per head for livestock.

In November Alfred Waddington returned to Victoria with

seventy men who had spent the season at Bute Inlet. To his share-holders he reported that twenty-three miles of trail had been completed and a further forty miles, up to the forks of the Homathko River, had been blazed and partly cleared. He regretfully announced that the difficulties of penetrating the Coast Mountains were greater than he had anticipated, and that the Homathko River was less suitable for navigation than he had expected. He reported, moreover, that the Indians were proving a nuisance. Nevertheless he was far from losing faith in the project.

The Bentinck Arm Company did not attempt construction this year, probably because it was awaiting the report of Lieut. Palmer, R.E., who with Sappers Edwards and Breakenridge had been sent by the government to survey the country between Bella Coola (at the head of Bentinck Arm) and Alexandria. It was well that the Company waited, for Palmer's final report plainly intimated that the proposed Bella Coola route, because of "its high continuous elevation, and from the general absence of good soil and pasturage in the districts which it traverses"[25] could not compete with the wagon road being built by way of the Fraser and Thompson canyons.

One of Palmer's liveliest reports is a letter of mid-July sent to Colonel Moody from his camp on the Bella Coola River:

A good trail can be made along the base of the hills skirting this valley, & the present distance materially shortened, for the Indian trail we are now on follows all the windings of the river. As for the Indians I can only say that they are the most extortionate, inconsistent thieving rascals I ever saw. The man who christened Bella Coola "Rascals' Village" [Sir Alexander Mackenzie] ought to be remembered by posterity as a discerning gentleman. The beggars have an unlimited affection for pannekins, knives etc. & I am getting rather short. One of them stole the inverting eye-piece of the theodolite. I hope to goodness he will be frightened when he sees the world upside down. As it is they think that, when I am observing with the sextant, I am having a "cloche nanitch" at the "Sockally Tihe" to find out whether the smallpox is going to be bad.[26]

---

[25] H. Spencer Palmer, *Report of a Journey of Survey From Victoria to Fort Alexander, via North Bentinck Arm* (New Westminster, Royal Engineers Press, 1863), p. 29.

[26] PAC, Transcript, Box 320, Frank Swannell, *Field Book "C"* (1926), pp. 128-29.

Alas, poor Indians! The smallpox would indeed prove bad. This year it would wipe out about one-third of the native population of British Columbia, reducing it from some 60,000 persons to around 40,000.

The disaster began in Victoria in May when the dreaded disease flared up among the visiting northern Indians. Soon there were far more cases than could be accommodated in the small Indian hospital adjacent to the Victoria Hospital. As noted earlier, each year had seen a growing demand for the expulsion of the northern Indians. Now, with their smallpox becoming a major threat to the health of the little town, that expulsion finally occurred. The Indians from upcoast were ordered to vacate their huts and start home. When they refused to do so, the police set fire to some hundred of their hovels. Only Indian women living with white men were exempted from the order which this spring sent the northerners in flight from Victoria. As the Indians worked their way upcoast they carried with them the smallpox, already mounting to epidemic proportions. Everywhere they put in, they brought the plague with them. Like wildfire the smallpox spread up the Coast. One party returning north from Victoria was attacked by the piratical Yucultas. The aggressors caught the disease from their victims and soon were lying dead on the beaches. Lieut. Palmer, in that letter to his colonel already noted, speaks of how the smallpox ravaged the Bella Coolas:

Poor creatures, they are dying and rotting away by the score, & it is no uncommon occurrence to come across dead bodies lying in the bush. They have now dispersed from the villages, but it seems to be spreading through the valley.[27]

Flight only spread the disease more widely. Soon it reached into the Interior:

Smallpox, brought up from the Coast, played havoc among the Chilcotins, decimating them until almost those parties only who were away in the mountains were left to represent the tribe. Coming north, the plague next attacked, in November, 1862, the Southern Carriers stationed in the valley of the Blackwater [Westroad River], who, flying through the woods crazed with fever and fright, communicated the contagion to the inhabitants of Peters [Uncha] Lake, where only eight persons survived. Then it extended its ravages from Hehn [Tatuk]

[27] *Ibid.*, p. 129.

Lake, at the source of Mud [Chilako] River, to St. Mary's [Cheslatta] and Morice [Eutsuk] Lakes, where the immense majority of the natives succumbed. . . .

At first corpses were hurriedly buried in the fireplaces, where the ground was free of snow and frost. Then the survivors contented themselves with throwing down trees on them; but soon the dead had to be left where they fell, and the natives still relate in their picturesque language that grouse used to do their wooing on the frozen breasts of human corpses.[28]

A party under Joseph Harrison, prospecting up the North Thompson, reported, "There were no Indians on the river, as they nearly all died of the small-pox this year."[29]

*   *   *

Mention of this prospecting for gold on the North Thompson reminds us that the quest for gold was by no means limited to the bars of the Fraser and the creeks of the Cariboo. Pete Toy, a Cornish miner who had worked both the areas, pushed far north this year and on the Finlay River, where the waters behind Bennett Dam now extend, found a bar containing the first gold discovered in the Omineca. Meanwhile, Alexander Choquette reported finding gold on the Stikine River, in British territory beyond the boundaries of British Columbia. After some eight hundred prospectors had rushed northwards, the British government on July 19th created a new area of government, Stikine Territory, which was to be administered by the Governor of British Columbia. The Stikine gold rush turned out, unfortunately, to be a real humbug. Headlines in the *Colonist* of August 23rd proclaimed:

Stickeen Under a Cloud
MINERS RETURNING.

The next year the greater part of Stikine Territory was quietly absorbed into British Columbia.

*   *   *

28 Morice, *History of Northern Interior of B.C.*, pp. 300-301. A number of these place names are ones given by Morice which failed to win official acceptance and so are not on the maps or in the gazetteer today.

29 *Colonist*, 18 Oct. 1862.

Various men, having failed to find gold in Cariboo or Stikine, were taking out land and starting farms. The amount of arable land around Victoria was limited, but Governor Douglas remembered the lush fertile valley of the Cowichan River which he had visited during the miniature campaign of 1853. In mid-August Douglas announced that prospective farmers would be taken upcoast to Cowichan Bay aboard H.M.S. *Hecate*, landed, and given an opportunity to take out land in the Shawnigan, Somenos and Quamichan districts. Mere occupation of the land would secure possession of it for the settlers. The Indians, in compensation for the land they surrendered, would each be given two blankets by the government.[30] Today a simple marker on Cowichan Bay commemorates the founding of this, the second agricultural settlement on Vancouver Island.

Except for a few special missions such as this one, the *Hecate* was continuing the detailed survey of the coast initiated a few years earlier by the *Plumper*. Late this year when she returned to England her work was continued by Her Majesty's Hired Surveying Vessel *Beaver*. The latter was none other than that famous old first steamboat in the North Pacific, which had flown the HBC flag for the last time. This transfer of the *Beaver* from the Hudson's Bay Company to the Royal Navy is an interesting historical curiosity. Much more significant is the fact that this year the Admiralty decided to transfer the Royal Navy's Pacific base from Valparaiso, Chile, where a floating supply depot had been maintained, to Esquimalt, Vancouver Island.[31]

The Admiralty decided that, in keeping with the harbour's new importance as a naval base, Esquimalt should be fortified. Hence the *Colonist* of September 6th carried the following item:

FORTIFYING ESQUIMALT HARBOR — The work of fortifying Esquimalt harbor has just been commenced. Ten or twelve large guns have been landed from the Bacchante on Hospital Point, where a fifty-gun battery will be erected. Two of these guns are 68-pounders and the others are long 32's or broadside guns. When the Topaze returns she will bring 15 more large barkers for the projected battery, which will be erected on Hospital Point — an admirable location for

---

[30] *Colonist*, 22 Aug. 1862.

[31] Gough, *Royal Navy and Northwest Coast of North America*, p. 186.

defensive purposes. In a week or ten days the Naval Hospital will be removed to the opposite side of the harbour, where the barracks now are.

*   *   *

Her Majesty's warships were not the only vessels which used Esquimalt harbour. Small coastal craft might thread their way through the tortuous entrance to Victoria harbour, but the mail steamers from Panama and San Francisco and merchant ships from Britain always preferred to enter the capacious harbour at Esquimalt. Late in the evening of September 17th one of the most famous ships in British Columbia history dropped anchor at Esquimalt. She was the "brideship" *Tynemouth*, which had brought out a number of single women badly needed in the two colonies whose white population was overwhelmingly male.

The project had originated in Lillooet one evening when the Anglican rector, the Rev. R. C. Lundin Brown, talking to some Cariboo miners, mentioned that brideships were being sent to other parts of the Empire. Why did they not try to get a shipment of eligible young women sent out to their part of the world? One miner at once declared, "Then, sir, I pre-empt a wife!" and his comrades all put in their bids too.[32]

In a letter read in England at the next annual meeting of the Columbia Mission, Brown's proposal was set forth. It made good sense at a time when there were 600,000 more females than males in England. The Columbia Emigration Society was set up and, in cooperation with the London Female Emigration Society, despatched in April this year an initial party of females. The main body of sixty women followed on the *Tynemouth*, under the supervision of a matron charged with protecting the girls from the lascivious attentions of the crew.

The arrival of the *Tynemouth* caused great excitement in Victoria. For a short time the young women were kept more or less incommunicado aboard the *Tynemouth* while arrangements were completed for their reception. However the *Colonist* managed to get a reporter on board:

[32] Peake, *Anglican Church in B.C.*, p. 40.

... we went aboard the steamer yesterday morning and had a good look at the lady passengers. They are mostly cleanly, well-built, pretty looking young women — ages varying from fourteen to an uncertain figure; a few are young widows who have seen better days. Most appear to have been well raised and generally they seem a superior lot to the women usually met with on emigrant vessels. Taken altogether, we are highly pleased with the appearance of the "invoice".... They will be brought to Victoria and quartered in the Marine Barracks, James Bay, early this morning by the gunboat Forward. A large number of citizens visited Esquimalt yesterday and endeavoured to board the vessel, but were generally ordered off and returned from their fruitless errand with heavy hearts.[33]

Unfortunately no sociologist or historian has made a detailed study of what became of the women in their new homeland. Some, we know, promptly married, and set about the business of being first a wife then a mother. Some others, finding that miners with pokes full of Cariboo gold were ready to pay handsomely for even very temporary possession of a white woman, lost no time in getting into the world's oldest profession. There was, in fact, a suspicion that a few of the girls had been prostitutes in England. However, the number of women who went wrong seems to have been fairly small.

* * *

Victoria became an incorporated city this August and its first mayor, Thomas Harris, and his council had plenty to require their attention when the Cariboo miners came down from the goldfields to winter in Victoria:

The fall of 1862 witnessed the return from Cariboo of a large number of miners with heavy swags of gold dust, and Victoria was the theatre of many uproarious gatherings and routs. The owners of ... very rich claims on William Creek congregated here and seemed to find difficulty in getting rid of their money....

Abbott [who was said to have wagered $5,000 on a single poker hand] with a number of friends entered the St. James bar one evening and called for drinks for the crowd. Having been served he asked what the mirror behind the bar was worth.

"Forty dollars," replied the barkeeper.

[33] *Colonist*, 19 Sept. 1862.

Taking a number of nuggets from his pocket Abbott discharged them full at the glass, breaking it into many pieces.

"Take its value out of that and keep the change," he said, as he left the place. The nuggets were sold at the express office for a figure exceeding $100.[34]

Thus D. W. Higgins recalled the riproaring days of the winter of 1862. Higgins, an old-time Victoria newspaperman, was given to dressing up the tales he published at the end of the century in an effort to be British Columbia's Bret Harte but, whatever his exaggerations, he caught the spirit of the time.

Those miners who were of a more thrifty character put their gold in a bank instead of showering it into the hands of harlots or hurling it at mirrors. Since 1859 the Bank of British North America had been doing business in the two colonies, and even earlier the quasi-banks of Wells Fargo and of McDonald and Company had been active. This spring a new colonial bank was incorporated in Britain by royal charter. Named the "Bank of British Columbia" and capitalized at £250,000, it sent out James D. Walker with three assistants to commence operations. On September 17th of this year the new bank opened its first branch, in Victoria; the next year branches were opened at New Westminster and at Richfield in the Cariboo. In 1864 the bank opened additional branches in Nanaimo, San Francisco, Quesnel and Yale, and moved its Richfield office to Camerontown.[35] This bank survived until 1901 when it was taken over by the Bank of Commerce. It bears no relationship to the present Bank of British Columbia which opened its first office in 1968.

*   *   *

On August 18th of this year Simon Fraser died. Near the mouth of the great river that bears his name, New Westminster was becoming a sizable settlement. Developments there this year included the setting up of a brief-lived mint, and the founding of the Royal Columbian Hospital. Moreover, New Westminster was taking on a

[34] Higgins, *The Mystic Spring*, pp. 227-28.

[35] R. N. Beattie, *Banking in Colonial British Columbia*, B.A. essay 1939, UBC, pp. 98-100.

character of its own. Whereas Victoria was increasingly English, New Westminster was increasingly Canadian. Whereas Victoria, on the whole, was friendly to Douglas as the resident governor of Vancouver Island, New Westminster was largely hostile to him as the absentee governor of British Columbia. This year a petition was circulated in New Westminster calling for the removal of Douglas. A Canadian politician, the Hon. Malcolm Cameron, was charged with laying this document "at the foot of the throne". Her Majesty's petitioners, after commenting on the failure of other petitions to have any effect upon the Duke of Newcastle, her Secretary of State for the Colonies, proceeded to beg for:

... representative institutions, and a resident Governor, of experience and ability, who shall be capable of carrying out the principles of free and liberal institutions — open up our lands to actual settlers, preventing jobbery and corruption. . . .

In conclusion, the petitioners implored Her Majesty:

... to grant to them "the image and transcript of the British Constitution" which time has only suited, tempered, and adapted, to the present exigence of the highest and most enlightened minds of the world.[36]

Among the signatories to the petition to the Queen was John Robson, editor of the *British Columbian*. If Robson was hostile to Governor Douglas, that hostility was mild compared with the intense animosity with which he regarded Judge Begbie. This reached its peak during the so-called "Cottonwood Scandal" of this year, a storm which centered around an anonymous letter which Robson printed in the *British Columbian* of November 26th. This interesting epistle, signed only "A" but probably written by a Methodist minister, the Rev. Arthur Browning, insinuated that the reason why Begbie had reversed a magistrate's decision that one Dud Moreland had not done sufficient work on his pre-emption to qualify for a certificate of improvement was that the said Dud Moreland had made a gift of twenty acres to the Judge. On December 1st Begbie, furious at this aspersion on his personal integrity, had Robson up before him, gave him his version of what had happened, and

---

[36] University of Nottingham, *Newcastle Papers*, No. 11,127.

demanded an apology. Robson replied that his own knowledge of the transaction was incomplete and that he had no way of questioning an unknown correspondent and so, *if* the matter was indeed as Begbie said it was, he, John Robson, was prepared to apologize. "Much virtue in your 'if' ", says Shakespeare. But Begbie could see none upon this occasion. What did Robson mean by his damnable *if*? He was only compounding his contempt by calling into question Judge Begbie's truthfulness. Finding the editor guilty of contempt of court, Begbie sent him to prison. Excitement reached fever pitch in the little town of New Westminster. The friends of the martyred editor held a public indignation meeting, and from his cell Robson sent his printer a notable editorial entitled "A Voice From the Dungeon". Although a trifle ungrammatical, it was one of the finest flowers of the old tradition of rhetorical and melodramatic journalism. It began:

> Fellow colonists! We greet you from our dungeon. Startled by the wild shrieks of a dying maniac on the one hand, and the clanking of the murderer's chains on the other, while the foul and scant atmosphere of cell, loaded with noxious effluvia from the filthy dens occupied by lunatics, renders life almost intolerable, our readers will overlook any incoherency or want of connected thought in our writings.[37]

What happened next was something of an anti-climax. Wearying of his dungeon, Robson, on December 5th, asked to be taken before Begbie. To him he handed a written statement, "one of those casuistical apologies, so frequent in libel actions".[38] Begbie accepted the apology and ordered the editor released. But the matter did not end here — there was another letter from "A", and a letter from Dud Moreland himself which in part undercut Begbie's version of the transaction. Today it is impossible to determine exactly what happened, but Professor Pettit is certainly right in giving Begbie, a man who was generally regarded as the soul of honour, the benefit of any doubt.[39]

*   *   *

[37] *British Columbian*, 6 Dec. 1862.

[38] Howay & Scholefield, *British Columbia: From Earliest Times to the Present*, II:664.

[39] Sydney G. Pettit, "His Honour's Honour: Judge Begbie and the Cottonwood Scandal", *BCHQ* 9 (1947):207.

It would be another twenty-four years until there would be a town of Vancouver on the map of British Columbia. Back in 1859, however, H.M.S. *Plumper* surveying Burrard Inlet had discovered the deposits which give Coal Harbour its name, but though several enterprising gentlemen hastily filed claims to land in the vicinity, the coal seams proved too narrow to be profitable and no settlement followed. Such was the situation this year when John Morton, a young potter fresh out from Yorkshire, saw a block of Burrard Inlet coal displayed in a store in New Westminster. Morton knew that there was generally clay to be found close to coal, and persuaded his cousin Sam Brighouse and their friend William Hailstone to pre-empt land adjacent to Coal Harbour and go into the business of manufacturing bricks. Accordingly the "three greenhorns", as they were mockingly known in New Westminster, pre-empted what is now Vancouver's West End, all the land between today's Burrard Street and Stanley Park. This was the "Brickmakers' Claim", which figures so prominently in the histories of Vancouver. On their land the partners built a shack and a brickyard, and put in a garden. They made friends with the Indians by letting them use their grind-stone, and were rewarded with copious gifts of fish. Other supplies they packed in over the trail which the Royal Engineers had put through from New Westminster to False Creek the previous year.

After the first few years, the brickmakers saw little of their property, though they contrived to keep their title alive. Theirs was the distinction of having been the first to settle on the site of British Columbia's future metropolis.[40]

*   *   *

These were the years when many of the first churches were being built. They ranged from the small but exquisite Roman Catholic cathedral in Victoria, built between 1858 and 1861 (whose architect became the first priest to be ordained within its precincts) to St. John's, the pre-fabricated iron church from England, erected in

---

[40] Those wishing to know more about the brickmakers and their claim are referred to Alan Morley, *Vancouver: From Milltown to Metropolis* (Vancouver, [1961]), pp. 20-23, and Eric Nicol, *Vancouver* (Toronto, 1971), pp. 18-21.

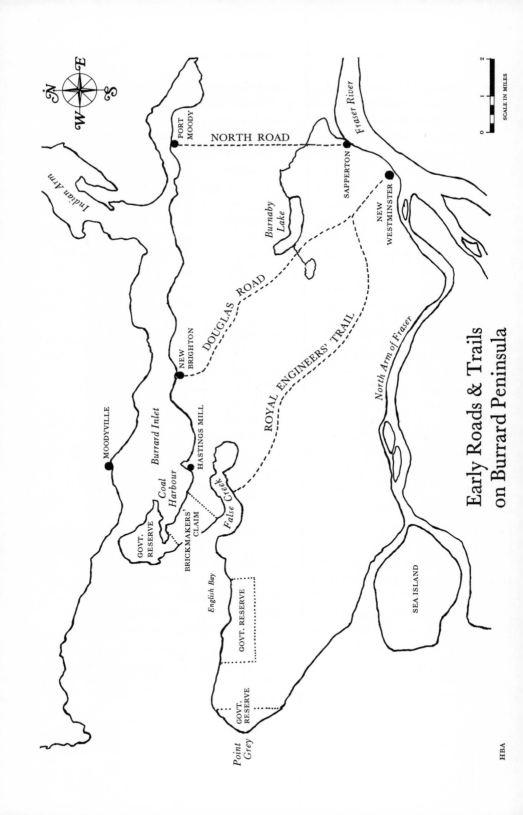

Early Roads & Trails
on Burrard Peninsula

SCALE IN MILES

0   1   2

HBA

NORTH ROAD

PORT MOODY

Indian Arm

Fraser River

MOODYVILLE

Burrard Inlet

Coal Harbour

GOVT. RESERVE

BRICKMAKERS' CLAIM

HASTINGS MILL

NEW BRIGHTON

DOUGLAS ROAD

Burnaby Lake

ROYAL ENGINEERS' TRAIL

SAPPERTON

NEW WESTMINSTER

North Arm of Fraser

False Creek

English Bay

GOVT. RESERVE

GOVT. RESERVE

Point Grey

SEA ISLAND

1860 for the second Anglican parish in Victoria. That same year, on the banks of Mission Creek, Father Pandosy built the first church in the Okanagan. The Methodists also were busy erecting churches. The Rev. Arthur Browning operated on a decidedly ecumenical basis while raising funds for a Methodist church at Yale in 1861 :

Catholics, Jews and the disciples of Confucius have alike subscribed to its erection; in fact the name of *but one* Methodist member is found on my subscription book. There is Kwong Lee $10; Yanloo Sang, $5; See Fo Chow and See Fo Hung, $5; Hie Fe $5; Quang Shong, $2; Ti Sung, $5. . . . [41]

Of the churches built in 1862, none deserves more attention than a great octagonal edifice, able to accommodate seven hundred persons, built at Metlakatla on British Columbia's remote north coast by the Anglican missionary William Duncan.

William Duncan was a most remarkable person, "a man of ten thousand" said Commander Mayne, who was not given to over-statement. Duncan owed his career on the Pacific Coast to the Royal Navy. When the pious Captain Prevost of H.M.S. *Virago* had returned to England in 1856, his mind was haunted by the depravity and deprivations of the heathen Indians he had seen at Fort Simpson and elsewhere. Accordingly, in a series of letters to the *Christian Missionary Intelligencer*, he appealed for funds for a missionary to carry the gospel to the Indians of the North-west Coast. Only a few weeks before returning thither himself in command of a fine new ship, H.M.S. *Satellite*, Prevost received the Admiralty's permission to supply a free passage for a missionary. Prevost immediately got in touch with the Church Missionary Society, whose choice fell on young William Duncan. Short, thickset, with what Dr. Helmcken called a "scrubby face", Duncan was one of those incredible Victorians whose simple faith and limitless energy made them capable of prodigies. A totally confident Christian, incapable of compromise where principles were concerned, William Duncan showed the measure of his integrity on his passage out on the *Satellite*. Assigned to the engineers' mess, he was so shocked by the blasphemous language of the second engineer that he reported the man to the captain and

---

[41] *Christian Guardian*, 12 March 1862, p. 43.

accepted a transfer to the gunners' mess. A heavy atmosphere of gloom prevailed among the gunners at his coming, so at Rio de Janeiro Duncan obtained a large supply of rusks and moved himself to a small dinghy hanging in the davits at the stern of the *Satellite*. Here for many weeks he lived on a diet of rusks and water until, on the last stretch of the journey, he was taken into the officers' mess. Meanwhile, the young lay preacher had been conducting an active Bible class among the crew.

When the *Satellite* arrived at Esquimalt in June 1857 an unexpected problem arose. In their eagerness to be about the Lord's work, neither Prevost nor the Church Missionary Society had thought to arrange matters with the Hudson's Bay Company. Douglas, in his capacity as Chief Factor, flatly refused to let young Duncan go to Fort Simpson, and urged him to work with the Indians around Victoria instead of getting himself killed up north. But Duncan insisted that he had been posted to Fort Simpson and that, if Douglas would not let him go there, he must return to England. Finally Douglas recognized that he was dealing with a man of his own calibre and not only gave the necessary permission but became Duncan's friend. On 25 September 1857 the young lay preacher sailed for Fort Simpson aboard the HBC steamer *Otter*. En route he got his first experience of what lay ahead for him when he saw mutilated and disembowelled human corpses on the beach at Fort Rupert.

During his stay in Victoria, Duncan had been working hard learning not only Chinook (the *lingua franca* of the Indians and whites) but Tsimpsean. Other missionaries might speak in English and then stand by while an interpreter passed on their message to the Indians, but Duncan was determined to speak to his people in their own tongue. At Fort Simpson Duncan spent his first eight months learning Tsimpsean from a young Indian, Clah, and teaching him English in return.

On Sunday, 13 June 1858, having at last secured what he trusted was sufficient mastery of the language, Duncan left the Fort, went to the house of Neyahshnawah, head chief of the Kitlootsah tribe, and preached his first sermon in Tsimpsean. Seven times that morning he repeated his words in the houses of other chiefs. In the afternoon he gave his Tsimpsean lesson in nine other houses speaking, in all, to almost nine hundred Indians. The head chief, Legaic, offered his house for a school, and at once Duncan began holding classes. In November Duncan, with the help of his converts, completed building a schoolhouse of his own. His classes now contained 140 children and 50 adults.

While many of the Tsimpseans were ready to accept Christianity and were eager to acquire the white man's learning, there were others who held by the old ways and the beliefs of their fathers. Despite the amazing personal ascendancy that Duncan was establishing in the community, these latter sought to frustrate his endeavours. Moreover, exposed to the persuasions of those continuing heathens, Duncan's converts were in danger of backsliding:

> As early as 1859, Mr. Duncan had come to the conclusion that if the work he was carrying on should have any permanent results, it would be necessary to remove those of the Indians who had become subject to the power of the Gospel, from the evil influences of the heathen homes and surroundings. And, more important still, be it said to our shame, was it, in his judgment, to get them away from the degrading influence of the white people at the Fort.[42]

After various trips of inspection, Duncan found the site he wanted for his new community. It was at Metlakatla, seventeen miles south of Fort Simpson. Here there was a beautiful well-protected harbour with good beaches for the canoes, and arable land suitable for the farms which were part of Duncan's plan. In the late spring of 1862, Duncan's Christian Indians moved to the new settlement. Each of them had made a solemn pledge:

1. To give up their "Hallied" or Indian deviltry
   [belief in pagan magic spirits].
2. To cease calling in conjurers [shamans] when sick.
3. To cease gambling.
4. To cease giving away their property for display [in potlatches].
5. To cease painting their faces.
6. To cease drinking intoxicating drinks.
7. To rest on the Sabbath.
8. To attend religious instruction.

---

[42] John W. Arctander, *The Apostle of Alaska: The Story of William Duncan of Metlakahtla* (New York, [1909]), p. 151.

9. To send their children to school.
10. To be clean.
11. To be industrious.
12. To be peaceful.
13. To be liberal and honest in trade.
14. To build neat houses.
15. To pay the village tax.[43]

By the autumn of this year, thirty-five houses had been erected, each with four windows. Governor Douglas provided both the windows and the nails for each house. The climax was the building of the great octagonal church. It had no flooring, and the smoke from the two great roaring fires in the centre ascended, as in the old Indian buildings, through a smoke hole high in the roof. Still it was with an overflowing heart that on Christmas Day of this year William Duncan conducted his first service here.

Thus there came into being an Indian community of clean well-ordered houses, where alcohol was unknown, the people industrious, peaceful, happy, and entirely obedient to Mr. William Duncan. Metlakatla was a revelation to all who visited it. It afforded visible proof that those they had scorned as degraded "Siwashes" could be made into civilized citizens. The word "Metlakatla" was to be echoed admiringly at thousands of missionary meetings in Britain and Canada. True, Duncan's Metlakatla was a bit like Calvin's Geneva. And the Church of England was to have increasing misgivings about Duncan's authoritarianism. He himself, curiously compounded of humility and ego, would refuse obedience to his bishop when he later found Metlakatla within the newly-created Diocese of New Caledonia. Though consistently refusing ordination for himself, he made life impossible for every ordained clergyman that the Church Missionary Society sent to work with him at Metlakatla. In the end, determined to do everything his own way, he moved to a New Metlakatla in Alaska. But all this lay far in the future. Certainly the founding of Metlakatla was one of the major developments of 1862.

[43] *Ibid.*, pp. 154-55.

1863

"Cariboo" Cameron brings out his dead wife — Her four funerals — The Gold Escort — Stagecoaches and roadhouses — Viscount Milton and Dr. Cheadle come overland from Canada — Whites murdered on Saturna Island by Lamalchi Indians — Punitive expedition by the Royal Navy — Governor Douglas learns of his retirement — Receives knighthood — Prize essay embroglio — Royal Engineers end their service in British Columbia.

The last day of January this year saw a strange cortege winding along the snowy slopes near Richfield, Cariboo. It consisted of twenty-two men on snowshoes drawing a toboggan loaded with bedrolls, food, fifty pounds of gold, and a long box containing the frozen corpse of a white woman. That woman was Sophia Cameron, wife of John "Cariboo" Cameron, who with her husband had arrived in Cariboo the previous summer. In August Cameron and his associates staked on Williams Creek the "Cameron claim", destined to prove one of the richest in the history of Cariboo. Mrs. Cameron was a tall, beautiful woman aged twenty-eight and Cameron, after ten years in the goldfields of the Pacific coast, could be forgiven the self-indulgence of bringing her to the hard life of the Cariboo mining camps. Early on the morning of October 23rd she died of typhoid fever despite the ministrations of a local doctor. Cameron in his sorrow made a resolution. Having brought her to this wilderness, he would see her body buried in the little Ontario town from which she had come. The preservation of the body posed no immediate problem, as the temperature of 30 degrees below zero (F.) soon froze it solid. After the funeral the icy corpse was put, in cases of tin and wood, in a cabin on the outskirts of Richfield.

Almost two months to a day after his wife's death, Cameron and

his company struck it rich. Dick Rivers, the partner who was working at the bottom of the shaft, suddenly shouted to the men at the
top, "Cameron or Stevenson — come here at once — the place is
yellow with gold". From here on Cameron and company took out
gold by the pound.

For a month Cameron stayed working at the claim, but it was
essential to get his wife's body to Victoria for embalming while the
winter cold still lasted. For the journey out, with his dead wife and
his new-found gold, Cameron had the company of Robert Stevenson,[1] one of his partners and his closest friend. Each of the men who
pulled the heavy toboggan had been hired for $12 a day, with a
bonus of $2000 upon completion of the journey. Even with remuner-
ation on this scale, all but eight of the twenty-two abandoned the
project when, with the temperature thirty-five degrees below zero,
very strong winds caused great drifting of the snow. Others gave up
at Keithley Creek. Finally just four men arrived at Quesnel Forks
with the body. On February 10th they reached Beaver Lake and
here Cameron was able to buy a horse to pull the toboggan, and he
and Stevenson pushed on alone, passing the "snow graves" of Indians
who had died of smallpox. At the beginning of March they were in
Victoria. Here an undertaker sealed Mrs. Cameron's remains in a
metal coffin filled with alcohol, and on March 8th she received her
second funeral when she was buried in the old Quadra Street
cemetery.

With Sophia Cameron at least temporarily at rest, Cameron and
Stevenson hastened back to their claim. With them they took
Cameron's brothers Roderick and Sandy. A three-shift system was
instituted, each shift yielding between 40 and 112 ounces of gold.
Two more shafts were sunk, the last the richest of all. By the end of
September Cameron, now a very wealthy man, was ready to take his
wife home to Canada. A hundred miners escorted him for the first
few miles of his journey, taking their leave of him with three rousing
cheers. With him he took gold worth $150,000 and a protective
escort of nineteen men. Late in October he once again was in
Victoria. Mrs. Cameron's grave was opened, and a new box was put

---

[1] For Stevenson's own recollections of his journey with Cameron, see Walkem,
Stories of Early B.C., pp. 262-68.

around the metal coffin. Then off Cameron and Stevenson went with it by steamer to Panama, by train across the Isthmus, by sea to New York, until their pilgrimage ended at Cornwall, Ontario. Before her third funeral there, Mrs. Cameron's kin wanted to have the coffin opened so that they could have their last sight of Sophia, but Cameron apparently found the thought unbearable and, despite Stevenson's urgings, refused to have the coffin opened. Stevenson, after doing so much to help Cameron, was furious that Cameron had gone against his advice and revenged himself by refusing to make a sworn statement as to how Mrs. Cameron came to her end. These two refusals gave plenty of scope for rumour and gossip. In a few years the story was all over the district that Cameron had really sold Sophia to an Indian chief and had returned with the body of another woman. Finally, to save his reputation Cameron ordered the grave at Cornwall opened, unsealed the coffin and exhibited the remains to a large group of spectators.

In 1940 Judge Howay received a letter from one of Cariboo Cameron's nephews, living on Salt Spring Island. This reads in part:

... I remember the last funeral well & the stories leading up to it. My Father & Mother attended the funeral, also my older brother and sister, I remember what my mother said, & she put her hand on Sophia's face, & it was as hard as a stone, her Father and Mother were also there, and her mother said that is SOPHIA, & the shawl under her head is the one I gave her when she went away.[2]

Following this macabre proceeding, Sophia Cameron received her fourth and final funeral when her remains were once more buried, this time at Summertown, close to the elaborate mansion which Cameron had built in 1865 for himself and his second wife. In the years which followed, Cameron's luck failed. Unsuccessful ventures in the lumber business and an unlucky Lachine Canal contract impoverished him. In 1888 he returned to Cariboo, but the time for making fortunes there was past. Soon after his return he died in a Barkerville hotel and was buried in a little cemetery above Camerontown, adjacent to the famous Cameron claim.

*   *   *

[2] UBC, *Howay Papers*, Folder I:20.

The best year of all for the Cariboo mines was 1863. When the winter of 1862-63 set in, the returns were already so great that some five hundred men, instead of wintering at the Coast, kept working at the deep rich claims. Billy Barker, the onetime Cornish potter and sailor who had struck it rich in the summer of '62, was one of those who kept his operation going:

The Barker Co. worked most of the winter; they washed out up to the 19th of January [1863] the sum of $137,000; from that time on they could not wash owing to the scarcity of water.[3]

After the water gave out, Billy Barker kept his men mining, building up a great pile of pay dirt to be washed once the spring thaws brought the water needed to wash it.

Reading the New Westminster and Victoria newspapers of the summer of 1863, one finds a succession of notices about Cariboo miners arriving from the Interior with fortunes. On June 24th, for instance, the *British Columbian* announced the arrival in New Westminster of J. E. Martin (the Black Jack claim), J. Loring (the Hard Curry claim), Jerry Woods (the Jerry Woods claim), Pat Murray (the Canadian claim), and J. Cook (the Beaver claim) with "a little over $100,000". On July 18th the same newspaper noted that the *Sierra Nevada* on her last voyage from Victoria to San Francisco had carried gold worth $3,564,777 for the Bank of British Columbia, and $1,947,648 for the Bank of British North America, plus an unknown amount for Wells Fargo. On August 12th the *British Columbian* reported the arrival of I. P. Diller with $130,000 taken out by his company:

Mr. Diller went up to the Cariboo Country in '60 and has remained there ever since. He now goes home to his native State (Pennsylvania) with a very handsome fortune, and right well he deserves it.

Diller's gold was only part of a shipment valued at $310,000 which arrived in New Westminster. A week later a further $125,000 worth of gold arrived. And so it continued. Official statistics on the total production of gold were largely meaningless, so much was taken out by Chinese and whites on their own persons without ever clearing it

---

[3] *British Columbian,* 18 April 1863.

through normal banking channels. Allen Francis, the American consul in Victoria, was probably not very far out when he estimated that in 1863 the Cariboo produced $6,000,000 worth of gold.[4] (It would perhaps be redundant to equate this with $150,000,000 in modern funds.)

The Gold Escort which Governor Douglas had provided in 1861, having proved expensive and not drawing much business, had been discontinued in 1862. Lacking protection, three traders coming down from Cariboo that year with their gold on them had been murdered and robbed. Possibly because of these murders, the Victoria Chamber of Commerce and the Bank of British Columbia urged that the Gold Escort be reintroduced this year. Reluctantly Douglas agreed to the measure. New Westminster was furious at the re-establishment of the escort — probably because, at British Columbia's expense, it carried the gold right through to Victoria in the colony of Vancouver Island, not to New Westminster, which dearly hoped to become the centre from which gold would be shipped to San Francisco or Britain. To the *British Columbian*, "this miserable abortion" the Gold Escort was "The Victoria Escort" or the "Bank of British Columbia's Escort". Since in its resurrected form the Escort still provided no guarantee to make good any losses of gold, many miners preferred not to use it. In its July 29th issue the *British Columbian* indignantly pointed out that, during the period when the Gold Escort had brought out gold worth $40,000 at a cost to the government of $10,000 (surely a wildly inflated figure), Dietz and Nelson's Express had brought out gold worth $103,037 at absolutely no cost to the colony. Gleefully it told of how one traveller, arriving at a roadhouse at three o'clock in the morning, had found the gold totally unattended in the wagon, and the escort all asleep in the inn.

The nature of gold-mining in the Cariboo was changing. Shrewd men had bought into the more profitable claims. An increasing number of the miners no longer worked claims of their own but hired themselves out to their more fortunate fellows. The latter looked more and more like capitalists and less and less like lucky members of the proletariat. The consequences were increasing labour

---

[4] Fred W. Ludditt, *Barkerville Days* (Vancouver [1969]), p. 37.

troubles and the first miners' industrial strike. In May of this year the hired hands struck for $12 for a ten-hour day. When this demand was granted, they struck within a fortnight for $12 for an eight-hour day. This demand was granted also. But then the bookkeepers of the companies found that a number of miners were moonlighting, working one shift for one company and another shift for a second, all in the same day, while various poor fellows were totally without employment. Moreover, the officers of the various companies declared that they had been closely investigating the ringleaders in the strikes, and had discovered that they were nearly all Americans. Foreigners could not be permitted to take over in this way! On these speciously patriotic grounds, the syndicates closed down their mines. The hired miners held out as long as they could, but at last they went back to work for the original wage of a dollar an hour for a ten-hour day.

*   *   *

Travel to and from the Cariboo was becoming easier, cheaper and faster as Governor Douglas' great program of road-building entered its final phases. In mid-August a Mr. Humphrey arrived at New Westminster with letters and gold only eight days after leaving Richfield in the heart of the Cariboo. He had been able to drive his own buggy from Soda Creek to Boston Bar. The reason why he could not continue in his buggy all the way to Yale was that Joseph Trutch had not yet completed his Alexandra Suspension Bridge across the lower Fraser Canyon. Finally opened to traffic in September, this bridge was the most ambitious piece of engineering yet attempted in British Columbia. Built at a cost of $45,000, it was meticulously constructed with a span of some three hundred feet. When it was tested by driving a four-horse team pulling a wagon with a three-ton load across it, Trutch was gratified to find that the total deflection had been less than a quarter of an inch.

With the completion of major portions of the highways, stage-coach lines came into operation. Each morning a stage left Port Douglas for Lillooet, as did one from Lillooet for Port Douglas. Dietz and Nelson's British Columbia & Victoria Express ran an advertisement announcing that it now connected both with Wells

Fargo at Victoria for California, and with Barnard's Cariboo Express at Yale and Lillooet. As longer and longer stretches of wagon road were completed, and stagecoaches and freight wagons became more in evidence, the old rough shanties which were the first roadhouses gave way to much more elaborate buildings. The Clinton Hotel, perhaps the most famous hostelry in British Columbia, opened this year where the Lillooet road joined the main Cariboo road at a new junction; while Loch Lomond House "at the Seventy-four-mile Post on the Lillooet-Alexander Road" advertised not only that stagers and teamsters would find good stabling and provender but that "The Bar will contain Civility and the best Liquors and Cigars".[5]

As the Great Cariboo Wagon Road neared completion, men's imaginations began to turn to an even greater project — a wagon road right across British North America, linking the colonies on the Pacific coast with Canada in the East. The intervening territory, Rupert's Land, was the fief of the Hudson's Bay Company, but this year the Colonial Office was corresponding with the HBC about the necessary transfer of property and rights so that not only a road but a telegraph line could follow a British route across North America.[6] Nor did speculation halt here. For years there had been occasional talk about the possibility of building a British transcontinental railway. In September of this year an advertiser in the *British Columbian* announced that in order to pay his debts and keep out of gaol he was prepared to sell sixty-five acres, "the very spot on which must terminate the great ATLANTIC & PACIFIC RAILWAY".[7]

*   *   *

Meanwhile, in the absence of either a transcontinental wagon road or railway, or indeed even a trail for part of the way, persons coming overland from Canada still had to make a most grueling journey. One very odd party came overland this year. It was headed by that Hon. C. W. Wentworth Fitzwilliam, whom we noted as a visitor at

[5] *British Columbian*, 18 April 1863.

[6] Great Britain, *Parliamentary Papers*, 1863, No. 438. Colonial Office, "Correspondence re a road and telegraph from Canada to British Columbia, and the transfer of property and rights of the HBC to other parties".

[7] *British Columbian*, 2 Sept. 1863.

Fort Victoria in 1853. Now Viscount Milton and heir to Earl Fitz-william, he was a tiny man, slender in build and only about five feet in height. Being an epileptic, he had chosen for his travelling companion a medical man, great bluff Dr. W. B. Cheadle. At Fort Pitt they had picked up a Métis, Louis Battenotte (who had a badly maimed left hand), along with his Indian wife and their thirteen-year-old son. To Battenotte they had given the nickname of "The Assiniboine". At Fort Edmonton the party had picked up a sixth member, a very queer fish indeed, named Eugene Francis O'Beirne. Middle-aged,[8] O'Beirne was an Irishman of good family who had studied at the University of Cambridge. Subsequently he had become a journalist, editing at one time a paper at Lahore in India. After migrating to the United States, he became secretary to a wealthy planter in Louisiana, but left hurriedly because of fear of involvement in the American Civil War. Briefly he was a professor of Classics in a tiny college in a northern state, and then appeared in Red River Colony. Supplied with a letter of introduction to Governor Douglas, he had joined the Overlanders of '62, but they refused to take him past Fort Carlton in Saskatchewan. Eventually he got as far west as Fort Edmonton. Here he earnestly begged Milton and Cheadle to let him complete his journey to the Pacific in their company. The man obviously belonged to their own class (one of his grandfathers had been a bishop), he was smooth, urbane and ingratiating, and so the two agreed to accept him. It was a decision they were to regret a thousand times in the next few months, for O'Beirne turned out to be hopelessly impractical. An appalling parasite, he would sit down to reread Paley's *Evidences of Christianity* when everybody else was hard at work making or breaking camp. One service he did unconsciously render them: when Milton and Cheadle got back to England and published an account of their journey, *The North-West Passage by Land*, "Mr. O'B", as they termed him, added a comic element which helped to put the book through edition after

[8] Milton and Cheadle (*The North-West Passage By Land*, London, [1865], p. 192) say he was between forty and fifty years old, but some notes on him in the office of the Canadian Permanent Committee on Geographic Names, Ottawa (File 0494) say he was sixty, and it is significant that to Battenotte he was always "Le Vieux".

edition. Some contemporaries accused Milton and Cheadle of having invented Mr. O'B, but the actuality of that blithering eccentric has been fully authenticated.

Setting out from Fort Edmonton on June 3rd, the strange little party entered British Columbia by the Yellowhead Pass on July 9th. The next day they struck the Fraser which, being in flood, had covered much of their trail. Here they had a signal instance of Mr. O'B's helplessness:

> Soon after we set out, he dropped behind the rest of the cavalcade, and before long, Cheadle, who was driving some of the hindmost horses, was arrested by a most tremendous bawling for help from the rear. He ran back in haste, and found Mr. O'B., in rather muddy condition, and with very disconsolate air, leading his horse by the bridle. It appeared the horse had shied and pitched him off amongst the logs and *débris* around, and he imagined himself severely hurt. But no important injury could be found, and, by dint of great persuasion, and some assistance, Cheadle induced him to re-mount, and exhorted him to keep close up to the rest. But he was too much afraid of his horse to urge him on by any but the most gentle verbal persuasion, and tender pattings on the neck. He was soon left behind again, and the ears of the party saluted by another succession of piteous cries from the rear. Cheadle again went back to his assistance, in very unamiable mood, but was unable to resist a burst of laughter when he came upon the unfortunate Mr. O'B. He was driving his horse before him, with the saddle under its belly, and the bridle trailing on the ground. He was covered with mud, his long visage scratched and bleeding, and his clerical coat, split asunder to the neck, streamed from his shoulders in separate halves. "Very nearly killed, Doctor, this time. I thought it was all over. '*Semel est calcanda via lethi*', you know."[9]

At Tête Jaune Cache they met a party of Shuswap Indians, and paused briefly to let their horses pasture in the meadows there. Then on July 20th they headed south along the trail made by the Kamloops Overlanders of the previous year. Crossing Canoe River, they nearly came to disaster when their improvised raft got hung up briefly on a "sweeper" (a tree which has fallen over from the bank, partly blocking the stream). Cheadle, Battenotte and his son managed to get ashore. Milton and Battenotte's wife were rescued before the torrent could tear them from their insecure hold on the fallen

[9] *North-West Passage By Land*, pp. 251-52.

tree. And Mr. O'B, in a state of shock, sat motionless on the raft as it continued on until stopped by another fallen tree.

At Slaughter Camp, the forlorn little party took stock of their situation. They correctly deduced that their predecessors had here abandoned land travel and constructed rafts. But with only food for three days, Milton and Cheadle decided that they had not the time to fell the trees and construct the large raft needed to go down the Thompson. In any case, they lacked enough hands to manage it, once constructed. Instead, on the last day of July, they continued through the vast trackless forests of the upper North Thompson. Gigantic fallen trees blocked them at every turn. Some days they travelled only two or three miles. For a while Battenotte cleared their way with the only axe that they had not lost amid their misadventures. When the Assiniboine's hand became hopelessly torn and swollen, Cheadle took over with the axe. On August 7th they ate the last of their pemmican. The only food left was one quart of flour. Their morale was really shaken the next day when they came upon the dessicated corpse of an Indian, inexplicably headless, who had plainly died of starvation since around him lay the splintered bones of the horse whose bone marrow had afforded him his last sustenance. Milton and Cheadle decided that the time had come to kill one of their own horses for food, and so Blackie was shot. On they continued, with two axes now since they had found one beside the dead Indian. At times, in addition to the dried horsemeat, they found food in the form of berries, skunk meat, and the flesh of a porcupine run down by their dog Papillon. Thus they managed to keep alive. Three days were spent clambering over the rocky bluffs along Murchison Rapids. At Hell's Gate they killed another horse, then pressed on. Five weeks had passed since they had last seen a living soul. On August 18th they heard the call of a crow, the first evidence they were getting out of the sunless, dismal forest, and the next day they found a river trail. Several days later they reached an open meadow, and paused while their horses, mere skin and bones, ate of the good green grass. On August 24th, by the Clearwater River they met Indians with whom they bartered for potatoes. The travellers were so famished that they ate the first ones raw. On August 28th they reached the home of the famous Indian chief Lolo, alias St.

Paul. The next day they entered Fort Kamloops and began to eat in earnest. In a short time Dr. Cheadle put on forty-two pounds.

Space does not permit us to follow the noble lord down to Victoria or on his jaunt up to Cariboo. Mr. O'B, having reached Victoria, told a pitiful tale to Bishop Hills and was given a cheque for $100 which, according to rumour, he converted into a cheque for $1000.[10] Then he moved to Australia. Milton and Cheadle returned safely to England in March 1864. And so ends the story of one of the most astonishing expeditions in the entire history of British Columbia.

*　　*　　*

On the coast there were renewed clashes between whites and the surviving Indian population. Two sleeping white men were shot at Bentinck Arm, the one slain and the other seriously injured. In this case a local chief, without white intervention, personally arranged for the murderer to be shot. In April while William Brady and a companion were asleep at Bedwell Harbour on North Pender Island, they were attacked by Cowichans and Brady was mortally wounded. Retribution was dealt by H.M.S. *Forward*, which managed to capture the murderers, three men and a woman, at Chemainus. Tried at Victoria, the men were sent to the gallows, but not before they had complained of the injustice of merely giving life imprisonment to the woman, who had incited them to commit the crime.

One of the worst Indian attacks was made by a notorious band of Cowichans, named the Lamalchi. This occurred in November of 1862 when a settler, Marks, was moving to Mayne Island. The trouble began when a gale separated the two boats carrying the Marks family and their effects. Mrs. Marks safely completed the crossing, but Marks and his daughter were unable to land until they reached Saturna Island. Here some Lamalchi Indians shot Marks dead while he was kindling a fire by the shore. His daughter was pursued and murdered. Only with the discovery, some months later, of her naked body buried under a pile of stones did public opinion in Victoria become fully aroused. Four warships, the gunboats *Forward* and *Grappler*, and H.M.S. *Devastation* and H.M.S. *Cha-*

---

[10] Holland Butterworth to Dr. Walter Cheadle (nephew of Milton's companion) 12 Nov. 1884. Original in McGill University Library's Rare Book Dept.

meleon, were sent to hunt down the Lamalchis. Despite the size of the force, the Navy found it extremely difficult to arrest the principal criminals, and in one of the clashes with the tribesmen a bluejacket aboard the *Forward* was killed. There was of course the usual burning of canoes and shelling of villages to force the surrender of the guilty Lamalchis. The Voltigeurs from Victoria aided in the capture, at Montagu Harbour, of A-chee-wun, the Lamalchi chief who had been implicated in other murders of both Indians and whites. In the end, seven Indians went to the gallows, four for the murder of Marks and his daughter, and A-chee-wun and two others for the attack on the *Forward*. An eighth Lamalchi had been shot by other Cowichans, who delivered his body to H.M.S. *Devastation* at Chemainus. Governor Douglas was unpleasantly aware, however, that some of those involved in the murders had fled to places so inaccessible or unknown as to make their capture impossible.

*   *   *

Douglas was now nearing the end of his days as governor of the twin colonies. His achievements had been truly great. He had throughout, by his blend of firmness and understanding, kept the allegiance of nearly all the Indians. (Although he was ready to use gunboats when necessary, he knew from long experience that more could usually be gained by giving the Indians their beloved gifts of biscuits and molasses.) During Governor Douglas' regime there had been no Indian wars like those to the south. He had expertly handled the American miners during the days of the Fraser Gold Rush and had ended any ideas they may have entertained about annexing British Columbia to the United States. During the Cariboo Gold Rush he had grasped the central importance of roads and, by building the Cariboo Wagon Road, had opened up the Interior. Sophisticated newcomers might laugh at "Old Square-toes", his pretentious manner, his fondness for wearing his uniform with its gold braid, his maintenance of a sword-bearing bodyguard who accompanied him through the streets of Victoria — but these vanities were incidental. They were really a continuation of the old Hudson's Bay Company tradition, a highly practical one when dealing with the Indians, that a major officer must manifest his position by a certain pomp and circumstance. But times were changing. Douglas, an autocrat through and through, had little patience with democracy. New arrivals from Britain and Canada, not knowing his background and hardly caring to assess his achievements, knew only that they were denied the representational system of government that was the birthright of British citizens. The Canadians in New Westminster, especially, kept up a flow of petitions against Douglas' "despotism", along with continuing complaints about having to endure an absentee governor who plainly preferred to live in Victoria. The petition presented by the Hon. Malcolm Cameron late in 1862, and the latter's conversations with the Duke of Newcastle were probably decisive in convincing the Colonial Secretary that, though Douglas had been the right man to look after matters during the crucial chaotic years of 1858 and 1859, he was not the man for the years that lay ahead.

On March 16th Newcastle wrote a friendly private letter to Douglas. After mentioning that Douglas would shortly be receiving permission for his government to borrow an additional £50,000 for his road program, and commenting upon his own attempts to get "a postal and telegraphic communication between Canada and British Columbia", the Duke broached the important news he had for Douglas personally:

I have now to communicate to you what I have no doubt will not surprise you and may possibly not be disagreeable to you. This year the Act of Parliament constituting the government of B Columbia expires and I propose to introduce a less autocratic form of government than that which now exists. My wish would have been to unite B Columbia & Vancouver Island under one government, but I fear that is at present impossible. I shall endeavour however to interpose no new obstacles to their future amalgamation. As you have now ruled over Vancouver Island for twelve years — twice the usual period of governorship — and as I do not think it would be desirable to replace you by a new Governor there and have you to take up your abode in New Westminster as Governor of British Columbia alone, I intend to relieve you of both governments. You may be assured however that I shall not carry out this decision in any way that can be disagreeable to you or shall give triumph to them who have desired your recall.[11]

[11] University of Nottingham, *Newcastle Papers.*

Newcastle was as good as his word. Later this year the colonists learned not only of the coming retirement of their governor but of his elevation to the dignity of Knight Commander of the Most Honourable Order of the Bath. On August 14th he became Sir James Douglas.

One pettiness marred Douglas' final months as governor. The previous year, 1862, had been that of the second Great Exhibition in London, one calculated to match the glories of the Great Exhibition of 1851. The colonial authorities had decided that visitors to the exhibition should be able to purchase booklets containing information and statistics about Vancouver Island and British Columbia. Accordingly, a prize essay contest had been set up in each colony, the winning entries to provide the pamphlets for the Great Exhibition. The award for Vancouver Island was won by Dr. Charles Forbes of the Royal Navy, stationed at Esquimalt; and that for British Columbia by the Rev. R. C. Lundin Brown, Anglican rector of Lillooet. But whereas Forbes' essay was published promptly in 1862, Brown's did not appear until September of this year of 1863. The reason for the delay soon came out. Douglas' pride had been hurt by various critical remarks contained in the British Columbia essay. Somehow or other, Brown was finally persuaded to omit the offending passages and to supply others more laudatory of the government. The *British Columbian* secured access to the earlier version and, shocked, offered the following specimens to its readers:

Passage as Contained in the Original Manuscript

The backward state of the country, the bad condition of the roads that exist, the waste of the revenue in the construction of roads now abandoned — because in districts not frequented, — and underdeveloped state of the agricultural resources, are owing to the maladministration of the Government.

Passage from the Printed Essay

The manner in which the Government is carried on and the laws administered, gives general satisfaction. So long as the Colony progresses, and its new necessities are met by new enactments, the colonists (with the exception of an uninfluential clique at New Westminster) are satisfied; they have not the wish, as in the present circumstances they would not have the time, to legislate for themselves.[12]

The hapless author, who had consented to these changes, got short shrift from the *British Columbian*:

Of the clergymen who for the paltry sum of £50 was found willing to betray his country and sacrifice a good conscience we dare hardly trust ourselves to write.[13]

The three judges who had awarded the prize (Archdeacon Wright, Henry Holbrook and W. E. Cormack) wrote to the government indignant letters which were swiftly published by the *British Columbian*. All three announced that what had been published was not the essay for which they had given the prize. They demanded release of the original text, a demand which was refused.

In his letter to Douglas, Newcastle had mentioned that he intended to provide British Columbia with "a less autocratic form of government than that which now exists." He kept his word, and his subordinates in the Colonial Office were charged with supplying a suitable constitution. The Colonial Office had no shortage of constitutions, having drafted them for colonies of the most diverse character all over the world. After some thought, it was decided that the best constitution for British Columbia would be the one that had been devised for Ceylon.[14] This provided for a Legislative Council consisting of five heads of governmental departments, five magistrates, and five elected representatives. In accordance with the new constitution, Governor Douglas set up five ridings:

> New Westminster
> Douglas, Pemberton and Lillooet
> Hope, Yale and Lytton
> Cariboo West
> Cariboo East

The election in October for the New Westminster seat was a lively one. The final vote was J. A. R. Homer 69, Henry Holbrook 58.[15]

---

[12] *British Columbian*, 12 Sept. 1863.

[13] *Loc. cit.*

[14] *British Columbian*, 26 August 1863.

[15] *British Columbian*, 7 Oct. 1863.

Holbrook's supporters were bitter about the part played in the election by Homer's "Canadian clique", and were confident their man would have won if only Colonel Moody had permitted the Royal Engineers to vote.

*   *   *

The Royal Engineers were, in fact, in the process of being disbanded. Governor Douglas, as we have seen, had not got along well with Colonel Moody;[16] the sappers had done most of the work that he required them for; and Douglas' thrifty soul was disturbed by the cost of the contingent. Writing to England on April 17th of this year, Douglas observed:

> The expense of the Royal Engineers is overwhelming, if relieved of that costly ornament we should be better able to cope with other difficulties. I have no complaint to make of the Corps, but their pay and allowances and charges of various kinds are far higher than they ought to be, and added to these the families of the whole detachment, both officers and men, are continually on the increase, and all are supported at the public expense. The disbursements for the Corps, on Colonial account for 1862 exceeds £16,900 against works executed by them, valued at £3,500. The R. Engineers are to British Columbia what the old man of the Sea was to Sinbad, with this aggravation, that H.M. Government helped to fasten the burden on the Colony and I have no power to relieve it.[17]

Douglas had conveniently forgotten how urgently he had sought troops from Britain five years earlier. But of course with the Americans now deep in a civil war there was no longer any threat of Yankee invasion. Whitehall considered Douglas' plaint, then decided to recall Moody and his sappers. On July 8th, Colonel Moody paraded his men at Sapperton, and read the order recalling their unit. Almost at once it became apparent that few of the sappers would be accompanying their officers back to Britain since most

---

[16] In an undated confidential report Douglas alleged of Moody: "I have in fact found it necessary to exercise the utmost vigilance over his public acts; and have narrowly escaped being involved in a ruinous contract for the survey of public lands, which he had entered into with Mr. Joseph Trutch". (Cope, *Col. Moody and the Royal Engineers in B.C.*, p. 197.)

[17] *Governor's Private Official Letter Book*, cited in W. N. Sage, *James Douglas and British Columbia* (Toronto, 1930), p. 299.

would be exercising their privilege of being demobilized in British Columbia. Many were probably attracted by the government's offer of 150 acres of free land for each man who chose to remain.

The autumn saw the Royal Engineers winding up their operations and disposing of their property. Two of the officers would be taking brides home with them. In New Westminster Lieut. Palmer married the eldest daughter of Archdeacon Wright, and in Victoria Captain Luard married Caroline Mary Leggett. When Luard and his bride, accompanied by Colonel Moody, arrived in New Westminster, they were greeted at the wharf by the Royal Engineers band playing "lively airs".

On November 5th the citizens of New Westminster held a grand testimonial banquet in honour of Colonel Moody and his officers. Although all but four of the colonial civil servants, probably anxious to keep on the right side of Sir James Douglas, absented themselves from that festive occasion, the room was packed with friends of the Royal Engineers. The repast, at which the Colonial Hotel served its choicest viands and wines, was presided over by the "President of the Municipal Council" who as yet lacked the title of "Mayor", seconded by the city's newly-elected member of the Legislative Council. After the food came the toasts:

The Queen

The Prince and Princess of Wales and the rest of the Royal Family

The Governor

The Army and Navy

The Red, White and Blue

Colonel Moody and the Officers of the Royal Engineers

The major speech of the evening was of course that delivered by the Colonel. He was glad to see the meeting "so entirely composed of the independent members of the community". (So much for Douglas and his sycophants!) Generously he acknowledged his debt to his officers:

Where should I have been without my valuable friend and officer Capt. Grant? (Great applause.) He is known and his labors appreciated throughout the whole Colony. His figure up-country, with shirt sleeves tucked up (laughter) is familiar to all. . . . To Capt. Parson's high scientific attainments how deeply am I indebted? (Great applause.) To Capt. Luard, ever with me, I find it difficult to express how much is due. His great value, however, is well known to everyone. (Loud applause.) Lieut. Palmer's assistance has proved to me his remarkable talents and acquirements, which, combined, cannot fail to lead him to distinction in whatever position he may be placed. (Enthusiastic applause.) Dr. Seddall you all know. He is individually known in the Colony and universally beloved. (Applause).[18]

Colonel Moody then paid tribute to "the intelligent, high class of excellent men who have served under the command of these officers and myself". He reviewed the circumstances under which the Royal Engineers had been sent to British Columbia, and noted what an experiment it had been "mingling thus military and civil duties". He reviewed the achievements of the Royal Engineers in the colony, and declared that he left "more truly a British Columbian than ever".

Next came a series of "volunteer toasts" by gentlemen already in a happy mood from the previous ones. There were toasts to:

> The Municipal Council of New Westminster
> The Press
> The Clergy
> The British North American Provinces
> Trade and Commerce
> The Agriculturists of British Columbia
> The Ladies

At the end everybody rose, took hands, sang "Auld Lang Syne" and "God Save the Queen", then concluded with three hearty cheers. It was, said the *British Columbian*, the best public dinner party in the history of British Columbia.

On November 11th, H.M.S. *Chameleon* sailed with the Royal Engineers who were returning to England — but British Columbia was not long to be left defenceless. At seven o'clock that same evening an organizational meeting was held for the New Westminster Volunteer Rifle Corps. Soon the volunteers (many of them recently Royal Engineers) had elected their officers, been issued rifles and ammunition left behind by the Royal Engineers, and were drilling in

[18] *British Columbian*, 7 Nov. 1863.

Royal Engineer fatigue uniforms while awaiting the arrival of their own uniforms of rifle green and black from England.

*　　*　　*

A brief calendar may best serve to set forth some of the other events of this year.

January. The Northern blockade having cut off shipments of cotton from the Confederacy, one Lancashire cotton mill after another had closed down, leaving their workers to starve. This month the Royal Engineers, at the pretty little theatre they had built for themselves at their camp, put on a benefit program for the Lancashire Cotton Hands. A little while later subscription lists were opened in New Westminster, and British Columbia sent some £250 for the relief of the starving Lancashire workers.

February. A spirited editorial in the *British Columbian* dealt with:

... the great difficulty and annoyance people are subjected to in this Colony in the matter of forming matrimonial alliances, on account of the absence of a marriage law, or any of the usual facilities for that purpose.

It was clearly outrageous that any British Columbian who desired to take unto himself a wife "must needs go to another Colony [i.e. Vancouver Island] for a marriage licence."[19]

March. As the sixth speaker in New Westminster's "Winter Lectures on Science and Literature", Lieut. Palmer, R.E., spoke on "Bentinck Arm and Cariboo". Admission to the single lecture was twenty-five cents, with any profit going to the Royal Columbian Hospital.

April. Dr. Edward B. Boggs, assistant surgeon, R.N., made a surprising discovery at Nanaimo:

The population consists almost entirely of miners and Indians, and is generally healthy. It is worthy of remark that those miners who have

---

[19] *British Columbian*, 11 Feb. 1863.

English wives generally have their houses in a dirty slatternly condition, while, on the other hand, those among the miners who have *married* Hyday [Haida] or Tsimshean women have their houses kept patterns of cleanliness, neatness, and comfort; this is not the case, however, when a man is simply co-habiting with an Indian squaw, then dirt and discomfort reign supreme.[20]

One of the things which made life tragic for the Indians and dangerous for the whites was the effect of alcohol on the native people. The government did all it could by legislation to protect the Indians, but there were always unscrupulous traders ready to sell them the illicit liquor. This month H.M.S. *Devastation* seized three Victoria ships, the *Kingfisher*, *Langley* and *Petrel*, which had been smuggling liquor to the mainland Indians. Passing judgment, Judge Brew observed that they would shortly have all the shipping of Victoria tied up as prizes in New Westminster's harbour.

John Robson was carrying on his feud with Judge Begbie. Begbie, aware of the trouble brought to the American mining camps by cheap lawyers bent on stirring up litigation, was afraid that Canadian lawyers might prove of the same breed. Accordingly, he preferred English-trained lawyers and raised obstacles when George A. Walkem, a Canadian-trained lawyer, sought to practise in the courts of British Columbia. Robson was ardently on the side of his fellow Canadian. Once more he savaged Begbie. In a remarkable editorial Robson, noting the light docket of the assizes over which Begbie was presiding, wrote:

> Once more the disgusting farce has been enacted. The painted, jewelled harlot has again been exhibited, adorned with all the habiliments of Justice, yet reeking with injustice and wrong. But none were found so infatuated as to submit to her fatal embrace; all stood aloof as though afraid even to inhale the polluted atmosphere which surrounded the mock throne of justice. . . . [21]

It is to be hoped Robson felt better when, a few months later at Begbie's own suggestion, the government passed a Legal Professions Act which allowed Canadian lawyers to be admitted to the British Columbia Bar.

[20] PRO, Medical Officers' Journal, # 155.
[21] *British Columbian*, 18 April 1863.

May. This month it was Lieut. Lascelles, R.N., who was having trouble with the press. The Victoria *Daily Evening Express*, dealing with the naval action against the Lamalchi murderers, suggested that the course followed by Lascelles with his gunboat *Forward* was dictated by the old adage, "He who fights and runs away lives to fight another day." Lieut. the Hon. Horace D. Lascelles was not amused. He sent a bluejacket around to the office of the *Daily Evening Express* to present his compliments to Mr. Allen, the editor, and to ask if he would be so good as to come aboard the *Forward* which had one of her boats waiting for him at the wharf. Once aboard the gunboat, Allen was told that if he cared to step below Lascelles would be glad to enlighten him about the movements of the fleet. Proceeding down the stairs towards which the lieutenant ushered him, Allen found Lascelles had not followed him. Instead he had posted a sentry at the head of the stairs with orders to keep Allen below. For several hours the unfortunate editor remained on the lower deck exposed to the insults of various sailors who had not relished his aspersions on their ship.

A couple of hours later, Lascelles having returned from a shore trip, H.M.S. *Forward* put to sea with her captive editor. Slipping past his guard, Allen got to Lascelles and insisted on being put ashore since he had important business which required his presence. Lascelles refusing, the editor suddenly jumped overboard and began swimming for Victoria. He was only half way ashore when Lascelles, who had reversed direction and lowered a boat, recaptured him. That evening Lascelles, either thinking he had sufficiently punished the cad for his sneer at the courage of the Royal Navy, or reflecting that his unusual behaviour might cause trouble with the Lords of the Admiralty, set Allen ashore near Beacon Hill Park. Shocked by this very literal infringement on the freedom of the press, Allen's fellow editors in the colonies called for Lascelles' scalp, but nothing much seems to have happened other than a lawsuit in which Allen won handsome damages and costs.

June. On the second of this month the cornerstone was laid for a synagogue in Victoria. Two ceremonies attended the laying of this particular cornerstone, a Jewish one and a Masonic one. Altogether the occasion was remarkably non-sectarian. The Freemasons' Lodge, the Germania Verein, and the Caledonian Society were all on hand for the great event, and the band of H.M.S. *Topaze* provided music.[22]

This month an English periodical, *The Gardener's Chronicle*, carried a report in which its correspondent in British Columbia noted that the Canadians seemed positively determined to run New Westminster.

July.   Things were going well in the Cariboo. Of the 3500 men at Williams Creek only 200 were unemployed. On the other hand, there were two disturbing cases of highway robbery, and a gruesome discovery:

> The skeleton of a man, 5 feet 8 inches high with light hair, was found on the 12th at Mud [McLeese] Lake, a few rods from the public house. He evidently met with foul play, as his skull was broken in and the body had been placed in a swampy hole and covered over with brush. The clothing was entirely gone, nothing remaining except a pair of English made boots.[23]

So still another family back in England would never know what became of the son who set out to find gold in Cariboo.

August.   A party of thirty, which included Henry Pering Pellew Crease, the new Attorney-General of British Columbia, came around from New Westminster to visit the Pioneer Mills located inside the First Narrows on Burrard Inlet. They travelled aboard the *Flying Dutchman*, whose Captain Deighton would later become famous as "Gassy Jack" of Vancouver's Gastown. They were generously wined and dined that evening, and next day returned to New Westminster towing a scowload of lumber.

September.   A new commander-in-chief for the Pacific, Rear-Admiral John Kingcome, had arrived with a fine new flagship, H.M.S. *Sutlej*, carrying 35 heavy guns and a crew of over 500.

[22] *vide Jewish Western Bulletin* (Centenary Number, 1958), 26:7.

[23] *British Columbian*, 22 July 1863.

Early this month Admiral Kingcome made his first visit to the mainland, the *Sutlej* anchoring in English Bay. No doubt there was much coming and going along the Royal Engineers' trail from New Westminster. Boatloads of excursionists from New Westminster came around Point Grey to see the warship.

October. There was satisfaction in Nanaimo this month with the expected completion of roads which would link the coal town with the white settlement at Comox and with the capital of Victoria.

On the mainland men talked of a new gold rush to the "Shuswap country". The *British Columbian*, after noting that the Cariboo still had most to offer for men with plenty of capital to invest, went on to observe:

... but for the man who lands in the Colony with his one, two, or five hundred dollars — for the masses — the Shuswap country is unquestionably preferable.[24]

Actually gold was to be found only in very modest amounts, almost entirely on Cherry Creek some thirty miles east of today's Vernon.[25]

There was a sensational accident on Kamloops Lake this month. A Hudson's Bay Company freight boat was eastbound with a white man, Burgess, and four Indians for her crew, and a cargo of fifteen tons of supplies for Fort Kamloops. Among these supplies was a stock of gunpowder. Somehow this ignited. There was a tremendous blast. Those who came to investigate found splintered wood and one white arm on the lakeshore. As the *British Columbian* somewhat luridly reported, the boat and its crew had been "blown to atoms".

November. Evidence that the Cariboo was increasingly for syndicates with plenty of capital was provided this month when Hard Curry, Loring & Co. became the first to use steam power at Williams Creek. It cost at least $4,000 for them to get the machinery up to the diggings over the practically completed Cariboo Wagon Road.

[24] *British Columbian*, 17 Oct. 1863.
[25] On the placer deposits here see A. G. Jones, *Vernon Map-Area British Columbia*, Geological Survey of Canada, Memoir 296 (Ottawa, 1959), p. 138.

December. New Westminster was decidedly proud of the fine muscular young men who made up its volunteer fire brigade, called the Hyack Company. ("Hyack" was a Chinook jargon word meaning "quick".) The by-laws of the Hyack Company prohibited the use of liquor in the firehall. A letter in the local press, signed "Admonitor", raised an interesting point: what was the avail of such a by-law "if the Company as such, can march round from saloon to saloon as they did on Thursday"? Apparently the Hyacks had put in at every groggery in town.

Christmastide was not all joy for the girls and boys in New Westminster. The *British Columbian* of December 19th carried an item:

SCHOOL EXAMINATION: The half-yearly examination of the New Westminster School will take place in the new school house on Wednesday, the 23ʳᵈ inst., commencing at 1 o'clock, p.m. Friends of education are invited to attend.

1864

Sir James Douglas retires — Rivalry between Victoria and New Westminster — Governor Kennedy acquires a Government House — The convivial Governor Seymour — The Chilcotin Uprising — Pursuit of Klatsassin — Ahousats capture the Kingfisher *— Indian submissiveness and their addresses to Seymour and Kennedy — The Wild Horse goldfield.*

On the afternoon of January 21st, Governor Sir James Douglas opened the first session of the new Legislative Council of British Columbia. In the speech from the throne, he dwelt on the great importance of roads, the need to promote settlement, and the existing good relationship with the Indians. The last he attributed to the government's granting of reservations, amounting to not more than ten acres for each family,[1] held communally and in perpetuity by the tribes. But he had two pieces of bad news, both financial. The first was that the government had incurred a deficit of £17,055 the previous year; the other was that the Imperial Government was charging the colony £10,700 for the barracks and other military buildings left by the Royal Engineers. Because of these two items, the new year was begun with a deficit of £27,755. Nevertheless, Douglas brought forth a budget which might produce a surplus in 1864:

Debtor balance remaining from 1863 of			£ 27,755
Road Bonds falling due in '64	£	4,250	
Interest on Loans		8,000	
Sinking Fund		6,500	18,750

[1] The Indians were not confined to these reservations which, as Douglas pointed out, were intended primarily to provide havens for "the aged, the helpless and the infirm." The Indians had the same rights as other British subjects to pre-empt and purchase lands outside these reserves.

Expenditures on Civil Establishment		
viz: Salaries, Allowances &		
Contingencies		33,915
Other ordinary Expenses, viz:		
Revenue Services	425	
Administration of Justice	1,900	
Police and Jails	3,650	
Charitable Allowances	400	
Education	500	
Rent	150	
Transport	3,265	
Conveyance of Mails	4,000	
Works and Buildings	3,900	
Roads, Streets & Bridges (repairs)	5,000	
Miscellaneous Services	3,500	
Light Houses	800	27,490

Which gives a total, of ordinary, necessary and probable expenditure for the year 1864 of	£ 107,910
The Revenue from all sources for 1864 is estimated at	120,000
Deducting the amount as above, say	107,910
There will remain a surplus of for the general service of the year	£ 12,090[2]

Douglas was now entering the final weeks of his administration. Although John Robson in the *British Columbian* sternly advised against any farewell banquet for Sir James, he and his clique of New Westminster merchants did not really speak for the colony as a whole. A well-attended banquet was given in honour of the retiring governor for, though few realized the full greatness of Douglas' achievement, most men knew that he deserved well of British Columbia. Douglas received complimentary messages from the Legislative Council, the civil service and various other groups. Four of the five popularly elected members of the Legislative Council presented Lady Douglas with a handsome medallion of her husband.

[2] *British Columbian*, 23 Jan. 1864.

The single abstainer was J. A. R. Homer, the member for New Westminster. A testimonial to Douglas' services, prepared for delivery to the Duke of Newcastle and signed by some nine hundred British Columbians, was read in Douglas' presence. Sir James, with a side glance at the Robson-Homer faction, replied:

Gentlemen,

Envy and malevolence may be endured, but your kindness over-whelms me; it deprives me of the power of utterance; it excites emotions too powerful for control. I cannot, indeed, express at this moment in adequate terms, my sense of your kindness. This is surely the voice and the heart of British Columbia — here are no specious phrases, no hollow or vernal [sic: venal?] compliments. This speaks out broadly, and honestly, and manfully. It assures me that my administration has been useful; that I have done my duty faithfully; that I have used the power of my sovereign for good and not for evil; that I have wronged no man, — oppressed no man; but that I have, with upright rule, meted out equal-handed justice to all men, and that you are grateful. A pyramid of gold and gems would have been less acceptable to me than this simple record.[3]

Douglas' leave-taking of the Indians of the Fraser Valley took the form of a government "potlatch" at which biscuits and molasses were distributed, and some final land grants were made by His Excellency.

Victoria, of course, gave a grand testimonial dinner in honour of Douglas. Only one incident marred that festive occasion. Judge Begbie, rising to reply to the toast "Our Sister Colony", got a hostile reception. This unpleasant though minor episode was symptomatic of the almost paranoic hostility now existing between Victoria and New Westminster, an enmity which the Duke of Newcastle had seen as making infeasible his desired union of the two colonies. John Robson was currently dismissing Vancouver Island as that "insignificant little Island which forms the natural breakwater to British Columbia". When H.M.S. *Tribune* grounded briefly on a sandbar at the entrance to the Fraser, having failed to spot a buoy marking the channel, Robson in the *British Columbian* half suggested that the pilot had been bribed by Victoria interests to run her aground in

---

[3] Alexander Begg, *History of British Columbia* (Toronto, 1894), pp. 364-65.

order to confirm their slanders that shipping could not safely come up the river to New Westminster.[4] As for Victoria harbour, the *British Columbian* did not hesitate to comment on "the submarine rocks with which that harbour, so-called, abounds."[5]

*   *   *

His two replacements having arrived, Sir James Douglas on May 14th left for a holiday in Europe. The first of Douglas' successors to arrive had been the new Governor of Vancouver Island, Arthur Edward Kennedy, who received an elaborate reception when he was sworn in on March 26th. A former captain in the British Army who had first entered the civil service in Ireland during the great potato famine, Kennedy later had served as Governor of Sierra Leone, and then of Western Australia. Those welcoming him met "a soldier-like man, with a resolute, handsome face, and firm voice."[6] With him he brought his wife and family. This fact made particularly disconcerting Kennedy's discovery that, since Douglas had always lived in his own house, there was no Government House in which the Kennedy family could take up residence. For a while they lived at the Colonial Hotel, then at "Fairfield", a house which he rented from Joseph Trutch, the Cariboo roadbuilder. Finally in 1865 he purchased for a Government House a large, partly completed, pretentious mansion. This had been started by the Hon. G. H. Cary, a former Attorney-General, before that brilliant, unstable, sharp-tongued lawyer and his little eccentric wife returned to England, where Cary would die in a lunatic asylum. Because the big house had been equipped with a lofty tower and crenellations in the Victorian Gothic fashion, it had been nicknamed "Cary Castle", a name still sometimes applied to the present Government House, the fourth one on the site. Victorians raised quite an outcry when they learned that Kennedy was spending $19,000 in government funds to acquire Cary Castle, and their outcry mounted when they learned that com-

---

[4] *British Columbian*, 27 Aug. 1864. New Westminster rejoiced when Lord Gilford, captain of the *Tribune*, certified that ships up to twenty feet in draught could safely come up to New Westminster.

[5] *British Columbian*, 29 Oct. 1864.

[6] Sproat, *Scenes and Studies of Savage Life*, p. 62.

pletion of the building and numerous repairs were costing an additional $21,000.

Even before his purchase of Cary Castle, Kennedy had become locked in an interminable struggle with the House of Assembly of Vancouver Island. Under Douglas' thrifty administration, the island colony's tiny white population of some 7500 persons had been paying taxes averaging only £8 per capita whereas British Columbians, with the enormous cost of Douglas' roadbuilding program, had been paying about £24 per capita.[7] But now that Kennedy was setting up a full-fledged colonial establishment, Vancouver Island found itself confronted with much higher taxes and these the Assembly was determined to prevent. To pay for the new Government House, Kennedy had to use his own direct powers of securing government funds, a step which did nothing to ease his troubles with the Assembly.

Frederick Seymour, the new governor for mainland British Columbia, was like Kennedy an experienced colonial administrator. Starting as Assistant Colonial Secretary of Van Dieman's Land (Tasmania), by 1862 he had risen to be Lieutenant-Governor of British Honduras. Unfortunately he had contracted "Panama Fever"[8] which had permanently impaired his health, and made him welcome the transfer to the salubrious climate of British Columbia.

New Westminster went mad with enthusiasm when, on April 20th, Seymour, a bachelor in his mid-forties, arrived and British Columbia finally had a governor who was entirely its very own. The little gunboat *Forward*, bearing the new representative of the Queen, announced its approach with the booming of its cannon. The volleying of the cannon was answered by the bugle call of the New Westminster Volunteer Rifle Corps. Thus alerted, the entire population of the little town thronged to the wharf. Disembarking from the gunboat, Seymour was greeted with a loyal address from the President of the New Westminster Municipal Council. Seymour inspected the honour guard provided by the Rifle Corps then, embarking in a

---

[7] H. H. Bancroft, *History of British Columbia 1792-1887* (San Francisco, 1887), p. 592.

[8] On Seymour generally, see Margaret A. Ormsby, "Frederick Seymour, The Forgotten Governor", *BC Studies* 22 (Summer 1974) : 3-25.

small boat, was taken up to Sapperton where the former residence of Colonel Moody was to serve as Government House.

Next morning at the Treasury Buildings in New Westminster, Judge Begbie, impressive in his robes, first read the revocation of Douglas' appointment and then the royal letters patent naming Seymour as his successor. Next Begbie administered the oath of office. The City Band played the national anthem; a seventeen-gun salute was fired; and the bells of all the churches and of the Hyack Volunteer Fire Company hall rang forth merrily. A welcoming address was read and answered. Then the new governor was taken in procession to Government House. The Rifle Corps marched with a military precision surprising those who knew how recently it had been formed. The Fire Brigade marched, having with them, decked out with ribbons and flowers, "The Fire King", the engine which was their pride. The City Band puffed, tootled and drummed. Onward they all marched under decorated arches raised to give "a right loyal and hearty welcome to the representative of the best of earthly Sovereigns".

Seymour seemed just the man for British Columbia — full of bonhomie and good cheer, swift to identify with the colony and to declare that the days must end when all the treasure of Cariboo went down past New Westminster, enriching Victoria and San Francisco while little benefiting the colony's capital. The condition of New Westminster was in fact grim when Seymour arrived. Subsequently he recalled the capital as he found it:

I had not seen even in the West Indies so melancholy a picture of disappointed hopes as New Westminster presented on my arrival. Here, however, there was a display of energy wanting in the tropics, and thousands of trees of the largest dimension had been felled to make way for the great city expected to rise on the magnificent site selected for it. But the blight had come early. Many of the best houses were untenanted. The largest hotel was to let, decay appeared on all sides, and the stumps and logs of the fallen trees blocked up most of the streets. [New] Westminster appeared, to use the miners' expression, 'played out'.[9]

Seymour set himself to restore morale and it was not long before

9 *Ibid.*, p. 6.

New Westminster began to feel that it really was a capital, especially when in November Governor Seymour gave a party the like of which British Columbia had never seen before. The guest list was headed by Governor Kennedy and his family, who came over from Vancouver Island with scores of other invited guests, including the new Commander-in-Chief of the Pacific Station, Rear-Admiral the Hon. Joseph Denman and his lady. Invitations had been showered over New Westminster and the "up-river towns". On hand to supply music for Governor Seymour's grand ball was the band of H.M.S. *Sutlej*, specially brought over from Esquimalt on one of the gun-boats. With extravagances like this, and the expenses of his own little steam yacht, the *Leviathan*, the Governor found it hard to live within the munificent salary of £3,000 allotted to him by the Duke of Newcastle. He began to dip into his private means. Aware of this fact, and proud of Seymour's style and dash, British Columbians in 1865 increased his salary by another thousand pounds. The *British Columbian* did not fail to contrast this munificence with the shoddy treatment that Vancouver Island was giving its governor.

*   *   *

Governor Seymour's greatest crisis came when, within weeks of taking over the government of British Columbia, he was confronted with very serious Indian trouble, the so-called "Chilcotin Uprising". As noted earlier, a Victoria syndicate headed by Alfred Waddington had launched a scheme to open first a trail, and then a wagon road, between the head of Bute Inlet and the Cariboo. In March of this year when a work party landed at Waddington, at the head of Bute Inlet, to commence the season's work, they found that some Indians had broken into a supply shed and had helped themselves to flour. Allegedly, Waddington's agent wrote down the names of the thieves and, to intimidate them, declared, "All the Chilcoatens are going to die. We shall send sickness into the country, which will kill them all."[10] The Indians were always frightened by the writing down of their names, thinking it gave the white men a magic power over them. Also, remembering the terrible smallpox of two years past, the

[10] R. C. Lundin Brown, *Klatsassan and other Reminiscences of Missionary Life in British Columbia* (London, 1873), p. 10.

Indians took all this as an indication that they would be punished by another visitation of the disease.

During April work on the trail progressed steadily. From Waddington at the head of the Inlet, the "road" followed the Homathko River upstream for some thirty miles, then crossed to the other side of the river by means of a ferry operated by a man named Tim Smith. Beyond the ferry the trail continued for something like nine miles before it reached the trailbuilders' main camp, where twelve men were established. About four miles farther up the trail was the advance camp, where Brewster, the foreman, was working with three men.

By now the trail was being built not in the territory of the relatively friendly Homathko Indians but through that of the savage Chilcotins. The latter were a tribe with whom even the Hudson's Bay Company had never been able to establish satisfactory relations. Almost entirely unvisited by missionaries, the scattered Chilcotins were as savage and ruthless a tribe as could be found. Yet amazingly Waddington's men had no armed escort, made no attempt to fortify their camps, and did not even maintain a night watch. They were now to pay a terrible price for this negligence.

On April 29th a small group of Chilcotins, led by the formidable Chief Klatsassin, arrived at Smith's ferry and apparently demanded food or goods. Probably it was a refusal by the ferryman that caused the Indians to kill him. They then started up the trail towards the main camp, laden with loot from the stores kept at the ferry. En route they met another Chilcotin chief, Telloot, and persuaded him to join in an attack on the main camp. Arriving at this base, they mingled with the Chilcotins employed there as packers by the Bute Inlet Company. Putting on an appearance of the greatest friendliness, they joked with their intended victims and sang as evening came on.

The next morning, just about dawn, when the twelve white men were still asleep in their small tents, the Chilcotins attacked, pulling the tents down upon the sleepers. Edwin Mosely, one of the three survivors, has left an account of his experience:

I was in a tent with Fielding and Campbell [both slain] . . . and

54. Waddington's Road, at the
head of Bute Inlet

55. Rifle pit dug by Macdonald's packers during Chilcotin Uprising

56. John A. ("Cariboo") Cameron

57. Mrs. John A. Cameron

58. "Steve" Tingley

59. A Chinese in British Columbia

60. The original Parliament Buildings ("The Birdcages"), Victoria

61. Government Street, Victoria

62. Victoria, view from Parliament Buildings towards James Bay Bridge

63.   Sir Edward Bulwer Lytton

64.   Governor Frederick Seymour

65.   Governor Arthur Edward Kennedy

66.   Governor Anthony Musgrave

about daybreak I was awakened by two Indians coming to the door of
the tent; they did not enter but raised it up and whooped; at the same
time each of them fired on either side of me. I was lying in the centre.
They then let the tent down; the ridge pole fell on the top of me, and
the tent covered all three of us. While lying in this position I saw knives
on each side of me come through the tent and pierce the bodies of my
two companions. I could see through the side of the tent, and observing
Indians going to the other tents, I jumped up and plunged into the
river which was about two steps from me. . . . After going down the
river about 100 yards, I got out and saw the Indians, men, women and
children, hallooing where the cook's tent and provisions were.[11]

Continuing up the trail, the Chilcotins reached the advance camp
where Brewster and his three men had just finished their breakfast.
Here there were no survivors.

On May 11th the steamer *Emily Harris* reached Victoria with
news of the massacre of fourteen of Waddington's men. Word was
sent to Governor Seymour at New Westminster who, on May 15th,
sent Chartres Brew to Bute Inlet with twenty-eight special constables
to pursue the murderers. On May 26th Seymour himself left for
Bute Inlet aboard the gunboat *Forward*, but five days later he was
back in New Westminster with Brew. The latter had found the
terrain beyond the advance camp so appalling that he had deemed
it impossible to make his way through it in pursuit of the band of
killers. The latter had, of course, long since disappeared from the
scenes of their crimes.

Brew had given burial to the mutilated remains of the murdered
men, and he had found evidence that helped to explain the Chilcotin attack: the white workmen had got involved with the Chilcotins' women. With decent reticence the *British Columbian* reported "the particular manner in which some of the unfortunate
victims were mutilated points to the secret cause of trouble".[12] Edgar
Fawcett, visiting the scene of the main massacre with a Canadian
Pacific Railway survey party in 1872, found not only drills, hammers,
spades, axes and tent poles still on the scene, but "women's shoes and
other articles of apparel". He had no doubt that the "Indian girls

[11] *Colonist*, 12 May 1864.
[12] *British Columbian*, 6 Aug. 1864.

having been enticed from their friends by the white men . . . had thus brought down the Indians' vengeance on the seducers."[13]

Back in New Westminster after Brew's failure at Bute Inlet, Governor Seymour followed another plan: to send to North Bentinck Arm a force which would proceed inland from Bella Coola and meet with Gold Commissioner Cox and fifty men proceeding westward from Alexandria. On June 1st His Excellency wrote to Vice-Admiral Kingcome at Esquimalt, requesting naval assistance and emphasizing the seriousness of the situation:

I need scarcely point out to you, the difficulties and enormous expense which an Indian War in this vast territory would entail on the Imperial and Local Governments, and the total ruin which would befall British Columbia, were access to the Gold mines of Cariboo rendered impracticable. I am doing all I can to avert such a serious catastrophe, and am dealing in a lavish manner with such resources in men and money as the Colony possesses.[14]

Admiral Kingcome gave the requested cooperation and was aboard his flagship, H.M.S. *Sutlej*, at Bentinck Arm when it landed, on June 18th, Governor Seymour, Chartres Brew, and a party of forty-eight members of the New Westminster Volunteer Rifle Corps, largely composed of former Royal Engineers.

Preparing for their journey inland, Seymour and Brew knew that they had to deal with more than the massacre of the Waddington party. The previous day, just after the *Sutlej* had entered Bentinck Arm, she had been hailed by two Englishmen in a canoe. They had a grim story to tell. Both had been members of a party of eight white men, headed by Alexander Macdonald, who had left Bella Coola with forty-two packhorses loaded with provisions, stores and ammunition for the Cariboo. After these men had travelled about 120 miles, they came upon an encampment of Indians (Chilcotins and others) near Nimpo Lake.[15] One of the white men, McDougall, had

---

[13] PABC, E/E/F28G, p. 4.

[14] PRO, ADM 1/5878.

[15] PRO, ADM 1/5878. Occasionally this encampment has been erroneously identified as being at Anahim Lake. The rifle pit and the historical marker several miles west of Nimpo, let alone the despatch carried in the *British Columbian* of 6 Aug. 1864, make it clear that Nimpo Lake is the correct location. The hilltop fortified village subsequently burned by Brew's men probably stood very close to the present Nimpo service station.

with him a Chilcotin woman, Klymtedza. Speaking to her newly-met tribesmen, she learned that Klatsassin, leader of the Bute Inlet murderers, had arrived here and was urging a general uprising against the whites, one which would culminate in an attack on Fort Alexandria. She learned moreover that the local Indians had already decided to attack Macdonald and his packtrain. Returning to the whites, Klymtedza revealed the plot. Urgently she told them that their only hope was to abandon their slow-moving packtrain, get on their horses and ride back to Bella Coola just as quickly as they could. But not all the whites were ready to leave to the Indians their valuable freight and their pack animals. After some discussion among themselves, they retreated a mile or two along the Bella Coola trail until they reached a good defensive position on an open knoll within a bend of the Dean River. Here they dug a rifle pit twenty-five feet long, with flanking trenches both of twenty feet,[16] and prepared to fight off any Indian attack.

When after two or three days the Indians had made no move against them, Macdonald and his men, growing impatient, decided to return to Bella Coola. Two Indian "bell-boys" sent out to help round up the pack animals were captured by Klatsassin's people and revealed to the chief the important news that the whites were preparing to leave their stronghold. Grimly the Indians prepared an ambush. Macdonald's party got their long train of loaded horses started down the trail. After travelling three miles they reached a branching of the trail, and here the Chilcotins were waiting for them. Two of the white men, Higgins and McDougall, and apparently McDougall's faithful Klymtedza, fell dead as the Indians opened fire. The other white men galloped off at top speed except Mac-donald, whose horse was shot from under him. Grabbing another horse, Macdonald mounted it, only to have it too shot down. Left alone, on foot, Macdonald took to the bush and prepared to make his last stand. When the Chilcotins moved in on him, he managed to kill one of the Indians before another, stealing up behind him,

---

[16] In 1927 F. C. Swannell, the well-known B.C. land surveyor, visited the site, measured and photographed the earthworks. He also got the story of Mac-donald's end from an old Indian who had witnessed it when a young boy. See PAC, Swannell, *Diary of Survey, Dean & Bella Coola Rivers, 1927*, entry for June 22nd.

smashed in the side of his head with a blow from his musket butt. The five survivors, only one unwounded, hastened on to Bella Coola. They arrived just in time to warn the first settler they met, a man named Hamilton, to get his family to safety. The survivors and the Hamilton family had barely pulled out in a canoe when the Chilcotins appeared on the scene and began looting the Hamilton house.[17]

Aware, then, of the fate of Macdonald's party, Seymour and Brew, after adding to their force a number of friendly Bella Coola Indians, started east. Their destination was Puntzi Lake, the focal point where trails from Bentinck Arm, Bute Inlet, and the Fraser River at Alexandria all converged. The amazingly steep ascent of five thousand feet from the valley of the Bella Coola River to the edge of the Interior Plateau provided the usual ordeal. At the top they rested for a day, then pushed on for Anahim Lake. Here they found Chief Anahim's village, Nacoontloon, deserted. Since Anahim had not joined in the uprising, the New Westminster Volunteers left unburned both the village and its palisaded fort. Continuing on their way, Seymour, Brew and their men began to find evidence of the attack on the packtrain: "Kegs of nails, boxes of carpenter's tools, gutted pack-saddles, broken agricultural instruments". Then they came to the grave of the Indian whom Macdonald had got with one of his last shots, "a Siwash tomb of logs, pompously adorned with stakes and flags".[18] Fifteen yards off lay the naked body of Macdonald, terribly gnawed by animals but with the features still recognizable. Half a mile farther along was the well-preserved body of Higgins, and a few hundred yards beyond were the remains of McDougall. Dead horses lay along the trail. Brew's men halted for the night. The next day they passed the earthworks where Macdonald and his people had briefly remained safe. Then they continued on a couple of miles to the abandoned blockhouse of the Nimpo Indians. Since there was no doubt of the band's complicity in the attack on the packtrain, Brew's men set fire to the fort. As dense clouds of black smoke arose from it, a protesting shot was heard from the far side of Nimpo Lake.

[17] E. S. Hewlett, "The Chilcotin Uprising of 1864", *BC Studies* 19 (Autumn 1973) :58.

[18] *British Columbian,* 6 Aug. 1864.

Pressing on, the Bentinck Arm Expedition hurried towards Puntzi Lake. They were passing through some of the most beautiful country in all British Columbia, scores of bright little lakes gleaming amid lush water meadows, dark clusters of pines rising out of the stretches of open parkland, occasional rolling hills with lighter deciduous trees and, to the west rising in breath-taking majesty, the great snowy peaks of the Coast Mountains. Yet it is doubtful if, after the horrors they had just witnessed, many had thoughts for scenery. On July 6th they reached Puntzi Lake and joined up with Cox's Alexandria force.

Gold Commissioner W. G. Cox was about the last man Seymour should have chosen to command a military force, even a ragged one made up of Cariboo goldseekers. Friendly, genial and easy-going, he had hardly the dimmest idea of how to set about his task. Leaving Alexandria on June 8th, he had arrived at Puntzi Lake on June 12th and ever since then had sat there achieving nothing other than building a "fort". Perhaps his nerves had been shaken by the discovery at Puntzi of the corpse of the only white settler in the country, William Manning. Although Manning had been on good terms with the Chilcotin Indians, they had not forgiven him for settling on an old and favourite Indian campsite, and Anahim ordered one of his band, Tahpit, to slay Manning. Afterwards the Indians put his body in a small stream and sought to conceal it under tree roots fetched from where Manning had been clearing his land. Klatsassin and his Chilcotins, who reached Puntzi Lake the evening of the murder, were still in the vicinity when Cox and his force arrived. Indeed, the sight of an Indian dog had revealed their presence to Cox, but Klatsassin and his followers managed to slip away. After that, Cox and his people just stayed put at Puntzi for an entire month, eating up the expensive provisions which they had brought from Alexandria, and sending for more. (It had cost Seymour £200 just to ship from the Coast their fifty unused rifles and a supply of ammunition.) Cox's excuse for his inactivity was that he had expected to find Chief Alexis at Puntzi, ready to supply him with Indian guides and trackers, but that since Alexis had never shown up, and a party sent to Chilcotin Forks to look for him there had been totally unsuccessful, he had concluded there was nothing really that he could do without the help of Alexis. One can imagine the blistering contempt that Sir James Douglas would have expressed if Cox had given such a report to him. Even the complaisant Seymour, who arrived at Puntzi on July 6th, ordered Cox and his expensive troops off to Tatla Lake the next day to start searching for Klatsassin, Telloot, and the other wanted men.

From this point on, the record becomes somewhat obscure, with parties penetrating into various regions in the vast Chilcotin country. At one point the pursuers had Klatsassin in open view, but he escaped by diving into a lake and hiding amid its reeds. During one of these forays the government forces suffered their only fatality. It could not have happened to a more unpleasant individual. Donald McLean, at one time the Hudson's Bay Company officer in charge of Fort Kamloops, was one of that New Caledonia gang of bullies who had between the mid-1840s and mid-1850s so signally stained the generally excellent reputation of that great company. Retired from the HBC service and running a ranch on the Bonaparte River, McLean had hastened to join Cox's force. Report had it that McLean had during his career personally slain nineteen Indians,[19] and some said he joined Cox only because he saw an opportunity to make his total a round score. Certainly the Indians dreaded and hated him, referring to him simply as "Küschte te' Kukkpé" ("The Fierce Chief"). Exasperated by Cox's incompetence, McLean seized any opportunity to get away from him and conduct the search in his own fashion. One day late in July, slipping away from the rest of his group north of Chilko Lake[20] and taking with him only an Indian boy, he headed up a gully where recent tracks of Indians were to be seen. Pressing eagerly ahead, McLean came in sight of a screen of fir boughs piled against a tall tree. Intently he stared for a glimpse of the Indians supposedly lurking behind the blind. But the fir branches were merely a decoy. The Indians were in a clump of willows on the opposite side of the trail. Suddenly a shot rang out, followed by another which got McLean through the heart.

After McLean's death, the abject Cox wanted to give up the

---

[19] *Klatsassan*, p. 69.

[20] See PRO, Map MPG 654, a contemporary map which has the sites of certain key events marked on it.

pursuit until winter stripped the trees of concealing foliage, but Seymour ordered him and Brew to continue harrying the Indians in an attempt to force the surrender of the wanted men. After all, His Excellency (who was continuing on to Richfield before returning to the Coast) could hardly return to New Westminster with nothing to show for all this expenditure of time and money!

Finally, on August 15th, Klatsassin, Telloot, and six others presented themselves at Cox's camp on the site of old Fort Chilcotin[21] and were immediately placed under arrest. Mystery surrounds this surrender. Klatsassin apparently thought that he had been granted some sort of guarantee of personal freedom which would permit him to negotiate with Governor Seymour. Possibly the Chilcotin had misunderstood a message from Cox, or Cox may have deliberately disregarded promised terms. In any event, two of the Indians were freed for lack of evidence, and on September 28th and 29th at Quesnel Judge Begbie conducted the trial of the remaining six Indians. Five of them were sentenced to death by hanging — Klatsassin, Telloot, Tahpit, Pierre and Chessus. Immediately after the trial Begbie wrote, "Klatsassin is the finest savage I have met with yet, I think."[22]

The hanging of the five Indians at Quesnel really ends the story of the Chilcotin Uprising. It had never become a general insurrection of the entire Chilcotin people, even though Klatsassin had endeavoured to make it one. The British Columbia government's punitive operation had proved a very expensive one, entailing an outlay of £18,000.[23] Old John Tod reflected that, back in the days when the Hudson's Bay Company held sway, the whole matter would have been looked after by "a mere handful of Fur Traders."[24]

*   *   *

[21] We are indebted to Mr. Gabriel Bayliff for showing us this site (Lot 416) on the Chilcotin River just above its junction with the Chilco River. This property continued to be owned by the Hudson's Bay Company until sold to the Bayliff family in the 1930s. In *British Columbia Chronicle, 1778-1846* we erroneously took the view of those who placed the fort on Chilcotin Lake.

[22] Hewlett, *op. cit.*, p. 54.

[23] Ormsby, *BC Studies* 22:7.

[24] Tod to Edward Ermatinger, 1 June 1864. PAC, *Ermatinger Papers.*

If Governor Seymour had his fill of Indian troubles this year, so had his opposite number, Governor Kennedy of Vancouver Island. The trouble there began in August when the trading sloop *King-fisher*, a mere ten tons in burden, put into Matilda Creek, Clayoquot Sound, to trade with the local Ahousat Indians. Here Chief Cap-chah (who already had a very bad reputation), with twelve men seized the *Kingfisher* in order to plunder its cargo. While two Indians held Captain James Stevenson's arms, Chief Cap-chah sank his dagger three times into his back. Three other Indians gave the same treatment to Wilson, the other white man aboard the little ship. The throats of Stevenson and Wilson were then slit, their bodies cut open and thrown overboard. The third and last member of the crew, a Fort Rupert Indian, was also stabbed and killed, and the vessel was pillaged and sunk.

Rumours of this outrage reached Victoria in mid-September and Commander Pike was sent to Clayoquot Sound with H.M.S. *Devastation* to investigate. He soon returned with confirmation of the loss of the *Kingfisher*, and brought with him some of the murderers of W. E. Banfield, the Indian agent there who had been killed back in October 1862. Informed of Pike's report, Governor Kennedy decided upon rigorous action against those who had attacked the *King-fisher*.[25] Coasters must be able to enter Clayoquot Sound, confident that they would not be in danger from the Indians.

On October 2nd Rear-Admiral Denman, with his flagship H.M.S. *Sutlej*, rendezvoused with Commander Pike and H.M.S. *Devastation* at Clayoquot to deal with the Ahousats. There was a standard procedure in such cases: seize some hostages, threaten to destroy the villages, deprive the Indians of some of their canoes, gradually increase the pressure until the Indians handed over their tribesmen whose crimes had brought this visitation upon them. Admiral Denman was to find the Ahousats too tough to crack by such tactics. This day, finding the village at Matilda Creek dismantled, Denman proceeded to the village of Sik-tok-kis. Here no Indian would risk coming aboard and being taken a hostage but somehow Hankin, the

---

[25] Kennedy to Denman, 27 Sept. 1864, PRO, ADM 1/5878, f.422. The following account of the *Kingfisher* operation is based largely on the reports of Rear-Admiral Denman contained in this file.

67. Victoria Pioneer Rifle Corps ("The African Rifles")

68. Queen Victoria's birthday celebration, New Westminster [?]

69. Government House, New Westminster

70. Croquet party at Fairfield House, Victoria

71. Indian bridge, Hagwilget, built with wire abandoned by Collins Overland
    Telegraph

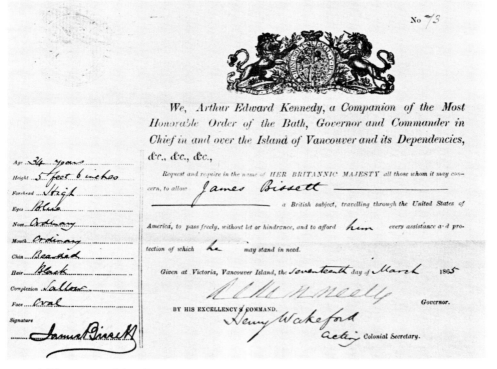

72. A Vancouver Island passport

73. H.M.S. *Sparrowhawk*

74. Ships loading lumber at Moodyville, Burrard Inlet

expedition's interpreter, did manage to secure an Indian, Ea-qui-ok-Shittle, who admitted being one of those who had boarded the *Kingfisher* but denied involvement in the actual murders. He subsequently supplied Denman with the names of the other attackers, and the parts played by each. Meanwhile Pike had taken the *Devastation* to another village, Moo-yah-hah at the head of Herbert Arm, where the Ahousats appeared in war dress and opened fire on his ship.

Admiral Denman, a very decisive man, felt that the time had come to get rough with the Ahousats. While Pike burned three Ahousat villages and seized their canoes (in the process recovering the compass, papers and other property belonging to the *Kingfisher*), Denman anchored off the village of Moo-yah-hah and announced that if the murderers were not handed over he would open fire on the houses. The Indians retorted that if he did so they would simply build new ones. At this, the *Sutlej* began cannonading the bush around the village while, under the cover of her guns, her gigs made for the shore. Moo-yah-hah was set on fire by the landing party, who seized the villagers' canoes and found the *Kingfisher*'s dinghy among them. The dismantled village at Matilda Creek was also totally destroyed. Next day the *Devastation*, living up to her name, destroyed Chief Cap-chah's own village as well as another, and seized the inhabitants' canoes. The seriousness of these measures can be understood only when one realizes the enormous amount of time required to raise the great posts of the house frames and to hand-hew the planks that were their siding; and appreciates also the time and skill required to make even a small dugout canoe. After all these losses, the Ahousats should surely have handed over Cap-chah and the other murderers; but nothing of the sort happened.

Clearly other tactics were required. Pike took the *Devastation* around to Sydney Inlet, where the services of the friendly Manu-wissett Indians were enlisted. They seized and turned over to the British an Ahousat who proved decidedly useful.

On October 7th Admiral Denman played his trump. Three miles from the ruins of Cap-chah's village he landed forty bluejackets and thirty marines. Guided by the Clayoquots, they threaded the forest trails with such stealth that they got within twenty yards of Cap-chah's temporary huts before a native dog started yelping, giving the alarm. The Ahousats raced into the forest and started firing. Ten of them were killed by the fire of the British, who sustained no casualties. And that was the end of the attempt to capture Cap-chah by a surprise onslaught. The Ahousats simply disappeared into the forest. Anybody who has hiked along the trails of the West Coast of Vancouver Island and seen the incredible thickness of the salal and other underbrush will agree with Denman that, once the Ahousats had gone into that practically impenetrable forest, pursuit would be impossible.

So Admiral Denman sailed back to Esquimalt. The Ahousats had seen seven of their villages totally destroyed. They had lost nearly all their precious canoes. A number of them had been killed or wounded. On the other hand, although two of the *Kingfisher*'s attackers had finally surrendered, Cap-chah and nine of his accomplices remained at large and, in fact, never were captured.

Although Denman returned to Victoria without the prime offenders, Governor Kennedy took the view that he had done what he could to arrest them. To the admiral, Kennedy wrote a letter of thanks and congratulation:

> I feel assured that the decisive measures which you have adopted will be productive of the best results to this and the neighbouring Colony, and check the piratical and blood-thirsty practices of the Coast Indians, which have been left too long unpunished.[26]

The Chilcotin Uprising and the *Kingfisher* episode more or less mark the end of Indian armed resistance to the white men. The Indians came to realize that they could not compete with the increasing number of whites and that they were helpless against their superior arms. The native population, indeed, had been so reduced through smallpox, venereal disease, measles, tuberculosis and the effects of alcohol that most whites expected the Indians to become extinct during the next century. Missionaries were turning more and more of the surviving Indians into the gentler Christian pattern of life, and in the process making them ashamed of their earlier savage "heathen" existence.

[26] Kennedy to Denman, 14 Oct. 1864. PRO, ADM 1/5878, f.428v.

Indicative of the breaking of the spirit of the Indians are two addresses which they presented this year to their white rulers. The first was offered to Governor Seymour by the chiefs of the Lower Mainland on May 24th, Queen Victoria's birthday:

GREAT CHIEF ENGLISH — We beg to speak to you. We, the native Indians, are gathered to welcome you, and to show you our good dispositions.

We know the good heart of the Queen for the Indians. You bring that good heart with you, so we are happy to welcome you.

We wish to become good Indians, and to be friends with the white people.

Please to protect us against any bad Indians, or any bad white men.

Please to protect our land, that it will not be small for us; many are pleased with their reservations, and many wish that their reservations be marked out for them.

Please to give good things to make us become like the good white men, as an exchange for our land occupied by white men.

Our heart will always be good and thankful to the Queen, and to you, Great Chief.

We finish to speak to you.[27]

The other address, translated by the missionary Thomas Crosby, was presented to Governor Kennedy at Nanaimo this November:

YOU, OUR GREAT CHIEF, —

We, the Nanaimo Indians, have long wanted to see you and speak our hearts to you; and we want Mr. Crosby to translate our words. This day our hearts are made very glad because we see you. You, Mr. Kennedy, have come from our great Queen, and we hope you have some good words to speak to us from her. We are poor dark Indians. You white people know more than we do. If all white people who come here were good, it would be better for us; but many teach our people to swear and get drunk. We hope you, our Governor, will speak strong words to them. Our hearts are very glad that good white people have sent ministers of the Gospel to us, who tell us good things about God, and teach our children to read. We want them to know more than we do. We want to keep our land here and up the river. Some white men tell us we shall soon have to remove again; but we don't want to lose these reserves. All our other land is gone, and we have been paid very little for it. God gave it to us a long time ago, and now we are very poor, and do not know where our homes will be if we leave this. We

[27] *British Columbian*, 28 May 1864.

want our land up the river to plant for food. Mr. Douglas said it should be ours, and our children's after we are gone. We hope you, our new chief, will say the same. We have over 300 people in our tribe, though a number are away fishing now. Many are old and not able to work, and some of our children, who have neither father nor mother, have no clothes. We hope you will be kind to them. Our hearts are good to all white people, and to you, our great white chief. We hope you will send our words to the great Queen. We pray that the Great Spirit may bless her and you. This is all our hearts to-day.[28]

*   *   *

Meanwhile the white population that was moving into the country which had once been solely the Indians' were curious to know more about it. Hence we have the exploration expeditions which are such a feature of this year. Kennedy, while Governor of Western Australia, had been associated with government-sponsored exploration expeditions, and thought similar expeditions might be useful for Vancouver Island. Accordingly a Vancouver Island Exploration Committee was set up and under its auspices, with the government paying two-thirds of the bill and private contributors one-third, an expedition was put in the field this June. This consisted of Dr. Robert Brown (leader), Lieut. P. J. Leech (astronomer), Mr. F. Whymper (artist), Mr. J. Buttle (naturalist), and "a staff of assistants, pioneers, miners and native hunters".[29] After exploring the Cowichan Lake district the group divided. Brown's party struck overland from the west end of Cowichan Lake, followed Nitinat River and Lake to the sea and rendezvoused at Port San Juan (Port Renfrew) with Leech's party which had travelled south-westerly from the eastern end of Cowichan Lake. Next, Leech led his party northwards from Sooke Harbour to Cowichan Bay; and later Brown travelled to Port Augusta (Comox Harbour) and explored the area around the Courtenay and Puntledge Rivers, finding some fine coal seams. Finally Brown's party travelled up Puntledge Lake (Comox Lake) and, heading south-easterly past a series of small lakes and rivers,

[28] Matthew Macfie, *Vancouver Island and British Columbia* (London, 1865), pp. 468-69.

[29] R. Brown, "Explorations in the Interior of Vancouver Island", *Proceedings of the Royal Geographical Society* 9 (1864-65):306.

reached first Central Lake, then Sproat Lake and finally the Alberni valley, where they were warmly received by the settlers. They returned to Victoria by way of Nanaimo. Gradually, the rugged interior of Vancouver Island was becoming known.

British Columbia felt an urge to match the Vancouver Island Exploration Expedition. In August the New Westminster Exploring Association was formed and money raised to send out a party to explore the country between Pitt Lake and the headwaters of Squamish River, but this appears to have achieved little. Another party was despatched up Coquitlam River to look for gold, found none, and returned after travelling no great distance. Meanwhile Lillooet organized an exploration expedition, headed by A. C. Elliott, the local magistrate, and H. Featherstone, which was to journey from Lillooet to the headwaters of Pitt River. Yale and Lytton also buzzed with talk about exploring expeditions.

All in all, the achievements of the "explorers" were far from impressive. Perhaps the most notable was that of Lieut. Leech who, on his trip from Sooke to Cowichan, found modest amounts of gold on the Leech River and so started a gold rush which proved a rather disappointing affair for all concerned.

*   *   *

The most important new gold strike of this year was made along Wild Horse Creek in the East Kootenay country. Wild Horse was one of the roughest and toughest of all the gold-mining camps. According to D. M. Drumheller, one of the Americans who had joined the rush, many of the prospectors had been ordered out of Montana by the "vigilance committee". There was, moreover, a constant feud between the men from east of the Rockies and those from the west, which culminated in a free-for-all in a saloon, with a man named Walker getting killed. For the events which followed we have "Uncle Dan" Drumheller's own recollections:

A mob was quickly raised by the friends of Tommy Walker for the purpose of hanging Overland Bob and East Powder Bill. Then a law and order organization numbering about 1000 miners, of which I was a member, assembled. It was the purpose of our organization to order a miners' court and give all concerned a fair trial. . . . The next morning we appointed a lawyer by the name of A. J. Gregory as trial judge and John McClellan sheriff, with authority to appoint as many deputies as he wished. That was the condition of things when Judge Haines, the British Columbia commissioner, rode into camp.

"Fifteen hundred men under arms in the queen's dominion. A dastardly usurpation of authority, don't cher know," remarked Judge Haines. But one little English constable with knee breeches, red cap, cane in his hand, riding a jockey saddle and mounted on a bob-tailed horse, quelled that mob in 15 minutes.[30]

Drumheller's "Judge Haines" was actually John Carmichael Haynes, gold commissioner for southern British Columbia, who had arrived to issue mining licences, register claims, collect duties, and attend to all the other miscellaneous chores which fell to a gold commissioner's lot. He found the miners making, on the average, between twenty and thirty dollars a day, with one lucky man the proud discoverer of a nugget weighing thirty-seven ounces.[31] When A. N. Birch, the Colonial Secretary, visited Wild Horse this September, he brought out some seventy-five pounds of gold with him.

Unfortunately the Wild Horse miners trafficked almost entirely with the United States, bringing in their supplies from Lewiston and Walla Walla. Understandably the merchants of New Westminster were far from happy at seeing this business going to the Yankees. Representations were made to Governor Seymour, who sent out two parties to look for a British route to this new gold area in the East Kootenay. The first of Seymour's parties, headed by George Turner, late of the Royal Engineers, travelled to Kamloops, went up the South Thompson River to Shuswap Lake, then crossed the Monashees and struck the Columbia River near Death Rapids. Here on the upper Columbia they found a little gold, foreshadowing the later Big Bend Gold Rush, but their supplies were running out and they had to head back without getting anywhere close to the Wild Horse Creek area. The second party, headed by J. J. Jenkins, was more

---

[30] "Uncle Dan" [Daniel Montgomery] Drumheller, *"Uncle Dan" Drumheller Tells Thrills of Western Trails in 1854* (Spokane, 1925), pp. 116-17. Actually the title of this book is misleading, since it deals with the period from Drumheller's arrival in California in 1854 to his experiences as a cattleman in Washington and British Columbia in the 1870s.

[31] For Haynes' report, see *British Columbian*, 19 Oct. 1864.

successful. After following the Dewdney Trail to the now abandoned Rock Creek gold settlement, Jenkins and his men pushed on to Grand Forks and Christina Lake, up Sheep Creek and over to the Columbia River, and from Fort Shepherd took the Moyie route to Wild Horse.

Encouraging though the Wild Horse diggings undoubtedly were, they did not for one minute approach in importance the Cariboo which this year continued to yield incredible treasure. Access to the Cariboo was becoming easier now that an uninterrupted road extended from Yale to Soda Creek, a route improved this year when Cook's Ferry was replaced by Spence's Bridge. From Soda Creek a Fraser River steamer made easy connection with Quesnel.

And what awaited the hopeful traveller bound for the goldfields once he disembarked at "Quesnelle City", *alias* "Quesnelmouth", *alias* "Quesnel"? — a rugged trail over which he had to travel by horse or foot some sixty-five miles before arriving finally at Barkerville, in the heart of the Cariboo. The government, however, was determined that a wagon road should be provided for this last stretch and this summer the ubiquitous Gustavus Blin Wright, probably the greatest of the roadbuilders, got a wagon road through as far as Cottonwood.[32]

The man who seized the opportunity to get a scheduled service operating to Cariboo over the newly-completed Yale to Soda Creek road was Francis Jones Barnard, proprietor of Barnard's Express & Stage Line, famous throughout British Columbia in the coming years as the "B.X." Barnard was not the first to operate an express service for British Columbians — that distinction went to Billy Ballou back in June 1858. Barnard appeared on the scene only in 1861 when, with incredible endurance, he made the 760 mile return trip to Cariboo entirely on foot, fighting his way through winter blizzards, with a pack of letters and papers on his back. Endowed with such energy and determination, Barnard had soon driven Ballou out of business. An advertisement proudly displayed in the *British Columbian* of May 4th this year announced Barnard's new Cariboo service:

[32] Gordon R. Elliott, *Quesnel: Commercial Centre of the Cariboo Gold Rush* (Quesnel, 1958), p. 123.

EXPRESS, FREIGHT

—AND—

PASSENGER LINE

STAGES.

AFTER THE FIRST DAY OF MAY, 1864, THE Coaches of this Line will run as follows:

UP TRIP:

LEAVES YALE ON

MONDAYS & FRIDAYS, AT 3 A. M.,

PASSING OVER THE

SUSPENSION BRIDGE

—AND—

THROUGH THE CANYONS

By daylight, and reaching

Soda Creek

in time to connect with the stern-wheel steamer

'ENTERPRISE'

on Thursdays and Mondays, at daylight, reaching

Quesnelle City

on the same day.

DOWN TRIP:

Leaves SODA CREEK on the arrival of the "ENTER-PRISE," on TUESDAYS and THURSDAYS, reaching YALE on THURSDAYS and SATURDAYS in time to connect with the stemers for NEW WESTMINSTER.

F. J. BARNARD.

Yale, April 30, 1864.   my4 1m

Some mention must be made of Barnard's future partner who was to buy him out in 1894 and rename the company the British Columbia Express. This man was the most famous of all British Columbia's stagecoach drivers, the redoubtable Steve Tingley. It was this year that, abandoning hopes of finding gold in Cariboo, he signed on as one of Barnard's drivers. Stories about Tingley, his nerve and his endurance are legion. One of the best tells of how on one occasion when Steve was careening along the narrow winding road through the Fraser Canyon, with no guard rail between his coach and the sheer drop to the river far below, a nervous lady passenger asked, "Mr. Tingley, what happens if the wheels go over the edge?" "Well, Ma'am," said Steve, "that depends strictly upon the sort of life you've been living up to that moment."

1865

The last of the "Golden Years" of the Cariboo — Cariboo Wagon Road completed — Cariboo Sentinel — The tragic, ironic death of a son of Simon Fraser — Britain fails to purchase the Alaska Panhandle — Admiral Denman favours disposing of British Columbia — Economic depression in Victoria and New Westminster — End of the Wild Horse diggings — The Big Bend gold rush — Moberly finds Eagle Pass — The Collins Overland Telegraph — Christmas Squaw Race at Takla Lake.

Old-timers would look back on 1863, 1864 and 1865 as the "golden years" of the Cariboo. Never again would its creeks and valleys yield so much gold as poured forth during these three wonderful years. Their pre-eminence stands forth clearly when we look at the most reliable tables we have for the value of gold production in British Columbia during the period covered by this chronicle:

YEAR.	Amount actually known to have been exported by banks, etc.	Amount added to represent gold carried away in private hands.	Total.	Number of miners employed.	Average yearly earnings per man.
	$	$			$
1858 (partial return)	543,000	......	705,000	3,000	235
1859	1,211,304	1-3rd 403,768	1,615,072	4,000	403
1860	1,671,410	" 557,133	2,228,543	4,400	506
1861	1,999,589	" 666,529	2,666,118	4,200	634
1862	1,992,677	" 664,226	2,656,903	4,100	648
1863	2,935,172	" 978,391	3,913,563	4,400	889
1864	2,801,888	" 933,962	3,735,850	4,400	849
1865	2,618,404	" 872,801	3,491,205	4,294	813
1866	1,996,580	" 665,526	2,662,106	2,982	893
1867	1,860,651	" 620,217	2,480,868	3,044	814
1868	1,779,729	" 593,243	2,372,972	2,390	992
1869	1,331,234	" 443,744	1,774,978	2,369	749
1870	1,002,717	" 334,239	1,336,956	2,348	569
1871	1,349,580	" 449,860	1,799,440	2,450	734 [1]

[1] Victor Ross, *History of the Canadian Bank of Commerce* (Toronto, 3 vols. 1920-34), I:473.

The citizens of the Cariboo could congratulate themselves this year on something besides continuing rich returns of gold, for 1865 saw the completion of the Cariboo Wagon Road with the building of the last stretch from Cottonwood to Richfield, the district's administrative headquarters. Early the next year the road would be extended the few miles to Barkerville and Camerontown.

Nor was this the only road construction in the Cariboo this year. While the river link, supplied by the *Enterprise* plying between Soda Creek and Quesnel, was fine for passenger traffic and light expresses, and continued to be used by them for a great many years, it was anything but satisfactory for the freighters travelling with their two or more heavy wagons fastened in tandem, and drawn by as many as ten or twelve horses or oxen. The freighters clamoured for a route which would let them drive from Yale to Barkerville without any transshipping, and this year they were able to by-pass the river stretch when a wagon road was built between Alexandria and Quesnel.

With the completion of "The Road", Sir James Douglas' vision had been brought to fulfilment. Visitors with a classical education would sometimes call the Cariboo Wagon Road the "Appian Way of British Columbia". Certainly its construction, chiefly by civilian contractors along routes surveyed by the Royal Engineers, was a tremendous achievement for a colony whose total white population was something like ten thousand. It had of course been a vastly expensive enterprise, costing £264,972 during the period 1862-1864 alone. Much of this had been borrowed money, carrying heavy interest charges. To meet these charges, and gradually pay off the principal, a burdensome set of tolls was charged on everything travelling up or down the road. Freight leaving New Westminster had to pay $3.00 per ton. At both Alexandra Bridge and Spence's Bridge it had to pay an additional $7.40 per ton, and at Lytton (or Lillooet if it had come up by the Harrison route) it had to pay $44.80, for a total toll of $62.60 per ton. Although these tolls were highly unpopular, the benefits for which they paid were patent. In 1861, when freight was still coming in over the old Harrison-Lillooet route, it cost 75¢ a pound to bring freight to the gold camps on

Williams Creek. In 1864, with the Cariboo Wagon Road largely completed, it cost 30¢, and this year the price went down to 15¢ a pound.[2]

Of the continuing prosperity in the Cariboo there is plenty of evidence. This summer, for example, the district acquired its first newspaper, the *Cariboo Sentinel*. It expressed the Barkerville view of the needs of British Columbia, which turned out to be noticeably different from the New Westminster view. Consequently, the *Cariboo Sentinel* had hardly printed its first number when the *British Columbian*, long engaged in a war with the Victoria press, gave the back of its hand to the newcomer, declaring that the *Sentinel*, in league with the Victoria papers, was attempting to split British Columbian sentiment by poisoning the minds of the Cariboo miners against the government in New Westminster.

The *Cariboo Sentinel* came into existence just a little too late to chronicle one of the most tragic happenings of the year. John Fraser was the eldest son of Simon Fraser, the explorer. Bright, personable and well-educated, he was obviously a man with a future. When he came out to Cariboo to practise his profession as a civil engineer, the Fraser family had raised, by mortgaging the family farm, between three and four thousand dollars for him to invest on their behalf in Cariboo gold properties. Young Fraser worked hard and chose his investments wisely, and his kinsmen's money increased. Moreover, John Fraser became very popular in Barkerville. He was active in the Literary Society, the Glee Club, the Library Association, and the choir of the Methodist Church. Then this May catastrophe struck. In the same mail he received two letters from home: the one informed him that the mortgage on the family home had been foreclosed and his sisters had been turned out to shift for themselves; the other letter told him that the girl to whom he was engaged had married somebody else. All through the night young Fraser paced his bedroom in a state of utter distraction. Just after dawn he cut his jugular veins with his penknife. He was rushed to a doctor, who vainly attempted to stitch the veins, and within a few minutes he

---

[2] *British Columbian*, 20 June 1865. The toll total is here given, incorrectly, as $62.20.

was dead. Hardly was his body cold when word came of a rich strike on the Saw Mill claim, in which Fraser held a major interest.[3]

*   *   *

When we turn our gaze from the Cariboo to the rest of British Columbia and to her sister colony of Vancouver Island, the view proves hardly heartening. For one thing, Britain this year missed an opportunity to acquire the Alaska Panhandle, that narrow strip of Russian territory which deprived nearly half of British Columbia of direct access to the sea. Negotiations had become pretty much dead-locked over the rent that the Hudson's Bay Company should pay for a renewal this year of its lease of the Panhandle as far north as Cape Spencer (58° N. Latitude), a lease which the Russians wanted to extend to as far north as Mount St. Elias (60° N. Latitude) at double the previous rent. Caught in something of a quandary, the London Committee of the HBC canvassed the views of veteran officers in North America. One of the men so consulted was Chief Factor W. F. Tolmie in Victoria. In his reply Dr. Tolmie noted that the Russian American Company's agent in these negotiations, Rut-kovski, had earlier mentioned the sale of the Panhandle as a possible way out, and that the same solution had been "verbally proposed to me by Prince Maksutoff [the Governor of Russian America] when last here."[4] Tolmie strongly urged that the Russian offer to sell be accepted. Unfortunately, by the time his letter reached London a new lease had already been negotiated. Accordingly, the proposed purchase received no attention. When the HBC's renewed lease ended two years later, it was the United States that purchased Alaska.

On the whole, it seems unlikely that, even if Tolmie's recommendation had been received in time, Britain would either have purchased the Panhandle itself, or have permitted the Hudson's Bay Company to do so. Britain at this time was gorged with empire, and had no interest in acquiring more territory on the other side of the world. In fact, this June the Royal Navy's Commander-in-Chief for the Pacific, Rear-Admiral the Hon. Joseph Denman, writing to the

---

[3] Walkem, *Stories of Early B.C.*, pp. 278-79.

[4] C. Ian Jackson, " 'A Territory of Little Value': The Wind of Change on the Northwest Coast 1861-67", *The Beaver* (Summer 1967), p. 45.

Admiralty from Esquimalt, recommended that Britain get rid of Vancouver Island and British Columbia! After noting that half of the total white population of 14,000 of these two colonies was foreign, that the colonies had to import food from Washington and Oregon, that they were incapable of their own defence, that they were very remote and hence would entail a dispersal of British forces during a war, he concluded:

Under these circumstances I consider it would be greatly for the interest of England to divest herself of these possessions by any means consistent with honor and with justice to the English settlers.[5]

Obviously if Admiral Denman had his way, Alaska would not be the only real estate offered for sale to the United States.

This spring the merchants of Victoria became aware of an ominous development — the miners who had gone to California to winter were not returning in their usual numbers. Business began to decline. By midsummer everyone could see that in Victoria "the mercantile population were far in excess of the demand at this depressed time."[6] Governor Kennedy tried to stimulate morale by getting a second Vancouver Island Exploring Expedition in the field. But Kennedy himself was becoming more and more unpopular because of the taxes with which he sought to finance his administration. The Vancouver Island House of Assembly spent endless hours locked in acrimonious conflict with the executive. Old John Tod expressed a growing feeling about Governor Kennedy:

. . . the most selfish, obstinately selfwilled man I ever met with.

. . . a man of the most despotic character — he will do nothing for the good of the country, and many of the people are leaving the colony in disgust.[7]

But Kennedy was not as bad as Tod depicted him. He was simply a rather autocratic governor attempting the impossible task of maintaining, during an economic recession, the governmental establish-

---

[5] Denman to the Secretary of the Admiralty, 3 June 1865. PRO, ADM 1/5924.

[6] Blakey Smith, *Helmcken Reminiscences*, p. 210.

[7] John Tod to Edward Ermatinger, Letters of 21 July and 12 Dec. 1865. PAC, *Ermatinger Papers*.

ment required by a full-fledged Crown Colony when he had only the tax base supplied by seven thousand white inhabitants. Even Kennedy's adversaries began to realize that their problems involved economics as well as the Governor's personality. Vancouver Island had on previous occasions flirted with the idea of forming a confederation with British Columbia. This year the two Victoria representatives in the House of Assembly, Amor De Cosmos and Leonard McClure, advocated total union with British Columbia — just what London had wanted all along.

Except for the Cariboo, British Columbia did not escape the depression which this year was elbowing Vancouver Island towards union. Admittedly, New Westminster was benefiting from developments on Burrard Inlet, which it liked to call its "outer harbour". Here Sewell ("Sue") Moody, a lumberman from Maine, had acquired the bankrupt Burrard Inlet Mills on the north shore of the inlet and, under Moody's energetic direction, the enterprise was prospering and expanding. For a competitor on the south side of the inlet, Moody had the haughty Captain Stamp, who this year acquired the "Sawmill Claim", where he started building a mill (later to be known as the Hastings Mill) for his British Columbia and Vancouver Island Spar, Lumber, and Sawmill Company at the foot of today's Dunlevy Street. Farther east on the south shore of the inlet, New Brighton, at the end of the Douglas Road from New Westminster, was becoming a favourite summer excursion place for people from the Royal City. After a hotel was opened at New Brighton, the *British Columbian* in an excess of enthusiasm declared the tiny holiday area was "rapidly assuming the appearance of a fashionable 'watering place'."[8]

But all was not well in New Westminster itself. Like Victoria, it was losing population. Writing late in October, the Methodist minister the Rev. Ebenezer Robson reported that half his congregation had left New Westminster during the preceding twelve months.[9] Sinking ever more deeply into economic depression, the people of New Westminster began to reflect, like the citizens of Victoria, that

[8] *British Columbian*, 12 Aug. 1865.

[9] *Christian Guardian*, 3 Jan. 1866, p. 3.

beneficial economies could be achieved by merging the two colonies. Certainly there was plenty of talk of union when Governor Seymour, at the end of August, left for England on extended leave.

One thing, of course, that could save British Columbia from the indignity of having to unite with Vancouver Island would be a great new gold discovery — a second Cariboo! Hopes ran high that the Wild Horse diggings in the remote Kootenay country would prove just such a bonanza, and accordingly this year the government engaged Edgar Dewdney to continue the original Dewdney Trail on to the Kootenay gold area. An 1861 extension had carried this famous trail eastward as far as Rock Creek. Now Dewdney continued it, using the Rock Creek — Grand Forks — Columbia — Moyie route that the Jenkins party had examined in 1864. Unfortunately, just about the time the Dewdney Trail reached Wild Horse, the miners there (having decided that the area was "played out"), were moving to other areas.

The destination of some three hundred of the Wild Horse men was the newly-found gold area on the "Big Bend" of the Columbia, north of the present city of Revelstoke. The Columbia River itself, with its north-south direction, gave ready access from the United States to this supposed new El Dorado, and one of the first parties to arrive on the Big Bend this spring was one from Washington Territory, led by the veteran William Downie. Soon those who followed them were washing gold out of a number of creeks (Downie, Carnes, Goldstream, French and McCulloch) which flowed westwards from the Selkirk Mountains into the Columbia. The returns were not inconsiderable. The La Fleur Company in two days took out gold worth five hundred dollars, and in some places gravel would yield from two to twelve dollars to the pan. But it soon became obvious that the Big Bend was not another Cariboo.

Apparently the Hudson's Bay Company had early information about the new gold area. Late in 1864, having explored a line "from Souswap to the Columbia River",[10] the Company had opened a post

---

[10] HBCA, B.226/b/26. Although Marten was ostensibly being stationed on Shuswap Lake "to protect the Fur trade in that direction", there seems little doubt that the Company was chiefly interested in the coming gold rush, and the profits to be made from supplying the miners.

at the head of Seymour Arm, at the north-east extremity of Shuswap Lake. From here miners and packers could cross the Monashee Mountains without any great difficulty, and descend into the valley of the Columbia close to the gold area. George Marten, whom the HBC had put in charge of this new Seymour Arm post, would be excellently placed for trade over this route.

A second British route eastward to the upper Columbia was found this summer when Walter Moberly discovered Eagle Pass[11] which today carries the Canadian Pacific Railway and the Trans-Canada Highway between Sicamous and Revelstoke. Moberly had made a magnificent discovery, but utilization of the new pass would have to wait some twenty years until the building of the C.P.R. This year those who used a British route to the Big Bend, rather than the shorter and more direct American one up the Columbia River from Washington Territory, took the trail from Seymour Arm, first in its rudimentary form hacked out by packers, and then in the much improved state completed by Moberly this October.

To realize just how sanguine were the hopes entertained in New Westminster for the new Big Bend gold area, one need only look at the *British Columbian* for February 8th of this year. Here was a great headline:

NEW DIGGINGS STRUCK
GREAT EXCITEMENT

The story which followed spoke of some 30,000 adventurers heading into the Big Bend this spring. A rush on that scale would indeed have boosted British Columbia's faltering economy. But that estimate was wildly unrealistic. It was all the most arrant wishful thinking.

*   *   *

One of the great inventions of the mid-nineteenth century was the electric telegraph. In 1861 San Francisco was linked with the eastern United States by a transcontinental line, and clearly it would be only

---

[11] Moberly mentioned his discovery in a report dated Sept. 10th, sent to Joseph Trutch, Surveyor-General and Moody's successor as Commissioner of Lands. This was reprinted from the government *Gazette* in the *British Columbian*, 4 Oct. 1865.

a matter of time until British Columbia and Vancouver Island were brought into the telegraphic network that was gradually encircling the world. In 1864 Dr. W. F. Tolmie informed A. N. Birch, the Colonial Secretary of British Columbia, that his employer, the Hudson's Bay Company, intended to lay a line between New Westminster and the Rockies, and there to connect with a line being carried westward from Fort Garry. But the HBC was slow off the mark, and it was an American company which in 1865 brought New Westminster into telegraphic communication with the outside world. The California State Telegraph Company having run a line north to Seattle, it was an easy operation to extend its service to New Westminster. On March 21st Governor Seymour in person, with his little yacht *Leviathan*, got the cable across the Fraser River, working under the direction of Mr. Gamble of the California company. A few weeks were required before the line from Seattle became fully operative. Then, on April 18th when direct communication was finally achieved, one of the first messages announced the assassination of Abraham Lincoln.

The opening of this first telegraph line was soon eclipsed by a much more important development, the coming of the Collins Overland Telegraph.[12] Perry McDonough Collins, banker, lawyer, and entrepreneur, was an American gifted with insight, imagination and energy. In 1857 he had made a journey across Russia to the mouth of the Amur River which, he thought, would provide a useful avenue for American commerce. Back in California in 1858, Collins found wide attention being given to the recent failure of the trans-Atlantic cable. This had gone dead within three months of its laying, and most people believed that the immense breadth of the Atlantic would defeat any further attempts to lay an operative line beneath it. With the problem of linking North America and Europe by cable yet to be solved, Collins came up with an answer: since the Russians were extending their telegraph system into Siberia, and since the Americans had already spanned North America with theirs, why not build a link through British Columbia, Alaska and eastern Siberia which would join the two networks?

[12] See Corday Mackay, "The Collins Overland Telegraph", *BCHQ* 10 (1946): 187-215.

Working closely with the United States State Department, Collins secured the necessary rights from the Russian, British and American governments. Then, in 1864, he sold his rights for a very handsome price to the Western Union Telegraph Company. Western Union promptly set up a subsidiary, the Western Union Extension Company, whose stock was almost entirely bought up by Western Union shareholders. Amply capitalized, the new company swung into action in August 1864. Everything was done with military precision. Colonel Charles S. Bulkley of the U.S. Army's telegraph system was appointed Engineer-in-Chief. Major Franklin L. Pope was appointed Chief of Explorations in British America (i.e., in British Columbia), and Captain Edmund Conway was named Chief of Construction Parties for the same area. Some time was needed to purchase and charter ships, and to accumulate vast supplies of wire insulators and other material, but on June 17th of this year the *Milton Badger* arrived at New Westminster with the supplies necessary for construction. Conway at once started work. By August 17th he had a line into Hope, where the welcome news was received that a new attempt to lay an Atlantic cable had failed. Stringing wire along the Cariboo Road with almost incredible speed, Conway reached Quesnel by September 14th. Meanwhile, Pope had mapped out a proposed route for the line to follow from Quesnel to Takla Lake via Fort St. James on Stuart Lake, and had built a winter headquarters, Bulkley House, on Takla Lake.

Christmas Day saw the telegraph men at Takla Lake joining with those from the nearby Hudson's Bay Company post in celebrating their Yule:

After our usual breakfast, the Indians (a few families camped in our vicinity) came gaily dressed to pay their respects, and were delighted to join in the festivities. An impromptu programme of sports was arranged, commencing with shooting matches, short ranges, 100 yards the distance, to give our savage friends a fair show with their antiquated weapons. . . . This amusement became decidedly chilly, and foot races were then entered to keep up the circulation of blood and fun. . . . The squaws' purse was a scene of great amusement, all the Indian women being invited to run a foot race 500 yds. over unbroken snow, about 2 ft. deep on the ice — prize, a red mouchoir. Six entered the course, dressed in line by the starter; they seemed to enter into the spirit of contest like old racers, much tobacco changed hands amongst the betters. Three of the dusky belles at once got odds in the ring, from their superior physique and the business-like way in which they girthed themselves for the race. Their ages varied from a sharp little girl of about 12 years rising to a tough looking old lady aged, say 85 years or upwards, pedigree uncertain. These two divided the favoritism with a third, a young squaw of 20 years, the other three seemed wanting in wind straining, tho' not deficient in age. The bets were made up, the 20 year older received some injunction from her husband and owner, no doubt to the effect, that it would be better for her health and future happiness in the family lodge, if she won the prize; the tough old lady and the little favorite looked defiance at each other, and off they went. The pace at first showed want of judgment on their part, and if not unsurpassed for speed, it was certainly fatiguing. At half the distance the three outsiders were breathless and distanced, the three favorites seemed rather distressed, but kept well together, the young squaw having the lead, her exertions doubtless stimulated by her lord's admonition. A few "purls" [falls] more amusing than elegant tried their endurance, but the last 50 yds. showed their qualities; the young squaw had a good lead, the little girl found both her wind and legs too short for the deep snow, the old one, tough as ever, passing the filley with a volley of chaff that did not seem to improve the filley's temper, made a gallant rush to pass the leading belle, but failed, the young squaw coming in first, amid loud acclamations and screams of laughter, not to forget the approving Waugh! of her now admiring owner. Time, 4 minutes.[13]

There followed an Indian snowshoe race, and then the call was "Dinner". The whites trooped in to enjoy a New Caledonian Christmas feast of grouse pie, roast beaver, apple and bread sauce, plum pudding, cheese and mince pies. Then came the toasts to the Queen of England and the President of the United States, and many, many others. The festivities ended with an evening's dancing, for which the Indians rejoined the whites. One of the Indians had brought with him a keg of rum and, a vote being taken, it was decided that it should be broached to add life to the dancing. Alas, the rum proved more than the Indian chief could handle, and at the end of the evening he took his leave riding on the back of his wife. Slipping on the ice outside, the two took a tumble. The wife refused to pack

---

[13] *British Columbian*, 11 April 1866.

him any farther, and was last seen dragging him through the snow, back to their encampment. Still, the Christmas had been a thoroughly happy one and, our reporter thoughtfully noted, not without benefits for the whites:

The whole celebration was a decided success. It cemented a friendship between the whites and the Indians the knowledge of which will travel far and wide, making us welcome as friends, amongst those tribes we shall meet on our way North.[14]

[14] *loc. cit.*

1866

End of the overland telegraph — Fenians threaten British North America — S.S. Marten's *maiden voyage on Shuswap Lake — The Big Bend gold rush peters out — Economic crisis forces union of British Columbia and Vancouver Island — Murder on the Cariboo Road.*

On May 14th work resumed on the Collins Overland Telegraph, with Captain Conway starting construction where he had left off the year before, a short distance north of Quesnel. By June 1st, work was in full swing with a force of 150 men and 160 animals. As Conway's reconnaissance north the previous autumn had left him dissatisfied with the proposed Stuart Lake-Takla Lake route, two trusted assistants had been sent to investigate a possible alternative route, one running up to Fraser Lake, then along Burns Lake and Decker Lake, down the Bulkley River to Hazelton and then up the Kispiox River. Satisfied by the reports of these two men, Conway decided upon the latter route. When, on October 2nd, work was suspended for the 1866 season, the line had reached a point some twenty-five miles up the Kispiox River. The nature of the work done this year is tersely set forth in Conway's report to Colonel Bulkley:

We constructed the Telegraph road, and line to Latitude 55.42N. and longitude 128.15W. The distance from Quesnel, by the road, is computed at 440 miles, and by the wire 378 miles. There are fifteen stations built, a log house, with chimney, door and windows, 25 miles apart. We built bridges over all small streams, that were not fordable, corduroyed swamps. All hillsides too steep for animals to travel over, were graded, from 3 to five feet wide. The average width of clearing the wood for the wire is, in standing timber, 20 feet; and in fallen timber, 12 feet. All underbrush and small timber is cleared to the ground, thus leaving the road fit for horses, travelling at the rate of, from 30 to 50 miles per day. Double wires are stretched across all large rivers. Number of poles put up 9246. Boats are built for crossing the Bulkley and Westroad Rivers.[1]

There was to be no further construction. This summer the steamer *Great Eastern* laid a new Atlantic cable from Ireland to Newfoundland. Sceptical of its success, the Western Union Extension Company had proceeded with its own Collins Overland line until winter brought the season's work to its scheduled end. By the spring of 1867, however, it was clear that Cyrus Field had been successful in his sixth attempt to lay a functioning cable on the bottom of the Atlantic. Accordingly, the Western Union Telegraph Company abandoned the Collins scheme, reimbursing out of its own great profits those who would have lost money since they had purchased shares in its now defunct extension subsidiary. Since Western Union deemed it not worthwhile to bring back the stores cached at various points along the uncompleted portion of the line, great dumps of insulators and wire were abandoned in the wilderness. The Indians, helping themselves to the wire, used it to build, among other things, a strange ramshackle suspension bridge across the Bulkley River at Hagwilget Canyon.

The labour that had gone into the Collins project was not entirely lost: the section of the line between New Westminster and Quesnel was kept in operation and, in fact, in 1868 the telegraph was extended eastward to Barkerville. Finally, in February 1871, British Columbia took over the New Westminster-Barkerville line on permanent lease.

And what of the hundreds of miles of completed line running northwards beyond Quesnel? These were left to go to ruin. In May 1873, the explorer Captain William Butler had a curious experience in north-central British Columbia:

Crossing the wide Nacharcole River, and continuing south for a few miles, we reached a broadly cut trail which bore curious traces of past civilization. Old telegraph poles stood at intervals along the forest-cleared opening, and rusted wire hung in loose festoons down from their tops, or lay tangled amid the growing brushwood of the cleared space.

[1] Conway to Bulkley, 19 Feb. 1867. Printed in Corday Mackay, "The Collins Overland Telegraph", *BCHQ* 10:207.

A telegraph in the wilderness! What did it mean? . . . this trail, with its ruined wire, told of the wreck of a great enterprise.[2]

A thoroughly cordial spirit prevailed between the British Columbians and the American officers and employees of the Western Union Extension Telegraph Company. This friendship was especially notable since, during these years of 1865 and 1866, the colonies in British North America were viewing the United States with increasing apprehension. During the Civil War, British sympathies had clearly been with the South, though after the resolution of the Trent Affair British intervention had grown less and less likely and neutrality had been scrupulously maintained. True, in Victoria a number of Americans with Southern sympathies met in a few favoured saloons, occasionally sallying out to tear down the Stars and Stripes and defiantly hoist the Stars and Bars. But most of the American community, both in Vancouver Island and British Columbia, were on the side of the North. When rumours circulated that a Confederate privateer was to be outfitted at Vancouver Island, U.S.S. *Saginaw* sailed into Esquimalt harbour and remained there so long beyond the period allowed a belligerent that the British naval authorities finally had to send her on her way. But there was no crisis.

The real danger came after the end of the Civil War. Still haunted by visions of Manifest Destiny, some Americans felt that, now that they had the world's largest and most experienced army, they should lose no time in taking over the British colonies to the north. Urging war were a great many Irish who had emigrated to the United States, especially during the great potato famine of the 1840s. The most bitterly anti-British of the Irish-Americans were the members of a secret revolutionary organization known variously as the Fenian Society and the Irish Republican Brotherhood. When in 1865 the British took decisive action against the Fenians in Ireland, the American Fenians went on the offensive and plotted to invade British North America from bases in the United States. They hoped, by carefully staged incidents, to spark a general Anglo-American war, and thereby win Irish independence. This year reports travelled

[2] W. F. Butler, *The Wild North Land, Being The Story of a Winter Journey, with Dogs, across Northern North America* (London, 1873), pp. 333-34.

northwards that in San Francisco 40,000 Fenians were preparing to invade the British territories beyond the 49th parallel.

Admiral Denman, pitifully weak in forces, assigned H.M.S. *Sparrowhawk* to maintain a guard off New Westminster, H.M.S. *Alert* to take up position off the entrance to Victoria harbour, and the little gunboat *Forward* to stand by at Cadboro Bay in case the Fenians should launch an attack from nearby San Juan Island. Meanwhile additional militiamen were signed up both in Victoria and New Westminster. This June two new units were raised in the latter city, the Home Guards (consisting of about 60 men), and the Seymour Artillery Company (made up of 40 men under Captain Holmes, formerly of the Royal Artillery). With these men added to the older-established New Westminster Volunteer Rifle Corps, the capital of British Columbia could put about 180 men[3] in the field should the alleged 40,000 Fenians come surging up from Washington Territory. Fortunately the accounts of Fenian activity proved grossly exaggerated, and the gallant militiamen of British Columbia and Vancouver Island did not have to lay down their lives for the colonies. For years, however, the Fenian threat bulked large in the minds of British Columbians. Three years later Rear-Admiral Hastings informed the Admiralty that, despites its objections, he was going to keep his flagship, H.M.S. *Zealous*, at Esquimalt since the Fenian threat still made this "a matter of imperative necessity".[4]

*   *   *

One American invasion of British Columbia, a peaceful one, did occur this year when hundreds of American miners again headed up the Columbia to the Big Bend goldfields. Among them was the entire garrison from the U.S. Army's Fort Colvile, who deserted to a man and headed north, taking their arms with them. They used them to fire a joyous salute upon their arrival at the diggings. Access to the Big Bend became much easier for Americans this year since an entrepreneur, Captain White, was now running a steamer, the *Forty-Nine*, on the Columbia between Fort Colvile, Washington

---

[3] *British Columbian*, 20 June 1866.

[4] Hastings to Secretary of the Admiralty, 16 April 1869, quoted in Gough, *The Royal Navy and the Northwest Coast of North America*, p. 212.

Territory, and the head of navigation at the commencement of the Dalles des Morts (Death Rapids). Some foolhardy souls tried taking boats through these Dalles, but the practice stopped after seventeen men got drowned this May while trying to run a large boat through this chaos of white water, eddies and boils.

The British remained determined that the profits of supplying the new gold area should go not to Fort Colvile or the new city of Portland near the mouth of the Columbia, but to New Westminster and Victoria. Accordingly, real effort went into developing and maintaining the British route, via Shuswap Lake, to the Big Bend. Throughout the winter of 1865-66, British Columbia packers contrived to keep supplies moving in from Seymour at the northern end of Shuswap Lake to the parties wintering on the creeks on the east side of the Columbia. Notable among these packers was "Thousand Dog Joe" Tellias, who sent in not only freight-laden toboggans drawn by seven-dog teams, but other dogs carrying loads fastened to their backs.[5]

Spring brought a host of gold miners from various parts of the colony, drawn by such declarations as that of the *British Columbian*: "The Big Bend mines bid fair to eclipse anything yet struck on the Pacific Coast...."[6] Who could hold back when the newspapers were proclaiming that a gold area richer than California, than the Fraser, than Cariboo itself, was opening up? By April of this year a wagon road had been hurriedly pushed through, linking Cache Creek on the Cariboo Wagon Road with Savona's Ferry at the lower end of Kamloops Lake. Once arrived at Savona's, newcomers found a strange assortment of boats and canoes waiting to take them up Kamloops Lake, along the placid South Thompson River, across the broad waters of beautiful Shuswap Lake to Seymour City, a shacktown in a setting as lovely as anything in the English Lake District. From Seymour City it was only thirty miles by the new "shortcut" trail leading directly to Wilson's Landing at the mouth of Gold Creek.

Travel by the Shuswap Lake route became easier in May when

[5] *British Columbian*, 28 April 1866.
[6] *British Columbian*, 11 April 1866.

the Hudson's Bay Company began running a steamer between Savona's and Seymour City. The S.S. *Marten* was built at Chase's ranch[7] (now Chase, B.C.), taken down to Savona's where her machinery was installed, and on May 26th started on her maiden run to Seymour City. Her arrival there, on May 27th, was a gala occasion. Seymour City was already quite a thriving settlement, boasting six saloons, thirteen stores, five bakeries, three restaurants, eleven shoemakers, two breweries etc., not to mention a coffee and doughnut stand. Once the *Marten* came into sight the entire population of 500, deserting their evening meals, flocked to the water's edge while an improvised "Royal Anvil Artillery" boomed forth each time the gunpowder between two anvils was ignited. Cheers split the air. Oratory flowed, and more than oratory, for the captain of the *Marten* poured out free champagne and free HBC rum for everybody on his boat and everybody on the shore.[8] Shuswap Lake has seen some pretty good parties, but nothing to match the one which greeted the *Marten*.

Ironically, the *Marten*'s arrival more or less coincided with the beginnings of disillusionment about the Big Bend. The goldfield on the upper Columbia was, to use the miners' own word, a "humbug". Any clear-sighted view of the record for 1865 should have induced scepticism in 1866: the official government return had shown that, with some thousand miners active in the area, only $40,000 worth of gold had been found.[9] It took time and courage to face the dismal truth. As late as July 31st, J. Turnbull, after a detailed survey, was submitting to Walter Moberly an estimate of $10,950 to put through a trail from the south-eastern end of Shuswap Lake (Sicamous) to the Columbia River at the "Big Eddy" (Revelstoke).[10] But by this

[7] For details, see Mary Balf, *Kamloops, A History of the District up to 1914* (Kamloops, 1969?), p. 14.

[8] For the full account, see *Colonist*, 4 June 1866. Excerpts from this report are reproduced in R. M. Patterson's useful article, "Trail to the Big Bend", *The Beaver* (Spring 1960) :38-43.

[9] Howay and Scholefield, *British Columbia* II:238. Of course it was well known that a lot of gold was taken out of the country without ever being reported, but even so these figures tell one a lot.

[10] McGill University Library, *Bissett Papers*, "Copy of Mr. J. Turnbull's Report on the Columbia River District."

time disillusioned miners were already evacuating the Big Bend. The pockets of gold found in the gravel were generally too scanty and thin. Sometimes one could do better by mining down to bedrock, though often one had to go very deep indeed and ended up with a flooded pit. Even the two best creeks, Gold and McCulloch, could hardly be worked at a profit. When the *Forty-Nine* made her last trip down to Fort Colvile late this year, three-quarters of the men aboard her were too destitute to pay their passage.

Today one strange monument remains to the Big Bend fiasco. The traveller who seeks to follow the old Seymour-Columbia trail finds near its summit a stack of slate slabs intended for two billiard tables which were to be set up at one or another of the gold camps. They may have been jettisoned by packers who, en route, received word that the Big Bend bubble had burst. Seymour City itself was abandoned in 1867. Even the Hudson's Bay Company closed its post there, boarding up the windows and doors, and taking all that was valuable and movable to Kamloops.

Something must be said of other gold areas. The Cariboo continued to do well, even if its heyday was past. The Chinese, who had taken over the rich Wild Horse Creek diggings after the Kootenay miners stampeded up to the Big Bend, prospered in their own secretive way. Bridge River, where gold had first been found back in 1858, became a centre of activity. Toby Creek, near the head of the Columbia, yielded some gold. Small quantities of gold were found along the Lillooet River above Harrison Lake. Gold was taken out from diggings on Perry Creek and Moyie River in the Kootenay country. In short, there was a great deal of prospecting, but no sensational new riches were found.

*   *   *

Vancouver Island and British Columbia drifted ever deeper into economic depression. Donald Fraser, correspondent of the London *Times*, revisiting Victoria in January, was shocked at the changes he found there:

In Victoria I find the population reduced: a large proportion of buildings of every class unoccupied; the rents of such as are occupied lowered in amount and many in arrear; real property sunk to a nominal value and unsaleable, except in a few exceptional cases — so few that I cannot learn of any *bona fide* sale at any price; trade dull and diminished in amount. One of the largest houses closed its business; bankruptcies numerous, and "skedaddlers" (the modern euphuism [*sic*] for fugitive debtors) abundant, money scarce, and the employment of labor limited. Nothing flourishing or buoyant but taxation and Government expenditure — much of the latter on unproductive objects and the former finding its reluctant way into the Treasury only under the coercive process of forced sales of real property by the Sheriff for delinquent taxes.[11]

The fact that the two colonial governments were getting deeper and deeper into debt did not go unnoticed by the imperial Board of the Treasury in London, which held strong convictions that colonies (especially gold-producing colonies) should pay their way. This year both British Columbia and Vancouver Island were on the verge of bankruptcy — British Columbia's net indebtedness being $1,002,983 and Vancouver Island's $293,698.[12] In May the Bank of British Columbia refused further loans to the government in New Westminster, and the Bank of British North America cut off credit for the government in Victoria.

Plainly things could not go on this way, and meetings were convened at the Colonial Office. Attention was given to a petition from the House of Assembly of Vancouver Island begging for union with British Columbia. That Assembly had earlier set conditions for a "federation", but now it was ready to accept any scheme that Whitehall might devise.[13] On the other hand, there was a counter-petition from British Columbia stoutly opposing union. Governor Seymour, vacationing in Paris, was consulted. In a long memorandum he endorsed the views of the British Columbia Legislative Council, saying that even under the existing arrangement Victoria had been a parasite living off the economy of British Columbia. One thing especially that rankled British Columbians was the fact that, while everyone on the mainland paid duties on all they consumed, the Islanders, while profiting in many ways from the gold rush, paid no

[11] Despatch dated "Victoria, January 24th, 1866", reprinted in *British Columbian*, 4 July 1866.
[12] Howay and Scholefield, *British Columbia*, II:225-26.
[13] Ormsby, *British Columbia: A History*, p. 217.

import duties. Seymour went on to say that at first British Columbia was a colony in name only — "There was a gold mine at one end of a line of road; a seaport town (under a different government) at the opposite terminus."[14] Seymour maintained that, since that time, British Columbia had become a truly full-fledged colony. (Quite incorrectly he painted a picture of a prospering British Columbia, sustained by new riches from the Kootenay country and the Big Bend.) All the same, concluded Seymour, he could see how the union of his colony with Vancouver Island would be in the interests of imperial policy.

Reviewing everything, listening to the pro-union lobbyists of the Hudson's Bay Company and the Bank of British Columbia, the gentlemen at the Colonial Office had no difficulty reaching their decision: there would have to be union. As Judge Howay later stated of this shotgun marriage of British Columbia and Vancouver Island:

Despite their local jealousies, Imperial interests, and an even stronger force, imperious financial necessity, required that a population less than that of a second-rate town should cease to have two Governors, two Chief Justices, two Colonial Secretaries, two Attorneys-General, and so on down the list.[15]

On August 6th Queen Victoria gave her royal assent to "The British Columbia Act", uniting the two colonies.

The citizens of Vancouver Island were aghast when they learned the terms of union — their little colony was to be totally absorbed into British Columbia. Victoria was to lose her precious privilege of being a free port. The revenue system of the mainland colony was to be extended forthwith to Vancouver Island. The laws which had been passed by the Vancouver Island House of Assembly were to remain in force only until new laws had been passed by the enlarged Legislative Council of the expanded British Columbia. That Council was to consist of twenty-three members of whom only nine would be elected, with five coming from mainland ridings and four from ridings on Vancouver Island. (There would be no wholly-elected legislative assembly to replace the one that had met in Victoria.)

---

[14] *British Columbian*, 11 Aug. 1866.
[15] Howay and Scholefield, *British Columbia*, II: 226.

On 23 October 1866 Governor Kennedy gladly took his leave of Vancouver Island, his deadlock with the House of Assembly still unresolved. Kennedy would go on to larger and more important governorships and a well-deserved knighthood. On November 7th Governor Seymour, back from England, reached Victoria, and three days later disembarked at New Westminster to preside over the enlarged colony of British Columbia. Victoria had received him with marked coolness — the mayor's address of welcome was limited to just eighty-two words. Replying to it, Seymour observed that, though he owed that address entirely to Victoria's loyalty to the Crown, he trusted that he and the Victorians would in time become friends.

There were no such reservations about the welcome that New Westminster had for its returning governor, popular before his departure and now even more popular because of the way he had swung the terms of the unwanted union so clearly in the mainland's favour. During his absence, His Excellency had acquired a bride, Florence Maria, daughter of the Hon. and Rev. Sir Francis Stapleton, 7th Baronet. All the bells of New Westminster sounded "a right merry peal", and the Seymour Artillery volleyed a salute as the government steamer *Sir James Douglas* bearing the Seymours came into sight. The colonial militia, together with the Hyack Volunteer Fire Company (fifty men carrying blazing torches), marched in procession to greet Governor and Mrs. Seymour at the landing immediately below Government House and, when the couple arrived at their destination, the band gently played "Home, Sweet Home". "Oh," exclaimed Mrs. Seymour, "Isn't it delightful". That evening she was serenaded by the Orpheus Glee Club.[16]

At exactly twelve o'clock noon on 19 November 1866 (eight years to the day since Douglas had been installed Governor of the original mainland colony), the High Sheriffs of British Columbia and Vancouver Island, in New Westminster and Victoria, proclaimed the union of the two colonies. There was no enthusiasm on either side of the Strait of Georgia. The British Columbians still did not want union, and feared Vancouver Island would be an expensive incum-

---

16 *British Columbian*, 14 Nov. 1866.

brance. In Victoria thoughts were dire and bitter. This day Sir James Douglas put his own comment in a daughter's diary:

The Ships of war fired a salute on the occasion — A funeral procession, with minute guns would have been more appropriate to the sad melancholy event.[17]

A month later John Tod, at Oak Bay, declared his feelings in a letter to an old friend:

The Colonial office . . . has lately deprived V.I. of its popular [i.e. democratic] institutions, and imposed on its inhabitants a form of Govt. than which nothing could be more unjust, or oppressive.[18]

*   *   *

A visitor to Quesnel this spring was a gambling man named James Barry, who met up with an ill-assorted pair who were travelling together to Barkerville. One was a Negro, W. D. Moses, who intended to open a barbershop there. The other was Charles Morgan Blessing, son of a well-to-do Boston family, who carried a thick wad of banknotes to finance him while he sought to make his own fortune in the Cariboo. Eager to get to Barkerville and set up his business, the Negro pushed ahead, leaving Blessing to follow in his own good time, along with his new friend the gambler Barry. Thirty miles along the Quesnel-Barkerville road, Barry shot Blessing through the back of the head and took his money. But before concealing the body, he also took the fancy stickpin that the dead man wore in his tie. This pin was rather unusual in its decoration: a golden nugget, roughly in the shape of a human head, which a careless jeweller had mounted upside down. In Barkerville Moses, who had now opened his barbershop, grew uneasy at the continued failure of his former companion, Blessing, to appear on the scene. Moses met Barry, however, and was very disturbed to see the gambling man wearing Blessing's distinctive gold nugget pin. He communicated his misgivings to the authorities. A search was made, and Blessing's body discovered. Somehow Barry got word of the finding of his victim

[17] Ormsby, *British Columbia: A History*, p. 219.
[18] John Tod to Edward Ermatinger, 16 Dec. 1866. PAC, *Ermatinger Papers*.

and hurriedly fled the Cariboo. Intercepted at Yale, he paid on the gallows the full price for the stickpin with the curious nugget.[19]

*   *   *

Leonard McClure, editor of the *Colonist* and one of the Victoria members of the House of Assembly of Vancouver Island, is remembered for a notable exploit this year. In the course of a successful filibuster he spoke continuously for eighteen hours,[20] despite catcalls, hootings, and sundry other interruptions from the other honourable members. The strain of McClure's oratorical feat was generally credited with ruining his health and sending him to his grave the following year.

Other bits of miscellanea may be noted. This year the Hudson's Bay Company, due to the incompetence of her captain, lost its fine steamer *Labouchere* when she struck a reef while on the Victoria-San Francisco run.

At year's end, Admiral Denman prepared to return to England with his flagship, H.M.S. *Sutlej*. Before their departure the *Sutlej*'s crew raised a monument listing the names of their shipmates who had died while on the Pacific Station. Among the names carved on the stone was that of Maggie Sutlej, a little Indian waif found during the action against the Ahousets in 1864. The Admiral's lady had adopted the little girl, but Maggie had died at sea, and the crew felt that her name should go on the monument also.

A fire this year consumed about one-quarter of the wooden shack-town that was Lillooet. Two years earlier Yale had had its big fire. Recovered, and growing in importance, Yale this year acquired a weekly newspaper, the *British Columbia Tribune*. Condescendingly the *British Columbian* remarked: "We congratulate Yale upon the possession of a newspaper, and wish our little contemporary success, so long as it keeps a clean mouth."[21]

---

[19] There are of course a number of variant details preserved in different accounts of this murder. For these see Robin Skelton, "The Cariboo Gold Rush Murder: The Blessing-Barry Case", *Sound Heritage* 5:3 (1976):28-31.

[20] Not a world record, though possibly a British Columbia one. *The Guinness Book of Records* notes that Senator Wayne Morse of Oregon, in April 1953, spoke for over twenty-two hours without once resuming his seat.

[21] *British Columbian*, 14 April 1866.

1867

*Constitution of the enlarged colony of British Columbia —
New Westminster or Victoria for capital? — Founding of the
Dominion of Canada — The Americans buy Alaska and eye
British Columbia — Colonial Secretary Birch, the Governor's
"dry nurse" — "The Grouse Creek War" — Continued de-
pression — Last days of the Harrison-Lillooet route — "Gassy
Jack" comes to Burrard Inlet.*

On January 24th the new Legislative Council of the enlarged colony
of British Columbia, now including Vancouver Island, held its first
meeting in New Westminster. The colony had not been granted
responsible government and this Council, although its decisions
carried a good deal of weight, could only advise the Governor.
Control of the machinery of government remained firmly in the
hands of the Governor.

The membership of the Legislative Council was tri-partite. The
first group, which may be equated with today's cabinet, consisted of
the five "official members", senior civil servants who made up the
Executive Council. The members of this group were:

Arthur N. Birch — Colonial Secretary
H. P. P. Crease — Attorney-General
W. A. G. Young — Acting Treasurer
Joseph W. Trutch — Chief Commissioner of Lands and Works
Wymond O. Hamley — Collector of Customs

The second group was composed of magistrates, nominated by the
Governor but not always as responsive to his wishes as the "official
members". Following instructions from Whitehall gradually to
enlarge the democratic element in the Council, Seymour had created
a few new magistrates who enjoyed a popular following in the
colony. The magisterial members were:

Thomas L. Wood — Acting Solicitor-General

H. M. Ball — Magistrate, Cariboo West

Chartres Brew — Magistrate, New Westminster

C. F. Cornwall — Magistrate, Thompson River District

W. G. Cox — Magistrate, Cariboo East

W. J. Macdonald — Magistrate, Victoria

C. S. Nicol — Magistrate, Nanaimo

Peter O'Reilly — Magistrate, Kootenay

E. H. Sanders — Magistrate, Yale and Lytton

The third group consisted of nine elected members returned by various ridings within the colony. Technically it was not their election which gave them their seats, these being granted by gubernatorial appointment, "in deference to the wishes of the people". The elected members of the Legislative Council were:

Amor De Cosmos — Victoria

J. S. Helmcken — Victoria

John [sic — i.e. Joseph] D. Pemberton — Victoria District

John Robson — New Westminster

R. T. Smith — Columbia River and Kootenay

J. J. Southgate — Nanaimo

Edward Stamp — Lillooet

G. A. Walkem — Cariboo

George Wallace — Yale and Lytton[1]

The last-named resigned his seat just before the session commenced and, after a by-election, his place was taken by F. J. Barnard. Every member of the Legislative Council — official, magisterial, or elected — had the right to inscribe "The Honourable" in front of his name.

The four elected members from Vancouver Island went over to New Westminster, the temporary capital, with dark thoughts in their minds. Dr. Helmcken has left his recollections of what he found when he went ashore:

Westminster was at this time a very small place — a village, with virtually one street along the water front, with three or four good

---

[1] *British Columbian*, 5 Jan. 1867 (reprinting the list announced in the official government *Gazette* of 28 Dec. 1866).

buildings. The people seemed peculiar — hated Victoria — sitting over hot stoves in stores or publics . . . eating crackers and drinking water or some apparently equally innocent beverage — indeed they seemed to live on these and politics — the latter being sufficiently exciting [for teetotallers from Ontario]. What was Victoria — nothing! . . . we did not want their friendship but their Capital.[2]

Convening in a large building nicknamed "Noah's Ark", in the former camp of the Royal Engineers, the new Legislative Councillors endured Governor Seymour's verbose opening address, then set about their business. They had passed a remarkable number of bills by the time they adjourned on April 2nd. These dealt with everything from the postal service to Indian graves, and from trade licences to the roads on Vancouver Island. In all there had been forty-nine sittings, some of which had lasted ten hours, and only once had the Council lacked a quorum. Governor Seymour gave his assent to thirty-eight of their bills, disallowed one, and reserved his opinion concerning three others.

More interesting than any of the bills passed were two resolutions endorsed by the Legislative Council. The first concerned the choice of the "seat of government" or, as we would say today, the capital. The act uniting the two colonies had been drawn up quickly and carelessly. In consequence, it had failed to designate either Victoria or New Westminster as the capital for the united colony. Before returning to British Columbia, Governor Seymour had pointed out the need for a decision on this point. In reply the Colonial Office, fully aware of Seymour's preference for New Westminster, had made it clear that he was free to make this choice himself. Had Seymour been a stronger man, he would have done what the Colonial Office clearly expected and, immediately after the proclamation of union, have issued his own proclamation designating New Westminster as the capital. Instead he shillied and shallied, putting off as long as possible a decision which he knew would anger either New Westminster or Victoria. Finally, on March 27th, he sent a message to the Legislative Council that he would recommend to the Queen that he and his successors reside permanently in New Westminster. By that indirect and indecisive move, he opened the way for that agile parlia-

2 Blakey Smith, *Helmcken Reminiscences*, pp. 225-26.

mentarian Dr. Helmcken to give notice of a resolution "recommending the removal of the Seat of Government to Victoria, and the assembling of the next session of the Legislature there."[3]

For nine and a half hours on March 29th, the Council debated the Helmcken resolution. Each side mustered arguments which had already been repeated in scores of newspaper editorials. The Island members argued that Victoria had priority as the first British colonial capital on the Pacific coast, that it was the largest city in the new British Columbia, and that it was the commercial centre of the colony. They also claimed that the proximity of the naval base at Esquimalt made Victoria more defensible than New Westminster, and that a government in Victoria could keep in close communication with the fleet. The proponents of New Westminster retorted that New Westminster had been proclaimed the capital of British Columbia by Governor Douglas years earlier, and that the fact that British Columbia had "annexed" Vancouver Island did not mean that New Westminster had ceased to be the capital of British Columbia. Moreover, they said, New Westminster was more central, and it had quicker communication with the gold areas which were the economic basis of British Columbia.

On the face of it, the champions of Victoria stood no chance at all. Even the four elected representatives from the Island were outnumbered by the five elected by mainland constituencies. But Seymour, although he wanted New Westminster chosen, had not instructed his five "official members" to vote against Helmcken's resolution. Left to their own personal choice, the senior civil servants preferred living in the relatively civilized larger community of Victoria to dwelling in the raw little town which was New Westminster. Accordingly, when the vote was taken, Helmcken's resolution was carried by a vote of thirteen to eight. But it was a non-binding resolution. Governor Seymour still had to make the final decision. Writing to London, possibly hoping for a directive instructing him that New Westminster was to be the capital, Seymour got a cool reply: if he himself were to decide on Victoria, he could say that the Home Government supported that view.

[3] *British Columbian,* 30 March 1867.

One reason why Seymour got no encouragement from London to opt for New Westminster was that the citizens of Victoria were lobbying with might and main to win support in England. From the first they had a powerful ally in the Hudson's Bay Company, which had its western headquarters in Victoria but not even a retail store or trading post in New Westminster. Predictably favouring Victoria was the great Sir James Douglas. And directing the campaign was the energetic Dr. Helmcken, Douglas' son-in-law. Later Helmcken was to recall his mighty exertions to get the capital moved to Victoria:

> I worked like a madman — got up petitions to H.M. Govt — Donald Fraser [of *The Times*], Dallas [of the HBC] in England gave great and awfully valuable assistance. All the Admirals and officers who had been here were solicited for assistance and they gave it. I sent telegraphic despatches to Dallas and Fraser — they cost me a considerable sum — most of which I had to pay myself — and in due course I had the reins — for the people in England were friends and relatives — and upon the partisans in England the battle depended, for they had to bring influence on HM Government in behalf of Victoria.[4]

While the pressures built up on the hapless Seymour, he protracted his agony by postponing his decision until the coming year.

The second important resolution of the Legislative Council related to a development in eastern British North America. Here the colonies of Canada West (Ontario), Canada East (Quebec), New Brunswick and Nova Scotia were on the verge of forming a federal union. On March 18th Amor De Cosmos proposed that the Legislative Council go on record as favouring "immediate entrance into the North American Federation". Objections were raised. How could there be one country extending from the Pacific to the Atlantic when the Hudson's Bay Company owned an enormous block of territory, Rupert's Land, between Canada and British Columbia? What about the need of first having a road, or perhaps even a railroad, linking British Columbia with Canada? These and other questions made the councillors unready to demand immediate union. They did, however, pass unanimously a somewhat milder resolution calling upon Governor Seymour:

---

[4] Blakey Smith, *Helmcken Reminiscences*, p. 233.

... to take such steps without delay as may be deemed by him most advisable to secure the admission of British Columbia into the Confederation on fair and equitable terms — this Council being confident that in advising this step they are expressing the views of the Colonists generally.[5]

They were indeed speaking for most of the colonists. Typical were the sentiments expressed by John Tod in one of his many letters to his old friend Edward Ermatinger in the province of Ontario in that new country, Canada:

Affairs here, I am sorry to say, continue in the same depressed state as heretofore, and that too without any prospect of future amendment — Meantime the country is being deserted of its white inhabitants as fast as the Steamers can take them away — the few who remain, and who, having lost their all, cannot well leave, sit brooding over their blighted prospects, and ruined fortunes in sullen silence and hopeless despair — Should the newly erected Kingdome [sic] of Canada refuse them the bond of universal brotherhood, or fraternal Union they will probably ere long pitition [sic] for annexation with the States. . . . [6]

Governor Seymour was aware that the dire depression in British Columbia partly explained the desire for union with Canada. When he belatedly forwarded to London the Legislative Council's resolution, he observed, "The resolution was the expression of a despondent community longing for change."[7]

John Tod was not alone in thinking that, if British Columbia could not join Canada, she would seek American annexation. Already, in fact, there was the beginning of an American annexationist party. Although the press overwhelmingly supported confederation with Canada one paper, the Victoria *Morning News*, strongly favoured joining the United States. In Nanaimo, the *Tribune* saw the British connection as a "fast sinking ship", whereas the United States was a "gallant new craft, good and strong, close alongside, inviting us to safety and success".[8] As for the Victoria

5 W. G. Shelton, ed., *British Columbia & Confederation* (Victoria, 1967), p. 78.

6 Tod to Ermatinger, 15 July 1867. PAC, *Ermatinger Papers*.

7 Shelton, ed., *British Columbia & Confederation*, p. 90.

8 Quoted in *British Columbian*, 18 May 1867.

Colonist, it wavered in its policy to the extent that John Robson, most unshakable of the pro-Canadians, ran in the *British Columbian* the following item:

CONVALESCENT: We are gratified to learn that our contemporary of the Victoria *Colonist,* who has recently been labouring under a very severe attack of the annexation fever, has quite recovered, and returned to his allegiance again.[9]

Actually, for a while it seemed that British Columbia might become American, not through any choice of her own but through purchase by the United States. William Henry Seward, the American Secretary of State, had been one of the most ardent supporters of the Collins Overland Telegraph project. He confessed that, even though he realized that the success of the Atlantic cable was an irresistible reason for abandoning the project, he still believed in its importance. Probably through his interest in the telegraph line and the reports of the American army engineers concerned with its construction, Seward became increasingly aware of the value of Alaska. On March 30th of this year he reached an agreement with the Russians to buy Alaska for $7,200,000. This agreement the United States Senate approved by a margin of just one vote.

British Columbia received with equanimity the prospect of having Americans on both its northern and southern borders. There was some talk about the Colony now being a mouthful, caught between the upper and the lower jaw, but in the main British Columbians regarded the purchase in much the same way as those Americans who made jokes about "Seward's Icebox". The *British Columbian* pitied the Americans:

... who have been mulcted in seven millions for the doubtful luxury of an Arctic preserve in which to cool the ardour of their "manifest destiny" aspirations. ... [10]

But soon rumours began to circulate that Seward was interested in buying not only Alaska but British Columbia as well, thus securing an unbroken line of territory along the Pacific Coast. On the face of it, the report was not unlikely. Britain, having tidily packaged four

[9] *British Columbian,* 22 May 1867.
[10] *British Columbian,* 3 July 1867.

of her eastern colonies into a new country which would inevitably grow more and more independent, was left with a semi-bankrupt and rather useless colony at the other end of the continent. Why should she not follow Admiral Denman's advice of a few years earlier and disencumber herself of British Columbia with its problems and responsibilities? Adding credence to the widespread reports of an imminent sale of British Columbia to the Americans was the fact that the United States was claiming reparations from Britain for permitting confederate cruisers to be built and outfitted in Britain during the Civil War. Ultimately, in 1872, an international tribunal would assess Britain $15,500,000 for the damage done by these rebel warships, the *Alabama, Florida* and *Shenandoah*. This year all the talk was that Britain would settle the Alabama Claim by handing over British Columbia, probably picking up some money in the process.

Talk of American purchase cut two ways. It heartened the annexationists in British Columbia, and it brought out displays of fervour among those who were determined that British Columbia should remain British by becoming Canadian. The eastern newspapers took notice of the story, and British Columbians were glad to see various Canadian politicians and editorial writers declaring that the admission of British Columbia was essential to the development of Canada. In any event, although Seward had indeed planned to use the Alabama Claim in a deal which would secure British Columbia for the United States,[11] nothing was to come of his manoeuvres. Probably the principal reason why Great Britain declined to enter into any deal which would make British Columbia American was that the Royal Navy felt it needed its base on Vancouver Island.

*   *   *

History's unsung heroes are the "number two men", who do the detailed planning, turn plans into real achievement, and remain quietly in the background while the attention, honours and titles go to the "number one men" who would have been helpless without them. Such a subordinate was Arthur Nonus Birch, whose name has

[11] G. G. Van Deusen, *William Henry Seward* (New York, 1967), pp. 505 and 548.

hardly a prominent place in our history. A very bright, very competent young clerk in the Colonial Office, he was seconded in 1864 to
be Colonial Secretary of British Columbia when Seymour took over
as governor of the mainland colony. G. M. Sproat described Birch as
"a tallish, lean, flexible-limbed youth, good-looking, well-mannered
and immaculately British".[12] Dr. Helmcken remembered him as "an
awfully nice fellow — lively and very gentlemanly — young and
bright."[13] It was Birch who straightened out the tangled situations
which developed in the days when the same individuals simultaneously held posts in two colonial services. When, after sixteen months
in office, Seymour took himself off on a fifteen-month furlough, it
was young Birch who, as Colonial Administrator, expertly looked
after the governing of British Columbia. When Seymour, dilatory,
ailing, vacillating and increasingly alcoholic, returned, it was Birch
who made most of the arrangements to merge the civil services of
Vancouver Island and British Columbia. When the new Legislative
Council was set up, it was Birch who presided over its sessions. To
his expert and urbane chairmanship must be largely credited the
amount of solid useful work that the Council accomplished during
its first session. So useful was Birch to Seymour, and so dependent
was Seymour upon Birch, that some irreverent wits described Birch
as Seymour's "dry nurse".[14]

But now, in June of this year, Birch was about to resume his career
in the Colonial Office in London, though en route home he would
stop off in Canada to discuss British Columbia's entry into Confederation. A testimonial dinner was given for Birch before he left
New Westminster and, in a lengthy tribute to him, the *British
Columbian* declared:

Probably British Colonial history affords few instances, if, indeed, it
affords any, of one so young filling so difficult and responsible a position
with so much credit to himself and satisfaction to the Colonists.[15]

*   *   *

[12] *History of British Columbia*, PABC, Transcript, p. 39. Quoted by Ormsby,
p. 200.

[13] Blakey Smith, *Helmcken Reminiscences*, p. 227.

[14] Ormsby, *British Columbia: A History*, p. 222.

[15] *British Columbian*, 26 June 1867.

Without Birch, Seymour was soon in trouble. The occasion was the so-called "Grouse Creek War" in the Cariboo. This arose out of a simple case of claim-jumping when a group of adventurers, calling themselves the Canadian Company, took over some very rich land within the claim held by the Grouse Creek Bed Rock Flume Company. The Grouse Creek Company filed a complaint before Spalding, the acting gold commissioner and, since the trespass was blatantly obvious, Spalding ordered the Canadian Company to remove themselves from the holdings of the Grouse Creek Company. Instead of complying, the Canadian Company continued to take out quantities of gold while lodging an appeal with Chief Justice Begbie. Begbie pointed out that the law quite unequivocally ruled that the decisions of the gold commissioners were final and without appeal, and accordingly he dismissed the case.

Since the Canadian Company then continued to loot the claim, the Grouse Creek Company complained to the authorities. As a result, Edgar Dewdney went with three constables to eject the Canadian Company and their supporters to the number of about thirty men. When the interlopers absolutely refused to withdraw, the outnumbered Dewdney and his three constables left.

On July 15th, Gold Commissioner Ball swore in some thirty of the more respectable citizens of Barkerville as special constables and next day led them to the disputed claim. They were met by John Grant, ringleader of the Canadian Company, who hypocritically declared that, justice having been denied them, he and his men were forced to rely upon their own strength. He announced that, rather than submit to Ball and his little force, his ruffians (now numbering several hundred) would spill blood. Under these circumstances, Ball withdrew with his hopelessly outnumbered special constables and telegraphed an account of the crisis to Governor Seymour. Ball requested that a force of Royal Marines be sent to his assistance.

It was now Seymour's direct responsibility to re-establish the rule of law in the Cariboo. The *British Columbian* put the situation very succinctly:

In our most important gold field the arm of Justice hangs powerless by her side, while a company of men, under the most hollow and hypocritical professions of a desire to respect the law, are wantonly and openly trampling it under foot and taking gold out of ground which the law has pronounced the property of others at the rate of $1600 a day. It is simply a question of British law *vs*. Lynch Law. Governor Seymour is called upon this very instant to say which we shall have.[16]

Seymour's handling of the Grouse Creek War is in pathetic contrast to Governor Douglas' handling of "Ned McGowan's War". Without providing himself with a force either of marines or militia, Governor Seymour started for the scene of trouble, taking with him only Joseph Trutch (who was Surveyor-General as well as Chief Commissioner of Lands and Works), Commander E. A. Porcher, R.N., and a secretary.

While Seymour was en route to the Cariboo, the Canadian Company set up an affiliate, the Sparrowhawk Company, which completed the takeover of the land owned by the Grouse Creek Company. Night and day the interlopers worked the rich Heron lead which made this property so valuable. They had heard that marines had been summoned, and were determined to get out all the gold they could before the arrival of government troops forced their capitulation.

Having arrived without any force to support the decisions already rendered under the law, Seymour could only suggest that the whole matter be turned over to Chief Justice Needham of Vancouver Island for arbitration. Not unnaturally, the Grouse Creek Company protested against further delay while its property continued to be looted. Seymour then ordered the arrest of the nine principal members of the Canadian Company, and each of these was sentenced to three months' imprisonment. Though Grant, their leader, surrendered to the authorities, the eight others flatly refused to do so, and Seymour was confronted with a major problem: what to do with eight convicted men who refused to go to jail, convicted men who had a large armed force ready to protect them.

This was the most shameful hour in the history of British justice in British Columbia. Having got himself into a hopeless situation, all that Seymour could do was negotiate a deal under which the eight recalcitrants would surrender and in return he, after receiving

---

[16] *British Columbian*, 27 July 1867.

a petition signed by their friends, would reduce their sentences from three months to two days each. After this notable vindication of the power and the majesty of the law, Seymour scuttled back to New Westminster. Here he met his Legislative Council, petulantly putting the chief blame on the wronged Grouse Creek Company for not accepting a proposal he had advanced that would have made Trutch an arbitrator.

The whole miserable affair ended in October with the arrival of Chief Justice Needham bearing a commission to investigate the situation. By now the Canadian Company, having pretty well exhausted the claim after four months of desperate activity, was ready to cooperate. It was agreed that, prior to a decision, both the Grouse Creek Company and the Canadian Company would deposit with the court the gold that they had taken out of the claim. The Grouse Creek Company delivered gold worth $1800 and the Canadian Company an amount worth $2600. The sums were farcical, little more than a day's production. On September 30th Needham heard the case and reached the inevitable verdict: the claim did indeed belong to the Grouse Creek Company and it was to receive the modest amount of gold deposited by the Canadian Company as well as its own. And so the whole abject episode ended amid the humiliation of Governor Seymour.

*   *   *

The law received another bad jolt in British Columbia this year. At Keremeos, Magistrate Haynes was hearing a charge against an Indian who had assaulted a Chinaman, when a friend of the accused, armed and wearing war paint, entered the courtroom. Seizing an inkwell, he hurled it at the court constable and then levelled his rifle at the magistrate. Haynes, with remarkable courage, wrestled with the intruder and got his rifle away from him, only to see the Indian drawing a revolver. Timely intervention by a white man who threw his arms around the Indian attacker saved Haynes, but by now another Indian had fixed his rifle on the magistrate. Amid all this excitement, the Indian who was standing trial escaped. When Haynes found a whole band of armed Indians outside, he deemed

the time had come for discretion to take the place of valour and did
not attempt to recapture the escapee.

*   *   *

In this "year of unprecedented depression"[17] there was little new
development in British Columbia. For the first time a stagecoach
ran twice a week between New Westminster and its "outer harbour"
of Burrard Inlet, but generally there was a contraction rather than
an expansion of services. The government, desperate to save money,
pretty much abandoned the old Harrison-Lillooet route to the
Interior, and settlers along the road began to leave their homesteads.
Persons who wanted to travel to the upper Fraser had to be content
with a single route, the Cariboo Wagon Road.

Optimistically, a couple of new roadhouses were opened at Cache
Creek this year: Bonaparte House, run by Semlin and Parke, and
Cache Creek House. Both counted heavily on being at the junction
of the routes to the Cariboo and to the Big Bend. But the Big Bend
mines attracted hardly anybody this year. The steamer *Forty-Nine*
brought only ten passengers on its first trip up the Columbia from
the United States, and fifteen on its second. The Hudson's Bay
Company kept the *Marten* tied up at Kamloops most of this year,
not having enough business to warrant sending her up to Seymour
City, which was already becoming a ghost town.

The government, officially committed to a program of retrench-
ment, was determined to cut expenses — provided their own fat
salaries were untouched. Somebody got the bright idea that money
could be saved if, on the Queen's birthday, the usual feast and gifts
were not provided for the four thousand Indians who traditionally
came down to New Westminster to celebrate the 24th of May.
Fortunately wiser counsels prevailed and the goodwill of the Indians
was not sacrificed to make a petty economy. They all got their
biscuits and molasses, and each member of a winning team in the
canoe races received a dollar.

Let us turn from the Indians enjoying their biscuits and molasses
to the plight of the thirsty loggers who worked at Stamp's sawmill on

<hr/>

[17] Letter of Rev. Dr. E. Evans, Nanaimo, 2 Oct. 1867. Printed in the *Christian
Guardian*, 18 Dec. 1867, p. 203.

the southern shore of Burrard Inlet. At the end of September their drought ended. Around from New Westminster came an Indian dugout canoe. In it was a great fat man, with a blotched purple face, a belly laugh, and a fund of Rabelaisian stories. He was "Gassy Jack" Deighton, a Fraser River pilot bent on a new career. With him he had his yellow dog, his Indian woman, her mother, her cousin, two chickens, two chairs and a barrel of whiskey. That barrel of whiskey was the key to the operation. Coming ashore through the customary Burrard Inlet drizzle, Gassy Jack greeted the millhands, ladled out free whiskey, and broached his scheme. He wished to provide them all with the amenity of a saloon. Of course he would need help in building it. Tradition has it that within twenty-four hours the millhands had run up "Deighton House". Gassy Jack pulled himself up to the roof, broke out a Union Jack, and:

... in a homely speech, pointing to the flag, told his hearers that it represented all that was good, the blood and guts of England; it bobbed up on every sea, had been his chum forty years, that he had pinned his faith to it and would stay with it; thanked everybody for their generous help, and regretted to inform them that he would have to postpone the christening for a few days. He anticipated a shortage and dispatched the Indian cousin with an order to New Westminster, the answer to which read thus: "Cannot deliver your order to Indian, particularly the fireworks part; risk too great."[18]

But the supply problem was soon solved, and the thirsty millworkers went thirsty no more, and Gassy Jack prospered. Others came and settled nearby, until a little shack-town came into being around Deighton House. "Gastown" they called it after their founding father and, inelegant though the name was, it got onto the charts of the British Admiralty. In 1870 Gastown officially became "Granville", named for the Earl of Granville, Secretary of State for the Colonies, though the name of Granville lost out to the Canadian Pacific Railway's "Vancouver". However, as any visitor to Vancouver today soon discovers, Gastown is still alive and well.

[18] "Vancouver in the Days of Yore" by Old Timer. *Vancouver World*, 6 Jan. 1912, p. 43.

1868

New Westminster loses a battle and Victoria becomes the capital — Moves towards confederation with Canada — "The Victoria Memorial" — The Yale Convention — Anti-confederationist strength in Victoria — Death at the Mystic Spring — The Barkerville fire — Indian reserves reduced in size — Philip Hankin, the new Colonial Secretary.

On March 21st Governor Seymour opened at New Westminster the second session of the first Legislative Council of the united colony of British Columbia. In his speech from the throne, Seymour observed hopefully that the colony's prolonged economic depression might be nearing its end. He blandly passed over his own failure to maintain the law during the Grouse Creek War by asserting:

...the good sense and love of order, so general among our Miners, allowed of a settlement of the question without a resort to force, and the law speedily resumed its sway.[1]

The session which followed was not a particularly notable one. It did, however, produce a resolution asking Seymour to change the constitution of his Council (as he was fully empowered to do) so as to increase its elected element from just over one-third to a full two-thirds of its membership. Proroguing the Council on May 1st, Seymour showed little sympathy for this mildly democratic motion and declared that it was inspired by "a too violent reaction from an unsatisfactory state of things". There were mutterings around New Westminster that Seymour was suspicious of Canadians and wanted

[1] *British Columbian*, 21 March 1868.

354

to see the Colony more completely "English" before he would enlarge the elected element in the government.

Still undecided when the Council was prorogued was the site of the capital. We have earlier seen how Seymour had come back from his European furlough fully empowered to designate the seat of government, and supported by the Colonial Office's complete agreement that it should be in New Westminster. We have also seen how he had procrastinated and, needlessly putting the matter before the Council, had got the verdict he did not want, that Victoria should be the capital. Continuing to procrastinate, Seymour had given the champions of Victoria time to start lobbying in London. Meanwhile a change of administration in London had produced a new Colonial Secretary, the Duke of Buckingham and Chandos, who came to favour Victoria. His Grace did nothing so crude as to take the decision out of Seymour's hands and designate Victoria himself but, at the end of a letter in October 1867, he had written:

I will add that, although I do not prescribe to you the choice of one or the other Capital, you will be at liberty, in case you should decide in favor of Victoria, to quote the authority of the Home Government in support of that course.[2]

With this letter the Duke forwarded submissions favouring Victoria which he had received from the Hudson's Bay Company, the Bank of British Columbia, the Bank of British North America, and various influential private individuals. Seymour was left in no doubt that the Duke would be displeased if the Governor chose New Westminster.

Possibly hoping that, by some miracle, the Legislative Council would change its mind and get him out of the corner into which he had manoeuvred himself, Seymour decided to have it vote once more on the site of the capital. Accordingly, in his speech from the throne, the unhappy Seymour declared:

... Her Majesty's Government are of opinion that in my Message of the 27th of March, 1867, I took an extreme view as to the extent to which public faith and honour are pledged to the purchasers of land in New Westminster. Further that I should consider the public convenience from time to time as the main guide in the selection of a Seat of

[2] *British Columbian*, 1 April 1868.

Government. I am commanded to come to a decision without further delay, and I desire to avail myself — although the matter is one of Executive prerogative — of your assistance in so doing.[3]

Just before convening his Legislative Council, Governor Seymour had appointed to it the Nanaimo magistrate William Hales Franklyn, a former P. & O. captain who, because he was "all British — bristled with it all over", was nicknamed "The British Lion". Nanaimo was rather hostile to Victoria, and Franklyn was an ardent champion of New Westminster. Accordingly the Victoria faction, by the most unparliamentary tactics, sought to eliminate him from the proceedings. Before the debate commenced, he had been thoughtfully liquored in advance. All the same, though "The British Lion's" head was made muzzy, he was not put out of action and rose to give a prepared oration. This opened:

Mr. President,

When I went up the Hoogley [Hooghly River] forty years ago, the navigation was very intricate, the river full of shoals and sandbanks, a very great deal worse than Fraser River.[4]

He then proceeded to argue that, just as dredging of the Hooghly had enabled Calcutta to become a great port, so dredging the Fraser would do the same for New Westminster. At this point he turned his page, which the adroit Mr. Cox (a member of the Victoria faction) slipped back on top of his sheaf, and the befuddled Captain Franklyn once more intoned about how forty years ago the navigation of the Hooghly had been very intricate. The trick was repeated, then worse followed. When Captain Franklyn paused and laid down his glasses, Cox quickly pressed the lenses out, leaving the "Lion" unable to read any further. Helmcken quickly proposed an adjournment, and sympathetic "friends" used it to get the "Lion" back to the bar, where they so plied him with drinks that, when the crucial vote was taken, no "British Lion" rose to cast his vote for New Westminster.

Actually these shenanigans were quite unnecessary since nearly all the civil servants and magistrates, who made up the majority of the

[3] *British Columbian*, 21 March 1868.

[4] Blakey Smith, *Helmcken Reminiscences*, p. 230.

Council, were firmly for Victoria, which could provide them with many more comforts than little New Westminster. This vote on April 2nd was even more decisively for Victoria (14 to 5) than it had been the previous year.

Fury mounted in New Westminster when the result was known. A mob assembled outside the hotel where Dr. Helmcken, leader of the triumphant Victoria faction, was staying; and the frightened landlord warned him and his friends not to venture out into the streets.

The logical time for Seymour officially to announce the decision which by now had been forced upon him was at the prorogation of the Legislative Council. But the unhappy Governor continued to delay. Then he announced that he would make his momentous decision known on the Queen's Birthday, May 24th. If anybody around New Westminster still entertained any unrealistic hopes that Seymour, their champion, would stand by them, these hopes must have evaporated when, on May 18th, His Excellency left for Victoria. Seymour did not want to be around for the unpleasantness that lay ahead for him if he made his long-delayed announcement at New Westminster.

The 24th of May came. It was a Sunday, and Victorian sabbatarianism kept all but the most urgent government business from being transacted on that day. On May 25th, however, Victoria was proclaimed the capital of British Columbia.

On Saturday, the 23rd, Victoria had begun celebrating the royal birthday with a regatta. Everybody who was anybody turned out except Governor Seymour who, knowing that the Victorians regarded him with coolness approaching contempt, stayed away on grounds of ill health, and sent Mrs. Seymour instead.

In New Westminster a certain sadness clouded the celebration of Her Majesty's birthday. The *British Columbian* reported:

There were fewer Indians; the Governor had sent them word that there would be no celebration, imagining, we presume, that there *could* be none in the absence of Vice-Regal Patronage. There were no Government House entertainments; no warships; few officials. These had all turned their backs upon us; but it is gratifying to know that loyalty with this people is an inborn principle; and that although the Colonial Office and its agencies may be capable of robbing us of vested rights and wantonly trampling upon plighted "faith and honor", it may not so easily extinguish that spark of loyalty to our noble, good and virtuous Queen which burns in every bosom.[5]

The citizens of New Westminster were apparently unready to face the fact that it was Seymour himself who, by delay and indecision, had let them down so badly. He remained uniquely their governor, and he soon fled from the contemptuous aloofness with which Victoria had received him, and enjoyed once more the friendliness of New Westminster. Two entries in the *British Columbian* tell the story:

6 June 1868

It is understood that Governor Seymour is coming back to reside here, on account of the great superiority of the climate. We regret to learn that His Excellency's health has even already suffered much from a residence at Bleak House [Cary Castle, the Government House in Victoria] and that the change is considered essential to recovery.

4 November 1868

We understand that it is the intention of His Excellency the Governor and Mrs. Seymour to take their departure by H.M.S. Sparrowhawk, this morning, for their bleak winter habitation on Vancouver Island. Our readers will be glad to learn that His Excellency has recovered his wonted health.

*   *   *

Apart from the transfer of the capital, the political issue that got most attention this year was the continuing debate over whether or not British Columbia should join the Canadian confederation. With a good deal of spirit the confederationists began to muster their forces. A public meeting in Victoria on January 29th, called by Mayor Trimble, resulted in the drafting of "The Victoria Memorial" calling for union with Canada and proposing terms.[6] Audaciously the committee, knowing Seymour would be unsympathetic and useless, by-passed him and sent their memorial directly to Lord Monck, the Governor-General of Canada. Monck received it with warmth

---

[5] *British Columbian*, 27 May 1868.

[6] The text of this "memorial" is printed in W. G. Shelton, ed., *British Columbia & Confederation*, pp. 92-94.

and approbation. On April 6th at a mass meeting in New Westminster presided over by Henry Holbrook, a committee headed by John Robson was charged with drawing up an address to the Legislative Council asking for speedy union with Canada and setting forth possible terms. In Yale a public meeting was held three days later at Sutton's billiard saloon to help the good cause along. Those attending the Yale meeting unanimously called for British Columbia's immediate entry into Canada on fair and equitable terms.

On April 24th the Legislative Council had before it the confederation address which Robson's committee had drawn up in accordance with its instructions from the New Westminster mass meeting. Possibly the Council was angered at the pressures being brought upon it. Perhaps the Governor's own distaste for confederation had communicated itself to various of the "official" and "magisterial" members of the Council, who feared that absorption by Canada would rob them of the inflated salaries that they currently enjoyed. Certainly some of the members from Victoria, knowing that they had already won the battle for the colonial capital, were not enthusiastic about Victoria being eclipsed by Ottawa. In any event, whereas the previous year the Legislative Council had unanimously accepted a resolution seeking membership in Canada, this year only four men could be found to favour forwarding to the Queen the address proposed by New Westminster. The four who voted aye were Robson, De Cosmos, Stamp and Walkem. The twelve who voted nay were Crease, Trutch, O'Reilly, Ball, Cox, Pemberton, Helmcken, Wood, Elwyn, Ker, Smith and Spalding.

After this disastrous defeat, the four confirmed confederationists decided that, since the Governor and the civil service would indefinitely try to keep British Columbia outside the Canadian fold, public opinion must be mustered to overcome Seymour's oligarchy. The result was the founding of the Confederation League this May, as the prelude to a convention at Yale to which delegates with confederationist convictions would be sent from all parts of the colony. In an editorial in the *British Columbian*, John Robson commented upon the forces which were bringing the Yale Convention into being:

Popular sentiment *will* find some mode of expression. Crushed in our unpopular and unrepresentative Legislature, it has recourse to a Convention, a tribune called into existence solely by the people.[7]

At nine o'clock on the morning of September 14th the Yale Convention, known to the anti-confederationists as the "Yale Conspiracy", met for its first session. The twenty-six delegates were:

Victoria:	R. Wallace
	Amor De Cosmos
	J. E. McMillan
	J. D. Norris
Salt Spring Island:	M. W. Gibbs
Metchosin:	Thomas Fulton
Esquimalt:	J. B. Thompson
	W. Fisher
New Westminster:	Henry Holbrook
	John Robson
	Dr. A. W. S. Black
	David Withrow
New Westminster District:	D. W. Miller
Yale:	Charles Evans
	Adam McLarty
	Henry Havelock
Yale District:	Alexander Rose
Lytton:	R. Smith
Quesnelmouth:	J. C. Armstrong
Williams Lake:	F. J. Barnard
Cariboo:	E. H. Babbitt
	W. C. King
Lillooet:	H. Featherstone
Burrard Inlet:	Hugh Nelson
Harrison River:	James Donnelly
Lac La Hache:	Dr. Browse[8]

This was a body of substantial and responsible men. Three of them (including Barnard of Barnard's Express) were members of the

---

[7] *British Columbian*, 9 Sept. 1868.

[8] *British Columbian*, 16 Sept. 1868. (*v.* also Howay and Scholefield, *British Columbia*, II:283.)

Legislative Council; Holbrook was the chief magistrate (not yet entitled "mayor") of New Westminster; and Hugh Nelson would one day be Lieutenant-Governor of the Province of British Columbia.

The principal resolution of the Yale Convention was, of course, the one calling for British Columbia's immediate union with Canada. But the convention was interested in more than confederation. Another resolution demanded that British Columbia be given representative, responsible government, like that enjoyed by the Canadian provinces. A third demanded real governmental economy, chiefly by dismissing some civil servants and reducing the salaries of others — and, for a start, it was decided that the lordly salary paid to Seymour himself should be cut in half. A fourth resolution called for a reciprocal trade treaty with the United States, one which would permit British Columbia lumber and other raw products to enter the United States duty free. All in all, the Yale Convention was a major landmark in the history of British Columbia.

Late this year, preparatory to summoning a new Legislative Council, Seymour called elections. The contests in the various ridings showed the extent of confederationist sentiment in the colony. With a single exception, every member returned by the mainland was a supporter of confederation. It was Vancouver Island that provided a stunning defeat for those wanting union with Canada: in Victoria, Helmcken and Drake, running on an anti-confederation platform in that two-seat riding, easily outpolled Amor De Cosmos and Dr. Powell,[9] the confederationists, and the two other Island constituencies went anti-confederation also. The lines were clearly being drawn for a future battle, one which might easily pit the mainland against Vancouver Island.

*   *   *

Amid the political developments of this year, sight must not be lost of other events.

January.   One of the little society of retired Hudson's Bay Company men at Victoria, survivors of the heroic age of the fur trade, was James Murray Yale. After initial difficulties in the Company's

---

[9] *Colonist,* 4 Nov. 1868.

service, Yale had gone on to a successful career which saw him finally commanding Fort Langley, and giving his name to Fort Yale. A thrifty man, Yale had retired with a handsome fortune. But, alas, all his wealth could not save Yale from tragedy. Early this month he was felled by a stroke. John Tod, a friend from those early HBC days, did what he could to help the stricken man. In a letter Tod reported:

Poor Yale, I am sorry to say, has lately had a paralytic stroke ... — No one seems to care about him — not even his own children — There he lays in his big house, (in one end of which I counted 27 windows) alone without attendance of any Kind — Altho' at the distance of 4 miles from me I assure You I have had my hands full in looking after him.[10]

February.   In view of the action taken by the Bonaparte Indians in 1974, when they stopped at gunpoint tourists travelling the highway near Cache Creek and demanded $5.00 on the grounds that they were trespassers, the following item carried in the *British Columbian* of 5 February 1868 has special interest:

A PETITION has, we learn, been in circulation amongst the settlers on the Bonaparte valley, asking the Government to reduce the Indian reserve there, and throw open to settlement what is not needed for the natives. It appears that the Indians in respect of whom the reserve is made do not number more than one hundred men, women and children, and yet a tract of most desirable land, having a frontage of three and a half miles upon the river, and entirely cutting out a large and important district, is locked up on their account.

March.   There were renewed fears of a Fenian attack. Elsewhere, from American bases, the Fenians had launched a number of raids that had taken Canadian lives. Now reports were rife that a Fenian force was about to sail from San Francisco to attack British Columbia. In the March 11th issue of the *British Columbian*, John Robson recommended that three "small Star forts" be built to protect New Westminster. One would be on the opposite shore of the Fraser, one on the hill by Douglas Road, and the third at Sapperton. He also

[10] John Tod to Edward Ermatinger, 14 Jan. 1868. PAC, *Ermatinger Papers.*

suggested forts at Point Grey and the First Narrows to guard the approaches to Burrard Inlet.

April. Victoria was shocked by a girl's personal tragedy. Out at Cadboro Bay, close to where Mystic Spring Lane now runs, there was at this time an actual spring to which was attached an Indian legend. That legend ran that any woman who looked upon the water when the moon was full would see reflected there the features of the man who loved her. A Miss Booth, a young lady with an impeccable reputation, had fallen ardently in love with a young gentleman who, not reciprocating her feelings, had taken to avoiding her. One afternoon she was seen walking out on the road to Cadboro Bay, where she asked her way to the magic spring. Next morning her body was found floating where she had drowned herself in its waters.[11]

May. At a "liquor feast" held at a village on the Nass River, drunken fighting resulted in the death of five Indians, including a member of one of the Fort Simpson bands, "the proud and murderous tribe called Kinniak-an-Geak". Seething with fury, the latter got into their canoes and paddled down the Nass towards a Christian Indian community presided over by an Anglican missionary, the Rev. Robert Tomlinson. Close to the mission they came upon a canoe containing two men and two boys, three of whom they murdered on the spot. Tomlinson himself being absent in Victoria, William Duncan, the missionary and magistrate at Metlakatla, undertook to communicate with the Governor. On May 16th he grimly wrote:

There no doubt exists a long pent up and growing hatred in the breasts of some few of the more heathenish parts of the Community aroused to the Mission settlements, or rather to the Indians who have dared to join them . . . now that they [the heathen Indians] have

[11] D. W. Higgins has a romanticized version of the incident, related in suitably purple prose, in his book *The Mystic Spring and Other Tales of Western Life* (New York, 1908), pp. 1-11. One would dismiss this as part of the fiction which infiltrates Higgins' books based on personal recollections, were it not that Edgar Fawcett who, as the last person to see the girl alive and who testified at her inquest, relates the episode in his book, *Some Reminiscences of Old Victoria*, pp. 176-77.

openly and fearlessly and for the first time vented their murderous spite upon a mission settlement it remains for them to be taught the consequences.

The little band at Kincaullith [Kincolith] though panic stricken at the sight of their slaughtered brethren, have again gathered heart and have determined to abide patiently by the Law under which they have enrolled themselves, and look to Your Excellency to avenge their loss.[12]

Seymour, forwarding a copy of Duncan's letter to the Colonial Office, informed the Duke of Buckingham that Rear-Admiral Hastings was up north with H.M.S. *Sparrowhawk* and would undoubtedly give the required assistance. Just for good measure, however, Buckingham ordered a note sent to the Admiralty:

His Grace considers it a matter of great moment that these infant Settlements of Native Christians should not be allowed to be destroyed and he would be glad to receive any intelligence that their Lordships may receive on the subject from Admiral Hastings.[13]

Further investigation made it very clear that the three Kincolith Indians were murdered, not because of resentment that they belonged to a Christian village, but because they belonged to the same Nass tribe as the murderer at the drunken party.

June.   There were by now two Roman Catholic bishops in British Columbia — in 1864 the mainland has been entrusted to Bishop D'Herbomez at New Westminster, while Bishop Demers' diocese had been limited to Vancouver Island. This month Bishop D'Herbomez visited New Caledonia, preparing for a permanent mission there. Everywhere he went, the Bishop explained to the Indians how they must conduct themselves in order to merit the permanent residence of a priest. As a result:

... polygamy was solemnly abolished never again to appear, gambling and conjuring were severely proscribed, and the use of intoxicants renounced by every adult kneeling to the Bishop. In consideration of these pledges each village received a flag whereon were engraved, round the symbol of our redemption, the significant words "Religion, Tem-

[12] PRO, ADM 1/6071.

[13] *loc. cit.*

perance, Civilization", than which no others could better express the aim of the missionaries.[14]

July. Heretofore the major celebration each July had fallen on July 4th, when the large American population incongruously celebrated on British soil their ancestors' rebellion against the British Crown. But this year for the first time there was another and more fitting celebration — July 1st was Dominion Day, the first anniversary of the founding of the Dominion of Canada. In New Westminster the large Canadian element observed the day with cheers and the firing of salutes. At Yale the Canadian residents put on a dinner for fifty guests.

August. Burrard Inlet was becoming increasingly active, with so many ships coming in to take on lumber at the sawmills and so many New Westminster people patronizing the holiday resort of New Brighton. This month no less than three stage coaches were competing on daily runs between New Westminster and Burrard Inlet.

September. Although Richfield, with its cluster of modest government buildings, was the administrative centre of the Cariboo, it was far eclipsed by the nearby centre of Barkerville, the real capital of the Cariboo. This summer had been a hot, dry one, and the wooden shacks which made up most of Barkerville were dry as tinder. Catastrophe came. On the afternoon of September 16th a fire broke out in Barry and Adler's Saloon. Some said a girl ironing her clothes started the flames, others that a miner had knocked over a lamp during a scuffle. Whatever the cause, within an hour almost the entire town was reduced to ashes. Scott's Saloon at the upper end of the town was providentially saved by water brought from the nearby flume of the Baker Company. Another saloon at the lower end of town and two nearby warehouses were the only other buildings saved. In all, goods worth about $700,000 were destroyed, along with property of approximately the same value. While the refugees took shelter in miners' cabins along Williams Creek, reconstruction

---

[14] Morice, *History of the Northern Interior of B.C.*, p. 330.

commenced. Within a week of the fire over twenty buildings had already been rebuilt.

Among the casualties of the Barkerville fire were apparently many copies of the first book of verse to be published in British Columbia, one which had appeared just a few months earlier. This loss was made good by an augmented second edition brought out in the spring of 1869. The bard was a sturdy Scot named James Anderson, and his little book (really only a pamphlet) was entitled *Sawney's Letters*. Anderson had recited or sung various of his compositions at concerts in the mining camps, and had published many of them earlier as contributions to the *Cariboo Sentinel*. A fervent admirer of Robert Burns, Anderson cast his poems in Burnsian moulds, dialect and all. They give a vivid picture of life in the Cariboo with its gambling men, barkeepers, stake-jumpers, experts in the salting of mines, and the hurdy-gurdy girls in the dance halls. The latter, beefy young German women shipped in from San Francisco, inspired Anderson to write a poem based on Burns' "Green Grow the Rashes O":

> Last summer we had lassies here
>   Frae Germany — the hurdies, O!
> And troth I wot, as I'm a Scot,
>   They were the bonnie hurdies, O!
>
> There was Kate and Mary, blithe and airy,
>   And dumpy little Lizzie, O!
> And ane they ca'd the Kangaroo,
>   A strappin' rattlin' hizzy, O!
>
> They danced at nicht in dresses light,
>   Frae late until the early, O!
> But oh! their hearts were hard as flint,
>   Which vexed the laddies sairly, O!
>
> The dollar was their only love,
>   And that they lo'ed fu' dearly, O!
> They dinna care a flea for men,
>   Let them coort hooe'er sincerely, O!
>
> They left the creek wi' lots o' gold,
>   Danced frae oor lads sae clever, O!
> My blessin's on their "sour krout" heads,
>   Gif they stay awa for ever, O!

CHORUS: Bonnie are the hurdies, O!
               The German hurdy-gurdies, O!
               The daftest hour that ere I spent,
               Was dancin' wi' the hurdies, O!

For a poem on the hardships of Cariboo mining, Anderson took for his model Thomas Hood's "Song of the Shirt", with its repeated "Stitch, stitch, stitch":

"SONG OF THE MINE"

Drift! Drift! Drift!
From the early morn till night.
Drift! Drift! Drift!
From twilight till broad-day light,
With pick, and crow-bar and sledge,
Breaking a hard gravel face;
In slum, and water and mud,
Working with face-board and brace;
Main set, false set, and main set —
Repeated, shift after shift —
Day after day the same song —
The same wearisome Song of the Drift.

Occasionally the dirty work of putting through the exploratory tunnels called "drifts" would result in striking a rich deposit of gold. In another poem Anderson tells what was likely to follow:

I kent a body mak a strike —
He look'd a little lord!
An' had a clan o'followers
Amang a needy horde.
Whane'er he entered a saloon
You'd see the barkeep smile —
His lordships' humble servant he,
Without a thocht o'guile!
A twal months pass'd an' a' is gane,
Baith freends an' brandy bottle.
An' noo the puir soul's left alane,
Wi' nocht to weet his throttle!
An' since, I've seen the barkeeper,
Wha seem'd sae sweet before,
Wi' some persuasion show this chiel
The ootside o' the door!

October.   With the growing number of settlers in the Fraser Valley, feeling mounted among the whites that the Indians had been granted too much land for their reservations. The *British Columbian* ran an insistent campaign for the Surveyor-General's men to "define" [i.e. contract] the boundaries of these reserves. In May the paper had run a list of thirteen existing Indian land reservations, totalling some 40,000 acres. Among these reservations were:

Matsqui	9600	acres
Whonock	2000	"
Lower Sumas	6400	"
Upper Sumas	1200	"
Nicomen	6400	"

By the middle of this month the "survey" was being carried out with results gratifying to the *British Columbian*:

A proper appreciation of the importance of settlement, and a becoming desire to consider the interests of the white settlers has, we are assured, characterized the survey, so far, at least. In one instance a reservation of something like six thousand acres has been reduced to about two thousand, and in no case has the re-adjustment of boundaries disturbed the property of the whites.[15]

November.   This month John Tod left his retreat at Oak Bay and revisited the "upper country" of British Columbia. In one of his letters he remarked on the changes in "that recently rugged and inhospitable country". He was also amazed to see how agricultural settlement was spreading through the Fraser Valley:

All along the banks of the Fraser may be seen, in striking contrast to that of former times, thriving little villages, well stocked farms, tastefully ornamented cottages, inhabited generally by a young, hardy and interprising [*sic*] race.[16]

There was renewed fear of the Fenians this month. In October Rear-Admiral Hastings had received a coded message from London which, deciphered, read:

---

[15] *British Columbian*, 14 Oct. 1868.

[16] John Tod to Edward Ermatinger, 12 Nov. 1868. PAC, *Ermatinger Papers*.

The Foreign Department have information, which may be correct, of Fenian Attack may be attempted on Vancouver Island.[17]

One of the fears was that the Fenians, raiding Victoria, might abduct Governor Seymour and hold him as a hostage for the release of their leaders held in prison in Ireland. Accordingly, this month for the first time a guard of Royal Marines was assigned to Government House.

December. Victoria was celebrating New Year's Eve when a new Colonial Secretary, Philip James Hankin, arrived from Britain. Hankin was no stranger to either Vancouver Island or the mainland. As Lieut. Hankin, R.N., he had served on the coast and had become so attracted by the country that he had resigned his commission rather than return to England. For a while he served on the staff of W. A. G. Young, the Colonial Secretary of Vancouver Island. Out of a job after the union of the two colonies, Hankin was appointed Colonial Secretary of British Honduras. This year he was in London, ready to take up a posting to Sierra Leone, when the Duke of Buckingham, Secretary of State for the Colonies, received a querulous letter from Seymour declaring his lack of confidence in the really excellent W. A. G. Young, his own appointee as Acting Colonial Secretary of British Columbia. The Duke agreed that a governor should not be saddled with a colonial secretary whom he did not trust. His Grace cancelled Hankin's appointment as Colonial Secretary of Sierra Leone and named him Colonial Secretary of British Columbia. The appointment was a sensible one — both Seymour and Kennedy had written in praise of Hankin when he had left British Columbia, and Buckingham himself had been most favourably impressed by the man. After being the guests of the Duke and Duchess of Buckingham at their mansion at Stowe, Mr. and Mrs. Hankin left for Victoria.

Aptly enough, it was a stormy evening when the new Colonial Secretary landed at Victoria. Seymour, more and more going to pieces under the double strain of poor health and alcoholism, had reacted absurdly to news of Hankin's appointment. Completely reversing all his previous statements, he had declared, to the be-

[17] PRO, ADM 1/6056, Y157.

wilderment of the Colonial Office, that Young had been doing a splendid job and must be retained. Making various slanderous statements, he insisted that Hankin's record showed him to be totally unsuitable. These representations had been made while Hankin was already on the long journey out from England. Now here he was in Victoria, with an appointment as Colonial Secretary. The opening weeks of the coming year would find Seymour stubbornly refusing to install Hankin in his office. Even when the Governor learned that Buckingham was standing behind Hankin's appointment, he insisted on retaining Young as Colonial Secretary. Finally, on 8 April 1869,[18] Seymour most unhappily accepted Hankin. Young left for England after a testimonial dinner and a torchlight procession given by Victoria to honour a man whose worth Seymour had recognized too late. The whole weird incident no doubt helped to confirm an opinion in Whitehall that it was about time to recall Seymour.

[18] Robert L. Smith, "The Hankin Appointment, 1868", *BC Studies* No. 22 (Summer 1974), p. 34.

1869

The wreck of the John Bright *and the subsequent hangings at Hesquiat — Governor Seymour's northern cruise — He is killed by a bottle of brandy — The Granville Despatch — The Annexationist Petition — Renewed Fenian threats — Gold in the Omineca.*

In these earlier years, whenever a ship was lost with all hands off the west coast of Vancouver Island or in the vicinity of the Queen Charlotte Islands, there were many whites ready to declare that the Indians must have massacred the crew and looted the ship. Such was the accusation in 1868 when the *Growler* was wrecked off the Queen Charlottes,[1] and again this year when the *John Bright* and all aboard her were lost off Hesquiat Harbour, near Nootka.

News of the latter tragedy reached Victoria in mid-March with the arrival of Captain Christensen and his schooner *Surprise*, from the west coast.[2] Christensen had found the barque lying on her beam ends, with much of her cargo of lumber spread along the shore. Boarding the *John Bright*, he had found that everything movable had been taken from the wreck. Questioned, the local Indians declared that they had seen nobody, dead or alive, from the ship. Suspicious of apparent contradictions in the Indians' stories, Captain Christensen made a search, and found the remains of a woman with long flowing hair, her flesh almost entirely gone. She was, in fact, the Chilean wife of the *John Bright*'s captain.

Several weeks later another schooner, the *Alert*, Captain Carleton, put into Victoria with more details about the disaster.[3] Carleton had

---

[1] See *Lewis & Dryden's Marine History of the Pacific Northwest*, ed. E. W. Wright (New York, 1961 reprint), p. 168, for an account of the *Growler* episode.

[2] *Colonist*, 13 March 1869.

[3] *Colonist*, 31 March 1869.

buried the woman's remains, a decency curiously neglected by Christensen, and he had talked with Anayitzaschist, commonly called
"John", the Indian who had first discovered the wreck. John said
that he had found the corpse of the woman, fully clad, exactly where
Christensen and Carleton had found her bones. Carleton observed
that the Hesquiats had their houses full of things off the *John Bright*
and were worried that a warship might arrive on the scene.

The *Colonist* of April 23rd carried sensational news: Captain
Christensen, revisiting Hesquiat, had been told by the Indians that
he would find the bodies of six white men on a beach outside the
harbour. He had found five of these bodies, some headless (a bad
sign since the Indians traditionally decapitated their enemies), and
one with a hole in his back. Even these grisly and ominous discoveries
were not enough to make Governor Seymour take any action. Only
after the *Colonist* reported that fifty white men were ready to leave
Victoria and wipe out the Hesquiats,[4] did His Excellency send
H.M.S. *Sparrowhawk* upcoast with the Attorney-General and an
assisting magistrate to investigate the whole bizarre affair.

About ten days later the *Sparrowhawk* returned. The bodies from
the *John Bright* had been exhumed, and examined by the *Sparrowhawk*'s surgeon, who could find no medical evidence indicating
decapitation by human hands.[5] He believed that the gnawing of wild
animals and the terrible pounding of the bodies in the surf on that
rocky coast sufficiently accounted for their mutilated condition.
Nevertheless suspicions of murder still persisted, and the *Sparrowhawk* brought to Victoria seven Indians whom Captain Christensen
had pointed out to the Attorney-General as either probable murderers or potentially valuable witnesses.[6]

At the subsequent grand jury hearing one of the Indians, Nee-ta-
Kim, gave a detailed account of how the white woman had landed
alive on the beach, had appealed to John for help, but had been
pistolled by him after he had knocked her off her feet. She had died
a little later. As for a white man who had come ashore with her, he

---

[4] *Colonist,* 30 April 1869.

[5] PRO, *Medical Officers' Journals,* No. 152, H.M.S. *Sparrowhawk,* 1869.

[6] *Colonist,* 12 May 1869.

had been so weak that he could only crawl on his hands and knees. In that condition he had been easily killed by a bullet which had struck him by the left shoulder. Allegedly, John had told other Indians that not he but one Katina had fired that second shot. In the end, the grand jury indicted three of the seven Indians.

On May 29th the case went before the Assize Court, presided over by Chief Justice Needham. As the case proceeded, the evidence pointed more and more towards John as the villain. Needham, who was an extremely capable judge, went to great pains trying to determine whether or not the other Hesquiats were making a scapegoat of John, but the trial ended with him and Katina being sentenced to death. The *Sparrowhawk* took the two men back to Hesquiat village and there they were hanged.

Five years later Father Brabant, a missionary who became greatly devoted to the local Indians and mastered their language, settled at Hesquiat. To him the Hesquiats affirmed that none of them had ever harmed any of the *John Bright*'s people. Father Brabant became convinced of the Hesquiats' innocence, and his written defence of them is in the Provincial Archives in Victoria.[7]

*   *   *

Governor Seymour need not have fretted too much on April 8th of this year, when he installed the unwelcome Hankin as Colonial Secretary. He would not have to endure Hankin for long, for by June 10th Seymour himself would be dead.

In May important business took Seymour north aboard H.M.S. *Sparrowhawk*. The attack made the previous year by the Tsimpseans on the Christianized Nass Indians at Kincolith had led to prolonged hostilities between the two tribes, locked in a war which neither really desired. The Governor deemed his personal intervention highly desirable. Accordingly, on May 26th, the *Sparrowhawk* delivered the Governor, Lowndes his personal secretary, and Joseph Trutch, the Commissioner of Lands and Works, to Metlakatla, William Duncan's northern Christian village. As Commander Mist brought

---

[7] *v.* PABC, E/D/B72.4.

his ship to anchor, Metlakatla made a notable impression upon the visitors:

From the distance at which we lay this Mission Station has quite a town-like appearance. Mr. Duncan's residence and store-house, a large octagon building near it used for School and Church purposes, the gaol — a bastioned block-house — over which the ensign was flying, and the town-hall and court-house — a large framed building at the water side, all newly whitewashed, produced altogether an imposing effect.[8]

When the Governor came ashore, amid cheers from the populace and salutes fired by cannon and musketry, he found a uniformed honour guard of Metlakatla Indians awaiting his inspection. The next day was largely devoted to conferences with Duncan about the Indian war.

On May 30th, having proceeded to Kincolith, the *Sparrowhawk* encountered the schooner which, allegedly, had earlier supplied the Indians with the forbidden alcohol which had started all the current Indian trouble. After taking the boat, the *Nanaimo Packet*, into custody, Commander Mist, Lowndes and Trutch went ashore and conducted a thorough investigation into the murder of Tomlinson's mission Indians the previous year. They soon reached the verdict that the dead Indians had been slain not because they were Christians but because they belonged to the Nass tribe. The avenging Tsimpseans had regarded a Nass as a Nass, no matter whether he was Christian or heathen.

By June 2nd careful negotiations with both the Tsimpseans and the Nass Indians had advanced to the point where a reconciliation between the two tribes could be effected at Fort Simpson:

All the events of their hostility during the past year were discussed, and the amount of compensation to be paid by each tribe for injuries done to the other having been finally settled among them, peace was concluded, and symbolized by the former enemies blowing swans' down over each other's heads. A document setting forth that peace had been that day concluded between the Chimpsean and Naas Indians in the presence of the Governor was then drawn up, and to this the Chiefs' names were all signed by their marks being set thereto as certified by

---

[8] [Joseph W. Trutch], *Report and Journal of the Proceedings in Connection with the Visit of His Excellency the Late Governor Seymour to the North-West Coast in Her Majesty's Ship Sparrowhawk* (Victoria, 1869), p. 3.

the Governor's signature and seal. . . . The Governor then, through Mr. Duncan, addressed the Chiefs, telling them that he had allowed them on this occasion, for the last time, to make compensation to each other, according to the custom hitherto in force among them for friends and relatives killed and injuries inflicted; but now they must understand that this barbarous system was abolished; that they must henceforth live according to English law; and that if they offended against that law by taking each other's lives, every means in the Governor's power should be employed to apprehend and punish them. All the Indians on board, to the number of one hundred and upwards, were then feasted, and presents of pipes, tobacco, &c., made to each. The previously hostile tribes now mixed together with the greatest cordiality.[9]

The next day Commander Mist and Commissioner Trutch, sitting as Justices of the Peace, heard the evidence against the *Nanaimo Packet*, then ordered the little schooner confiscated and her captain fined $500 for selling liquor to Indians.

Seymour's business on the north coast was now satisfactorily concluded and he was free to return to Victoria. However, a visit had been planned to Skidegate Inlet so that the Governor and his staff could visit the workings of the Queen Charlotte Coal Company. A sudden deterioration now manifested itself in the Governor's health. At Skidegate he was unable to come up on deck, much less go ashore to visit the mine which the others inspected in his absence. From Skidegate the *Sparrowhawk* headed first to Kynumpt Harbour and then to Bella Coola. Here, shortly before ten o'clock on the morning of June 10th, His Excellency Frederick Seymour, C.B., Governor, Commander-in-Chief and Vice-Admiral of British Columbia, departed this life.

Late on the night of June 13th H.M.S. *Sparrowhawk* arrived in Esquimalt with the dead governor. At two o'clock on the morning of June 14th news of the tragedy reached Government House. The Rev. Dr. Hayman, roused from his bed, broke the news to the widowed Mrs. Seymour, while plans were made to swear in Hankin as Colonial Administrator.

Next day Victorians read in the *Colonist* an account of the last days of their governor. "The cause of death," they were informed,

<hr>

[9] Trutch, *Report*, p. 5.

"was dysentery."[10] Joseph Trutch, in his *Report and Journal* shortly printed by the Government Printing Office, appeared to confirm this statement when he spoke of Seymour having been for three days "so much exhausted from the effects of diarrhaea." Not surprisingly, historians have ever since declared that Governor Seymour died of dysentery.

But the historians have been wrong, deceived by that Victorian sense of propriety which concealed discreditable matters concerning personal representatives of the Sovereign. In fact, Governor Seymour died not of dysentery but of alcoholism. The evidence is to be found in the medical report of Dr. Comrie of H.M.S. *Sparrowhawk*, which is incisive and specific:

Governor Seymour who had for some time been debilitated, called upon me for medical advice June 6th and I found him suffering from great gastric irritation, nervous tremors, sleeplessness and other symptoms of alcoholism.

Dr. Comrie reported that, while using certain medicines, he had endeavoured to reduce the Governor's dependence on alcoholic stimulants:

... for which the patient had an inordinate craving which he gratified in spite of the vigilance of his servant and private secretary. The evening previous to his death he succeeded in getting hold of a bottle of brandy and drinking it off.[11]

In a little town like Victoria, everybody soon knew the truth about Seymour's end. John Tod, writing to Edward Ermatinger on June 16th, flatly declared the Governor's death was due to "a long course of intemperance, which he had fatally indulged in." D. W. Higgins who, as editor of the *Colonist*, inevitably knew the truth of Seymour's end, printed a somewhat bowdlerized account of it in *The Passing of a Race*, discreetly substituting a bottle of medicine for the fatal bottle of brandy.[12]

Governor Seymour was given a magnificent funeral. Ward 1 of

[10] *Colonist*, 15 June 1869.
[11] PRO, *Medical Officers' Journals*, No. 152, H.M.S. *Sparrowhawk* 1869.
[12] P. 186.

the Naval Hospital had been draped in black cloth and white satin and here Seymour lay in state, with silver candelabra flanking the "elegant mahogany coffin". Flowers were heaped high around a large cross of white satin set by the head of his coffin. From the Naval Hospital an impressive funeral procession conducted Seymour to his last resting-place in the Naval Cemetery. Among the pall-bearers was old Sir James Douglas. In a somewhat qualified encomium the *Colonist* paid tribute to the dead governor:

> Whatever His Excellency's shortcomings as a politician may have been, his character as a gentleman stands unblemished. His was a kindly nature, ill-adapted perhaps to the rough spirits with whom he was brought in contact as the Governor of a new Colony . . . but those who found most fault with his gubernatorial actions, were always ready to accord him the warmest praises for his courtesy and ready sympathies in any public movement that tended to promote the welfare or enjoy-ment of the people. He may not have originated any very brilliant measures, but he did all he could to sustain the reputation of the Colony; and in this, at least, he was successful.[13]

Judge Howay summed it all up when he described Seymour as "A genial, pleasant gentleman, fond of good living, of society, and of social functions . . . [but] vacillating, lymphatic, procrastinating, anxious to do what was right, but lacking the firmness to carry it through."[14]

*   *   *

News of Seymour's death was telegraphed to London on June 14th. The next day an answering cable announced that Anthony Musgrave, recently Governor of Newfoundland, had been appointed Governor in succession to Seymour and would be sailing at once. In fact, before Seymour made his fatal voyage on the *Sparrowhawk*, he was aware that Musgrave was in England, preparatory to taking over from him. Although Seymour had known Musgrave as his capable secretary in Antigua, he expressed a private opinion that the fellow could not be a gentleman since, even before getting his

---

[13] *Colonist*, 15 June 1869.
[14] Howay and Scholefield, *British Columbia*, II : 288-89.

appointment, he had written to him about the value of the furnishings in Government House.

Musgrave was a warm friend of the new Dominion of Canada and enjoyed the confidence of Sir John A. Macdonald, the Canadian Prime Minister, who, indeed, had been instrumental in securing for him his new appointment. Musgrave's instructions from the Colonial Office were simple: he was to get British Columbia into Canada as soon as he could secure the support of his Legislative Council.

On August 23rd Musgrave, accompanied by two maiden sisters and a private secretary, arrived in Victoria. The good impression which he had made on his fellow passengers on the steamer from San Francisco was rapidly confirmed in Victoria. Later Dr. Helmcken had pleasurable recollections of him:

He was a very pleasing man — gentlemanly in manner — had a fine appearance — clear intellect — and of persuasive tho rational conduct. He wished to do the best for the Colony — and gave reasons for his ideas and measures, which however he never forced down our throats — and apparently were never brought forward without previous deliberative thought.[15]

Opening the *Colonist* on his first morning in Government House, Governor Musgrave would have read the following assessment of the job lying before him:

Well, he has a great work to do; a large Colony to be populated; immense and varied resources to be developed; an empty exchequer to be replenished; important public works to be undertaken; a declining commerce to be restored; withering confidence to be revived; new political machinery to be constructed, and last, though not least, a bloated Civil List to be reduced.[16]

Musgrave had arrived with a reputation for administrative acumen and formidable energy. That energy was evident almost immediately — fifteen days after landing at Victoria he was off on a tour of the mainland, accompanied by Hankin the Colonial Secretary, and Trutch the Commissioner of Lands and Works. Musgrave knew already that confederation with Canada was not very popular on

---

[15] Blakey Smith, *Helmcken Reminiscences*, p. 251.

[16] *Colonist*, 24 Aug. 1869.

Vancouver Island. He wanted to sound out sentiment on the mainland, and to acquire a first-hand knowledge of the country.

The British Columbia which Governor Musgrave was touring was very different from that of a few years earlier. The hordes of transients brought by the gold rushes had pretty much disappeared:

Only about 8,500 people remained in the whole of British Columbia, but these were people with the courage to face economic reverses; people with the energy to hew down the forests, clear the land and harvest the wealth of the seas. . . . [17]

Although New Westminster did its best to give Governor Musgrave a real welcome, New Westminster was but a ghost of what it had been when it was the capital of the mainland colony, with a burgeoning civil service accelerating its growth, not to mention the Royal Engineers at adjacent Sapperton. Now the once proud "Royal City" was just a little river town, so depopulated that it could no longer sustain a newspaper — John Robson had taken the *British Columbian* over to Victoria in March. Burrard Inlet with its booming lumber industry was, in fact, more alive than New Westminster.

On September 9th Governor Musgrave, having spent the night at the old Government House at New Westminster, travelled over to the Inlet. First stop was at the Hastings Mill, operated by the British Columbia and Vancouver Island Spar Lumber and Sawmill Company, and at its satellite settlement of Gastown, presided over by Falstaffian Gassy Jack, proprietor of Deighton House. The flying of flags and firing of salutes welcomed His Excellency to these establishments on the south shore of Burrard Inlet. He next crossed over to English Bay to see where Mr. Jerry Rogers was logging on Point Grey. Mr. Rogers had recently been in trouble for logging on the government reserve that Colonel Moody had set up on the Point, but presumably nobody was tactless enough to mention this fact. His Excellency professed great interest in Jerry's "lumber slides". From Jerry's Cove (now Jericho) the Governor travelled to the northern shore of Burrard Inlet to visit the extensive sawmill operated by S. P. Moody and Company, and its settlement of Moodyville (in

---

[17] Ormsby, *British Columbia: A History*, p. 239.

time to become North Vancouver). After partaking of a fine lunch, His Excellency travelled back to New Westminster.

The next day saw Musgrave off on a long journey to the Cariboo. On September 12th he was at Yale, where he attended the Church of England before catching Barnard's stage, at eight that morning, for the Interior. The following day saw him in Lytton, and the 14th at Ashcroft Manor, home of the Cornwall brothers. The previous year the Cornwalls had brought out three foxhounds from England, via Cape Horn, the beginnings of the pack which for twenty years, with the Duke of Beaufort's fresh contributions to its breeding stock, set up the rousing "music" of the chase as they ran down coyotes instead of foxes in that vast, unfenced country.[18] On the whole, it seems unlikely that His Excellency got in any hunting at Ashcroft Manor since he was pushing through to Barkerville, where he arrived on September 18th.

Barkerville received Musgrave in style. Fifty uniformed firemen met him as he approached the town. (Ever since the Great Fire the fire brigade had been very important!) At the entrance to the settlement an arch, constructed of evergreens, carried an inscription — "Welcome". A second arch a bit farther along repeated the message in English and Chinese. Fireworks and guns provided reverberating evidence of the enthusiasm of the Cariboo for Queen Victoria's representative. Governor Musgrave passed under more arches including the Firemen's Arch, replete with ladders, hooks and buckets. Replying to an address of welcome, His Excellency expressed his gratification at seeing signs on some of the arches reading "Success to the Dominion" and "Union Forever".[19] By now the new governor knew that sentiment for confederation, although lukewarm in Victoria, was strong on the mainland. On October 14th His Excellency arrived back in Victoria.

Awaiting Musgrave on his desk at Government House was an important despatch from Earl Granville, Colonial Secretary in the new Gladstone ministry back in England. Gladstone's cabinet had

[18] For C. F. Cornwall's history of the Ashcroft Hunt, see PABC, E/C/C81/2A1. There were of course foxes in the country, but the coyote was found a more suitable prey.

[19] *Colonist*, 30 Sept. 1869.

reached a decision about British Columbia. More emphatically even than the Disraeli ministry, it had decided that British Columbia should be transferred to Canada. Granville declared that, now that arrangements had been completed for the Hudson's Bay Company to transfer Rupert's Land to Canada, and thus the Dominion's border would extend to the Rockies, no reason existed for postponing British Columbia's entrance into the Dominion. The government in London was convinced that British Columbia's own best interests would be served by union with Canada.

On October 30th, following instructions from the Colonial Office, Musgrave published the "Granville Despatch" in the government *Gazette*. The publication of this document made British Columbians aware that they could expect neither help nor sympathy from Britain if they avoided entry into the Canadian confederation. Some felt almost betrayed by this eagerness to get them into Canada. The Englishmen who almost entirely staffed British Columbia's civil service realized that the home government was making an irrevocable decision, and that they themselves must now decide whether or not to remain in a British Columbia that was obviously going to become Canadian. Those that had no great liking for the heavy Ontario Methodists who, to them, were "the Canadians" (and who had sneered at these same Canadians as "North American Chinamen" because of their stolid, unimaginative thrift) may have found the decision to remain rather a hard one.

On November 2nd, just when Musgrave was coping with the repercussions of the Granville Despatch and preparing for the coming session of the Legislative Council, he suffered an accident which crippled him for life. Mounting a filly at Government House, he was thrown by the horse. As he struck the ground, his entire weight came down on his right leg, breaking it so badly that a splinter of broken bone stuck out through the side of his riding-boot. Drs. Helmcken, Powell, Trimble and Davie were summoned to examine the fractures, and to endeavour to set the leg — no easy task in an era before X-Rays. In fact, the doctors soon divided into two parties: those who were for setting the leg, and those who deemed the job hopeless and urged amputation. In the end Musgrave put the Canadian Dr. Powell in charge of his case and kept his leg. He was bedbound for months while the leg partly mended, and limped until his dying day.

While Musgrave was enduring this painful injury, a part of the population of Victoria (not uninfluenced by the Granville Despatch) were signing a petition asking the President of the United States to annex British Columbia. This development was not surprising. The business depression was continuing. Britain was obviously unwilling to subsidize the colony; and her scheme to unite British Columbia with Canada was unpopular on the Island. Under the circumstances inevitably some people decided that British Columbia could do better for itself by joining the United States than by uniting with the Dominion of Canada. The only surprising thing is that so few were found to sign the Annexationist Petition. When, in mid-November this was handed to Vincent Collyer, the United States Indian Commissioner for Alaska (who was en route to Washington) for delivery to President Grant, it carried only forty-three signatures out of a community of three thousand. Recirculated, the petition picked up another sixty-one names. Oddly enough, as Willard Ireland has demonstrated, the main support for the Annexationist Petition came not from the American colony in Victoria but from Germans and Jews.[20]

Most Victorians did not take the Annexationists very seriously. The *Colonist*, after noting that the petition had been principally signed by foreigners, made a jocular suggestion that what was really needed was:

... a petition to the Queen praying Her Majesty to annex all the American territory north of the Columbia River — our natural boundary.[21]

There had been rather more excitement in the spring of this year when a voluble, plausible Fenian leader named George Francis Train had arrived in San Francisco with the avowed purpose of recruiting an Irish-American expedition against Vancouver Island. The San Francisco *Chronicle* was impressed both by Train's "astonishing knowledge of all the resources of the island" and his "remark-

[20] W. E. Ireland, "The Annexation Petition of 1869", *BCHQ* 4 (1940):281. Ireland provides biographical notes identifying each of the signatories.

[21] *Colonist*, 13 Nov. 1869.

ably practicable" secret plan for its conquest. The *Chronicle* opined: "Our impression is that Train will have that Island before Cuba will be wrestled from Spain." The *Colonist*, in the same column in which it ran the *Chronicle*'s story, had an item of its own:

THE FENIANS — The public mind is uncommonly tranquil over the threatened Fenian raid. Most people believe that, on the principle that "threatened men live long," Victoria will enjoy an immunity from attack. If Train were to come alone to British Columbia, he might give a performance at the theatre with considerable pecuniary advantage to himself and amusement to our citizens; but if he were to lead a gang of misguided men, he would stand a chance of having a few crevices added to his already badly cracked head. The authorities are on the alert; but if the Irishmen wait for Train to lead them upon British Columbia they will grow grey waiting.[22]

Of course it is a matter of history that, despite this and other alarms, there never was a Fenian raid on British Columbia.

*   *   *

Once more deaths from smallpox were diminishing the native population, though not on the scale of the appalling epidemic of 1862. Interestingly enough, Dr. Comrie of the *Sparrowhawk*, while describing smallpox as "almost invariably fatal" among the Indians, and declaring measles to be "very fatal", singled out syphilis and "scrofula" (a form of tuberculosis) as "the blight and curse of the whole native race, diseases working their extermination".[23] Years were yet to pass before the arrival of medical missionaries would help to save the Indians of British Columbia from the extinction which had overtaken the Indians of Newfoundland.

One piece of news gave some hope this year for the still depressed economy of British Columbia. A new gold area was discovered in Omineca, in the north of the colony. Michael Burns and Vital La Force were the pioneers who first prospected this remote country, spending the winter of 1868-69 on the headwaters of the Omineca River. Back in Quesnel they gave secret reports in the right quarters, thus obtaining backers who financed a new expedition this May. For

[22] *Colonist*, 5 June 1869.

[23] PRO, *Medical Officers' Journals*, No. 152, H.M.S. *Sparrowhawk* 1869.

the general public, however, Burns and La Force carefully circulated reports that Omineca was another humbug. Not everybody was taken in by this fiction. After setting out once more for the north, Burns and La Force found their party being shadowed by pursuers who were convinced the two men had found a new El Dorado. Unable to get rid of these parasites, the two made the best deal they could. They would show the way to a creek where they had already taken out over $8,000 in a little over a month, but the interlopers must agree to let them stake their own claims first.

When, late this year, it became generally known that gold and silver had been found on various streams in the Omineca country, a rush was soon under way. The Omineca would yield rather handsomely though unevenly for a few years. It was not a humbug like the Big Bend. But neither was it another Cariboo.

1870

The terms for confederation drafted — Trutch, Helmcken and Carrall journey to Ottawa — Agreement on the terms of union — The Flying Squadron at Esquimalt — Governor Musgrave takes an American wife — The Nanaimo coal strike — An election to ratify the terms of confederation.

This was a year of negotiations, long and complicated, which in 1871 would make British Columbia a Canadian province.

After adding to his Executive Council Helmcken and Carrall, two of the elected members of the Legislative Council, Governor Musgrave asked it to draft a set of terms for British Columbia's entrance into confederation. When, on February 16th, the Legislative Council convened for its annual session, these terms were ready for it to debate. Musgrave being still incapacitated by his broken leg, Hankin, the Colonial Secretary, read the speech which the Governor had prepared for the opening of the session. Although calling on the existing Legislative Council to vote on the proposed terms of confederation, the Governor promised that the ultimate decision would lie with a new Legislative Council that would be specially elected for the purpose of either accepting or rejecting whatever terms were finally negotiated with Ottawa.

Men were startled almost into disbelief at the boldness of the demands which the Executive Council had drafted. One of the most audacious requirements was that, although the total population of British Columbia (white, Chinese and Indian) was at the very most around 60,000,[1] Ottawa was to accept it as being 120,000 for pur-

---

[1] In 1870 British Columbia had a white population of 8,576, a Negro population of 462, and a Chinese population of 1,548. (British Columbia: *Report of the Hon. H. L. Langevin* (Ottawa, 1872), Appendix Z, p. 152.) The Indian population was estimated at anywhere between 30,000 and 50,000, though the smaller figure seems the more probable.

poses of its per capita grant to the proposed new province. Moreover, all British Columbia's debts were to be assumed by Canada, surveys were to start immediately for a transcontinental railway, and a wagon road across the Rockies was to be built within three years.

Attitudes had changed in the Legislative Council since its anti-confederation days. The official members, heeding the will of White-hall and the new Governor, no longer opposed union with Canada. The magisterial members had been won over by Musgrave's assurance that, once they were Canadians, they would cease to be magistrates and become county court judges. Some of the elected members from Vancouver Island may still have lacked enthusiasm about joining Canada, but just about all of those from the mainland were ardent confederationists.

From March 9th to 19th the Legislative Council debated the terms of union. The main onus of supporting these articles fell upon Attorney-General Crease, who only recently had switched from the anti-confederationist camp. Some minor opposition was offered, but a motion to postpone action for six months was easily defeated. The unrepentant Dr. Helmcken sardonically observed that the whole exercise was one in futility since the United States would inevitably take over Canada sooner or later. But finally the crucial vote was taken and the Legislative Council accepted the terms which the Executive Council had put before it. With only one dissenting vote, the Legislative Council authorized the sending of delegates to Ottawa.

The next step was to see if Ottawa would accept these British Columbian terms or insist upon substantial changes in them. Musgrave's choice of the three delegates to carry the terms of union to Ottawa was at once judicious and daring. One of the three men chosen was Dr. R. W. W. Carrall from the Cariboo, who all along had been an ardent confederationist. The second was Joseph W. Trutch, the Commissioner of Lands and Works. Under Seymour, Trutch had opposed confederation, but he had changed sides since Musgrave's arrival. The third was Dr. Helmcken, who had opposed confederation right up to the very last. Musgrave's audacious choice of Helmcken took various factors into account. For one thing, the little doctor was an experienced and wily parliamentarian, notably adroit at the fine footwork required in committee sessions. Secondly, he could be counted upon to fight for the best conceivable terms. Finally, with Helmcken identified with the confederation terms, the Colony's remaining anti-confederationists would be without their leader.

On May 10th the three delegates left Victoria for Ottawa, at San Francisco boarding a Union Pacific train for the eastern states. As their carriage clickety-clacked through mountain canyons and over sunbaked plains, the three men, looking about them, began to feel that the Canadian Pacific Railway (the name was already being used), was no impossible dream. What the Americans had been able to do, the Canadians might be able to do also.

On June 4th, Carrall, Trutch and Helmcken arrived in Ottawa. As Sir John A. Macdonald was ill, Sir George Cartier, the acting Prime Minister, headed the Canadian negotiating team. Everywhere hospitality was showered upon the British Columbians, who were gratified to find that the Canadians were not bent on driving a hard bargain. In surprisingly little time agreement was reached upon the terms for British Columbia's admission.

The citizens of British Columbia first learned of the success of their representatives when, on July 8th, the *Colonist* published a telegram just received from the special correspondent whom the paper had sent east with the delegation. It read:

The Terms agreed upon will be published first in British Columbia. Canada is favourable to immediate union and guarantees the railway. Red River affairs favourable. Trutch has gone to England. Carrall remains one month. Helmcken and your correspondent are on way home.

H. E. SEELYE[2]

One would like to report that British Columbia was seething with suspense and excitement during these fateful months. But in fact people were beginning to tire of the long confederation debate and, as the *Colonist* rather sadly noted, union with Canada sparked less interest than the Franco-Prussian War which had just erupted.

On August 30th Governor Musgrave made public the terms

[2] *Colonist*, 8 July 1870.

agreed upon in Ottawa. Their official publication came as an anti-climax since, leaked to the Toronto *Globe*, they had been reprinted in the *Colonist* of July 20th. Since the full text of these terms has been printed in an appendix to Howay and Scholefield's history of British Columbia,[3] their full legal terminology need not be reproduced here. Let it suffice to state briefly the principal terms:

1. Canada assumed British Columbia's existing debts and liabilities.

2. British Columbia "not having incurred debts equal to those of the other Provinces now constituting the Dominion", she was to receive certain equalization payments.

3. Accepting 60,000 as the figure for British Columbia's total population, Canada was to pay an annual subsidy of $35,000 plus a grant of eighty cents per capita for the support of the new province's government and legislature.

4. Canada was to provide an efficient mail service between Victoria and San Francisco, and between Victoria and Olympia, Washington.

5. Canada was to pay the salaries of the Lieutenant-Governor and of the judges of the supreme and county or district courts. Canada was to pay also for the customs service, the post office and telegraph system, fisheries protection, militia, lighthouses, quarantine and marine hospitals, and penitentiary, as well as the geological survey.

6. Suitable pensions were to be paid to colonial civil servants adversely affected by the union.

7. British Columbia was to retain its own customs tariff and excise duties until the completion of the transcontinental railway.

8. British Columbia was to have three members in the Senate and six members in the House of Commons at Ottawa.

9. Ottawa was to seek to persuade Britain to maintain the Royal Navy's Esquimalt naval base.

10. Apart from some special exceptions, the British North America Act was to apply to British Columbia.

11. The construction of a trans-Canada railway was to commence, from both east and west, within two years of the date of union, and be completed within ten years of the union. British Columbia was to cede a belt of public land extending for twenty miles on either side of that railway.

---

[3] Howay & Scholefield, Vol. II, Appendix VI, pp. 695-97.

12. Subject to certain limits, the Dominion Government was to pay for ten years the interest charges involved in building the drydock at Esquimalt.

13. The Government of Canada was to assume responsibility for the Indians, and management of their lands, pledging itself to as liberal a policy as that pursued by the colony.

14. The constitution of the executive authority and legislature of British Columbia would continue unaltered except when changes were made to secure accordance with the British North America Act. The Dominion Government accepted the introduction of "responsible government" into British Columbia.

Finally it was agreed that the union should take effect upon a day to be designated by Her Majesty, after she had received addresses ratifying the agreement from both the Legislature of British Columbia and the government of the Dominion of Canada.

Such then were the terms that would be submitted for final ratification to a new British Columbia Legislative Council specially elected at the end of the year to make the final decision.

*   *   *

Men gave their attention to much else besides the confederation negotiations during this last full year of the colonial regime.

January. Although the Annexationist Petition circulated on Vancouver Island attracted remarkably few signatories, it aroused much interest south of the border. Intimations of manifest destiny once more fluttered in American hearts. On January 18th, the Hon. Elwood Evans, a local politician, delivered before the Tacoma Library Association, at Olympia, a rousing address which was subsequently published under the title *The Re-Annexation of British Columbia to the United States: Right, Proper and Desirable.*

February. By oversight the Act of Parliament which had united Vancouver Island and British Columbia in 1866 had left the resultant colony with two Chief Justices. For a time there were unfortunate clashes of authority and resultant hard feelings. Such was the case especially during the Grouse Creek War when Seymour sent

Chief Justice Needham into the Cariboo, which Chief Justice Begbie regarded as his domain. Peace was at last established by creating Needham Chief Justice of British Columbia on Vancouver Island, and Begbie Chief Justice of British Columbia on the mainland. But this absurd anomaly could not long be tolerated, and this year it ended. Early this month Needham was preparing to leave, having been appointed Chief Justice of Trinidad.

March. This month we get a picture of the aging Sir James Douglas from the pen of John Tod, who had known him for half a century:

> Friend Douglas has of late become very unsteady of step, shaky of hand, and dim of eye, but as he gets older, seems more and more engrossed with the affairs of this world notwithstanding his ample means, he is as eager and grasping after money as ever and, [I] am told, at times Seized with gloomy apprehensions of dying a beggar at last. . . . [4]

April. When the U.S.S. *Newburn* arrived from San Francisco, she had on board Lady Franklin, whose earlier visit had been one of the events of 1861. Although now approaching eighty, that indomitable globetrotter was as energetic as ever. Once again she had her niece, Miss Cracroft, as her companion. After a few days in Victoria, she and her niece were off to see Alaska.

May. A visitor at Esquimalt this year might have thought that Britain and the United States had gone to war. Some 3500 blue-jackets and "lobsters" (marines) were in evidence, while in the harbour, instead of the usual gunboat *Boxer*, gun-vessel *Sparrow-hawk*, and whatever frigate was serving as Esquimalt's "post ship", there were no less than nine men-of-war. To show the flag, the Admiralty had sent round the world a "Flying Squadron", under the command of Rear-Admiral Hornby. Now for a fortnight the ships which used Esquimalt as their base — H.M.S. *Zealous, Charybdis, Sparrowhawk* and *Boxer* — had been joined by Admiral Hornby's

[4] Tod to Edward Ermatinger, 22 March 1870. PAC, *Ermatinger Papers.*

H.M.S. *Liverpool, Liffey, Endymion, Phoebe, Scylla* and *Pearl.* It was Esquimalt's finest hour as a British naval base.

June. The long years of economic depression seemed to be coming to an end, and British Columbia was no longer losing population. A census taken this year showed that the white population of the Victoria area now numbered 5313,[5] a notable advance over the 4208 of only a year before. Victoria exhibited the preponderance of males over females, so often found in frontier settlements — 3218 vs. 2095. This imbalance was rectified somewhat this month when a locally-based Female Immigration Board received from England, aboard that "fine and well appointed" ship *Alpha*, twenty-two girls intended to provide badly needed domestic help. Noting their arrival, the *Colonist* pleaded, "Do not quite lose sight of the sister in the servant."[6]

July. At ten o'clock in the morning of July 2nd, a signal gun at Government House alerted the town that H.M.S. *Sparrowhawk*, returning from San Francisco, had been sighted off Race Rocks. Hers had been no ordinary cruise, for she had taken British Columbia's widower governor to San Francisco to be remarried. Shortly after the *Sparrowhawk* had arrived at San Francisco, Governor Musgrave had gone to the railway terminal at Oakland to greet his fiancée, Miss Jeannie Lucinda Field, and her father, David Dudley Field, who had arrived on a Pullman palace car. (Mr. Field was a distinguished constitutional and corporation lawyer, and the brother of Cyrus Field, of trans-Atlantic cable fame.) Early in the afternoon of June 20th Miss Field was married to Governor Musgrave.

A curious contretemps marked the return of the *Sparrowhawk*. She had been expected to put in at Esquimalt, where Admiral Farquhar and sundry colonial dignitaries were waiting to welcome the returning governor and his lady. However to everybody's surprise the *Sparrowhawk*, probably at Musgrave's insistence, bypassed Esquimalt and made directly for Victoria, where only about one hundred and fifty persons assembled in time to see their governor

[5] *Colonist,* 24 June 1870.
[6] *Colonist,* 15 June 1870.

and his bride come ashore. The *Colonist* noted "His Excellency walked to his carriage with apparent pain and difficulty."[7] Driving through the streets en route to Government House, the Musgraves found them bright with bunting and paired British and American flags. The international aspect of the match was fully appreciated. Some indeed felt that it would have been nice if the Governor had extended his honeymoon by a few days so that his lady would arrive at her new home on July 4th then generally, though incongruously, observed throughout British Columbia as a public holiday. Earlier, announcing the marriage, the *Colonist* had quaintly observed, "Here it is that the tail of the British Lion and the tip of the American Eagle meet."[8]

When the vice-regal and bridal couple arrived at Government House, they found a scene exquisite in its Victorian sentimentality. A carpet extended from the carriage steps to the doors of Cary Castle. Flanking the carpet were rows of the comeliest young ladies of good family that Victoria could muster. Each was dressed in white and adorned with a blue sash. As Musgrave limped with his bride to the door where his spinster sisters waited to greet them, the virgins of Victoria strewed roses in their path.

August. Those who today traverse the coastal waters of British Columbia in the fine fleet of ferries maintained by the provincial government may be surprised to know that long before the establishment of the "Dogwood Fleet" in 1958, it had its precursor in colonial British Columbia. Although private entrepreneurs could profitably maintain ships on the Victoria-New Westminster-Yale runs, no private company was prepared to lose money on a service linking Victoria with the settlements at Cowichan Bay, Nanaimo and Comox. Accordingly, since 1866 the colonial government had operated the steamer *Sir James Douglas* on this route. The return fares from Victoria were $4.00 to Cowichan, $6.00 to Nanaimo and $13.00 to Comox. These prices were far too high, thought the *Colonist*, which this month launched a campaign to cut the fares in half.

[7] *Colonist*, 3 July 1870.
[8] *Colonist*, 23 June 1870.

September. This month Victoria had its very own gold rush when two hunters discovered what they took to be gold quartz on the slopes of Mount Douglas. Claims were optimistically staked all around the little mount, and the *Colonist* raised the possibility that Mount Douglas was "A MOUNTAIN OF GOLD". Unfortunately, all that the Assay Office could report was that traces of gold and silver had been found in the specimens submitted to it.[9]

October. The first of the bitter strikes which, from time to time, were to flaw the history of the Nanaimo coalfields started this month. This strike was precipitated by the action of the employers in cutting by "one bit" (12½ cents) the price per ton they paid to the miners. On October 3rd the pitmen went on strike and on the 5th they were joined by the men who loaded the coal at the wharves. That same day matters turned ugly when a crude homemade bomb was hurled through a window of the house where one of the non-striking engineers lived.[10] For seven unhappy months the strike dragged on, with a warship stationed in Nanaimo harbour to deal with any violence. After the stores cut off all credit, the strikers nearly starved. Young single men fared not too badly by digging clams and fishing, but life was dire indeed for the married men and their families. Later the Wesleyan lay preacher C. M. Tate, who had been laid off as an engineer, recalled:

> During the winter we organized a begging party to wait on the few settlers on the various islands between Nanaimo and Victoria. We hired an old Indian named Kwal-a-kup, with his large war canoe, and picked up potatoes, and other vegetables, besides an occasional sack of flour, some groceries, salt meat, and other edibles.[11]

November. In the spring Governor Musgrave had promised that any union terms agreed upon in Ottawa would be submitted for ratification to a specially elected new Legislative Council. This month brought the election, which was really a referendum on those terms.

[9] *Colonist,* 6 Sept. 1870.

[10] *Colonist,* 7 Oct. 1870.

[11] C. M. Tate, "Autosketch", United Church Archives, Toronto, G6i, Box 22, # 13.

It was a fiercely fought campaign, partly because Musgrave had changed the constitution of the Legislative Council so that, for the first time, it would be predominantly composed of elected members. When all the clamour at the hustings had died away, it was found that the confederationists had carried the day. The membership of the new and final Legislative Council was:

Elected members:

Victoria City	Dr. J. S. Helmcken
	Henry Nathan
Victoria District	Amor De Cosmos
Nanaimo	Arthur Bunster
New Westminster	Hugh Nelson
Hope, Yale & Lytton	Clement F. Cornwall
Lillooet & Clinton	Thomas B. Humphreys
Cariboo	Dr. R. W. W. Carrall
Kootenay	R. J. Skinner

Appointed members:

Colonial Secretary	Philip J. Hankin
Attorney-General	George Phillippo[12]
Chief Commissioner of Lands & Works	Joseph Trutch
Collector of Customs	Wymond O. Hamley
A. F. Pemberton, J.P.	
E. G. Alston, J.P.[13]	

December.   The terms of union drawn up in Ottawa, providing for a Canadian Pacific Railway, had scarcely been made public when the people of New Westminster began to realize that, if only the railway's western terminus were established at the Royal City, they could more than regain what they had lost when the seat of government had been transferred to Victoria. New Westminster could gloriously rehabilitate herself by becoming the commercial centre if not the political capital of British Columbia. Discussion led to further

---

[12] Crease, the former Attorney-General, had been promoted to the bench.
[13] Howay & Scholefield, II: 294.

discussion, there were meetings, and finally a petition was presented to Governor Musgrave setting forth reasons why the railway should end at New Westminster. Alarmed at New Westminster's initiative and presumption, the *Colonist* declared on December 2nd, "We conceive Victoria to possess pre-eminent claims to become the western terminus of the transcontinental railway". The next day a delegation called upon Governor Musgrave with a petition signed by some 550 citizens demanding that Victoria's suburb of Esquimalt, with its fine harbour for deepsea shipping, be designated as the terminus for the coming C.P.R.

Musgrave was not pleased. He remarked that petitions had already arrived from other places besides New Westminster, and that more were expected. He pointed out that, if British Columbia became embroiled in internal rivalry about a hypothetical rail terminus before the terms of union had been finally ratified, the whole confederation enterprise might fall apart. Acidly he remarked that geography rather than petitions would determine the route of the railway. But the first shots had been fired in a propaganda war which would continue until Sir William Van Horne decided, in 1884, that the western terminus of the Canadian Pacific Railway would be on Burrard Inlet at a place to be named "Vancouver".

1871

Robert Dunsmuir discovers the Wellington coalfield — British Columbia and Canada ratify the Terms of Union — "The glorious Twentieth of July".

In an earlier volume[1] we commenced our long adventurous journey, extending from Captain Cook's landing at Nootka on 29 March 1778 to British Columbia's union with Canada on 20 July 1871. That journey is now almost finished. But before recording British Columbia's entry into confederation, let us note a few of the happenings during the final months of British Columbia's existence as a Crown Colony.

January. Scanning the early newspapers, one cannot help but observe how, even in these early days, British Columbia's population was markedly multi-national. The *Colonist* of January 14th noted that Victoria's German colony had appointed a new arrival, Prof. E. O. Seliger, to lead its choir, the "Germania Sing Verein". The next day the same newspaper mentioned a meeting of the French Benevolent Society.

February. Excitement ran high in Victoria when, on February 24th, the *Colonist* appeared with headlines proclaiming:

A Captive Girl
AMONG THE MITINAHTS [*sic*]
THRILLING INCIDENTS

Apparently a little girl, supposedly lost after the wreck of the *John Bright* in 1869, had survived and was now a slave among the Indians. The very next day Governor Musgrave despatched H.M.S.

---

[1] G. P. V. Akrigg and Helen B. Akrigg, *British Columbia Chronicle, 1778-1846* (Vancouver, 1975).

Sparrowhawk to Neah Bay, Washington Territory, where the report had originated. Alas, when the *Sparrowhawk* returned it was to report that the captive "white girl" was partly Indian, a slave two years before the wreck of the *John Bright*.

March. Victorians examined with fascination "Thompson's Patent Steamers", newly brought from Britain on the Hudson's Bay Company's supply ship, *Prince of Wales*. These "road steamers" were ponderous steam tractors, "the thick india-rubber tire being enclosed within an endless chain of iron bands".[2] The mechanical monsters were for use on the Cariboo Road, with each pulling several wagons (very much like English railway goods cars) loaded with freight. Whereas existing horse-drawn freight trains, moving at a walking pace, required well over a month to get from Yale to Barkerville, these "road steamer" trains were to make the journey in ten days, and halve the freight rates. Alas, the steam tractors were to prove total failures!

April. British Columbia was already developing an interest in her own history. Men who had come out in the famous gold rush year of 1858 took pride in being "Fifty-Eighters". "Fifty-Niners" regretted that fate had not brought them out a few months earlier and allowed them that aura also. A small group of aging men could remember the great days of the Hudson's Bay Company when Dr. McLoughlin had ruled at Fort Vancouver, and the Company's red flag, carrying the Union Jack on its canton and the initials HBC on its fly, had floated in the breeze as far south as Umpqua in southern Oregon. On April 28th, the British Columbia Pioneer Society was organized.

May. Since his stroke in 1868, James Murray Yale had dragged out a miserable existence. Death came finally on May 7th of this year. An age had passed since he had first arrived in New Caledonia in 1820.

June. The Americans were building another transcontinental railway — this time it was the Northern Pacific. Running their rails

[2] *Colonist*, 23 Feb. 1871.

close to the Canadian border, and for a time talking of making Bellingham Bay their terminus, the promoters of the Northern Pacific Railway were out to take the place of a Canadian transcontinental railway. In a map published this year, the eager propagandists of the Northern Pacific printed the following declaration across the face of British Columbia:

British Columbia is a sea of Mountains, the Rocky Mountains, the Cascades, and the Coast Range, all heaped together and covered with densest forest. It has been pronounced by British Ordnance officers Impracticable for a Railroad.[3]

This month the gold rush to the Omineca country crested, with some nine hundred men arriving at the new diggings by way either of the Fraser or the Skeena rivers.

July. On July 13th the *Colonist* reported that men were already being recruited for the Canadian Pacific Railway's survey crews. On that magic day of July 20th, when British Columbia became part of Canada, these newly-recruited parties would leave for the mainland.

Early this month Robert Dunsmuir made his greatest discovery.[4] Dunsmuir had prospered moderately since he had arrived at Fort Rupert in 1851 to dig coal for the Hudson's Bay Company. When the Fort Rupert mines were abandoned, Dunsmuir moved to Nanaimo, where he worked in various managerial posts connected with the HBC mines, the Vancouver Island Coal Mining Company and the Harewood Coal Mining Company (the latter founded by Lieut. the Hon. Horace Lascelles of H.M.S. *Forward*). But Dunsmuir was an ambitious man — after all, he had promised his wife that he would build her a castle in the New World — and he kept his eyes open for a new coal area which he could claim for his own.

His first significant find occurred in October 1869 when, during his rambles, he recognized some rock as belonging to the stratum overlying the lowest known coal deposits. Beneath it he found a coal

---

[3] E. H. Knight, *Map of Country Tributary to the Northern Pacific Railway*, 1871. Huntington Library 43237.

[4] Writing to H. L. Langevin, 20 Sept. 1871 (Langevin, *British Columbia*, Ottawa, 1872, pp. 86-7), Dunsmuir said he had made the discovery "about ten weeks ago".

seam 3½ feet deep. Encouraged, he obtained a Crown permit to prospect further in the area. A second test shaft struck the seam where it was 8 feet thick, though under 132 feet of overlay. But now, this July, came the real breakthrough. On an outing, when he was not particularly engaged in prospecting but was keeping his eyes open, he happened to look under the roots of a fallen tree several hundred yards from his second test shaft. Under those roots he saw coal. Shrewdly reasoning that much of this surface showing had been lost through forest fires, Dunsmuir, after studying the lay of the formation, sent men to dig some eighty yards farther off. After penetrating only nine feet of overlay, they struck a coal seam nine feet deep. The situation was perfect for an open pit mine. In short order, Dunsmuir was building a tramway to carry the coal to a wharf which he constructed at Departure Bay.

Dunsmuir needed financial backing to continue development of the rich Wellington coalfield. Remembering how Lieut. Lascelles had financed the Harewood mine, he sought backers in the Royal Navy. Admiral Farquhar put up $12,000 and Captain F. W. Egerton $10,000,[5] but the chief investor was Lieut. W. N. Diggle, who had served on the coast with H.M.S. *Grappler*. With each acre of the Wellington coalfield yielding some 7000 tons of easily accessible coal of good quality, the Dunsmuir, Diggle Company prospered mightily. Dunsmuir bought out Farquhar and Egerton; and in time Diggle for a reputed $600,000. Cannily using his growing fortune, Dunsmuir invested in real estate, timber holdings, an ironworks, ships, and the Esquimalt and Nanaimo Railway. In Victoria he would build his wife her promised castle — Craigdarroch Castle. When he died in 1889 he would be British Columbia's first industrial magnate. But the start of Dunsmuir's great wealth had come when he looked under that fallen tree in the last weeks of British Columbia's colonial regime.

*   *   *

The time had come for the final steps which would bring British Columbia into Canada. On January 5th the new Legislative Council,

---

[5] James Audain, *From Coalmine to Castle: The Story of The Dunsmuirs of Vancouver Island* (New York, 1955), pp. 51-2.

the one elected to make British Columbia's ultimate decision on the terms hammered out in Ottawa, convened. Governor Musgrave knew that some members had no real heart for confederation and for them and the population at large he offered a special inducement. Although His Excellency did not believe that British Columbia was yet ready for self-government, he knew that a great many of the colonists wanted the responsible government enjoyed by the existing Canadian provinces. Accordingly, in his speech from the throne, Musgrave declared that, if the proposed terms were accepted, he would proclaim a new colonial constitution which would replace the partly-appointed Legislative Council with a wholly-elected Legislative Assembly. British Columbia then would enter confederation with responsible government.

On January 18th, Joseph Trutch moved and Dr. Helmcken seconded a motion that the Legislative Council go into committee and consider "The Terms". These, Trutch insisted, could not be amended but must be either accepted or rejected. One day sufficed for the debate. On the morrow the *Colonist* joyfully proclaimed:

Confederation Accomplished

'Tis done. The great transaction's done. The Legislature has unanimously accepted the Terms of Union and passed an address to the Queen praying that British Columbia may be admitted into the Dominion of Canada, in accordance with the provisions of the British North America Act 1867.[6]

But confederation had not been accomplished. The real battle lay ahead in the Parliament of Canada. There, some of the federal Conservative members were full of misgivings about the extremely generous terms that their government had granted British Columbia. The Liberal opposition, spearheaded by the sardonic and cynical Edward Blake, was unanimously opposed to the deal. When Trutch arrived in Ottawa bearing British Columbia's ratification, he soon found himself very busy strengthening the resolve of wavering Conservatives and supplying the government with ammunition in its fierce campaign against the thrifty Liberals, who felt that Sir John A. Macdonald, with his promise of a railway, was bankrupting the

[6] *Colonist*, 19 Jan. 1871.

country in his determination to bring into Canada that "sea of mountains" so incredibly far to the west.

It was on April 1st, April Fool's Day, that the House of Commons approved British Columbia's entry into confederation. The *Colonist* got the news overnight by telegraph. The next morning its subscribers read:

CANADA!!
Confederation before
Parliament!

The Terms Pass the
Commons by 18
Majority

The last battle was fought in the Senate. Here on April 5th, by a majority of seventeen, the senators voted for the address craving Her Majesty to authorize the union of British Columbia and Canada.

The final scene was enacted in Britain, at Windsor Castle. Here on May 16th Her Majesty the Queen, attended upon by the Secretary of State for the Colonies, graciously accepted the addresses from both Victoria and Ottawa and approved an imperial Order-in-Council that:

... from and after the twentieth day of July, one thousand eight hundred and seventy-one, the said Colony of British Columbia shall be admitted into and become part of the Dominion of Canada upon the terms and conditions set forth in the hereinafter recited addresses.[7]

There was some disappointment that Her Majesty had chosen July 20th rather than July 1st, Dominion Day, for the grand occasion. And a grand occasion it was to be. British Columbians knew that they had real occasion for rejoicing because of "the super-excellent terms obtained".[8] On July 6th a large and enthusiastic public meeting was held in Victoria to arrange suitable celebrations for "The Twentieth". At New Westminster, Burrard Inlet, Yale, Lytton,

---

[7] For the full text of the order see *Colonist*, 29 June 1871, p. 3, where it is printed along with Musgrave's proclamation of the new constitution for the colony.

[8] *Colonist*, 21 April 1871.

Lillooet, Barkerville and the rest of the Cariboo mining camps, the day was looked forward to with equal anticipation.

On July 19th, the last day of colonial rule, Governor Musgrave, true to his promise, proclaimed a new constitution providing for a democratically elected Legislative Assembly of twenty-five members, thirteen from the mainland and twelve from the island. British Columbia would enter Canada as emancipated politically as any of her sister provinces. The same day the *Colonist* printed an editorial in which, amid its fervent rejoicing, it believed it had found a better name than "Canada" for the country north of the 49th parallel:

> To-day it is the last in the life of British Columbia as a distinct colony of the British Crown. Tomorrow by the Grace of God and Royal proclamation, this Colony becomes a Province of the Confederated Empire of British North America. It is about to lay off the chrysalis shell of Crown colonial existence and don the garb of a full-fledged self-governing people.[9]

At twelve midnight British Columbia became Canadian. Nowhere was the rejoicing more exuberant than in the new provincial capital, though some felt the exultation was more for winning responsible government than for merging with Canada:

> At 12 o'clock last night there were manifestations of great rejoicing in this city. Bells were rung, guns fired, blue lights and Roman candles burned and crackers snapped. And people met on the streets and shook hands with and congratulated each other, and cheered, and cheered, and cheered! Everybody seemed happy and jolly and the manifestations were kept up long late in the small hours.[10]

Before British Columbia lay its Canadian era.

[9] *Colonist*, 19 July 1871.
[10] *Colonist*, 20 July 1871.

Epilogue

The Hon. H. L. Langevin arrives from Ottawa — His report on British Columbia — Some events of 1871-1878 — David Sallosalton, the amazing Indian boy — "The Carnarvon Terms" — Loss of the Pacific *— Lord Dufferin's visit — Death of Douglas — March 1878: The centennial of Captain Cook's landing at Nootka.*

In 1871, shortly after British Columbia's entry into the Dominion of Canada, the federal Minister of Public Works, the Hon. H. L. Langevin, was sent out to the Pacific Coast to make a comprehensive report on the new province and, incidentally, to attend to the interests of the Conservative Party. Published early in 1872 but depending upon the final statistics available from the colonial period, Langevin's 246-page report[1] is invaluable for those who want detailed information about the social and economic state of British Columbia when the colonial period was drawing to its close.

Perhaps the most interesting of the numerous statistical tables in the report is Appendix Z (reproduced on the following page) which, though unfortunately leaving the Indians out of account, analyses the population in terms of residence, sex, race and employment.

The portion of the Langevin Report entitled "Manufactures"[2] reveals both the paucity of secondary industry in British Columbia and the extent to which Victoria dominated over New Westminster as far as the colony's few manufactures were concerned:

Victoria is credited with:

> 1 Iron Foundry
> 2 Sash Factories
> Gas Works

[1] *British Columbia: Report of the Hon. H. L. Langevin, C.B.* (Ottawa, 1872).

[2] Pp. 21-22.

Return of the Population of British Columbia; also showing the Births, Deaths, and Marriages, for the year 1870.

County, District or Parish	WHITE		COLORED		TOTAL		CHINESE		PERSONS EMPLOYED IN				Births	Deaths	Marriages
	Males	Females	Males	Females	Males	Females	Males	Females	Agriculture	Manufacturing	Trading	Mining			
Cariboo	835	85	29	3	864	88	670	15	125	17	87	1,450	6	3	7
Comox	74	28	—	—	74	28	—	—	54	—	20	—	3	—	—
Cowichan	134	87	—	—	134	87	—	—	—	—	—	—	—	—	—
Esquimalt Town	74	58	2	—	76	58	7	—	3	—	42	—	—	—	—
Esquimalt and Metchosin	147	80	9	2	156	82	—	—	80	—	12	—	—	—	—
Hope, Yale, and Lytton	640	93	20	3	660	96	305	6	480	30	259	350	31	2	6
Kootenay	103	5	2	—	105	5	139	—	6	—	20	222	—	—	2
Lake and Highland	67	42	3	3	70	45	—	—	119	—	—	—	—	—	—
Lillouet	200	35	3	—	203	35	80	—	90	8	90	95	2	1	2
Nanaimo	395	206	44	48	439	254	35	1	39	—	22	161	20	5	4
New Westminster	891	401	34	3	925	404	26	1	286	198	38	—	43	13	9
North and South Taanish [sic]	114	70	19	10	133	80	—	—	112	—	2	—	—	—	—
Sooke	24	15	—	—	24	15	—	—	23	—	1	—	—	—	—
Victoria City	1,645	1,197	128	89	1,173	1,286	181	30	196	150	609	70	108	17	11
Victoria District	439	392	4	4	443	396	52	—	214	—	101	—	—	—	—
Total	5,782	2,794	297	165	6,079	2,959	1,495	53	1,827	403	1,303	2,348	213	41	41

4 Breweries
2 Distilleries
1 Soap Factory
2 Tanneries
1 Shipyard
2 Lumber Yards

New Westminster, including apparently Burrard Inlet, is credited with:

3 Saw Mills
1 Grist Mill
1 Distillery

The rest of British Columbia could provide only ten sawmills, ten flour mills, and a single quartz mill at Williams Creek in the Cariboo. The output of these flour mills and sawmills would be sold locally.

British Columbia, then, when she entered Canada, was practically without secondary industry and depended almost entirely upon the export of raw materials for her livelihood. The Langevin Report gives British Columbia's five main export industries and their 1870 values as:

Gold	$1,333,745[3]
Furs and hides	177,094[4]
Lumber products	128,257[5]
Coal	96,687[6]
Fish products	31,861[7]

[3] P. 7.

[4] Pp. 148-51.

[5] Pp. 148-51 and p. 5. This figure is lower than normal due to the lengthy closure of one of the Burrard Inlet mills. (In 1869 the value had been $252,154.) Under normal conditions, lumbering was already British Columbia's second most important export industry. The main markets for B.C.'s forest products were, in order of importance this year: Peru, the United Kingdom, China, the colony of Victoria in Australia, the Hawaiian Islands and Mexico.

[6] Langevin, pp. 148-51. Because of the miners' strike this figure is down from the previous year's $119,820 (Langevin, p. 13). Due to the development of the Wellington field, coal mining would increase rapidly and, with the growth in the lumber industry, would soon push furs and hides down into fourth position. The United States provided the market for B.C.'s coal.

[7] Langevin, pp. 148-51. Important in achieving this modest figure were shipments of fish oil (notably dogfish liver oil). Apparently left out of account were 300 cases of salmon shipped to England from the new Annieville cannery in 1870. It was, of course, the coming of the canneries which was to make fishing a major exporting industry.

Agriculture does not figure in this list of exporting industries since it was mostly carried on by small pre-emptors who sold their excess produce locally.

Apart from its gold, $1,047,245 of which still came from the Cariboo, British Columbia at this point had little to offer Canada. It was as a gold colony that it entered confederation.

*   *   *

The first years of British Columbia's Canadian era began to slip past.

1872.   David Sallosalton, the amazing Indian boy missionary, died at the age of nineteen. Born of a pagan family of the Nanaimo tribe, he had by the eloquence of his preaching achieved mass conversions of the Fraser Valley Indians to Methodism. No more would they hear David's famous "Steamboat Whistle Sermon" telling how, just as the Fraser River sternwheelers gave three warning blasts of the whistle before leaving the wharf, so Christ gave repeated calls to those who would travel with him to Heaven, and woe to those who did not heed His call and were left behind.[8]

Sandford Fleming, the Canadian Pacific Railway's engineer-in-chief, came overland through the Yellowhead Pass, convinced that it provided the best route through the Rockies. The old Hudson's Bay Company underwent a major re-organization, but the veteran Roderick Finlayson considered its affairs west of the Rockies beyond recovery.[9] In December Amor De Cosmos became the second premier of British Columbia, succeeding J. F. McCreight.

1873.   The Most Reverend Modeste Demers, first of the Roman Catholic bishops, having gone to his rest, Bishop Charles J. Seghers was consecrated in his stead in St. Andrew's Cathedral, Victoria. Up at Fort St. James, Father Blanchet and Father Le Jacq built the Church of Our Lady of Good Hope. At Gastown, Mr. and Mrs. Richard Alexander had a son, Henry, the first white child born within the limits of the future city of Vancouver.

[8] Thomas Crosby, *David Sallosalton* (Toronto, [1906]), pp. 27-29.

[9] George Barnston to Edward Ermatinger, 11 Sept. 1872. PAC, *Ermatinger Papers.*

1874. A new Liberal government in Ottawa decided to renegotiate the railway clause in the terms of union which had brought British Columbia into Canada. From British Columbia came an answering cry: "The Terms, the whole Terms, and nothing but the Terms". The British Colonial Secretary, the Earl of Carnarvon, was reluctantly accepted by both sides as an arbitrator. "The Carnarvon Terms" proposed that the completion date for the Canadian Pacific Railway be postponed to the end of 1890 but, while C.P.R. surveys were actively continued on the mainland, a railway be built immediately between Esquimalt and Nanaimo.

This year saw the culmination of a tremendous row between the slightly High Church Bishop Hills, and the decidedly Low Church Dean Edward Cridge, with Chief Justice Sir Matthew Begbie (knighted in 1871) granting an injunction forbidding Cridge to continue either as the Dean of Christ Church Cathedral or as a clergyman in the Church of England. Thereupon Cridge transferred his allegiance to the Reformed Episcopal Church and built, close to the cathedral on land donated by Sir James Douglas, the Church of Our Lord. Here he presided as Bishop Cridge. It was all very petty but full of the stuff for a Trollope novel, and it cleft polite society in Victoria in two.

1875. British Columbians were aghast when, in March, the Canadian Senate voted against building the Esquimalt and Nanaimo Railway, the key provision of the Carnarvon Terms. Joseph Trutch, now the Lieutenant-Governor of British Columbia, warned "unless a change of policy be adopted towards us this community will become so alienated from its loyalty to Canada as to be a source of weakness to the Dominion".[10] There was growing separatist feeling and some said that British Columbia should have joined the United States.

A great tragedy marked the year's close — the loss of the steamship *Pacific*. Sailing from Victoria on the morning of November 4th, she sank that same evening after colliding with another vessel off the entrance to the Strait of Juan de Fuca. Of almost two hundred and

[10] Quoted by Ormsby, p. 269.

fifty persons aboard the *Pacific* only two survived. Corpses of the drowned were washed up for forty miles along the shores of Vancouver Island — the body of one young girl being found only a short distance from her Victoria home.

1876. To improve relations between an embittered British Columbia and the government in Ottawa, the elegant Earl of Dufferin, Governor-General of Canada, and his vivacious Countess, journeyed to this remotest of all the provinces. Victoria, out of feeling for the Queen and the homeland, gave them a tremendous reception. Welcoming arches decorated their route through Victoria. The Chinese had erected no less than three, emblazoned with the mottoes "Glad to See You Here", "English Law is Liberal", and "Come Again". Forewarned that one of the arches carried the inscription "Carnarvon Terms or Separation", Lord Dufferin ordered a detour so that he could bypass it. In conversation with prominent British Columbians, and in a speech delivered in Victoria, Dufferin did everything in his power to assure them of the honest intentions and good faith of Alexander Mackenzie, the Canadian prime minister.

The Governor-General and his lady contrived to see a fair amount of British Columbia. Aboard H.M.S. *Amethyst*, which had brought them from San Francisco, they travelled up the northern coast and visited Duncan's famous Christian village at Metlakatla. En route, Lord Dufferin had the ship put into Bute Inlet, which he decided was unsuitable for a terminus for the C.P.R. A second extensive trip took Their Excellencies through the Fraser Canyon and on to Kamloops. ("The Dufferin Coach" is today preserved in the Irving House Museum at New Westminster.) On the last stretch of their drive back to Yale, the Earl and the Countess rode with Steve Tingley up on the "box" of their coach. It was a hair-raising experience careering along the Canyon's narrow road, with no guard rail between the coach and the precipices, but Lady Dufferin enjoyed the thrills. Said Steve Tingley, "There isn't a scare in her."[11]

1877. On the evening of August 2nd old Sir James Douglas experi-

[11] Molyneux St. John, *The Sea of Mountains: An Account of Lord Dufferin's Tour Through British Columbia in 1876* (London, 1877), II:124.

enced pains in his chest and his son-in-law Dr. Helmcken was summoned. The two were conversing cheerfully when suddenly Douglas' head fell back. "The Father of British Columbia" was dead.

Douglas' funeral was the most notable Victoria had ever seen. Schools and places of business were closed. Public buildings and private dwellings were hung with black. The tolling of church bells mingled with the volleying of H.M.S. *Rocket*'s guns. The funeral procession was over a mile long. And so British Columbia's great man departed from the scene. Well nigh half a century had passed since young James Douglas, a clerk in the service of the Hudson's Bay Company, had welcomed Sir George Simpson to Fort St. James.

1878. This March a new sound was heard in British Columbia, the ringing of a telephone.[12] A demonstration was being given in the office of the *Colonist* newspaper in the city of Victoria. One hundred years earlier, in March 1778, H.M.S. *Resolution* and H.M.S. *Discovery* had come gliding into Nootka Sound, and furled their sails and dropped their anchors. Then Captain Cook and his crews had become the first white men ever recorded to have set foot upon the soil of British Columbia.

British Columbia could look back with pride on her first century, and forward with hope to her second.

[12] *Colonist*, 26 March 1878.

Bibliography

1. *Bibliographies of British Columbia*

Strathern, Gloria M. *Navigations, Traffiques & Discoveries 1774-1848: A Guide to Publications Relating to the Area now British Columbia.* Victoria, 1970.

Lowther, Barbara J. *A Bibliography of British Columbia: Laying the Foundations 1849-1899.* Victoria, [1968].

Devoted to books, serials, monographs and offprints, these basic bibliographies unfortunately do not contain periodical articles.

2. *Manuscripts and Typescripts*

Major repositories in Canada include the Provincial Archives of British Columbia (Victoria); the Public Archives of Canada (Ottawa); the Provincial Archives of Manitoba (Winnipeg) where the Hudson's Bay Company's Archives are now deposited; and the Special Collections of the Library of the University of British Columbia. For unpublished theses and dissertations in the latter, see the library's *Reference Publication No. 35 (Theses on British Columbia History and Related Subjects).*

An enormous amount of manuscript material is preserved in Britain, especially in the Admiralty and Colonial Office papers, in the Public Record Office in London. Interesting items are preserved in the Library of the National Maritime Museum at Greenwich. Among the private archives which merit examination are the Newcastle Papers on deposit in the Library of the University of Nottingham.

For American documents and maps, a prime source is the National Archives and Records Service in Washington, D.C. In the Bancroft Library of the University of California, Berkeley, are the materials which H. H. Bancroft, in preparation for his histories of the North-west Coast, obtained from retired officers of the Hudson's Bay Company. Among the more valuable items are:

Anderson, A. C. *History of the Northwest Coast*

Cooper, James. *Maritime Matters on the Northwest Coast and Affairs of the Hudson's Bay Company in Early Times*

Finlayson, Roderick. *History of Vancouver Island and the North-west Coast*

McKay, J. W. *Recollections of a Chief Trader in the Hudson's Bay Company*

Tod, John. *History of New Caledonia & the Northwest Coast*

Typed transcripts of the above, and many other Bancroft items, are in the Public Archives of Canada. Here also may be found the originals of John Tod's letters to Edward Ermatinger.

3. *Newspapers*

Correspondents for *The Times* of London and the San Francisco *Bulletin* were reporting from British Columbia as early as 1858. For a typed transcript of Donald Fraser's British Columbia articles printed in *The Times* between 4 August 1858 and 15 August 1862, see Item E/B/F86 in the Provincial Archives of British Columbia.

This same year of 1858 saw the founding of the first of numerous newspapers, generally short-lived, in British Columbia and its sister colony of Vancouver Island. The two most important are the *Colonist* (originally the *British Colonist*), and the *British Columbian*. For the dates of publication of these and other pioneer newspapers, see pp. 1-7 of the University of British Columbia Library's *Reference Guide 52 (Canadian Newspapers in the UBC Library)*.

4. *A Select Bibliography of Other Printed Materials*

Akrigg, G. P. V. & Helen B. *British Columbia Chronicle, 1778-1846: Adventurers by Sea and Land*. Vancouver, 1975.

Anderson, A. C. *Hand-Book and Map to the Gold Region of Frazer's and Thompson's Rivers*. San Francisco, [c. 1858].

Anderson, James. *Sawney's Letters and Cariboo Rhymes*. n.p. [1862].

Arctander, John W. *The Apostle of Alaska: The Story of William Duncan of Metlakahtla*. New York, [1909].

Bancroft, H. H. *History of British Columbia 1792-1887*. San Francisco, 1887.

Barrett-Lennard, Capt. C. E. *Travels in British Columbia, With the Narrative of a Yacht Voyage Round Vancouver's Island*. London, 1862.

Begbie, Matthew B. "Journey into the Interior of British Columbia". *Journal of RGS* 31 (1861): 237-48.

Begg, Alexander. *A History of British Columbia*. Toronto, 1894.

Brown, Robert. "Explorations in the Interior of Vancouver Island". *Proceedings of RGS* 9 (1864-65) :305-308.

Brown, Rev. R. C. Lundin. *British Columbia: An Essay*. New Westminster, 1863.

———. *British Columbia: The Indians and Settlers at Lillooet: Appeal for Missionaries*. London, 1870.

———. *Klatsassan and other Reminiscences of Missionary Life in British Columbia*. London, 1873.

[Bushby, A.] "The Journal of Arthur Thomas Bushby, 1858-1859", ed. Dorothy Blakey Smith. *BCHQ* 21 (1957-58) :83-198.

Cheadle, W. B. *Cheadle's Journal of Trip Across Canada 1862-1863*, ed. A. G. Doughty and Gustave Lanctot. Ottawa, 1931.

Conway, Alan. "Welsh Gold-Miners in British Columbia During the 1860's". *BCHQ* 21 (1957-58) :51-74.

[Cracroft, S.] *Lady Franklin Visits the Pacific Northwest, Being Extracts from the Letters of Miss Sophia Cracroft. . . .* ed. Dorothy Blakey Smith. Victoria, 1974. (PABC Memoir No. 11.)

Creech, E. P. "Similkameen Trails, 1846-1861". *BCHQ* 5 (1941): 255-67.

Cronin, Kay. *Cross in the Wilderness*. Vancouver, [1960].

Dalzell, Kathleen E. *The Queen Charlotte Islands, 1774-1966*. Terrace, B.C., 1968.

Douglas, James. "Report of a Canoe Expedition along the East Coast of Vancouver Island". *Journal of RGS* 24 (1854) :245-49.

Downie, William. "Explorations in Jarvis Inlet and Desolation Sound". *Journal of RGS* 31 (1861) :249-56.

———. *Hunting for Gold. Reminiscences of Personal Experience and Research in the Early Days of the Pacific Coast from Alaska to Panama*. San Francisco, 1893.

Draper, W. N. "Some Early Roads and Trails in New Westminster District". *BCHQ* 9 (1945) :25-35.

Drumheller, "Uncle Dan". *"Uncle Dan" Drumheller Tells Thrills of Western Trails in 1854*. Spokane, 1925.

Duff, Wilson. "The Fort Victoria Treaties". *BC Studies* 3 (Fall 1969) :3-57.

[Ella, Martha]. "The Diary of Martha Cheney Ella, 1853-1856", ed. J. K. Nesbitt. *BCHQ* 13 (1949) :91-112 and 257-70.

Elliott, Gordon R. *Quesnel: Commercial Centre of the Cariboo.* [Quesnel, 1958].

Fawcett, Edgar. *Some Reminiscences of Old Victoria.* Toronto, 1912.

Fitzgerald, J. E. *An Examination of the Charter and Proceedings of the Hudson's Bay Company with Reference to the Grant of Vancouver's Island.* London, 1849.

Forbes, Charles. *Prize Essay: Vancouver Island: Its Resources and Capabilities as a Colony.* [Victoria], 1862.

Forsyth, J. "The Pioneer Press of British Columbia". B.C. Historical Assn.: *First Annual Report and Proceedings.* [1924]:22-28.

Galbraith, John S. "James Edward Fitzgerald versus the Hudson's Bay Company: The Founding of Vancouver Island". *BCHQ* 16 (1952):191-207.

Gough, Barry M. *The Royal Navy and the Northwest Coast of North America 1810-1914: A Study of British Maritime Ascendancy.* Vancouver, [1971].

Grant, W. Colquhoun. "Description of Vancouver Island". *Journal of RGS* 27 (1857):268-320.

————. "Remarks on Vancouver Island, principally concerning Townsites and Native Population". *Journal of RGS* 31 (1861): 208-13.

Great Britain, Parliament ... *Correspondence Relative to the Discovery of Gold in the Fraser's River District.* London, 1858 (Cmd. 2398, 1st series).

————. *Papers Relative to the Affairs of British Columbia.* Parts 1-4. London, 1859-1862 (Cmd. 2476, 2578, 2724 and 2952, 1st series).

————. *Correspondence Relative to the Discovery of Gold at Queen Charlotte's Island.* London, 1853 (P.P. 788 and 788-I).

[Guillod, H.] "Harry Guillod's Journal of a Trip to Cariboo, 1862", ed. Dorothy Blakey Smith. *BCHQ* 19 (1955):187-232.

Hacking, Norman R. "Steamboat 'Round the Bend': American Steamers on the Fraser River in 1858". *BCHQ* 8 (1944):255-80.

————. "Steamboating on the Fraser in the Sixties". *BCHQ* 10 (1946):1-41.

Harper, J. Russell, ed. *Paul Kane's Frontier.* Toronto, [1971].

Haynes, Bessie D. "Gold on Queen Charlotte's Island". *The Beaver* (Winter 1966):4-11.

[Helmcken, J. S.]. "Helmcken's Diary of the Confederation Negotiations, 1870". ed. W. E. Ireland. *BCHQ* 4 (1940) : 111-28.

[Helmcken, J. S.] *The Reminiscences of Doctor John Sebastian Helmcken*, ed. Dorothy Blakey Smith. Vancouver, [1975].

Hendrickson, J. E. "Two Letters from Walter Colquhoun Grant". *BC Studies* 26 (Summer 1975) : 3-15.

Hewlett, E. S. "The Chilcotin Uprising of 1864". *BC Studies* 19 (Autumn 1973) : 50-72.

Howay, F. W. *The Early History of the Fraser River Mines*. Victoria, 1926. (PABC Memoir No. 6.)

————. "Early Settlement on Burrard Inlet". *BCHQ* 1 (1937) : 101-14.

————. "Early Shipping in Burrard Inlet 1863-1870". *BCHQ* 1 (1937) : 3-20.

————. "The Negro Immigration into Vancouver Island in 1858". *BCHQ* 3 (1939) : 101-13.

————. "The Raison d'Etre of Forts Yale and Hope". *Trans. of the Royal Society of Canada* (1922), Sec. II: 49-64.

Howay, F. W. and E. O. S. Scholefield. *British Columbia from the Earliest Times to the Present* (4 vols.) Vancouver, 1914.

[Inskip, G. H.] "Account of the Plunder of the 'Susan Sturges' ". *Nautical Magazine* 23 (1854) : 209-12.

Ireland, Willard E. "The Annexation Petition of 1869". *BCHQ* 4 (1940) : 267-87.

————. "The Appointment of Governor Blanshard". *BCHQ* 8 (1944) : 213-26.

————. "Captain Walter Colquhoun Grant: Vancouver Island's First Independent Settler". *BCHQ* 17 (1953) : 87-121.

Jackson, C. Ian. " 'A Territory of Little Value': The Wind of Change on the Northwest Coast 1861-67". *The Beaver* (Summer 1967), pp. 40-45.

Jeffcott, P. R. *Nooksack Tales and Trails*. Ferndale, 1949.

Johnson, E. P. "The Early Years of Ashcroft Manor". *BC Studies* 5 (Summer 1970) : 3-23.

Johnson, F. Henry. *John Jessop: Goldseeker and Educator: Founder of the British Columbia School System*. Vancouver, 1971.

Kane, Paul. *The Wanderings of an Artist among the Indians of North America from Canada to Vancouver's Island and Oregon through the Hudson's Bay Company's Territory and Back Again.* London, 1859.

Kemble, J. H. "Coal from the Northwest Coast, 1848-1850". *BCHQ* 2 (1938) : 123-25.

Laing, F. W. "Hudson's Bay Company Lands on the Mainland of British Columbia 1858-1861". *BCHQ* 3 (1939) : 75-99.

————. "Some Pioneers of the Cattle Industry". *BCHQ* 6 (1942) : 257-75.

Lamb, W. Kaye. "Correspondence Relating to the Establishment of a Naval Base at Esquimalt, 1851-57". *BCHQ* 6 (1942) : 277-96.

————. "Early Lumbering on Vancouver Island". *BCHQ* 2 (1938) : 31-53 & 95-121.

————. "The Governorship of Richard Blanshard". *BCHQ* 14 (1950) : 1-40.

————, ed. "Memoirs and Documents relating to Judge Begbie". *BCHQ* 5 (1941) : 125-47.

————, ed. "Two Narratives of the Fraser River Gold-rush". *BCHQ* 5 (1941) : 221-31.

Langevin, H. L. *British Columbia: Report of the Hon. H. L. Langevin, C.B., Minister of Public Works.* Ottawa, 1872.

LeBourdais, Louis. "Billy Barker of Barkerville". *BCHQ* 1 (1937) : 165-70.

Lord, John Keast. *At Home in the Wilderness. What To Do There and How To Do It. A Handbook for Travellers and Emigrants.* London, 1867.

————. *The Naturalist in Vancouver Island and British Columbia.* 2 vols. London, 1866.

Ludditt, Fred W. *Barkerville Days.* Vancouver [1969].

Lugrin, N. deB. *The Pioneer Women of Vancouver Island.* Victoria, 1928.

Macfie, Matthew. *Vancouver Island and British Columbia.* London, 1865.

McGowan, Edward. "Reminiscences". *The Argonaut,* 5 May, 25 May and 1 June 1878.

Mackay, Corday. "The Collins Overland Telegraph". *BCHQ* 10 (1946) : 187-215.

McKelvie, B. A. "The Founding of Nanaimo". *BCHQ* 8 (1944): 169-88.

———. "Lieutenant-Colonel Israel Wood Powell, M.D., C.M.". *BCHQ* 11 (1947):33-54.

McNaughton, Margaret. *Overland to Cariboo*. Toronto, 1896.

Martin, R. M. *The Hudson's Bay Territories and Vancouver's Island*. London, 1849.

Mary Theodore, Sister. *Heralds of Christ the King: Missionary Record of the North Pacific 1837-1878*. New York, 1939.

Mather, Barry. *New Westminster: The Royal City*. n.p. 1958.

Mayne, R.C. *Four Years in British Columbia and Vancouver Island*. London, 1862.

———. "Report on a Journey in British Columbia in the Districts bordering on the Thompson, Fraser, and Harrison rivers". *Journal of RGS* 31 (1861):213-23.

———. "Route in Exploring a Road from Albernie Canal to Nanaimo, in Vancouver Island, in May, 1861". *Journal of RGS* 32 (1862):529-35.

———. "Sketch of the Country between Jervis Inlet and Port Pemberton, on the Lilloet River, a Branch of the Fraser River, British Columbia". *Journal of RGS* 31 (1861):297-302.

[Melrose, R.] "The Diary of Robert Melrose". *BCHQ* 7 (1943): 119-34; 199-218 & 283-95.

Milton, Viscount and W. B. Cheadle. *The North-West Passage by Land*. London, [1865].

[Moody, R. C.] "First Impressions: Letter of Colonel Richard Clement Moody, R.E., to Arthur Blackwood, February 1, 1859", ed. W. E. Ireland. *BCHQ* 15 (1951):85-107.

Moore, James. "The Discovery of Hill's Bar in 1858". *BCHQ* 3 (1939):215-20.

Morice, Rev. A. G. *The History of the Northern Interior of British Columbia*. Toronto, 1904.

Morley, Alan. *Vancouver: From Milltown to Metropolis*. Vancouver, [1961].

Mouat, A. N. "Notes on the Norman Morison". *BCHQ* 3 (1939): 203-14.

Nicol, Eric. *Vancouver*. Toronto, 1970.

Ormsby, Margaret A. *British Columbia: A History.* [Toronto], 1958.

———. "Frederick Seymour, The Forgotten Governor". *BC Studies* 22 (Summer 1974) :3-25.

———. "Some Irish Figures in Colonial Days". *BCHQ* 14 (1950) : 61-82.

Palmer, H. Spencer. "Remarks upon the Geography and Natural Capabilities of British Columbia and the Condition of its principal Gold-Fields". *Journal of RGS* 34 (1864) :171-95.

———. *Report of a Journey of Survey from Victoria to Fort Alexander via North Bentinck Arm.* New Westminster, 1863.

Patterson, R. M. "Trail to the Big Bend". *The Beaver* (Spring 1960) : 38-43.

Peake, Frank A. *The Anglican Church in British Columbia.* Vancouver, 1959.

Pethick, D. *James Douglas: Servant of Two Empires.* Vancouver, [1969].

Pettit, Sydney G. " 'Dear Sir Matthew': A Glimpse of Judge Begbie". *BCHQ* 11 (1947) :1-14.

———. "His Honour's Honour: Judge Begbie and the Cottonwood Scandal". *BCHQ* 11 (1947) :187-210.

———. "Judge Begbie in Action: The Establishment of Law and Preservation of Order in British Columbia". *BCHQ* 11 (1947) : 113-48.

———. "Judge Begbie's Shorthand: A Mystery Solved". *BCHQ* 12 (1948) :293-96.

———. "The Trials and Tribulations of Edward Edwards Langford". *BCHQ* 17 (1953) :5-40.

———. "The Tyrant Judge: Judge Begbie in Court". *BCHQ* 11 (1947) : 273-94.

Reid, Robie L. "How One Slave became Free". *BCHQ* 6 (1942) : 251-56.

———. "John Nugent: The Impertinent Envoy". *BCHQ* 8 (1944) : 53-71.

Reinhart, H. F. *The Golden Frontier: The Recollections of Herman Francis Reinhart 1851-1869,* ed. D. B. Nunis Jr. Austin, [1962].

Richardson, David. *The Pig War Islands.* Eastsound, Wash., 1971.

Rickard, T. A. "Gilbert Malcolm Sproat". *BCHQ* 1 (1937) :21-32.

Robson, Rev. E. *How Methodism Came to British Columbia.* Toronto, [1924?].

Sage, W. N. *James Douglas and British Columbia.* Toronto, 1930.

Sampson, H. S. "My Father: Joseph Despard Pemberton". *BCHQ* 8 (1944): 111-25.

[Sheepshanks, Rev. J.] *A Bishop in the Rough,* ed. D. W. Duthie. London, 1909.

Shelton, W. G., ed. *British Columbia & Confederation.* Victoria, 1967.

Simpson, D. H. "Henry Press Wright: First Archdeacon of Columbia". *BCHQ* 19 (1955): 123-86.

Slater, G. H. "Rev. Robert John Staines: Pioneer Priest, Pedagogue and Political Agitator". *BCHQ* 14 (1950): 187-240.

Smith, Dorothy Blakey. "The First Capital of British Columbia: Langley or New Westminster?". *BCHQ* 21 (1957-58): 15-50.

―――. *James Douglas: Father of British Columbia.* Toronto, 1971.

Smith, Robert L. "The Hankin Appointment". *BC Studies* 22 (Summer 1974): 26-39.

Sproat, G. M. *Scenes and Studies of Savage Life.* London, 1868.

Spry, Irene M., ed. *The Papers of the Palliser Expedition 1857-1860.* Toronto, 1968. (Champlain Society Vol. 44.)

Stenzel, Franz. *James Madison Alden: Yankee Artist of the Pacific Coast, 1854-1860.* Fort Worth, [1975].

[Thomson, James]. *For Friends at Home: A Scottish Emigrant's Letters from Canada, California and the Cariboo 1844-1864,* ed. R. A. Preston. Montreal, 1974.

[Trutch, Joseph]. *Report and Journal of the Proceedings in Connection with the Visit of His Excellency the Late Governor Seymour to the North-West Coast.* Victoria, 1869.

Vancouver Island. *House of Assembly Correspondence Book 1856-1859.* Victoria, 1918. (PABC Memoir No. 4.)

―――. *Minutes of the Council of Vancouver Island 1851-1861.* Victoria, 1918. (PABC Memoir No. 2.)

―――. *Minutes of the House of Assembly of Vancouver Island 1856-1858.* Victoria, 1918. (PABC Memoir No. 3.)

Waddington, A. *The Fraser Mines Vindicated.* Victoria, 1858.

Wade, M. S.   *The Overlanders of '62*. Victoria, 1931. (PABC Memoir No. 9.)

Waites, K. A.   "Responsible Government and Confederation: The Popular Movement for Popular Government". *BCHQ* 6 (1942): 97-123.

Walbran, Capt. J. T.   *British Columbia Coast Names 1592-1906*. Ottawa, 1909.

Walkem, W. W.   *Stories of Early British Columbia*. Vancouver, 1914.

Wild, R.   *Amor De Cosmos*. Toronto, [1958].

[Wilson, C.]   *Mapping the Frontier: Charles Wilson's Diary of the Survey of the 49th Parallel, 1858-1862. . . .* ed. G. F. G. Stanley. Toronto, [1970].

Wolfenden, R., ed.   *The Emigrant Soldiers' Gazette and Cape Horn Chronicle*. [Victoria], 1907.

Woodward, Frances M.   "The Influence of the Royal Engineers on the Development of British Columbia". *BC Studies* 24 (Winter 1974): 3-51.

Wright, E. W., ed.   *Lewis & Dryden's Marine History of the Pacific Northwest*. Portland, 1895. (Reprinted with corrections, New York, 1961).

Index

Abbott (miner), 212, 257-58
Active Pass, 109, 202
"African Rifles", *See under* Militia
Agriculture, 28, 40, 80, 159, 171, 187,
   191, 201, 208-209, 245, 255, 320,
   368, 404, 406
Alaska, 76, 319, 346
Alberni Inlet, 88, 189, 311
Albreda River, 237
Alcohol, 57-58, 59, 61, 71-72, 79, 133,
   182-83, 225, 286, 353, 375
Alexander, Henry, 406
Alexander, Richard, 406
Alexandra Bridge, 9, 123, 272, 317
Alexandria. *See* Fort Alexandria
Allard, Jason, 233
Allard, Ovid, 129
Allen, Charles William, 287
Alston, E. G., 394
Alta Lake, 166
Americans, 1-2, 7, 17, 26, 34, 46, 49,
   50, 97, 106-08, 109, 112, 120,
   121, 123-27, 128, 129, 130-31,
   135-36, 141, 142, 146, 152, 155,
   168, 171-75, 194, 196, 197-98,
   199, 217, 272, 330, 331, 382
American Civil War, 225, 231, 330
Anahim Lake 300n, 302
Anarchist Mountain, 196
Anderson, Alexander Caulfield, 7-9,
   12-13, 86, 117
Anderson, James, 366-67
Anderson Lake, 117, 169, 170, 195
Anderson River, 8-9, 13, 123
Annexation to U.S., 134, 175, 345-46,
   347, 382, 386, 389, 407
Annieville, 405n
Antler Creek, 211-12, 217, 247
Armstrong, Anson, 246, 247
Armstrong, J. C., 360
Ashcroft Manor, 234, 380
Aspinwall, William Henry, 23-24
Australia, 235

"B.X.". *See* Barnard's Express
Babbitt, E. H., 360
Babine Lake and River, 167
Baillie (H.B.C. farm manager), 75
Ball, H. M., 341, 349, 359
Ballads, 165, 244
Ballou, "Billy", 313
Balls, 68, 176, 180, 181, 297
Banfield, W. E., 306
Bank of British Columbia, 250, 258,
   270, 271, 335, 336
Bank of British North America, 258
   270, 335
Barker, Billy, 241-42, 270
Barkerville, 214, 242, 313, 317, 318,
   329, 338; fire of 1868, 365-66,
   380
Barkley Sound, 81, 88
Barnard, Francis Jones, 313, 341, 360
Barnard's Express (B.X.), 273, 313-15
Barnston, John G., 215
Barr, Mr., 95
Barrett-Lennard, Capt. C. E., 204
Barry, James, 338-39
Battenotte, Louis, 274-76
"Battle of Cape Mudge", 223
Bauerman, Dr. Hilary, 113
Bayley, John, 175
Bayliff, Gabriel, 305n
Baynes, Rear-Admiral Robert
   Lambert, 112, 134, 140, 174, 206
Bazalgette, Capt. George, 175
Beam, Adam, 164, 217
Beardmore, Charles, 32, 33
Beaver Harbour, 24, 32
Beaver Lake, 268
Bedwell Harbour, 277
Begbie, Chief Justice Matthew Baillie
   (later Sir Matthew), 134, 140,
   148-49, 151-52, 162, 167-68, 175,
   178, 179, 187; described 216;
   Bowie Knife Speech, 217; 242,
   259-60, 286, 293, 296, 305, 349,
   390, 407

Bella Bella, 59
Bella Coola, 215, 252, 300, 301, 302, 375
Bella Coola River, 252, 302
Bellingham Bay, 61, 106, 121
Bentinck Arm, 252, 277, 300, 302
Bentinck Arm Company, 251, 252
Big Bend of the Columbia, 322-23, 331-34, 352
"Big Jim" (miner), 193
Birch, Arthur Nonus, 312, 324, 340, 347-48
Birkenhead ("Mosquito") Portage, 195
Black, Dr. A. W. S., 360
Blackeye's Trail, 16
Blake, Edward, 400
Blake, Lieut. G. S., 170
Blanchet, Father George, 406
Blanshard, Governor Richard, 28-29, 32, 34, 36, 40, 42-44, 55
Blenkinsop, George, 61
Blessing, Charles Morgan, 338
Blinkhorn, Mrs., 74
Blinkhorn, Thomas, 39, 67
Bogart, Doug., 244-45
Boggs, Dr. Edward B., 285
Bonaparte House, 352
Bonaparte River, 168, 196, 304, 362
Booth, Miss, 363
Boston Bar, 123, 214, 247, 250, 272. See also Quayome
Boucher, Jean Baptiste, 37
Boundary, International, 1-3, 98, 99-101, 171-75. See also British Boundary Commission
Brabant, Father, 373
Brady, William, 277
Breakenridge, Archibald T., 252
Brew, Chartres, 139, 153, 286, 299, 300, 302, 305, 341
Brewster, William, 298, 299
Brideships, 256
Bridge, Admiral Sir Cyprian, 85-86
Bridge River, 334
Brierley Hill Colliery, Staffordshire, 78
Brigades and Brigade Trails, 7-9, 12-16, 26-27, 83-84, 106, 121, 123, 167, 179, 197
Brighouse, Samuel, 261
British Boundary Commission, 98, 99, 101, 112-15, 177, 196

British Columbia
  capital of (mainland colony), 142, 153-54
  capital of (united colony), 342-44, 355-57
  constitution of 1863, 281
  Executive Council, 340, 385
  Legislative Assembly, 402
  Legislative Council, before union with V.I., 281, 291, 292, 335
    after union with V.I., 336, 340-45, 348, 351, 354-57, 359, 378, 385-86, 393-94, 399, 400
  mainland Crown Colony, 112; proclaimed 137; 140-41, 320, 321, 334, 335-36; united with V.I., 336
  naming, 137
British Columbia and Vancouver Island Spar, Lumber, and Sawmill Company, 321, 379
British Columbia Pioneer Society, 397
British North American Exploring Expedition, 179
Brown, Peter, 55
Brown, Rev. R. C. Lundin, 229-30, 256, 280-81
Brown, Dr. Robert, 310
Browning, Rev. Arthur, 157, 158, 159, 214, 243, 259, 263
Browse, Dr., 360
Bruce, Rear-Admiral H. W., 89
Bryant, Cornelius, 158
Bryant, J. C., 241
Buchanan, President James, 175
Buckingham and Chandos, 3rd Duke of, 355, 364, 369
Bulkley, Colonel Charles S., 325, 328
Bulkley House, 325-26
Bulkley River, 166, 328, 329
Bunster, Arthur, 394
Burdett-Coutts, Angela, 184, 220
Burgess, Mr., 289
Burnaby Mountain, 171
Burns (member of McGowan Gang), 146
Burns, Michael, 383-84
Burns Lake, 328
Burrard Inlet, 47, 109, 170-71, 232, 261, 288, 321, 352, 360, 365, 379, 395, 405
Burrard Inlet Mills, 321
Bushby, Arthur, 167, 197

Bute Inlet, 215-16, 252, 297, 299, 302, 408
Bute Inlet Company, 251, 297, 298
Bute Inlet Route, 166, 215-16
Butler, Capt. William, 329-30
Buttle, John, 310
Byam, Lieut., 221

Cache Creek, 168, 250, 332, 352
Cache Creek House, 352
Cadboro Bay, 48, 331, 363
Cadboro Bay Farm, 75, 207
Caledonian Society, 288
California, 26, 105-06, 106-07, 108
California State Telegraph Company, 324
Camels, 251
Cameron, Chief Justice David, 69, 73, 91, 140, 162, 189, 198
Cameron, John "Cariboo", 267-69
Cameron, Mrs. J. (Sophia Groves), 267-69
Cameron, Hon. Malcolm, 259, 279
Cameron, Roderick, 268
Cameron, "Sandy", 268
Camerontown, 258, 269, 317
Campbell, Archibald, 99, 101
Campbell, James, 298
Canada, Dominion of. See Confederation
Canada West. See Ontario
Canadian Company, 349-51
Canadian Pacific Railway, 27, 216, 299, 323, 353, 386, 387, 388, 394-95, 398, 400, 406, 407, 408
Canadians, 160, 199, 249, 286, 288, 365, 381
Cann, Sergeant-Major George, 201
"Canoe Country", 126
Canoe River, 275
Cape Mudge, 202, 222, 223
Capital, controversy over location, 342-44, 355-57
Cardinal, Andre, 237
Cariboo, The, 211-14, 313, 316, 341, 349-51, 360, 394, 404, 406; Cariboo East, 341; Cariboo West, 341
Cariboo Lake, 191
Cariboo mining claims
  Barker, 242
  Beaver, 270
  Black Jack, 270

Cameron, 267, 268
Canadian, 270
Diller, 241, 270
Hard Curry, 270
Saw Mill, 319
Sebastopol, 193
Cariboo Wagon Road, 211, 214, 247, 249-51, 272-73, 289, 313, 317, 325, 332, 397
Carleton, Capt., 371
Carnarvon, H. H. M. Herbert, 9th Earl of, 407
Carnarvon Terms, 407
Carnes Creek, 322
Carpenter (Overlander), 239
Carrall, Dr. R. W. W., 385, 386, 394
Cartier, Sir George, 387
Cary, George Hunter, 139, 180, 186, 198, 294
Cary Castle, 294-95. See also Government House, Victoria
Cayoosh. See Lillooet
Census of 1854, 80
Central Lake, 311
Chain Gangs, 222, 224
Chapman's Bar, 250
Charles (Slave), 198
Charles, William, 239
Chase, 333
Chase River, 57
Cheadle, Dr. Walter Butler, 274-77
Cheakamus River, 166
Chemainus, 277, 278
Cheney, Martha, 67
Cherry Creek, 289
Cheslatta Lake, 254
Chilako River, 254
Chilcotin Forks, 303
Chilcotin Plateau, 215
Chilcotin Uprising, 297-305
Chilko Lake, 304
Chilliwack Lake and River, 121
China Bar, 128
China Rapids, 239
Chinese, 128, 141, 191, 199, 263, 270, 334, 385, 404, 408
Chinook, 264
Choquette, Alexander, 254
Christina Lake, 313
Christensen, Capt., 371, 372
Church Missionary Society, 98, 263, 266

Churches
Anglican, 25, 84, 98, 108, 151, 180,
184-85, 229, 261, 263, 266,
363, 407
Methodist, 157-59, 235, 263, 321,
406
Roman Catholic, 11, 48, 261, 364-
65, 406
See also Missionaries
Clark, Charles, 79
Clayoquot Sound, 306
Clearwater River, 276
Clinton, 250, 273, 394
Coal, 16-17, 23-24, 35-36, 49, 60, 78,
261, 310, 398-99, 405, 405n
Coal-miners, 24, 30, 31, 60, 78
Coldwater River, 8
Collins, Perry McDonough, 324
Collins Overland Telegraph, 324,
328-30, 346
Collyer, Vincent, 382
Colonization, 19-22, 30, 36, 39, 40, 48
Columbia Emigration Society, 256
Columbia River, 1, 93, 179, 312, 322
Columbia River and Kootenay
Electoral District, 341
Colvile Town. *See under* Nanaimo
Colwood Farm, 40, 187
Commercial Inlet, 35
Communications, 48, 58, 60, 115-18,
119, 120-21, 122-23, 123-27, 148-
49, 165-66, 167-68, 169-70, 170,
171, 193, 196, 197, 201, 211,
213-14, 215-16, 218, 219, 232,
235, 251, 252, 272, 273, 289,
297, 302, 313, 322, 332, 352, 392
Comox, 289, 310, 392, 404
Comox Lake, 310
Compton, Sergt., 164
Comrie, Dr. P., 376, 383
Confederation, 225, 344, 348, 358-61,
378-79, 381, 385-88; terms, 388-
89; 398, 398-402; subsequent
discontent, 407, 408
Confederation League, 359
Connolly, Cdr. Matthew, 90
Constance Cove, 16
Conway, Capt. Edmund, 325, 328
Cook, J., 270
Cook, Capt. James, 409
Cook's Ferry, 250, 313
Cooper, Capt. James, 39-40, 44, 57-59,
68, 69, 72, 73, 93

Coquihalla River, 7, 13
Coquitlam River, 311
Cormack, W. E., 281
Cornish Bar, 143, 149
Cornwall, Clement Francis, 234, 341,
380, 394
Cornwall, Henry Pennant, 234, 380
Cottonwood Canyon, 239
Cottonwood House, 214, 313, 317
"Cottonwood Scandal", 259-60
Courcy, Major John de, 174
Courcy, Capt. Michael de, 174
Courtenay, Capt. G. W. C., 16-18
Courtenay River, 310
Cowichan Bay, 255, 310, 392
Cowichan Gap, 64
Cowichan Lake, 310
Cowichan River, 55
Cowichan Valley, 90, 255, 404
Cox, William George, 197, 300, 303,
304, 305, 341, 356, 359
Cracroft, Sophia, 220-21, 390
Craigdarroch Castle, 399
Craigflower Manor and Farm, 221
Craigflower School, 79
Crease, Henry Pering Pellew, 288,
340, 359, 386, 394n
Cricket, 31, 144
Crickmer, Rev. W. Burton, 184
Cridge, Rev. Edward, 84, 107, 108,
184, 185, 407
Cridge, Mrs. E. (Mary Winnell), 84
"Crimea Huts", 85, 102, 203
Crimean War, 75, 77
Crosby, Thomas, 309
Crowley (Jailer), 207
Cultus Lake, 121
Cunard, Samuel, 16, 23
Cunningham, William, 240
Currency, 158, 176
Customs Duties, 119, 194, 335-36
Cutler, Lyman, 171-72
"Czar of Salt Spring Island", 226-27

Dallas, A. G., 139, 172, 177, 181, 344
Dalles des Morts. *See* Death Rapids
"Dancing Bill", 126
Darrah, Capt. Charles J., 113
Davidson, Mr., 248
Davie, Dr. J. C., 381
De Cosmos, Amor, 160-62, 177, 178,
186-87, 218, 321, 341, 344, 359,
360, 361, 394, 406

Deadman's Bend, 128
Dean River, 301
Death Rapids, 312, 332
Decker Lake, 328
Decker's Portage, 195
Deighton, Capt. John ("Gassy Jack"), 288, 353
Deighton House, 353
DeLacy, Capt. W. W., 121
Demers, Bishop Modeste, 11, 48, 364, 406
Denman, Rear-Admiral the Hon. Joseph, 297, 306, 319-20, 331, 339
Departure Bay, 399
Derby (old Fort Langley), 142, 153, 154
Dewdney, Edgar, 197, 322, 349
Dewdney Trail, 197, 313, 322
D'Ewes, John, 230
D'Herbomez, Bishop L. J., 364
Dietz and Nelson Express, 271, 272
Diggle, Lieut. W. N., 399
Diller, I. P., 270
Dixon, Mr., 146-47
Dolan, Major, 150
Donnelly, James, 360
Douglas, Cecilia. *See* Helmcken, Mrs. J. S.
Douglas, James (later Sir James), **7,** 9, 16, 23, 26, 29, 34, 42-43, 44, 47, 49, 50, 55-57, 57-59, 60, **63,** 69, 72-73, 74, 75, 76, 80, 84, 85, 89-90, 93-94, 97-98, 107, 118-19, 130, 136, 140-41, 142, 154, 160-62, 173, 174, 175, 177, 179, 194, 200, 208, 231, 255, 259, 264, 266, 282, 294, 338, 344, 377, 390, 407
appearance, 31, 85
appointed governor of V.I., 43
extends authority to mainland, 98
investigates "Fraser Canyon War", 130-33
resigns from H.B.C. service, 139
becomes governor of British Columbia, 139
relations with Indians, 55-57, 162, 163, 205-08, 278, 293, 310
visits Fraser gold area in 1858, 111
mainland tour of 1860, 195-97
decides to build Cariboo Wagon Road, 214
urges invasion of U.S.A., 231
achievements, 278
knighted, 280
retirement, 279-80, 292-93
death, 409
Douglas, Mrs. J. (Amelia Connolly, later Lady Douglas), 221, 292
Douglas, Mount, 393
Douglas Portage, 9, 12, 123, 201
Douglas Road, 321
"Douglas Vein", 36
Downie, William, 166-67, 215-16, 322
Downie Creek, 322
Dowson, Rev. Richard, 184
Dozier, Mr., 118, 170
Drake, M. W. T., 361
Drumheller, D. M., 311-12
Duels, 143, 180, 217
Dufferin, Frederick Temple Blackwood, 1st Earl of, 408
Dufferin, Countess of, 408
Duncan, William, 98, 263-66, 363, 374
Dundas, Rev. R. J., 185, 227
Dunsmuir, Robert, 398-99

Eagle Pass, 323
East Anderson River, 9
"East Powder Bill", 311
Eayres, Harrison P., 123
Economic Conditions, 145, 191, 296, 320, 321, 334-35, 345, 352, 382, 391
Education, 24, 38, 73, 79, 143, 220, 265, 290
Edwards, William, 252
Egerton, Capt. F. W., 399
Elections, 91, 186-87, 281-82, 361, 393-94
Elliott, Andrew Charles, 311
Elwyn, Thomas, 240, 359
Emory Bar, 131
Enderby, Charles, 20
Englefield Bay, 44
English Bay, 219, 289, 379
Esquimalt, 2, 16, 18, 26, 30, 41, 42, 60, 76-77, 81, 85, 91, 102, 154, 186-87, 225; becomes Royal Navy's Pacific base, 255-56; 330, 347, 360, 388, 389, 404
Esquimalt and Nanaimo Railway, 399, 407
Esquimalt Farm. *See* Colwood Farm
Eutsuk Lake, 254
Evans, Charles, 360
Evans, Dr. Ephraim, 157, 158, 159

Exact Point, 46
Exploration, 7-9, 81-83, 166-67, 215, 310-11, 320
Exports, 405

Falardeau (HBC engagé), 83
"Falls of the Fraser, The", 9
False Creek, 219
Fannin, John, 240
Farquhar, Mr., 95
Farquhar, Rear-Admiral Arthur, 391, 399
Farrell (member of McGowan Gang), 146
Fawcett, Edgar, 227-28, 299-300
Featherstone, H., 311, 360
Female Immigration Board, 391
Fenians, 330-31, 362-63, 368-69, 382-83
Fielding, Joseph, 298
Fifer, Dr., 147, 151, 152, 218
Finances, 119, 250, 279, 291-92, 294, 295, 297, 305, 317, 320, 335-36, 352, 378, 386
Finlay River, 254
Finlayson, Roderick, 4, 6, 17, 25, 26, 35, 37, 57, 81, 205, 406
Fisher, W., 360
Fisheries, 405, 405n
Fitzgerald, James Edward, 20-21
Fitzwilliam, Earl, 58, 59
Fitzwilliam, Hon. C. W. Wentworth. See Milton, Viscount
Fleming, Capt., 198
Fleming, Sandford, 406
"Flying Squadron, The", 390
"Foot of the Rapids, The", 9, 12
Forbes, Dr. Charles, 203, 280
"Forks, The". See Lytton
Forts
    Fort Alexandria, 9, 164, 191, 215, 252, 300, 301, 302, 303, 317
    Fort Bellingham, 172, 173
    Fort Chilcotin, 305 & n
    Fort Colvile (H.B.C.), 12, 86, 93, 179
    Fort Colvile (U.S. Army), 331
    Fort Dallas, 134
    Fort Edmonton, 237, 274
    Fort Garry, 236
    Fort George, 167, 239
    Fort George Canyon, 239
    Fort Hope. See Hope

Fort Kamloops. See Kamloops
Fort Langley, 7, 13, 72, 93, 108, 121, 130, 137, 140-41, 142, 148, 151, 158, 184, 197
Fort Nisqually, 23, 29
Fort Rupert, 24, 31-34, 35, 42, 49, 60, 61, 67, 264
Fort St. James, 167, 325, 406, 409
Fort Shepherd, 93, 180, 313
Fort Simpson, 36, 44, 46, 52, 59, 61, 63, 64, 94, 166, 263, 264, 374
Fort Thompson. See Kamloops
"Fort Union" 131
Fort Vancouver, 1, 2, 7, 25
Fort Victoria. See Victoria
Fort Walla Walla, 2, 11n, 77, 312
Fort Yale. See Yale
Fortier, Jean Baptiste, 78
Fortune, Alexander Leslie, 240
Fountain (The), 118, 143, 168
Foxhounds, 380
Francis, Allen, 271
Franklin, Lady Jane, 220-21, 390
Franklin, Selim, 186
Franklyn, William Hales, 356
Fraser, Donald, 130, 132, 134, 162, 212, 233-34, 334, 344
Fraser, John, 318-19
Fraser, Paul, 83-84
Fraser, Simon, 258, 318
Fraser Canyon, 8-9, 109, 122-23, 128-30, 131-33, 167-68, 191, 201, 214, 249, 408
"Fraser Canyon War", 129-33
Fraser Lake, 328
Fraser River, 13, 94, 219, 250, 275
Fraser Sandheads, 170, 219, 293
Fraser Valley, 201, 368
Freight Charges, 118
French Benevolent Society, 396
French Creek, 322
Fulton, Thomas, 360
Funerals, 227-28, 267, 268, 269, 376-77, 409
Fur Trade, 181, 405

Galiano Island, 101
Gallows Point, 57
Gamage, Rev. James, 184
Garrett, Rev. A. C., 185, 220
Garro, Count Paul de, 160, 218
Geology, 203-04

Georgia, Strait of, 102
German Community, 288, 382, 396
Germany, Kaiser, 175
Gibbs, M. W., 360
Gladstone, Rt. Hon. W. E., 20
Gold
  claims, 131. *See also* Cariboo
    mining claims
  dry diggings, 131
  returns from claims, 193, 212,
    240-42, 268, 270
  value of production, 105, 212-13,
    270, 271, 316, 333, 405, 406
Gold Areas
  Big Bend of the Columbia, 312,
    322-23, 331-34, 352
  Cariboo, 191, 211-13, 233-35, 240-
    48, 249, 268, 270, 271, 288,
    313, 334, 406
  Columbia River near U.S., 93
  Fort Colvile, 86
  Fraser River, 94, 97, 109, 111, 115,
    128-33, 143, 164-66, 191;
    routes to Fraser gold areas,
    106, 108-09, 117-18, 120-21,
    122-23
  Goldstream, 143
  Leech River, 311
  Omineca, 254, 383-84, 398
  Queen Charlotte Islands, 36, 44-46,
    49-50
  Rock Creek, 164, 194-95, 196
  Shuswap, 289
  Similkameen, 164, 193
  Stikine, 254
  Thompson River, 93, 97
  Wild Horse Creek, 311-12, 334
Gold Creek, 332, 334
Gold Escort, 216, 271
Gold Harbour. *See* Mitchell Harbour
Gold-miners, 104, 109, 111, 115, 120,
    122, 123, 130-31, 134, 141-42,
    143, 145, 158, 164, 176, 191, 196-
    97, 216, 221, 228, 229
  attire, 128
  casualties, 128, 129, 133
  clashes with Indians, 124-25, 128,
    129, 130, 133
  cost of provisions, 115, 165, 247,
    317-18
  destitution, 115, 165, 239, 250, 334
  disappointments, 165, 239, 244
  hardships, 165, 212, 214, 246, 367

  licences, 50-51, 98, 119, 121-22, 195
  numbers, 316
  reasons for failures, 243-45
  rewards, 270. *See also* Gold, returns
    from claims
  squander wealth, 257-58
Goldstream River (near Revelstoke),
    322
Goldstream (near Victoria), 143
Golledge, Richard, 90, 95-96
Gooch, Lieut. Thomas S., 99
Gordon, G. Tomline, 186-87, 230-31
Gosset, Capt. W. D., 139
Government House, New Westminster,
    296, 337, 379
Government House, Victoria, 294,
    358, 369, 392
Graham, "Capt.", 129, 133
Grand Forks, 313, 322
Grand Rapids, Fraser River, 238, 239
Grant, Capt. John Marshall, 140, 148,
    151, 211, 283
Grant, John, 349, 350
Grant, Capt. Walter Colquhoun,
    22-23, 28, 30, 31, 38-39, 68-69, 76
Granville, G. G. Leveson-Gower, 2nd
    Earl, 353, 380
Granville, 353
"Granville Despatch", 381
Gray, Willie, 193-94
Gregory, A. J., 312
Grenham, Thomas, 75
Grey, Earl, 19, 20, 21, 28
Griffin, C. J., 174
Grouse Creek, 212
Grouse Creek Bed Rock Flume
    Company, 349-51
"Grouse Creek War", 349-51, 354
Guillod, Harry, 245-46

Hagwilget, 166, 329
Haig, Capt. Robert Wolseley, 113
Hailstone, William, 261
Hall (Fort Constable), 60
Hamilton family, 302
Hamilton, Gavin, 167
Hamley, Wymond O., 139, 340, 394
Hankin, Philip James, 306, 369-70,
    378, 385, 394
Harbottle, Thomas, 247
Hard Curry, Loring & Co., 270, 289
Harewood Coal Mining Company, 398

Harney, General William S., 172-75,
    197-98
Haro Strait, 99, 101, 171
Harris, Thomas, 257
Harrison Hot Springs, 168
Harrison, Joseph, 254
Harrison Lake, 7, 117, 201, 204
Harrison-Lillooet Route, 117-18, 167,
    168, 169-70, 204, 214, 244, 251,
    317, 352
Harrison River, 117, 143, 360
Harvey's Creek, 191, 193
Hassan (Turkish naval officer), 63
Hastings, Rear-Admiral the Hon.
    George F., 331, 364, 368
Hastings Mill, 321, 379
Hat Creek, 168, 196
Havelock, Henry, 360
Hawaii, 25, 28, 204
Hawkins, Lt.-Col. John Summerfield,
    113
Hayman, Rev. Dr. W. E., 375
Haynes, John Carmichael, 312, 351
Hazelton, 166, 328
Hector, James, 180
Heffley, Adam, 251
Hell's Gate, North Thompson River,
    238, 276
Helmcken, Dr. John Sebastian, 30-31,
    32-33, 37, 53-54, 72, 91-92, 106,
    142, 341, 343, 344, 348, 356, 357,
    359, 361, 378, 381, 385, 386-87,
    394, 400, 409
Helmcken, Mrs. J. S. (Cecilia
    Douglas), 31, 53-54
Heron Lead, 350
Hesquiat Harbour, 371
Higgins (Packer), 301, 302
Higgins, D. W., 132, 258, 376
Hills, Rt. Rev. George, Bishop of
    British Columbia, 184-85, 220,
    242, 277, 407
Hill's Bar, 109, 111, 146, 150, 151,
    152
Holbrook, Henry, 281, 359, 360, 361
Holmes, Capt., 331
Holmes (Contractor), 170
Homathko River, 215, 252, 298
Homer, J. A. R., 281, 293
Homfray, Robert, 216
Hope, 16, 27, 120, 124, 128, 133, 134,
    141, 143, 148, 149, 150, 179, 180,
    191, 193, 197, 325, 394, 404

Hornby, Capt. Geoffrey Phipps (later
    Admiral), 174, 390
Hornby, Rear-Admiral Phipps, 16, 41
Horne (Musician), 202
Horne, Adam, 81-83, 88
Horne Lake, 82
Horsefly River, 164, 193
Horseguards Camp, 121
Hospitals, 77, 85, 175, 178, 253, 256,
    258
Houston Stewart Channel, 66
Howay, Judge F. W., 269, 336, 377
Howe Sound, 99, 166
Hubbs, Paul K., 172-73
Hudson's Bay Company, 1, 2, 3, 4, 10,
    12, 13, 16, 17, 18, 19-22, 23, 24,
    25, 26, 27, 28, 29, 31-32, 34-35,
    37, 38, 39, 40, 41, 42, 43, 44, 46,
    48, 49, 50, 55, 59, 69-70, 71, 72-
    73, 74, 75, 77, 78, 80, 81, 82, 83-
    84, 86, 88, 90, 93, 95-96, 97, 129,
    134, 139, 141, 148, 153, 157-58,
    167, 171-72, 176, 177, 181, 209,
    213, 221, 226, 264, 273, 304, 319,
    322-23, 324, 333, 334, 336, 344,
    381, 397, 406
    colonization of Vancouver Island,
        19-22, 40
    "Fur trade reserve", Victoria, 22,
        36, 41
    grant of Vancouver Island, 21
    grant of Vancouver Island
        cancelled, 141
    profits, 84, 213
    revocation of special rights on
        mainland, 141
    See also Forts
        Brigades and Brigade Trails
Humphrey, Mr., 272
Humphreys, Thomas B., 394
Hurdy-gurdy girls, 366

Immigration, 30, 40, 104, 106-07, 108,
    112, 233, 240
Indians, 143, 148, 162, 167, 220, 351,
    352, 389
    alcohol, 59, 133, 144, 182-83, 225,
        286, 308, 326, 363-64, 374, 375
    Christian, 265-66, 308, 363-64, 365
    clashes with whites, 34, 66, 111,
        124-27, 128, 129-30, 222, 277-
        78
    diseases, 37, 206, 252-54, 308, 383

gold, 44, 46-47, 93, 96-97, 111, 128, 191
inter-tribal fighting, 36-37, 64-65, 67, 75, 81-82, 159, 163, 205-08, 224, 253, 373
lands, 190-91, 196, 255, 293, 309
land treaties, 34-35
military or naval action against, 42, 55-57, 89-90, 203, 223-24, 277-78, 306-08
mistreatment by whites, 124, 125, 128-30, 131-33, 304
individuals
  A-chee-wun, Chief, 278
  Alexis, Chief, 303, 304
  Anahim, Chief, 302, 303
  Anayitzaschist ("John"), 372-73
  Bear Skin, Capt. (Chief), 61
  Bear Skin, Mr., 61
  Blackeye, 13
  "Canary", 225
  Cap-Chah, Chief, 306, 307, 308
  Chamutstin, 35
  Chessus, 305
  Clah, 264
  Coochaps, 35
  Dick, 92
  Ea-qui-ok-Shittle, 307
  Edensah (Edensaw?), 225
  Edensah, Chief, 51-53, 61, 65, 66
  George, Chief, 162
  Hay-hay Kane, 35
  Hoquymilt, 35
  Jefferson, Capt. (Chief), 223
  John, Capt. (Chief), 206-07
  Kalsaymit, 35
  Kamostitchel, 35
  Katina, 373
  King Freezy (Chief), 86
  Klatsassin, Chief, 298, 301, 303, 304, 305
  Klymtedza, 301
  Kwal-a-kup, 393
  Legaic, Chief, 265
  Lolo, Jean Baptiste (Chief), 169, 277
  Minayiltin, 35
  Nee-ta-Kim, 372
  Neyahshnawah, Chief, 264
  Nicholas, Chief. See Nicola, Chief
  Nicola, Chief, 10-11, 125, 127
  Pahallak, Chief, 8
  Pee shaymoot, 35
  Pierre, 305
  "St. Paul". See Lolo, Jean Baptiste
  Scowell, Chief, 52
  See-sachasis, 35
  Shawstun, Chief, 6
  "Sir Robert Peel", 225
  Suseechus, Chief, 129
  "Sweet William", Chief, 64
  Tahpit, 303, 305
  Telloot, Chief, 298, 304, 305
  Thlamie, 35
  Tsatsulluc, 35
  Winnets, 225
Northerners trouble Victoria, 74-75, 159, 162-64, 205-08, 222, 253
policemen, 225
population, 18, 253, 385
potlatches, 64-65
"prophets", 11
relations with whites, 33, 82, 97, 278, 308, 325-27
reservations, 291, 309, 362, 368
seize ships, 46, 51-53, 162, 223, 306
slaves, 6, 64, 82
superstitions, 5-6, 11, 97, 297, 363
thievery, 182, 202, 222, 223, 252, 297
Tribes and bands
  Ahousat, 306-08
  Alberni. See See-shaad
  Babine, 11
  Bella Bella, 163
  Bella Coola, 252, 253, 302
  Bonaparte, 362
  Cape Mudge, 82
  Carrier, 253
  Charcheena, 163
  Chilcotin, 253, 297-305
  "Couteau" or "Knife", 128-30
  Cowichan, 55-56, 75, 88-90, 277
  Duncash, 163
  Haida, 36, 44, 46-47, 66-67, 81-82, 162-63, 206-08, 223-24, 286
  Hesquiat, 372-73
  Kinniak-an-Geak, 363
  Kitlootsah, 264
  Kwakiutl, 163
  Lamalchi, 277-78
  Lillooet, 168, 196
  Manu-wissett, 307
  Masset, 51-53, 66

Nahwitti, 32, 41-42
Nanaimo, 35, 56-57, 67, 78, 309-10, 406
Nass, 364, 373
Nicola, 126, 127
Nitinat, 99, 162
Okanagan, 124-27
Qualicum, 81-82
See-shaad, 82-83, 88, 189-91
Shuswap, 125, 237, 275
Sinahomas, 6
Skidegate, 64-65
Songhees, 5, 86, 162, 163
Stikine, 163
Teechamitsa, 34
Thompson, 97
Tongass, 74, 206
Tsimpsean, 37, 64-65, 67, 74, 163, 264, 286, 373
Yuculta, 202, 224, 253
Villages
    Kincolith, 364, 374
    Sik-tok-kis, 306
    Moo-yah-hah, 307
    Nacoontloon, 302
    See also Masset, Nitinat, Skidegate
Women, 229-30, 253, 286, 299, 325-26
Industries, 403, 404
Ingram, Henry, 251
Inskip, George Hastings (Master, R.N.), 66
Ireland, Willard, 382

Jackass Mountain, 123, 201
James Island, 101
Jamieson, Archibald, 218
Jamieson, James B., 218
Jamieson, Capt. S. B., 218
Jenkins, J. J., 312
Jervis Inlet, 166
Jews, 287, 382
Johnson, Cdr. Charles Richardson, 30
Jourdain (gold-miner), 212

Kamehameha, Prince Lot, 204
Kamloops, 8, 9-11, 12, 83, 86, 94, 97, 126, 127, 169, 179, 238, 277, 289, 408
Kamloops Lake, 127, 168, 289, 332
Kanakas, 34

Kananaskis Pass, 77
Kane, Paul, 4-7
Keefers, 129
Keithley Creek, 191, 193, 211, 244
Kekuanoa, Hon. M., 204
Kelly, Mr., 241
Kennedy, Governor Arthur Edward, 294, 297, 306, 308, 309, 310, 320, 337
Kennedy, Dr. John F., 66, 91, 92
Kequeloose, 9
Ker, Robert, 359
Keremeos, 179, 196, 351
Kettle River, 197
King, W. C., 360
"King George Men", 163, 190
Kingcome, Rear-Admiral John (Vice-Admiral 1864), 288, 300
Kispiox River, 328
Kootenay Lake, 179
Kootenay River, 3, 179
Kootenays, 311, 322, 341, 394, 404
Kuper, Capt. Augustus L., 50
Kynumpt Harbour, 375

Labine, Leon, 78
Labouchere, Rt. Hon. Henry, 89, 94, 97
Lac La Hache, 250, 360
Lacourse, Francois, 70
Lady Franklin Pass, 221
Lady Franklin Rock, 9, 221
La Fleur Company, 322
La Force, Vital, 383-84
Lake boats. *See* Ships
Lancashire Relief Fund, 285
Land, acquisition of, 22, 133, 153, 154, 160, 170, 190-91, 208-09, 255, 283
Langara Island, 51
Langevin, Hon. H. L., 403
Langford, Capt. Edward E., 40, 60, 61, 91, 187-89
Langford, Mrs. E. E., 40, 61
Langford, George, 40
Langford, Mary, 61
Lascelles, Lieut. the Hon. Horace D., 287, 398
Laumeister, Frank, 251
Law, 131, 141, 167-68, 197, 198, 207, 217, 336, 350
Law Courts, 43, 69, 89, 135, 152, 179, 182-83, 217, 286, 305, 351, 373

Lawyers, 135-36, 286
Leech, Lieut. P. J., 143, 310, 311
Leech River, 311
Lefevre (cook), 10
Legace, Pierre, 46
Legarre, Pierre. *See* Legace, Pierre
Leggett, Caroline Mary, 283
Leigh, Mr., 96
Le Jacq, Father J. M., 406
Leon (cook), 59-60
Lewis, Thomas B., 250, 251
Libraries, 180, 318
Lieutenant-Governor, 145, 200
Lightning Creek, 212, 245
Lillooet, 7, 117, 168, 185, 196, 229-30, 250, 256, 272, 311, 339, 341, 360, 394, 404
Lillooet Lake, 117, 195
Lillooet River, 117, 334
Lira, Mr., 140
"Liverpool Jack", 143
Loch Lomond House, 273
Lodestone Mountain, 16
Lord, John Keast, 113-15
Loring, J., 270
Lowe, Rev. R. L., 185
Lowhee Creek, 212
Lowndes, Mr., 373, 374
Luard, Capt. Henry Reynolds, 155, 283, 284
Lulu Island, 205
Lumbering, 18, 28, 189, 191, 288, 365, 379, 405, 405n
Lyall, Dr. David, 113
Lytton, Sir Edward Bulwer, 112, 119, 133, 137, 138-39, 142, 176, 178
Lytton, 117, 143, 164, 168, 196, 250, 311, 341, 360, 380, 394, 404

Macaulay, Donald, 60, 63
Maitland, Rear-Admiral Sir Richard, 221
Maka Creek, 8
Maksutoff, Prince, 319
Manning, William, 303
Manson, Donald, 12-13, 69, 83-84
Manson Mountain, 13, 83
Mara, John Andrew, 240
Marble Canyon, 168
Margary, Mr., 95
Marks, Frederick, 277
Marten, George, 322, 323
Martin, J. E., 270

Martin, "Paddy", 147
Martin, R. M., 20
Mary Hill, 153
Masonic Order, 288
Masset, 51, 65, 66
Matilda Creek, 306
Matsqui, 368
Mayne, Lieut. Richard Charles, 148-49, 151, 152-53, 167, 168-69, 203, 263
Mayne Island, 101, 109, 277
Mead, James, 182
Measles, 383
Melrose, Robert, 71-72, 79
Metchosin, 39, 58, 360, 404
Metlakatla, 263-66, 373-74, 408
Military reserves, 201
Militia: "African Rifles" (Victoria). *See* Victoria Pioneer Rifle Corps
  Nanaimo, 224
  New Westminster Home Guards, 331
  New Westminster Volunteer Rifle Corps, 284-85, 295, 296, 300, 302
  Seymour Artillery Company (New Westminster), 331, 337
  Vancouver Island Rifle Volunteers. *See* Victoria Rifle Volunteers
  Victoria Pioneer Rifle Corps, 224
  Victoria Rifle Volunteers, 224
  Victoria Voltigeurs, 55, 57, 90, 278
  Victoria Volunteer Regiment of Rifles. *See* Victoria Rifle Volunteers
Miller, D. W., 360
Milton, C. W. Wentworth Fitz-william, Viscount, 58, 273-77
Miners' Bay, 109
Mission Creek, 217, 263
Missionaries
  Protestant, 98, 157-59, 184-85, 229-30, 263-66, 363, 406
  Roman Catholic, 11, 364-65, 373, 406
Mist, Cdr. H. W., 373-75
Mitchell, Capt. William, 44
Mitchell Harbour (Mitchell Inlet), 44, 49-50, 61
Moberly, Walter, 250, 251, 323, 333
Moffett, Hamilton, 67
Monashee Mountains, 312, 323

Monck, Charles Stanley Monck, 4th
    Viscount, 358
Montagu Harbour, 278
Moody, Col. Richard Clement, 139,
    145, 148-53, 153-54, 170, 177,
    180, 200-01, 205, 209, 252, 282-
    84
Moody, Mrs. R. C., 145, 177
Moody, Sewell ("Sue"), 321, 379
Moodyville, 379
Moreland, Dud, 259
Moresby, Rear-Admiral Fairfax, 41,
    50
Moresby, Lieut. John, 55
Morice, Father A. G., 11, 254n
Morton, John, 261
Mosely, Edwin, 298-99
Moses, W. D., 338
Mosquitoes, 114-15, 248
Moyie River, 313, 322, 334
Muir, John, 24, 68, 91, 92
Mule Tax, 170
Munro, Thomas, 38
Murchison Rapids, 238, 276
Murderer's Bar. See Cornish Bar
Murders and Massacres, 32, 55, 67,
    81-82, 99, 109, 125, 126, 205,
    227, 271, 277, 288, 298, 299,
    301-02, 303, 304, 306, 338, 363
Murray, Pat, 270
Musgrave, Governor Anthony, 377-82,
    391-92, 396, 400
Musgrave, Mrs. A. (Jeannie Lucinda
    Field), 391-92
Music, 63, 202, 226, 396
Musqueam, 47
Mystic Spring, The, 363

McClellan, John, 312
McClure, Leonard, 321, 339
McCreight, J. F., 406
McCulloch Creek, 322, 334
Macdonald, Alexander, 300, 301
McDonald, Angus, 86
MacDonald, Ben, 212
Macdonald, Sir John A., 378
Macdonald, Ranald, 215
Macdonald, William John, 90, 95-96,
    341
McDonald & Co., 212, 258
McDougall (Packer), 300, 301, 302
McGowan, Ned, 145-47, 150-53
McIlmoyl, James, 247

McKay, Joseph William, 35, 59-60,
    90, 91, 92, 95-96, 118, 166, 238
Mackenzie, Sir Alexander, 215, 252
Mackenzie Alexander, 408
McKenzie, Colin, 215
McKenzie, Kenneth, 182
McKibben, Lieut., 197
McLarty, Adam, 360
McLean, Donald, 86, 94, 97, 127, 141,
    304
McLeese Lake, 288
McLennan, Jack, 129
McMicking, Robert Burns, 240
McMicking, Thomas R., 236
McMillan, J. E., 360
McNeill, Lucy, 67 & 67n
McNeill, Capt. William Henry, 31, 46,
    94
McRoberts (contractor), 201

Nagle, Capt., 230
Nanaimo, 49, 56, 60, 67, 81, 91, 158,
    222, 258, 285-86, 289, 341, 356,
    392, 393, 394, 398-99, 404
    Coal discovered, 35-36
    Princess Royal pioneers arrive, 78
Nanaimo River, 35, 49
Nass River, 363
Nathan, Henry, 394
Nechako River, 167
"Ned McGowan's War", 145-53
Needham, Chief Justice Joseph, 350,
    351, 373, 390
Negroes, 106-08, 146, 186, 198, 224,
    338, 385, 404
Nelson, Hugh, 360, 361, 394
Nevin, Charles A., 37
New Brighton, 321
New Caledonia, 3, 11, 12, 69, 83, 137,
    213, 364
New Westminster, 153-54, 156, 157,
    158-59, 170, 199-200, 215, 219,
    232-33, 251, 258-59, 271, 281-82,
    283, 288, 290, 294, 295, 297, 311,
    312, 321, 324, 329, 331, 337, 341-
    42, 352, 357-58, 359, 360, 362,
    365, 379, 394, 404, 405, 408
    designated capital, 154
    assay office, 176-77
    described 1860, 200
    described 1864, 296
    Holy Trinity Church, 185, 233
    Hyack Fire Company, 290, 296, 337

mint, 258
Royal Columbian Hospital, 258, 285
ceases to be capital, 355-57
New York Bar (Fraser River), 128
New Zealand, 235
Newcastle-Under-Lyme, Henry
 Pelham Pelham-Clinton, 5th
 Duke of, 20, 59, 76, 178, 230-31,
 259, 279
Newspapers:
 British Colonist (later *The
  Victoria Colonist*), 160-62, 409
 British Columbia Tribune (Yale)
  339
 British Columbian, 218, 318, 339,
  379
 Cariboo Sentinel, 318, 366
 Christian Guardian, 159
 Courier de la Nouvelle Caledonie,
  160
 Emigrant Soldiers' Gazette, 155
 Nanaimo Tribune, 345
 New Westminster Times, 218
 San Francisco Bulletin, 120, 130
 San Francisco Herald, 135
 Times, (London), 92, 130, 233-34.
  See also Fraser, Donald
 Victoria Daily Evening Express, 287
 Victoria Gazette, 108, 160
 Victoria Morning News, 345
Newton, William, 95-96
Nicol, C. S., 341
Nicola Lake, 8, 121, 168, 196
Nicola River, 8, 168, 196
Nicoamen River, 93
Nicomen, 368
Nimpo Lake, 300, 300n, 302
Nind, Philip Henry, 211, 215
Nitinat, 99, 162, 310
Nobili, Father John, 11
Nootka Sound, 219
Norris, J. D., 360
North Pender Island, 101, 102, 277
North Road, 171
North Thompson River, 237-38,
 254, 276
Northern Pacific Railroad, 397-98
Nugent, John, 135-36

Oak Bay, 226
O'Beirne, Eugene Francis, 274-77
Ogden, Peter, 70, 213
Ogden, Peter Skene, 16

Okanagan District, 7, 179, 240, 263
Okanagan Lake, 124
Okanagan route to the goldfields,
 106, 123-27
Oliver, Mr. (actor), 205
Omineca, 254, 383-84, 398
Ontario, 160, 235
Oppenheimer, Charles, 250, 251
O'Reilly, Peter, 195, 341, 359
Ormsby, Margaret A., 250
Osoyoos Lake, 196
Ottawa, 386
Otter Lake, 16, 121
"Overland Bob", 311
Overland immigrants, 77
Overlanders of 1862, 235-40, 274, 275
 companies
  Acton, 236
  Chatham, 236
  Goderich, 236, 238
  Huntingdon, 236, 239
  London, 236
  Montreal, 236
  Ogdensburgh, 236
  Ottawa, 236
  Queenston, 236, 239
  Redgrave, 239
  St. Thomas, 236
  Scarborough, 236
  Symington, 239
  Toronto, 236, 238
  Waterloo, 236
  Whitby, 236

Pacific Mail Steamship Company,
 24, 35
Pakington, Sir John, 55
Palliser, Capt. John, 179-80
Palmer, Lieut. Henry Spencer, 155,
 167, 169-70, 179, 252, 253, 283,
 284, 285
Palmer, "General" Joel, 164
Pandosy, Father Charles Marie, 263
Parke, Lieut., 101
Parke, Philip, 352
Parliament, Canadian, 401
Parsons, Capt. Robert Mann, 138,
 140, 283-84
Pavilion Lake, 168
Pearse, Benjamin William, 95-96
Peers, Henry Newsham, 13, 16
Peers Creek, 13
Pelly, Sir John, 19

Pemberton, Augustus F., 162, 180,
    182-83, 206, 394
Pemberton, Joseph Despard, 41, 91,
    92, 95-96, 341, 359
Pemberton, 166, 170
Pender, Cdr. Daniel, 102-03
Pender Harbour, 102
Pender Hill 102
Pender, Mount, 103
Pender Point, 102
Pender Rock, 103
Pender Street, Vancouver, 103
Pend-d'Oreille River, 86
Perrier, George, 146-47, 151
Perry Creek, 334
Petropavlovsk, 76, 85
Pettit, Sydney G., 260
Phillippo, George, 394
Picken, Mr., 247
Pickett, Capt. George E., 172-74
Pidwell, John T., 157, 158
"Pig War", 171-75
Pike, Cdr. John W., 306, 307
Pike Guards, 129
Pike's Riffle, 250
Pioneer Mills, Burrard Inlet, 288
Pitt Lake and River, 311
Plays. See Theatre
Podunk Creek, 16
Point Grey, 379
Point Roberts, 3, 122, 140
Police, 134, 139, 143
Polk, President James A., 2
Pope, Major Franklin L., 325
Population, White, 59, 80-81, 104,
    143, 199, 200, 249, 256, 295, 317,
    320, 321, 379, 385, 391, 403
Porcher, Cdr. Edwin A., 350
Porlier Pass, 64
Port Augusta. See Comox
Port Douglas, 118, 143, 170, 195, 272
Port McNeill, 17
Port Moody, 171
Port Pemberton. See Pemberton
Port Renfrew, 310
Port San Juan. See Port Renfrew
Port Townsend, 106
Powell, Dr. Israel Wood, 361, 381
Powers (contractor), 201
Pre-emption of land, 208-09
Press. See Newspapers

Prevost, Capt. James Charles, 60, 61,
    64, 66, 98, 99, 101, 111, 140, 162,
    263
Princeton, 196, 197
Pringle, Rev. A. St. D. F., 184
Prize essays, 280-81
Prostitution, 163, 228, 229, 257
Protection Island, 57
Puget's Sound Agricultural Company,
    40, 81, 187
Puntledge River, 310
Puntzi Lake, 302, 303, 304

Qualicum River, 81
Quamichan district, 255
Quayome, 123, 168
Queen Charlotte Islands, 36, 44-47,
    49-53, 61, 63, 66, 166, 371
Queen Charlotte Coal Company, 375
Queenborough or Queensborough. See
    New Westminster
Quesnel (Quesnelmouth or Quesnelle
    City), 214, 239, 258, 305, 313,
    317, 325, 328, 329, 338, 360, 383
Quesnel Forks, 191, 217, 244, 247
Quesnel River, 164, 193

Railways, 27, 166-67, 273
Raney, Irvine, 247
Reinhart, Herman Francis, 123-27
Responsible government, 160-61, 218,
    259, 361, 389, 400, 402
Revelstoke ("The Big Eddy"), 322,
    333
Richards, Capt. George H., 101-02,
    143, 163, 201, 203, 219, 220
Richfield, 214, 258, 267, 305, 317, 365
"Ride and tie", 194n
Ring, D. Babington, 180
Rivalry between Victoria and New
    Westminster, 178-79, 215, 219,
    251, 271, 293, 296, 318, 341-44,
    356-57, 358, 394-95
Rivals, The, 95-96
River Boats. See Ships
Rivers, Dick, 268
Roadbuilding, 166, 170, 195, 197,
    201, 211, 214, 247, 249-51, 272-
    73, 279, 289, 298, 313, 317, 332.
    See also Communications
Roadhouses, 118, 169, 273, 352
Robinson, "Major", 127

Robinson, George, 78
Robson, Lieut. Charles R., 202, 220, 223, 227
Robson, Rev. Ebenezer, 157, 158, 218, 321
Robson, John, 218, 259-60, 286, 292, 293, 341, 346, 359, 360, 362, 379
Rock Creek 164, 194-95, 196-97, 313, 322
"Rock Creek War", 195, 197
Rogers, Jerry, 379
Rooney, Capt. Matthew, 51-53
Rosario Strait, 99, 171
Rose, Alexander, 360
Rose, John, 212
Rose Harbour, 66
Rose Spit, 51
Rouse, "Capt.", 129
Rowe (lunatic surveyor). See "Czar of Salt Spring Island"
Royal Engineers, 112, 130, 138-39, 140, 145, 151, 153, 155, 157, 169, 170, 177, 181, 195, 201, 211, 214, 249, 282-84, 285, 291. See also British Boundary Commission
Royal Marines, 130, 153, 154-55, 157, 175, 183, 195, 206, 257, 369
Royal Navy, 2, 16, 26, 41, 75, 85, 89-90, 143, 154, 174, 183, 202, 208, 221, 225, 227, 255, 287, 347. See also Ships
Rupert's Land, 273, 344, 381
Russia, 75-77, 324, 346
Russian American Company, 77, 319
Rutkovski, A., 319

Saanich, 55, 207, 227, 404
Sailors Bar, 115
St. Agnes' Well, 168
St. Alice's Well, 168
St. Paul, Mount, 169
Sallosalton, David, 406
Salt Spring Island, 101, 107, 222, 223, 226-27, 360
San Francisco, 105, 107, 108, 177, 202, 258, 323, 331
San Juan Boundary Dispute, 99-101, 171-75
San Juan Islands, 99, 100, 101, 171-75
Sanders, E. H., 341
Sansum, Lieut. Arthur, 56
Sapperton, 157, 159, 171, 177, 181, 282, 296

Saturna Island, 101, 277
Savona's Ferry, 332, 333
Sawmill Claim (Burrard Inlet), 321
Sawney's Letters, 366-67
Schubert, August, 236, 238
Schubert, Catherine, 236, 238
Schubert, Rose, 238
Scott, General Winfield, 175
Seabird Island, 120
Seddall, Dr. John Vernon, 284
Seelye, H. E., 387
Seghers, Bishop Charles J., 406
Seliger, E. O., 396
Selkirk Mountains, 322
Semiahmoo Bay, 114, 197, 232
Semlin, Charles Augustus, 352
Seton Lake, 117, 170, 195
Seward, William Henry, 346
Seymour, Governor Frederick, 295-97, 299-300, 302-05, 309, 312, 322, 324, 335-36, 337, 342, 344, 345, 348, 349-51, 354-57, 358, 361, 364, 369-70, 372, 373-75; death, 375-76; 377-78
Seymour, Mrs. F. (Florence Maria Stapleton), 337, 357
Seymour Arm, Shuswap Lake, 323, 332
Seymour City, 332, 333, 334, 352
Shaw, "Lieut.", 133
Shawnigan district, 255
Shay (Indian spirit), 204
Sheep Creek, 313
Sheepshanks, Rev. John, 185, 233
Shepherd, Capt. John, 26
Sheridan, Richard Brinsley, 95
Ships
  H.M.S. Alert, 331
  H.M.S. Amethyst, 408
  H.M.S. Bacchante, 221, 255
  H.M.S. Boxer, 390
  H.M.S. Brisk, 85
  H.M.S. Chameleon, 277-78, 284
  H.M.S. Charybdis, 390
  H.M.S. Constance, 16-17
  H.M.S. Cormorant, 17
  H.M.S. Daedalus, 34, 41
  H.M.S. Daphne, 42
  H.M.S. Devastation, 277-78, 286, 306, 307
  H.M.S. Dido, 85
  H.M.S. Driver, 29, 30
  H.M.S. Endymion, 391

H.M.S. *Forward*, 202, 219-20, 223-
24, 227, 257, 277-78, 287, 295,
299, 331
H.M.S. *Ganges*, 134, 174, 206
H.M.S. *Grappler*, 202, 227, 277,
399
H.M.S. *Havannah*, 112
H.M.S. *Hecate*, 102, 203, 219, 225,
227, 255
H.M.S. *Inconstant*, 26
H.M.S. *Liffey*, 391
H.M.S. *Liverpool*, 391
H.M.S. *Monarch*, 85
H.M.S. *Pandora*, 16, 18
H.M.S. *Pearl*, 391
H.M.S. *Phoebe*, 391
H.M.S. *Pique*, 76
H.M.S. *Plumper*, 101, 102, 103,
111, 143, 148, 154, 174, 176,
177, 202, 203, 219, 261
H.M.S. *Portland*, 41, 98
H.M.S. *President*, 76, 85
H.M.S. *Pylades*, 154
H.M.S. *Rocket*, 409
H.M.S. *Satellite*, 98, 111, 121, 122,
130, 140, 144, 148, 162, 174,
176, 203, 263
H.M.S. *Scylla*, 391
H.M.S. *Sparrowhawk*, 331, 358,
364, 372, 373-76, 383, 390,
391, 397
H.M.S. *Sutlej*, 288, 297, 300, 306,
307, 339
H.M.S. *Termagant*, 202
H.M.S. *Thetis*, 50, 55
H.M.S. *Topaze*, 203, 227, 255, 288
H.M.S. *Tribune*, 154, 163, 174, 293
H.M.S. *Trincomalee*, 67, 68, 89
H.M.S. *Virago*, 52, 60-61, 63-67,
76, 263
H.M.S. *Zealous*, 331, 390
U.S.S. *Active*, 85
U.S.S. *Newburn*, 390
U.S.S. *Saginaw*, 330
Albion, 34
Alert, 371
Alice, 40
Alpha, 391
Beaver, 32, 55, 57, 78, 102, 140,
172, 255
Cadboro, 34
Caledonia, 143, 212
Cariboo, 218

Cecil, 50
Champion, 195
Colonel Moody, 195
Columbia, 25, 39
Commodore, 106
Consort, 219
Cortez, 108, 222
Demaris Cove, 46
Duchess of San Lorenzo, 73
Eagle, 50
Eliza Anderson, 198
Emily Harris, 299
Emma Rooke, 204
England, 32
Enterprise, 148, 149, 317
Exact, 46
Florencia, 219
Flying Dutchman, 233, 288
Fort Yale, 218
Forty-Nine, 331, 334, 352
George Emery, 73-74
Georgianna, 46-47
Growler, 371
Harpooner, 23, 24
John Bright, 371-73, 396
Kingfisher, 286, 306-08
La Plata, 138
Labouchere, 158, 339
Lady of the Lake, 195
Langley, 286
Leviathan, 297, 324
Marquis of Bute, 84
Marsella, 195
Marten, 333, 352
Mary Dare, 33
Massachusetts, 174
Meg Merrilies, 189
Mexican, 50
Milton Badger, 325
Nanaimo Packet, 374-75
Norman Morison, 30, 31, 32, 40, 78
Orizaba, 108
Otter, 69, 89, 111, 140, 212, 264
Pacific, 407-08
Palerma, 50
Petrel, 286
Prince of Wales, 397
Princess Royal, 78
Recovery, 50, 55, 78, 121, 140, 157
Royal Charlie, 206
Sea Bird, 120
Sierra Nevada, 270
Sir James Douglas, 337, 392

Surprise (1), 120, 122
Surprise (2), 371
Susan Sturges, 50, 51-53, 65
Swiss Boy, 162
Templar, 204
Tepic, 50
Thames City, 155
Tory, 40
Tynemouth, 256-57
Umatilla, 117, 121
Una, 44, 46
Woodpecker, 189
Shushartie Bay, 33
"Shuswap Country", 289
Shuswap Lake, 312, 322-23, 332-34
Sicamous, 333
Sidney Island, 101
Sidolia (an Italian), 126
Similkameen River, 13, 124, 164, 193
Simon Fraser University, 171 ·
Simpson, Sir George, 4, 5, 70, 210, 409
Sinclair, James, 77
Sinnett, Charles, 155
Sitka, 76
Skagit River, 121
Skeena River, 166-67
Skidegate Inlet, 46, 61, 375
Skinner, R. J., 394
Skinner, Thomas J., 91, 92
Slaughter Bar, 129
Slaughter Camp, 237, 276
Smallpox, 252-54, 383
Smith (police constable), 182
Smith, R., 360
Smith, R. T., 341, 359
Smith, Tim, 298
Smyth, Robert Carmichael, 27
Snider, "Capt.", 128, 129
Snowshoe Plateau, 211
Society for the Propagation of the
    Gospel, 184
Soda Creek, 250, 272, 313
Somenos district, 255
Sooke, 23, 38-39, 68, 73, 91, 310, 404
South Pender Island, 101, 102
South Thompson River, 312, 332
Southgate, J. J., 341
Sowaqua Creek, 16
Spalding, Josiah C., 204
Spalding, W. R., 349, 359
Sparrowhawk Company, 350
Spence, Thomas, 250
Spences Bridge, 8, 250, 313, 317

Sproat, Gilbert Malcolm, 189-91, 348
Sproat Lake, 311
Spuzzum, 9, 123, 201
Squamish River, 311
Squa-zowm River. *See* Anderson River
Stagecoaches, 214, 272, 313-15, 352,
    365
Staines, Rev. Robert John, 24-25, 43,
    59, 69, 72-74, 185
Staines, Mrs. R. J. (Emma
    Tahourdin), 24, 74
Stamp, Capt. Edward, 321, 341, 359
Steamboat Explosions, 218
Steam Tractors, 397
Steele, William H., 240, 241
Stevenson, Capt. James, 306
Stevenson, Robert, 196, 268-69
Stikine River, 254
Stikine Territory, 254
Strikes (industrial), 31, 177, 272, 393
Stuart, Capt. C. E., 91
Stuart Lake, 167, 325
Stuart River, 167
Sumas, 368
Sumas Lake, 114-15, 201
Sutlej, Maggie, 339
Swanson, Capt., 95-96
Sweet, Lulu, 205
Sydney Inlet, 307

Takla Lake, 325
Tate, C. M., 393
Tatla Lake, 304
Tatuk Lake, 253
Tease (police constable), 182
Telegraph, 273, 279, 323-24
Telephone, 409
Tellias, "Thousand Dog Joe", 332
Tenas (Little Lillooet) Lake, 195
Tête Jaune Cache, 235, 237, 275
Theatre, 95-96, 108, 181, 205, 285
Thompson, J. B., 360
Thompson River, 8, 250
Thompson River Electoral District, 341
Thomson, James, 246-49
Thomson, Mary, 246, 248-49
Thomson, Walter, 170
"Three Greenhorns, The", 261
Tilton, Major James, 198
Tingley, Steve, 315, 408
Toby Creek, 334

Tod, John, 9-10, 44, 57, 63, 226, 228, 305, 320, 338, 345, 362, 368, 376, 390
Tolls, 123, 250, 251, 317
Tolmie, Dr. William Fraser, 36, 319, 324
Tolmie, Mrs. W. F. (Jane Work), 36
Tomlinson, Rev. Robert, 363
Toy, Pete, 254
Trading Licenses, 119
Train, George Francis, 382-83
Transcontinental Wagon Road (projected), 273
Treaty of Washington, 2, 17
Trevan, Henry, 60, 61, 64, 67
Trimble, Dr. James, 358, 381
Trutch, Joseph W., 250, 272, 294, 340, 350, 351, 359, 373-75, 376, 378, 386, 394, 400, 407
Tulameen River, 16, 179
Turnbull, J., 333
Turner, George, 312

Uncha Lake, 253
Union Bar (Fraser River), 218, 233
Union of B.C. and V.I., 321, 322, 335-36; proclaimed, 337
United States: possible purchase of B.C., 346-47
United States: proposed reciprocal trade, 361
United States Army, 46, 173-75, 197, 331
University of British Columbia, 202
Uplands Farm. See Cadboro Bay Farm
"Upper Country", 191
Uzakle, 11
Uztlius Creek, 8-9

Van Winkle Creek, 164, 214
Vancouver, 47, 261, 353, 395
    Brickmakers' Claim, The, 261
    Coal Harbour, 261
    Gastown, 353, 379, 406
    Hastings Mill, 321, 379
    Jerry's Cove, 379
    Stanley Park, 202
Vancouver Island, 2, 18, 19-22, 28, 43, 48, 49, 57, 59, 68, 69, 80-81, 81-83, 101, 107, 141, 173, 204, 293, 319, 320, 321, 334, 336

granted to Hudson's Bay Company, 21
    Provisional Council, 44
    Legislative Council, 44, 57-58, 91, 93, 174
    House of Assembly, 91-93, 295, 320, 321, 335, 337, 339
    grant to H.B.C. cancelled, 141
Vancouver Island Coal Mining Company, 398
Vancouver Island Exploration Expedition of 1864, 310-11
Vancouver Island Exploration Expedition of 1865, 320
"Vancouver Island Waltz", 202
Vancouver's Island Steam Sawing Mill and Agricultural Company, 40
Vavasour, Lieut. Mervin, 2
Vermilion Forks. See Princeton
Verse, 37, 96, 165, 244, 366-67
Victoria, Queen, 137, 157, 309, 401; birthday celebrations, 177, 352, 357
Victoria, 2, 4-6, 16, 17, 18, 22, 29, 36, 37, 53-54, 63, 71-72, 75, 81, 85-86, 91, 104, 106, 107, 119, 143-44, 145, 159, 176, 177, 178, 180, 182-83, 186, 198, 204, 205, 215, 218, 219, 227-28, 233, 253, 256-57, 259, 261, 271, 287, 293, 294, 320, 331, 337, 341, 359, 360, 391, 392, 393, 394, 403-05, 407, 408, 409
    "Bachelors' Hall", 38, 91-92
    Beacon Hill, 63, 144, 177, 206
    "Birdcages" (govt. buildings), 178
    Christ Church Cathedral, 185, 227, 407
    described 1858, 113-14
    described 1866, 334-35
    H.B.C.'s Pacific headquarters, 25
    incorporation, 257
    Indian problems, 74-75, 159, 162-64, 205-08, 222, 253
    Philharmonic Society, 175, 226
    police force, 107, 144, 182-83, 206, 225
    prison, 178, 182-83, 197, 207
    proclaimed capital of B.C., 357
    Royal Victoria Hospital (later Royal Jubilee Hospital), 175, 178

Townsite, 41
"Victoria Memorial, The", 358
Virago Rock, 64
Virago Sound, 66

Waccan. *See* Boucher, Jean Baptiste
Waddington, Alfred, 143, 216, 251-52, 297
Wadley, John, 217
Walkem, George Anthony, 286, 341, 359
Walker, James D., 258
Walker, Thos., 311
Wallace, George, 341
Wallace, R., 360
Warre, Lieut. Henry James, 2
Water power, 177
Wattie, James, 239
Wellesley, Capt., 41
Wellington coalfield, 398-99
Wells Fargo & Co., 212, 258
Wemyss, John, 225
"Wesleyan" (canoe), 158
Western Union Extension Company, 325, 329-30
Westroad River, 253, 329
Whannell, P. B., 146-47, 152
Whatcom Company, 129, 133
Whatcom Trail, 121-22
Whistler Mountain, 166
White (gold prospector), 124
White, Rev. Edward, 157, 158, 199, 235
Whiteman Pass, 77
Whonock, 368
Whymper, Frederick, 310

Wild Horse Creek, 311-12, 313, 322, 334
William (Bishop Hills' servant), 185
Williams Creek, 212, 214, 240, 242, 247, 267, 288, 289, 317-18, 405
Williams Lake, 214, 217, 246, 360
Williams, Thomas, 88-89
Wilson, Lieut. Charles, 113, 165, 176, 213
Wilson, D., 306
Wilson's Landing, 332
Winthuysen Inlet, 36, 78
Wishart, Charles, 32, 42
Wishart, George, 32, 42
Withrow, David, 360
Wood, Thomas L., 341, 359
Woods, Jerry, 270
Work, John, 36, 44, 73, 92, 226, 228-29
Work, Mrs. John (Susette Legace), 36
Wright, Gustavus Blin, 250, 313
Wright, Archdeacon Henry Press, 281, 283

Yale, James Murray, 8, 12, 47, 130, 148, 226, 361-62, 397
Yale, 9, 12, 13, 121, 128, 129, 132, 133-34, 136, 143, 146, 148-53, 158, 184, 185, 218, 221, 247, 250, 258, 263, 311, 313, 339, 341, 359, 360, 380, 394, 404
Yale Convention, 359-61
Yates, James, 58, 59, 69, 73, 91, 92
Yellowhead Pass, 275, 406
Young, William A. G., 162, 340, 369-70

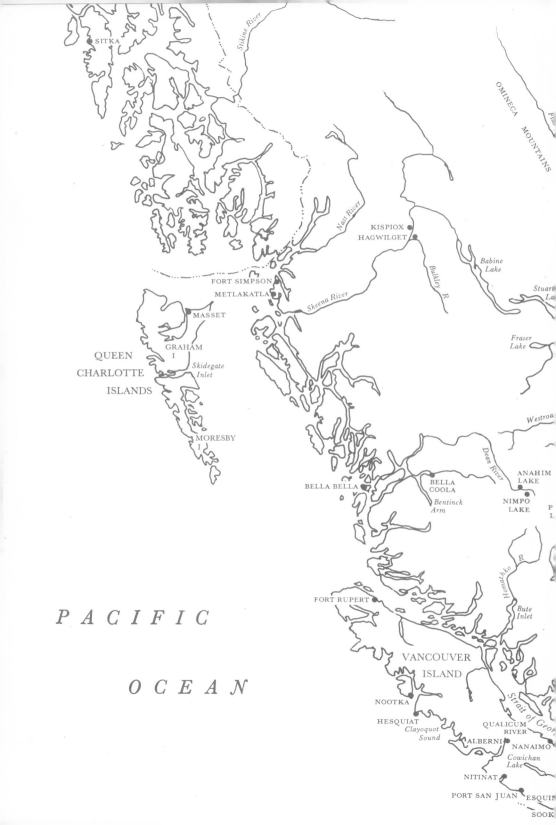